Kant in Brazil

North American Kant Society Studies in Philosophy

Kant's Aesthetics (Vol. 1, 1991)
Edited by Ralf Meerbote

Minds, Ideas, and Objects (Vol. 2, 1992)
Edited by Phillip D. Cummins and Guenter Zoeller

Kant's Early Metaphysics (Vol. 3, 1993)
Alison Laywine

The Table of Judgments (Vol. 4, 1995/6)
Reinhard Brandt

Logic and the Workings of the Mind (Vol. 5, 1997)
Edited by Patricia A. Easton

Selected Essays on Kant (Vol. 6, 2002)
Lewis White Beck, Edited by Hoke Robinson

Kantian Virtue at the Intersection of Politics and Nature (Vol. 7, 2004)
Scott M. Roulier

Understanding Purpose (Vol. 8, 2007)
Edited by Philippe Huneman

Kant and the Concept of Community (Vol. 9, 2011)
Edited by Charlton Payne and Lucas Thorpe

Kant in Brazil (Vol. 10, 2012)
Edited by Frederick Rauscher and Daniel Omar Perez

KANT IN BRAZIL

Edited by Frederick Rauscher and Daniel Omar Perez

Volume 10
North American Kant Society
Studies in Philosophy

UNIVERSITY OF ROCHESTER PRESS

First published 2012

University of Rochester Press
668 Mt. Hope Avenue, Rochester, NY 14620, USA
www.urpress.com
and Boydell & Brewer Limited
PO Box 9, Woodbridge, Suffolk IP12 3DF, UK
www.boydellandbrewer.com

ISBN-13: 978-1-58046-415-4

Library of Congress Cataloging-in-Publication Data

Kant in Brazil / edited by Frederick Rauscher and Daniel Omar Perez.
pages cm. — (North American Kant Society studies in philosophy ; volume 10)
Includes translations from Portuguese.
Includes some articles previously published in Portuguese as: Kant no Brasil. São Paulo, SP : Escuta, 2005.
Includes bibliographical references and index.
ISBN 978-1-58046-415-4 (pbk. : alk. paper) 1. Kant, Immanuel, 1724–1804. 2. Kant, Immanuel, 1724–1804—Influence. 3. Philosophy, Brazilian. I. Rauscher, Frederick, 1961– editor of compilation. II. Perez, Daniel Omar, editor of compilation. III. Kant no Brasil.
B2798.K2232 2012
193—dc23

2011048263

A catalogue record for this title is available from the British Library.

This publication is printed on acid-free paper.
Printed in the United States of America

In memory of Valerio Rohden

(1937–2010)

Cofounder and longtime president of the Sociedade Kant Brasiliera, who supported and encouraged this project from its inception

Contents

Acknowledgments

The editors could not have produced this volume without the advice and assistance of many individuals and institutions in both the United States and Brazil. In particular we would like to thank William Levine, who, as an undergraduate Portuguese major at Michigan State University, helped us to identify terminological inconsistencies and stylistic obscurities with the draft translations. William worked dozens of hours with us, pouring over various versions of the texts and making useful improvements that make the papers more accessible to English readers than if left to us alone. We are grateful to the College of Arts and Letters and, more broadly, Michigan State University for funding William's work. We would also like to thank two other student researchers, Glen Connolly and Mark Bogner, for devoting part of their research time to working up the bibliography and ensuring that all passages from Kant followed the Cambridge Edition.

Both editors are indebted to CAPES, the Brazilian counterpart to the Fulbright program, for funding Perez's stay at Michigan State University to allow intensive work on the volume. Rauscher benefited from advice from other CAPES scholars who choose to work at Michigan State: Juan Bonaccini, Darlei Dall'Agnol, Milene Consenso Tonetto, and Julio Esteves. Juan in particular was generous and patient with my numerous questions, and helpfully reviewed some of the translations.

Numerous Brazilians provided us with advice and encouragement throughout the course of work on the volume. The initial conception of this volume stemmed from conversations with Maria de Lourdes Borges, Darlei Dall-Agnol, Ricardo Ribeiro Terra, and Cauê Cardoso Polla in São Paulo. Valerio Rohden provided much encouragement and advice, including the best advice Rauscher received, namely, to bring in Perez as coeditor. The contributors to this volume were generous in providing their own translations and working with us as we altered their translations from the point of view of English readers. Other Brazilians who provided advice, encouragement, information, or recommendations on this project, small or large, and hospitality and intellectual stimulation during Rauscher's visits to Brazil are Guido de Almeida, Vera Bueno, José Humberto de Brito Cruz, Andrea Faggion, José Heck, Christian Hamm, Orlando Bruno Linhares, Zeljko Loparic, Rogério Passos Severo, and Latin America's most well-known Kant scholar, Mario Caimi of Argentina.

Robert Louden, as general editor of this book series, and Patricia Kitcher, as president of the North American Kant Society, supported this project from its inception. The long delays in work on this book saw Robert's axis of support shift from his editorship of the book series to his current position as NAKS president. His patience throughout the process helped keep the project on track.

Individually, Perez would like to thank Rauscher and Valerio Rohden for sharing moments of their lives that stimulated his thought, and Rauscher would like to thank Perez for helping to introduce him to the Brazilian corpus and community. Rauscher would also like to thank his wife, Delores, and children, Konrad, Bennett, and Audrey, for their patience while he spent time in Brazil: você também irá em breve começar a conhecer o Brasil.

Note on Sources and Abbreviations

The original Portuguese language versions of the essays included in this volume cited many secondary works in Portuguese, French, Italian, Spanish, German, and English. All of these references are retained in their original language. On occasion the author also chose to include a translation of the title into English in brackets; these have also been retained. The exception to this rule is the introductory essay "Two Centuries of Kantian Studies in Brazil," where translations of all the original titles are included in brackets to aid the reader in following the history of Brazilian Kant literature. In all cases for all articles, translations into English were done by the article's translator, except for quotations from Kant and from English sources.

The original essays also used Portuguese translations of Kant's writings. In the translations included below, quotations from Kant are presented in English using the *Cambridge Edition of the Works of Immanuel Kant* edited by Paul Guyer and Allen Wood (New York: Cambridge University Press, 1992–). When the material quoted does not appear in the published volumes of the Cambridge series, the translator of the essay has provided a translation. In all cases citations are given parenthetically in the text with reference to *Kants gesammelten Schriften* (Berlin: Walter de Gruyter, 1900–) by volume and page number, except citations to the *Critique of Pure Reason*, which follow the convention of referring to the pagination of the first and second ("A" and "B") editions. The parenthetical references use the abbreviation system that follows to identify particular works by Kant. Correspondence is identified by writer, recipient, and date, unless obvious from the surrounding text.

Abbreviations of Works by Kant

Anthropology	*Anthropology from a Pragmatic Point of View*
Anthropology Mrongovius	*Mrongovius Anthropology Lecture Transcript*
Conflict	*The Conflict of the Faculties*
Conjectural	*Conjectural Beginning of Human History*
Doctrine of Right	*Doctrine of Right*
Doctrine of Virtue	*Doctrine of Virtue*
End	*The End of All Things*
Enlightenment	*An Answer to the Question: What Is Enlightenment?*

First Introduction	*First Introduction to the Critique of the Power of Judgment*
Groundwork	*Groundwork of the Metaphysics of Morals*
Idea	*Idea of a Universal History from a Cosmopolitan Point of View*
Jäsche Logic	*Immanuel Kant's Logic: A Handbook for Lectures*
Judgment	*Critique of the Power of Judgment*
Metaphysics L	*Metaphysics L Lecture Transcript*
Metaphysics of Morals	*The Metaphysics of Morals*
Natural Science	*Metaphysical Foundations of Natural Science*
Only Possible Argument	*The Only Possible Argument in Support of a Demonstration of the Existence of God*
Opus Postumum	*Opus Postumum*
Orient	*What Does it Mean to Orient Oneself in Thinking?*
Perpetual Peace	*Toward Perpetual Peace*
Practical Reason	*Critique of Practical Reason*
Progress in Metaphysics	*What Is the Real Progress That Metaphysics Has Made in Germany Since the Time of Leibniz and Wolff*
Prolegomena	*Prolegomena to Any Future Metaphysics*
Pure Reason	*Critique of Pure Reason*
R	*Reflection*
Religion	*Religion within the Boundaries of Mere Reason*
Review of Schulz	*Review of Schulz's Attempt at an Introduction to a Doctrine of Morals for All Human Beings Regardless of Different Religions*
Soemmerring	*From Soemmerring's On the Organ of the Soul*
Theodicy	*On the Miscarriage of all Philosophical Trials in Theodicy*
Theory and Practice	*On the Common Saying: That May be Correct in Theory, But It Is of No Use in Practice*
Vienna Logic	*Vienna Logic Lecture Transcript*

Introduction

Frederick Rauscher

In 2005 the Brazilian Kant Society hosted the International Kant Congress, the first time it has ever been held outside Germany and the United States. Hundreds of Kant scholars from throughout the world joined hundreds of Brazilian professors and students for five days of keynote lectures, contributed session papers, and discussion. Nonetheless language barriers prevented extensive interaction. While most of the Brazilian scholars understood English or German, very few of the non-Brazilian scholars understood Portuguese. The keynote lectures in Portuguese that were simultaneously translated into English and the handful of Brazilian contributed session papers read in English or German testified to the high level of work that one could assume lay behind the other papers presented in Portuguese. A desire on both sides to break through this barrier sparked the idea for this book of translations.

The publication of the proceedings from the São Paulo Congress in 2008 has contributed to alleviating the language barrier.[1] All contributions presented at the Congress in Portuguese were translated into English, French, or German for publication. In one stroke, the amount of Brazilian work on Kant accessible to US Kant scholars increased severalfold. The extensive scope of this work goes a long way toward showing the multitude of approaches to virtually every aspect of Kant scholarship undertaken in Brazil. The Congress proceedings serve as a snapshot that captures the breadth of this work at one time. The current collection is intended to perform a different function. Here some of the most influential and important papers on Kant from the last few decades are presented to showcase some of the very best and most influential work done by Brazilians over time.

These essays have been translated into English in part to stimulate Brazilian-US interaction on Kant and in part because English is becoming the lingua franca of international Kant scholarship. Work on Kant is truly international, encompassing scholars working in English, French, German, Italian, Japanese, Korean, Norwegian, Portuguese, Romanian, Russian, and Spanish—and these reflect only languages associated with some kind of organized Kant society known to this writer. While German is of course expected for work on Kant, the most common language for work in philosophy in general is English. It is hoped that by offering these papers in English translation, the vast majority of Kant scholars worldwide will have access to some of the best work done in Portuguese.

The project is also part of an attempt to encourage interaction between US and Brazilian Kant scholars. Brazilian scholars already travel to Europe and the United States to study, teach, or participate in conferences. There are many opportunities for the reverse. Conferences in Brazil accept papers written and read in English. Graduate programs encourage or require their students to know English and would welcome visitors who would teach English language seminars. Published papers in Brazilian journals are sometimes in English. Further, advances in computer translation software allow one to download or obtain a paper published in Portuguese (or many other major languages) and translate it into English—very bad English, of course, but close enough so that, if one already has sufficient knowledge of the general area of the paper, one can get the gist of the author's argument.[2] Increased contact between Brazilian and US Kant scholars in all these ways can only help the international Kant community. To this end a new website has been created devoted to interaction between Brazilian and US Kant scholars, and more broadly the Portuguese-speaking and English-speaking Kant communities. The website includes more background information about Kant in Brazil, announcements of conferences and other opportunities, links to electronic journals in Brazil, bibliographies of work in English, German, and Portuguese, and other information. The address is www.msu.edu/~rauscher/brazil-us-kant, and a link to the site will always be available through the NAKS website.

The work being done in Brazil to present Brazilian Kant scholarship to the world reached a high point, of course, at the Tenth International Kant Congress in São Paulo in September 2005. International recognition of the maturity and extent of Brazilian work came earlier with the decision by the Kant Gesellschaft to authorize the Brazilian Kant Society to host the Congress. Brazilians on their part used the opportunity to showcase their work to the world. In some ways, the Tenth Kant Congress represented a rite of passage as a growing scholarly community stepped up to claim a place among its peers. One of the many manifestations of this aspect was the release of the book *Kant no Brasil* (Kant in Brazil), edited by Daniel Omar Perez, a collection of articles that gave this collection of translations its title, its core material, and its coeditor, as will be described below.[3]

The achievement embodied in the Tenth Kant Congress must be seen in the context of decades of work in creating, sustaining, and expanding Kant scholarship in the world's fifth most populated and fifth largest country. The history of this development is detailed in the first essay in this volume, "Two Centuries of Kantian Studies in Brazil," an expanded version of the editor's introductory essay in *Kant no Brasil*. Complementing the temporal story presented in that review of the origin and development of the organized Kant community in Brazil, the next sections of this introduction will provide a snapshot of the current extent and institutional structure of Kant studies in Brazil, including resources for future interaction. This overview will look at three general aspects of the current institutional structure: (a) organizations and conferences, (b) the university system, and (c) resources for scholarly interaction with Brazilians.

Organizations and Conferences

The national framework for Kant scholarship is provided by the Brazilian Kant Society, which organized and carried out the Kant Congress in 2005. It is the primary but not the only organization for Kant studies in Brazil. Its website (www.sociedadekant.org) is a useful portal for information about conferences and related matters. The current president of the society is Ubirajara Rancan of the Paulista State University in Marília, and the president during the time up to and including the Kant Congress was Valerio Rohden, who, along with Guido Antônio de Almeida and Ricardo Ribeiro Terra, played a pivotal role in the International Kant Congress.

The Brazilian Kant Society publishes a journal, *Studia Kantiana* (not to be confused with the Italian Kant journal *Studi Kantiani*), which is sent to all members. This journal began publication in 1998. *Studia Kantiana* is not currently indexed in *The Philosopher's Index*, but the list of articles published in it is available on the society's website as well as in the *Kant-Bibliographie* published by the Kant-Forschungsstelle of the Universität Mainz. At present the society is working on other sponsored publications, much like the North American Kant Society's series of publications of collections and monographs.

The society has also sponsored nationwide Brazilian Kant Congresses four times since 1989, with a fifth planned for Florianopolis in 2013. Large meetings like this are well enough funded to include several invited speakers from within Brazil and around the world but also include a large number of submitted, refereed papers. Most papers at these conferences are read in Portuguese. Many of the invited speakers read their papers in English or German. In the case of the nationwide Brazilian Kant Congresses, the invited papers have recently been translated into Portuguese, if necessary, and published in *Studia Kantiana*.

Under the umbrella of the Brazilian Kant Society are several regional sections associated with different universities or metropolitan areas that engage in intense work on Kant. There is no official requirement that work done by the society be assigned to a section, nor is activity around Brazil limited to the sections. Rather, these sections are to different degrees relatively independent groups affiliated with the nationwide society. In this way they are similar to the NAKS regional study groups, with the exception that they are not limited to annual meetings and the meetings tend to include more or less the same people each time.

The Campinas Section is centered on the State University of Campinas (UNICAMP) in the state of São Paulo outside the metropolitan São Paulo area, and emphasizes a semantic approach to Kant. This section hosts one or two conferences ("colloquium") each year on Kant in Campinas. The Campinas Section has its own website (www.kant.org.br) with conference announcements, downloads, and other information. It also publishes an online journal, *Kant e-Prints* (www.cle.unicamp.br/kant-e-prints), with some articles in German and English. Articles published in this journal are freely available for download.

The Rio Grande do Sul Section, centered around several universities in Porto Alegre in the southernmost state in Brazil, Rio Grande do Sul,[4] has a strong connection to the Goethe Institut in Brazil. Much of this section's activity consists of less formal reunions rather than formal conferences, but members have played a large part in the national society. Some of the activity of this section spills over to the Federal University of Pelotas further south, which has hosted four conferences on Kant. Other sections in Rio de Janeiro and Minas Gerais and Kant scholars at other universities also arrange for conferences on Kant and meet under other circumstances. The president of the Brazilian Kant Society, Ubirajara Rancan, has been arranging a series of conferences in Marília for the past several years as well.

Distinct from the activities of the Brazilian Kant Society and its sections is a new Center for Kantian Studies, founded at the Federal University of Santa Catarina in Florianopolis (www.cik.ufsc.br). The Center houses the official library of the Brazilian Kant Society, which aims to collect bibliographical material concerning Kant publications in Brazil and to amass a large collection of primary and secondary works in any language. The goal of the Center is to become a focal point for the study of Kant in Brazil. So far the Center has hosted four of its own conferences on Kant.

University System

The university systems in Brazil consist principally of four types. The federal universities are named for the states or cities in which they are found (for example, the Federal University of Rio Grande do Sul), but are funded by the central government. Each state also has its own state university system funded by the state. Of these the state universities in São Paulo—Brazil's wealthiest state and a central economic engine for the country—are most prominent. A system of Catholic universities, usually called Pontifical Catholic University followed by the name of the city or state in which it is located, is not as extensive as the federal university system, but reaches most major urban areas. Other private religious universities exist, such as a few Lutheran universities. Finally there are some community universities that have a mixture of public and private funding.

In general the library holdings of all these universities falls below the average for a flagship state university in the United States and far below the best academic libraries in Europe or the United States. These universities tend to be much younger than those in the United States or Europe and with smaller budgets. In recent decades the government has substantially increased funding for universities, and of course the internet increases the availability of sources as well. Kant's main published works, several minor works, and some unpublished works such as correspondence and course lectures have been or are in the process of being translated into Portuguese (some in Portugal, some in Brazil).

Resources for Scholarly Interaction

Increased funding is also reflected in government support for international scholarly interaction. The Brazilian government funds the Brazilian Federal Agency for Support and Evaluation of Graduate Education (CAPES) and the National Council for Scientific and Technological Development (CNPq).[5] CAPES is centered on work that supports graduate programs, while CNPq aims at promoting scholarship and research, although their missions overlap to some degree. Both sponsor Brazilian philosophy professors annually for up to twelve-month research visits abroad. The recipients have used these to do research in the United States and other countries as visiting scholars, postdocs, and the like. One editor of this volume (Perez) was awarded a CAPES grant to work at Michigan State University on, among other things, preparation of this collection of translations. Facing stiff competition, applicants for these funded research visits must have a strong letter of invitation from US professors. Both CAPES and CNPq also fund graduate students, mainly dissertation level, for study abroad. These students not only work with a US scholar on Kant but also have the opportunity to improve their language skills. Both also underwrite many conferences in Brazil, allowing US and other international scholars to be invited routinely.

On the US side, the Fulbright Program can fund visitors from Brazil, allowing them to teach in the United States, and fund US scholars who wish to teach in Brazil. Kant scholars are unlikely to be awarded Fulbright Scholar grants for research work in Brazil; however, Fulbright Scholar grants for teaching are available. The other editor of this volume (Rauscher) has been awarded a Fulbright Scholarship to teach graduate-level courses conducted in English at the Federal University of Santa Catarina, home of the new Kant Center, in 2012. Fulbright awards are also available to bring Brazilian scholars to the United States to teach. The US host university must make the application on behalf of the candidate Brazilian professor.

Interaction between Brazilian and US Kant scholars is not an isolated phenomenon. Many Kant scholars from many different countries worldwide already travel across oceans to attend conferences or pursue research. Books and some articles are translated from one language to another. Some conferences feature simultaneous translation. The internet allows individuals to keep track of the doings of Kant societies around the world. Still, much of the scholarship flows in a single direction: from Germany and the English speaking nations out to the rest of the world. International Kant scholars read work in German and English. Translations tend to be from German or English into the local language. If an individual wants to come to the attention of scholars in Germany or the English-speaking world, that individual strives to publish in German or English. The current collection of translations from Portuguese into English bucks that trend. Some scholarship will now flow to the German and English speaking nations. It is hoped that future publications can perform similar functions for Kant scholars from other nations, allowing their work to be translated into English as well.

* * *

The papers collected here have been chosen by one of the editors (Rauscher) in consultation with the other editor (Perez) and dozens of Brazilian scholars. The original conception of this book was to translate *Kant no Brasil*, the collection edited by Perez, which reprinted three papers from each of four major scholars pursuing work on Kant from different angles: the late Valerio Rohden, who practiced detailed linguistic and textual analysis; Ricardo Ribeiro Terra, who stresses Kant's political and aesthetic philosophy, in part influenced by French work; Guido Antônio de Almeida, whose work is highly analytical in style; and Zeljko Loparic, who has pioneered a semantic interpretation of Kant. In order to expand the book to include an even greater diversity of Brazilian approaches to Kant, the editors decided to include work by other, especially younger, scholars, and to reduce the number written by these four prominent scholars. Three of these four scholars are now represented with two papers each; since some of Loparic's work is already available in English or German, the editors decided to include only one of his essays. The resulting set retains about half the essays from *Kant no Brasil* and now encompasses twenty essays by eighteen different scholars. The substantial continuity of content and purpose is reflected in retaining the original's title, *Kant in Brazil*.

The selection of these essays was difficult. In a nation as vast as Brazil, one with just as diverse a set of approaches to philosophy in general and to Kant in particular as in the United States, and one with a relatively recent proliferation of excellent work on Kant, no collection could hope to perfectly represent Brazilian work on Kant. No single individual concurs that the precise set of essays included here represents the best Brazilian essays. Healthy disagreement made the selection of texts both frustrating and rewarding. Undoubtedly many excellent essays were left out; monographs were not even considered. In some cases the availability of work by that author in German or English precluded inclusion of similar work here. There is probably a bias toward living scholars since the terms "best" and "most influential over time" are not synonymous. There is also an attempt to include various representations of different approaches to Kant in order to present a picture of Brazilian work as a whole. Although dozens of Brazilian scholars contributed to the process of selection, this editor (Rauscher) alone is responsible for the final selection. No set is perfect. This set, at least, provides a good balance among diversity, influence, originality, and age in order to present the reader with a representation of Brazilian work on Kant.

Befitting the diversity of Brazilian work, this collection ranges from detailed analysis of epistemological issues in the *Critique of Pure Reason* to broader considerations of the relation between Kant and his contemporaries. In general there is a tilt toward work in practical philosophy and aesthetics in this collection. Strikingly, the number of papers on practical philosophy is more than triple the number related to the *Critique of Pure Reason*. In part this emphasis stems from the historical importance of political issues in Brazilian philosophy, in part from the availability in English of some material that otherwise might have been selected.

The first essay, "Two Centuries of Kantian Studies in Brazil" by Daniel Omar Perez and Juan Adolfo Bonaccini, is a much expanded version of Perez's introductory essay to *Kant no Brasil*. The essay provides an overview of the history of Kant studies from the early nineteenth century to the present. Diverse influences contributed to the development of various interpretive schools. The present diffusion of Kant work represents the flowering of decades of preparatory work by many who founded graduate programs and other institutions to encourage this work.[6]

"Self-Consciousness and Objective Knowledge in the Transcendental Deduction of the *Critique of Pure Reason*" by Guido Antônio de Almeida questions the extent to which self-consciousness is necessary for objective judgments. Kant requires all judgments to relate in some way to the "I think," but the precise relation need not be one in which self-consciousness is explicit. The *unity* of self-consciousness requires only that an objective judgment be made, in contrast to actual self-consciousness, which requires that the cognizer relate subjective unity of perceptions to objective knowledge. Thus de Almeida argues that self-consciousness in the broad sense is not necessary in relation to objective knowledge.

João Carlos Brum Torres in "Intuitive Knowledge and *De Re* Thought" compares Kant's empirical intuition with the contemporary conception of de re thoughts. He argues that Kant's intuitions seem ill suited to this comparison since cognition of the objects requires the intervention of subject-dependent conditions. By showing that the structure of objects corresponding to those conditions should be understood to be given with the form of intuitions, he preserves Kant's insight while viewing it under this contemporary lens.

In "Predicative Judgments and Existential Judgments: Apropos Kant's Critique of the Cartesian Ontological Argument," Raúl Landim assesses the basis of Kant's claim that existence is not a real predicate. He distinguishes categorical, assertoric judgments from existential judgments, drawing from Kant's early work *The Only Possible Argument in Support of a Demonstration of the Existence of God.* This distinction establishes the basis for Kant's rejection of the Cartesian version of the ontological argument as provided in the *Critique of Pure Reason.*

Opening the series of essays on practical matters is "An Experiment with Practical Reason" by Valerio Rohden. While investigating previous editions of Kant's *Critique of Practical Reason* for his translation into Portuguese, Rohden found a seemingly minor correction made by an acquaintance of Kant in his own copy of the book. Rohden argues that the change from "*nur*" to "*nun*" in the passage best expresses Kant's intention regarding the analogy between an experiment in chemistry and the relation between practical reason and personal interest.

The selection by Darlei Dall'Agnol, "On the *Faktum* of Reason," places the fact of reason in the *Critique of Practical Reason* into a larger context. Dall'Agnol collects every reference to a fact (*Faktum*) of reason by Kant before attempting to provide his interpretation. He allows that Kant might have in mind several *Facta*, including the connotation of "deed" as well as more familiar interpretations such as consciousness of the moral law or the moral law itself. His main point is that, rather than seeing the invocation of this *Faktum* as an admission of a failure of a deduction of freedom in *Groundwork* III, one should see a smooth extended argument from the first *Critique* through the *Groundwork* to the second *Critique*.

A second selection from Guido Antônio de Almeida, "Critique, Deduction, and the Fact of Reason," takes on the same topic.[7] De Almeida tries to correlate seemingly contradictory problems in that Kant sees a deduction of the principle of morality as impossible yet does not believe that resorting to the fact of reason leaves it without foundation. His approach is to understand the moral principle in terms of a law, in which case it is analytic for perfectly rational beings, and in terms of an imperative, in which case it is accessible to imperfectly rational beings.

Groundwork III's labrynthical argument is the subject of Julio Esteves, "The Noncircular Deduction of the Categorical Imperative in *Groundwork* III." He defends Kant's argument from the charge of circularity and holds that Kant provides a plausible practical rather than theoretical argument. Kant's method of resolving the apparent circle, Esteves argues, is successful and was thought so by Kant in later writings. Determinism understood universally is self-defeating in practice since any claim to its truth would need a justificatory element that cannot be seen as the product of prior causes. From this practical claim of a necessary presupposition of freedom, Kant is able to justify the self-ascription of freedom of human agents.

Ricardo Ribeiro Terra, "The Distinction between Right and Ethics in Kant's Philosophy," dating from the 1970s and thus the oldest article included in this anthology, clarifies this important distinction in the context of conceptual confusion that Terra found in French and Italian interpretations of the time. Terra defends the a priori status of Kant's principle of right and the subsequent political claims built upon it. He sets out the different ways in which virtue and right are derived from fundamental practical law, and thus puts to rest the idea that Kant was merely a positivist in his theory of rights.

"Right and the Duty to Resist, or Progress toward the Better" by José Nicolau Heck tackles the tension in Kant between the a priori approach to right and the reliance on specific contingent institutions in history to realize right. The denial of a right to resist a government exemplifies this problem. Heck stresses the role of the inevitability of historical progress in resolving this tension.

Zeljko Loparic applies his semantic approach to interpreting Kant's philosophy[8] to practical issues in "The Fundamental Problem of Kant's Juridical Semantics." His semantic interpretation focuses on the performability of actions governed by practical concepts rather than on any metaphysical considerations. He sees the main issue in Kant's *Doctrine of Right* as showing the way in which pure practical concepts of right are able to be understood in terms of physical activity, particularly the application of force. Loparic further argues that his semantic interpretation shows that the overall systematic unity of theoretical and practical considerations is not resolved by teleological judgment but by this focus on the applicability of practical concepts to physical actions.

In "Right, History, and Practical Schematism," Daniel Tourinho Peres connects Kant's pure a priori political principles to his theory of history. The pure principles of right are not themselves directly instantiated in any institution but remain abstract concepts. Their actualization unfolds in human history and particular institutions reflecting right. History is thus akin to a schema for concepts of right. Peres notes that this interpretations shows that

Kant predates Hegel in the use of history as the necessary means for a gradual realization of practical concepts.

The article by Soraya Nour, "Cosmopolitanism: Kant and Kantian Themes in International Relations," provides an overview of Kant's work *Toward Perpetual Peace* and traces its influence. She stresses the relation between republican government and international peace in Kant. Her approach shows the interaction between historical events since World War II and the reception and interpretation of Kant's claims by both philosophers and public intellectuals. She concludes that structural deficiencies in international economic and political relations prevent Kant's dream of perpetual peace from realization at the present.

Maria de Lourdes Borges offers an assessment of Kant's various treatments of love and related emotions in "A Typology of Love in Kant's Philosophy." Noting the tension between these emotions and the aprioricity and purity of the moral law, she draws out the ways in which various emotions contribute to fulfillment of duty. Sympathy, gratitude, and benevolence support human beings as sensible agents in their efforts to follow the moral law. Some variations of love can be detrimental to morality, in particular the passion of love that can cause others to be treated unequally.

The second selection from Valerio Rohden, "The Meaning of the Term *Gemüt* in Kant," stems from his translation work on the third *Critique*. Here he dissects the shades of meaning in *Gemüt*, which indicates an integration of mental faculties, and related terms such as *Geist* and *Seele*. Since Portuguese is a romance language, the direct translation of Kant's terms can be based upon Latin equivalences identifiable by Kant's own reliance on Latin textbooks; however, Kant identifies two for *Gemüt*, namely, *animus* and *mens*. Philosophical considerations, in particular related to the free activity of *Gemüt* in Kant's aesthetic theory, favor the Portuguese *ânimo* (from Latin *animus*) over *mente* (from *mens*), a sense unavailable in an English equivalent differentiated from soul (*Seele*), mind (*mens*), and spirit (*Geist*).

Ricardo Ribeiro Terra's second contribution follows. "Between Prescriptive Poetics and Philosophical Aesthetics" argues that Kant is a transitional figure between discussion of poetry's (and art's) technique on the one hand and a genuine philosophy of art on the other. Kant's crucial move was to recognize the autonomy of aesthetic judgment, an insight that was able to explain the response to beautiful technique while opening the path to fuller assessments of the aesthetic in a broader sense. Autonomy links the aesthetic to morality, morality is the aim of cultural formation, and culture is a product of history. The broader historical turn taken by Schiller, Hegel, and others in the age of Goethe stems from Kant's introduction of the free faculty of judgment.

Pedro Costa Rego's "The Purposiveness of Taste: An Essay on the Role of *Zweckmässigkeit* in Kant's *Critique of Aesthetic Judgment*" places purposiveness in the center of Kant's theory of aesthetic judgment. A judgment of taste requires some way to join together a feeling and a universally valid principle. Purposiveness provides that link between the sensible and the universal not for reasons limited to aesthetic judgment but because the principle of purposiveness is a principle for the whole of reflecting judgment. Rego looks at purposiveness in both epistemological and practical senses in relation to taste.

The next selection, by Christian Hamm, turns to the Kantian influence on one of his successors. "Freedom in Appearance: Notes on Schiller and His Development of Kant's Aesthetics" traces Schiller's attempt to move beyond Kant's aesthetics while remaining within Kant's framework and retaining Kant's insights, in particular the transcendental aspect of his theory. Schiller tightens the link between beauty and morality by having aesthetic judgment recognize an analogy between a free will and freedom "in appearance" in the expression of beauty. This leads Schiller to stress that actions themselves can be beautiful, and thus to overcome what he saw as a false division between duty and inclination.

Pedro Pimenta discusses the other role of judgment in "Reading the Appendix to Kant's *Critique of the Teleological Power of Judgment.*" He shows the role of teleological judgment in connecting theoretical and practical reason into one faculty, but stresses that this role is integral both to the critical philosophy and the third *Critique* as a whole. Teleological judgment offers a way to understand concepts of practical objects, in particular God, not as transcendent but as the hypothetical basis of a transcendental point of view that reveals that natural and moral ends are fundamentally the same. Kant unites the theoretical and practical by using a teleological judgment of nature that incorporates reason's moral aims.

In the final article, "Symbolization in Kant's Critical Philosophy," Joãosinho Beckenkamp takes as his starting point the famous fragment "The Oldest System Program of German Idealism," attributed to the early Hegel or, sometimes, to Schelling, which called on philosophy to further Kant's subsumption of metaphysics under morals by introducing a new, rational, and aesthetic mythology. Beckenkamp examines the way in which Kant had already succeeded in symbolizing ideas of reason using the mythology of Christian religious symbols, thus paving the way for the later rational mythology advocated by the fragment.

The papers in this collection span a broad area of Kant research. Other areas, such as the metaphysics of space and time, have received significant attention as well. The diversity of Brazil is mirrored in the diversity of approaches to Kant. Just as Brazil's political and economic growth is propelling it into the top of the rank of emerging powers like China and India, so also the growth of Brazil's academic infrastructure is raising the profile of Brazilian Kant studies in the international scholarly community. Latin America in general is receiving more attention in the Kant community—witness the awarding of the Kant Prize at the most recent International Kant Congress in Pisa to Argentina's Mario Caimi (who frequents Brazilian Kant events). The next decades will likely see a continuation of this trend not only regarding Brazil and the remainder of Latin America, but more broadly other communities of Kant scholars whose work becomes available to the English- and German-speaking world. Genuine internationalization of Kant scholarship will benefit everyone as the work of each becomes available to all.

Notes

1. *Recht und Frieden in der Philosophie Kants: Akten des X Internationalen Kant-Kongresses*, 5 vols., ed. Valerio Rohden, Ricardo Terra, Guido de Almeida, and Margit Ruffing (Berlin: Walter de Gruyter, 2008). The bibliography at the end of this collection lists the names of Brazilian as well as Portuguese contributors to the proceedings from the Congress.

2. Once one gets the gist, one will know whether it is worth expending the effort required to make a more accurate translation, or to contact the author for more information since the author is likely to know English. The translation software freely available on the Internet falls short of even this minimal standard. Recent advances such as "Google Translate," for example, still produce confusing translations. For example, the famous first sentence of *Groundwork* I is renderd as "There is nothing anywhere in the world, indeed even to think outside it possible, which could well be held without limitation, as a good will." The worst feature of many translation systems is an imprecision in philosophical vocabulary. This writer has experimented with commercial translation software (SYSTRAN) that enables translation of entire Word or PDF documents and allows specification of vocabulary. The program can be taught to use specific terms universally or in particular textual contexts (allowing one to parse related terms such as "knowledge" and "cognition") and can translate short phrases into specific short phrases (useful for book titles and common terms such as "transcendental ideality of space and time"). Even with these user-directed improvements the software falls far short of smooth readability, let alone publishable quality.

3. Daniel Omar Perez, ed., *Kant no Brasil* (São Paulo: Escuta, 2005).

4. While in the United States members of the pairs of states with geographically related names such as North and South Dakota and North and South Carolina are adjacent, in Brazil the states of Rio Grande do Norte and Rio Grande do Sul are separated by nearly the entire remainder of Brazil outside the Amazon region.

5. The state of São Paulo has a similar funding institution known as FAPESP. Funding for conferences is also sometimes provided by the Goethe Institutes in various Brazilian cities.

6. Another recent overview of the development of Kant studies in Brazil that stresses the influence of French thought more than the present essay does is Ubirajara Rancan, "Bemerkungen über die Kant-Forschung in Brasilien," *Kantstudien* 100 (2009): 369–78.

7. A third famous article on this topic is not included here, although a shorter version is available in German: Zeljko Loparic, "Das Faktum der Vernunft—Eine semantische Auslegung," in *Akten des IX Internationalen Kant-Kongresses*, vol. 3, ed. Volker Gerhardt, Rolf-Peter Horstmann, and Ralph Schumacher (Berlin: Walter de Gruyter, 2001), 63–71.

8. Loparic's semantic interpretation is presented in his book *A semântica transcendental de Kant* [Kant's transcendental semantics] (Campinas: Col. CLE, 2000). An English translation of this book is in preparation.

1

Two Centuries of Kantian Studies in Brazil

Daniel Omar Perez and
Juan Adolfo Bonaccini

The Beginning: Kant in Brazil during the Empire

When Napoleon invaded Portugal in 1807, Prince Regent Dom João de Bragança decided to move his family and transfer the whole court to Brazil, departing on November 29, 1807, and arriving in Brazil in March 1808. That same year the Royal Library was installed in the hospital of the Third Order of the Carmelites (Carmo) in Rio de Janeiro.[1] Might *Philosophie de Kant, ou principes fondamentaux de la philosophie transcendantale* (Kant's philosophy, or the fundamental principles of the transcendental philosophy) (1801) by Charles Villers, a work that arrived in Brazil as part of the library of the prince regent and future emperor along with the royal family, have been the first text to publicize the thought of the German philosopher in Brazil? We certainly do not have information of any earlier references.

Historians, in any event, maintain that Francisco Bento Targini, Viscount of São Lourenço, also known as Francisco Vilela Barbosa Targini, Marquis of Paranaguá, was one of the first to transmit the ideas of Immanuel Kant, in addition to writing several books himself and translating Milton's *Paradise Lost* and Pope's *Essay on Man*. This task was no mere leisure activity. It is worth noting that the empire's censorship decree of July 27, 1801, had prohibited the circulation of Pope's *Essay on Man*, along with Swift's *Gulliver's*

This essay, translated by William Levine, is a much shorter version of a paper written by Perez and Bonaccini, "On Kantian Studies and Kant's Influence in Brazil," published in *Kant e-Prints*, 2nd ser., 4, no. 1 (2009): 23–41, which in turn is an expansion and revision of Perez's introductory essay "Dois séculos de leitura de Kant no Brasil," in *Kant no Brasil*, ed. Daniel Omar Perez (São Paulo: Escuta, 2005), 5–22. Space requirements prevent the full version, which provides extensive reference to particular individuals and publications, from appearing here. Rauscher is solely responsible for the deletions made to create the shorter version and does not intend by them to imply that work not mentioned is unimportant.

Travels and Sterne's *Sentimental Journey*, whose possession and reading all depended on the authorization of the censors. Freedom of the press in Brazil was only authorized later by Dom Pedro I by a specific law of August 28, 1820. Thus, in a certain way, the translation of forbidden writings tells us of the qualities and weight of the translator. But at the same time it allows us to speculate that the thought of Kant, an enthusiastic admirer of the French Revolution and a defender of the freedoms of press, religion, and thought, had begun to penetrate into Brazil as an example of rational thinking in harmony with a large part of the political, liberal ideology being debated. Still, for all of the effort Targini put into them, his attempts to print and spread Kantian ideas did not prosper. His influence on Kantian studies was just as short as his stay in Brazil, which only lasted until the return of Dom João and his family to Portugal in April 1821.

Also during the early years of the nineteenth century, another of the court's intellectuals, Martim Francisco, offered a course and wrote a book called *A filosofia transcendental de Kant* (Kant's transcendental philosophy). The book nonetheless disappeared, and apparently its contents never received any commentary.

In the second and third decades of the nineteenth century, Kant's works continued to spread in Brazil. In this respect, a distinguished scholar notes that "when the São Paulo College of Law was created in 1827, Kant's doctrine was already known in some way, to the extent that a priest named Father Mimi, who offered the preparatory courses, usually exposed his students to the Kantian theory of space and time as *a priori* forms of sensibility."[2]

Although incipient, the presence of Kant in philosophical thought in São Paulo at the time even earned an explicit mention in the work of Wilhelm Gottlieb Tennemann, *Grundriss der Geschichte der Philosophie für den akademischen Unterricht* (Outline of the history of philosophy for academic instruction), where he speaks of "São Paulo Kantianism."[3] This book dates from 1829, making it clear that Kantian influence already existed for some time, since a school of philosophy does not come into being overnight. In addition to this, the testimony lets us speculate that Kant's influence could have survived into the following decade. If it is true that a school needs years to be consolidated, it is also correct that neither is it possible for it to be extinguished from one hour to the next. Thus, it is valid to say that it could have continued to exist during the whole of the following decade. The reference in Tennemann's book can be understood as a demonstration of the endurance of São Paulo Kantianism.

Another São Paulo thinker influenced by Kant, the politician and later regent of Brazil Father Diogo Antônio Feijó (1784–1843),[4] could be the source of São Paulo Kantianism. In *Cadernos de filosofia* (Philosophical notebooks),[5] written between 1818 and 1821, Feijó began to develop a sui generis way of interpreting Kantianism. Distancing himself from scholasticism and combating the political conservativism of some sectors of the rural aristocracy, his appropriation of Kant developed along the lines of the new liberalism.[6]

From the 1830s onward, in terms of writings and publications, the flame of Kantianism appears to have been practically extinguished; at least until it was relit by the Recife School in the final quarter of the nineteenth century. But we can also suppose that the influence of Kant's ideals had left the page for the streets and animated the political transformations from the end of the so-called First Empire through the period of the Regency and up to the beginning of the so-called Second Empire. The very trajectory of Feijó, who assumed the Regency in 1835, appears to suggest something along these lines.

Ironically this first stage of Kantian thought in Brazil, with its ties to liberalism, is due to the authoritarian Napoleon. As we have seen, Kant's thought first arrived in Brazil around 1808, as everything indicates, with the library of the future emperor. It was Napoleon's invasion of Portugal that prompted the transfer of the Royal Library to Rio de Janeiro. Although in the beginning the presence of Kantian thought was tenuous and reduced to a half dozen scattered references, it would wind up influencing Brazilian thinking in a marked way.

The Kantianism of Tobias Barreto

Kant's thought began to reappear in Brazilian scholarship with *Teoria transcendtal do direito* (Transcendental theory of right) (1876) by João Theodoro Xavier, and with texts by Tobias Barreto such as "Recordação de Kant" (Reminiscences of Kant) (1887) and other writings from the last years of his life. In "Deve a metafisica ser considerada morta?" (Should metaphysics be considered dead?) (1875), for example, Barreto wrote: "All of philosophy up until the appearance of Kant, as Schopenhauer teaches, was nothing more than a sterile dream of falsehood and intellectual servitude, from which later days only freed itself thanks to the *Critique of Pure Reason*."[7]

Aside from the weight of this declaration, there is an interesting detail that these emblematic and loaded words of strength and universality hide. They were written the same year that Barreto, in the small interior city of Escada, edited a curious German-language newspaper called *Deutcher Kämpfer*, of which—writes Luís W. Vita—Tobias Barreto was the only writer and, perhaps, the only reader.[8] But, like thinking that manifests itself in little details such as a love of the German language and a consciousness of the importance of Kant, the episode of the newspaper revealed the character and work of an author who wound up setting a certain agenda for the future Recife

School. Thus, Antonio Paim sees Barreto's importance in that, in opposition to the positivist project of creating a social physics, in which human beings were the subject of determinist schemes, Barreto stressed human beings as consciousness, reorienting the center of philosophical investigation toward the world of culture. In doing so, he drew his inspiration directly from Kant, following the example of some contemporary European thinkers, and also inspired the main orientation of the Recife School.[9] So profound was his influence that in the first half of the twentieth century Brazilian studies on Kant did not just take the southwest Baden neo-Kantianism as their base, but also, above all else, they took the legacy of Tobias Barreto in his emphasis on German Idealism. This has already been amply documented by historians of Brazilian thought who emphasized his capabilities as an eminent thinker.[10]

Brazilian Neo-Kantianism in the Early Twentieth Century: The Recife School and Culturalism

In the beginning of the twentieth century, various works that are about Kant or related to his thought appeared. First, there were those texts by Father Charles Sentroul, a professor at the University of Louvain in Belgium who taught at the University of São Paulo, who wrote, among other texts, *La philosophie religieuse de Kant* (Kant's religious philosophy) and *L'objet de la métaphysique selon Kant et selon Aristote* (The object of metaphysics according to Kant and Aristotle) (1905), both published in France. The latter was later translated into German (*Kant und Aristoteles*, 1911). In 1908, the second edition of Silvio Romero's *Ensaio de filosofia do direito* (Essay on the philosophy of right) was published with a part that corresponds to *Kant e a metafisica* (Kant and metaphysics). In 1909, Januário Lucas Gaffrée wrote, under the influence of the Marburg School, *Teoria do conhecimento de Kant* (Kant's theory of knowledge), published in Rio de Janeiro.[11] In 1912 Pedro Lessa, ex-chief of police and judge of the Supreme Federal Tribunal, published a paper against Kant ("O idealismo transcendental ou criticismo de Kant" [Transcendental idealism, or critique of Kant]) in *Estudos de filosofia do direito* (Studies in the philosophy of right). Although it is a text that is worth the trouble of reading more as a curiosity within the history of Brazilian Kantianism, its contents are rather poor and its criticisms irrelevant.

In 1924, a "Commemorative Party for the Bicentennial of Kant's Birth" was organized that resulted in the publication of a collection of papers edited in Rio de Janeiro by the publishers Canton & Bayer. Amoroso Costa, "Kant e as ciências exatas" (Kant and the exact sciences), Abelardo Lobo, "Kant e o direito" (Kant and right), Nuno Pinheiro, "Kant," and Pontes de Miranda, "Kant em face à cultura geral" (Kant with regard to general culture) are found in this collection. The work offers a general overview of the relation between Kant's philosophy and the sciences and culture and is generally well executed.

Already in the so-called Recife School, authors such as Sílvio Romero, Clóvis Bevilacqua, Arthur Orlando, and some other thinkers forged a Brazilian kind of neo-Kantianism as a response to spiritualism and positivism. They thought of philosophy as a theory of knowledge, but they also thought about the difference between nature and freedom, and consequently, they considered culture to be a free anthropologic dimension of the human universe and not merely a natural one. They sought to distance themselves from the explanatory model of the positivists, whose naturalist determinism defended a type of social engineering that conflicted with the ideas of the Recife School. Kantian philosophy furnished them with another perspective to think of human actions in society and of the products of culture.

The *culturalist current* succeeded the Recife School as its heir, and signified, for Kantian studies, a type of theoretical-institutional continuation that sought to recreate a historical-geographical identity. It is in this sense that, as Paim notes, the culturalist current considered itself the heir of Tobias Barreto, and took his meditations as a framework. Paim continues by claiming that this event anticipated the German neo-Kantian movement by several decades.[12]

During the 1940s, Miguel Reale initiated the culturalist current movement with works in a neo-Kantian vein such as *Fundamentos do direito* (Elements of right) and *Teoria do direito e do estado* (Theory of right and the state). Several years later, after the foundation of the *Instituto brasileiro de filosofia* (Brazilian institute of philosophy) and of the *Revista Brasileira de Filosofia* (*Brazilian journal of philosophy*), Reale extended his criticism of the formal concept of culture and reformulated his reflections on right, culminating in such seminal texts as *Experiência e cultura* (Experience and culture) (1977) and *Verdade e conjetura* (Truth and conjecture) (1983), in which he used a systematic analysis partially inspired by Kant's work to address the fundamental problems of philosophy, first in dialogue with Husserl and later with Heidegger and other contemporary philosophers. His work appears to recreate an arc that goes from the neo-Kantianism of the Baden School, represented by Rickert and Windelband (in opposition to the Marburg School, represented by Cohen and Natorp), to the reflection about right and culture in a clearly phenomenological tenor.

Kant's Presence in Journals and Books in the Twentieth Century

Production in the form of specialized journal articles as a result of university research appeared in the second half of the twentieth century. During the 1950s, 1960s, and 1970s, the *Revista Brasileira de Filosofia* (Brazilian journal of philosophy)[13] and the *Revista Convivium* published many texts about Kant, both from culturalists and also from other authors (Ubiratam de Macedo, François Hubert Lepargeneur, Fritz Joachim Von Rintelen, Romano Galeffi, etc.).

During the first thirty years of the publication of philosophy periodicals in Brazil (the 1950s, 1960s, and 1970s) the space occupied by research on Kant is not voluminous and was sustained the whole time with some effort. Kant was the subject of numerous articles, some dedicated solely to him, some to comparison with other philosophers. But Kant was one subject among many and held no special importance.

The 1980s marked a turning point in Kantian studies—a true change that we can cite as a return to Kant. The substantial increase in the number of publications and the expansion of research about Kant are tendencies that emerged at this time and were accentuated in the following decades. Compared to prior periods, the 1980s saw the appearance of a torrent of works about Kant. Many dozens of articles and books appeared, stimulating even more interest among students. Many of the active writers at this time continue to be active and influential today. Here we must limit ourselves to mentioning just a handful of these texts.

In 1981, Valério Rohden published his celebrated book about Kant's philosophy, *Interesse da razão e liberdade* (The interest of reason and freedom), in which he explains the relationship between freedom and universality from the point of view of the practical interest of human reason and argues for the universality of freedom in ethics, right, and history.[14] Rohden has also contributed to recent Kant studies through his series of careful translations, described below.

Around this time an important symposium about Kant was organized at the University of Brasília, the papers from which were later published (1984) in a notable collection.[15] Such important scholars as Andrés Raggio, Wolfgang Röd, Manfredo Oliveira, and Gérard Lebrun participated in this symposium. The topics of debate encompassed a variety of Kantian themes, such as the relationship between the Inaugural Dissertation and the first *Critique* (Lebrun), Kant's constructivist theory of mathematics (Raggio), and well-known critiques of Kant by Hegelians and contemporary continental philosophy (Oliveira, Röd).

In 1987 Ricardo Terra published "A distinção entre direito e ética na filosofia kantiana" (The distinction between right and ethics in Kant's philosophy),[16] translated in this volume. Terra responds to certain misunderstandings of the relation of right and virtue to morality by showing how both reflect morality through different applications of autonomy and different understandings of duty.

In 1989 Marco Zingano published *Razão e história em Kant* (Reason and history in Kant), an acclaimed book in which he asked how to think about history purely rationally and argued that Kant's philosophy, by starting from the concepts of free action and free will, could be explained without attributing any hidden plan or any kind of eschatology to history.

The increase in publications during this period indicates a considerable change in the course of philosophical research in comparison with previous decades when one group and a handful of scholars dealt with Kant. The samples seen above are part of a list of publications that embrace a whole range of possible studies about Kant.

Kant, Graduate Studies, and the Brazilian Kant Society

The academic work of teaching, research, and mentoring on Kant began to be systematized in Brazil at the same time as the boom in publications on Kant. In fact, the 1970s saw, gradually, the birth of the academic circles and research groups on Kant that consolidated during the 1980s and 1990s and that still are bearing fruit today. Intellectuals linked to some of these groups founded the Sociedade Kant Brasileira (Brazilian Kant society) in the 1980s and paved the way for the Tenth International Kant Congress in 2005 in Sao Paulo.

Although various colleges were in existence throughout the nineteenth century, the first universities were founded only in the first half of the twentieth century, and philosophy professors were usually trained abroad. New professional and financial possibilities for research that were created or consolidated at this time had an enormous influence on the academic structure of Brazilian universities. They were beneficial not only to university research in general but to Kant studies in particular. As the 1970s gave way to the 1980s, graduate programs in philosophy were created in Brazil. Leading funding institutions such as the German Academic Exchange Service (DAAD), the Brazilian Federal Agency for Support and Evaluation of Graduate Education (CAPES), the National Council for Scientific and Technological Development (CNPq), and the Foundation for the Support of Research in the State of São Paulo (Fapesp) strengthened research groups and permitted interaction with foreign universities. They supported the education of many Brazilian doctoral students in Brazil and also allowed them to study abroad in France, Germany, and other countries. Institutions such as the Universidade de São Paulo (University of São Paulo), the Universidade de Campinas (University of Campinas), the Universidade Federal de Minas Gerais (Federal University of Minas Gerais), the Pontifícia Universidade Católica do Rio de Janeiro (Pontifical Catholic University of Rio de Janeiro), the Universidade Federal do Rio de Janeiro (Federal University of Rio de Janeiro), and the Universidade Federal do Rio Grande do Sul (Federal University of

Rio Grande do Sul) consolidated a model of teaching and research in philosophy, particularly in Kant studies, that later spread to the whole country. In this sense, a large step forward was also taken by the foundation of the Sociedade Kant Brasileira made possible by the work of Zeljko Loparic, Ricardo Ribeiro Terra, Balthazar Barbosa Filho, Guido A. de Almeida, Valério Rohden, José Nicolau Heck, and Christian Hamm, among others.[17] The society, in turn, was strengthened by its local affiliates in Rio de Janeiro, Campinas, and Porto Alegre, where various colloquia were organized and the diffusion of Kantian studies was institutionalized.

Besides the work of Miguel Reale and the culturalists in the specific areas of right, philosophy of law, and culture, the notable work and teaching of Gérard Lebrun of the Universidade de Campinas and the Universidade de São Paulo (both universities in the state of São Paulo), starting in the 1970s, inspired various articles, theses, and dissertations. Although his famous book, *Kant et la fin de la métaphysique* (Kant and the end of metaphysics), published in Paris in 1970, was only published in a Portuguese translation in 1993, the seed planted by Lebrun marked an epoch and set down roots in Brazil. Thus it was that in the two following decades studies of Kant were expanded at the Universidade de São Paulo thanks to the undertaking and initiative of Professors José Arthur Gianotti, Ricardo Ribeiro Terra, Franklin Leopoldo de Silva, and Luis Henrique Lopes dos Santos, as well as at the Universidade de Campinas by the tireless work of Professor Zeljko Loparic, the first president of the Sociedade Kant Brasileira, and Professor Lutz Müller and other Kant and Hegel scholars. In general we can say that a French style of interpretation developed at the Universidade de São Paulo, while a more German or even American style developed at the Universidade de Campinas. The former pursued interpretations of Kant stressing history, judgment, and practical philosophy, as exemplified in Terra's essays. The latter is known for semantic interpretations of Kant advocated by Loparic, although his book *A semântica transcendental de Kant* (Kant's transcendental semantics) was published only in 2000.

The role played by the group founded in the late 1970s around Professors Guido Antônio de Almeida and Raúl F. Landim at the Pontifícia Universidade Católica de Rio de Janeiro was also of fundamental importance. This group migrated in the 1980s to the Universidade Federal do Rio de Janeiro and founded the *Seminário de filosofia da linguagem* (Seminar on philosophy of language). In the 1990s they founded the journal *Analytica* and participated in the foundation of the Kant Society, in the foundation of the journal *Studia Kantiana* (Kantian Studies), and in the organization of large colloquia on Kant. As a whole this group tends to apply analytical methodology to assess Kant interpretations and well as Kant's own arguments, as well as to engage German- and English-speaking scholarship.

The examples of these three universities (São Paulo, Campinas, and Rio) reveal the institutionalization of Kant studies in Brazil. Similar consolidation of Kant work took place in Porto Alegre, where a section of the Brazilian Kant Society continues to thrive, and in Belo Horizonte, where Kant and Hegel studies developed in tandem. At other universities some Kant scholars such as José Henrique dos Santos and Roberto Markenson stood out and helped train the new generation of Kant scholars.

The 1990s and Beyond

Starting in the 1990s philosophy in Brazil decentralized. Not only did graduate courses (masters and doctorate) multiply throughout the country, but so too did highly qualified professional groups. As a result, we find today in this new context many Kant scholars and groups of scholars in various universities outside of the Rio de Janeiro, Campinas, São Paulo, and Belo Horizonte axis.

In the 1990s philosophy journals also multiplied. In Kantian studies, two of them mentioned above deserve to be singled out: *Analytica* and the journal of the Kant Society *Studia Kantiana*.

Between the end of the 1980s and into the new century there were many national and international congresses in Brazil. Perhaps most important were the large Brazilian Kant congresses in 1989, 1997, 2001, and 2008 organized by the Brazilian Kant Society. Other conferences were dedicated to specific subjects such as the congress "Belo, sublime, e Kant" (Beauty, the sublime, and Kant), in Belo Horizonte, or allowed smaller groups of scholars with similar interests to meet, such as the annual Campinas Colloquium on Kant at the Universidade de Campinas, primarily but not exclusively from a semantic approach.

It should also be noted that the translation of Kant's three *Critiques* by Valério Rohden, as well as several events and books he organized with the support of the Goethe Institute, made possible the greater diffusion of Kant's ideas, both among specialists and among the larger public. Previous translations into Portuguese had been published in Portugal. Rohden's translations offered a consistent vocabulary across Kant's works.

In the late 1990s the Kantforschungsstelle of the University of Mainz requested as complete a collection of Brazilian work on Kant as possible. Professor Juan Bonaccini created an extensive bibliography of Portuguese language work on Kant and, in addition, ensured that the Kant-Forschungsstelle had copies of much of the work for its archives. This collection allows for the work of Brazilian scholars to be accessible to Kant scholars around the world.

The organization of congresses and colloquia on Kant mentioned above; the interaction with other Kant scholars from the Americas and Europe; the publications of many members of the Brazilian Kant Society in journals and books from Germany, the United States, France, Mexico, Argentina, and elsewhere; the presence of several Brazilian scholars in international congresses on Kant; Professor Rohden's constant dialogue with the Kant Gesellschaft; the inclusion of a large part of the recent Brazilian work on Kant in the archives of the Kant-Forschungsstelle; all built on the past and culminated not only in Brazil hosting the Tenth International Kant Congress in 2005 in São Paulo, but also in achieving outstanding scholarship in Kant studies today.

During the 1990s, authors we can call the "new Kantians" began to publish. Some are Kant scholars, while others work in contemporary philosophy in dialogue with Kant. But there are too many of them to discuss in detail here. Their debt to the scholars discussed above lies both in direct student-teacher relations and in the legacy of published work. Of course, many of those older scholars who brought Kant work to maturity in the 1970s and 1980s are still active in the new century. They have the privilege of seeing the fruit of their mentoring in the active careers of the new Kantians.

So-called new Kantians are writing numerous essays, books, and articles; they also have been organizing colloquia, seminars, and symposia; they have been advisors for undergraduate, masters, and doctoral studies; they have been participating in national and international congresses; and they have published in various countries. These new Kantians are the ones who more and more are guiding the new debates on Kantian themes and directing the course of research in Brazil.[18] Some of them have papers included in this volume; but many others deserve attention and, perhaps, another collection like this one.

In Closing

A more thorough history of the whole of Kantianism in Brazil over the past two centuries should propose a new periodicization on the basis of the reading of the texts. It would need to indicate the currents in Kantian scholarship starting from their structure and the arguments in the writings. It should also research the records and documents and events that have marked the course of research—not only in congresses, colloquia, and symposia, but also in dissertation defenses that from the 1980s onward have been creating the latest generation of Brazilian philosophers. Perhaps this paper will set a framework for Brazilian Kant scholarship and will contribute to the writing of a new page in this history.

Notes

1. However, the inauguration of the Royal Library, allowing scholars access only with an explicit request, did not occur until May 13, 1811.

2. Tercio Sampaio Ferraz Jr., "A filosofia do direito no Brasil" [Philosophy of right in Brazil], in *Revista Brasileira de Filosofia* 45, no. 197 (2000): 16.

3. As noted by Ferraz, ibid. See Wilhelm Gottlieb Tennemann, *Grundriss der Geschichte der Philosophie für den akademischen Unterricht* (Leipzig: J. A. Barth, 1829).

4. Priest, professor, politician. São Paulo representative in the Constitutional Convention in Lisbon (1821); later senator, minister of justice, and regent of the empire. He had an extremely important role during the Liberal Revolution of 1842.

5. Diogo Antônio Feijó, *Cadernos de filosofia*, ed. Miguel Reale, 1st ed. (São Paulo: Grijalbo, 1967).

6. See Miguel Reale, "Feijó e o kantismo (a propósito de uma crítica imatura)" [Feijó and Kantianism (with regard to an immature criticism)], *Revista da faculdade de direito* (São Paulo: n.L, 1950), 330–51.

7. Tobias Barreto, "Deve a metafísica ser considerada morta?," in Barreto, *Estudos de filosofia* [Studies in philosophy], ed. Luiz Antonio Barreto (São Paulo: Editorial Grijalbo, 1977), 188.

8. Luís W. Vita, *Panorama da filosofia no Brasil* [Overview of philosophy in Brazil] (Porto Alegre: Editora Globo, 1969), 88.

9. A. Paim, "A corrente culturalista" [The culturalist current], in *As idéias filosóficas no Brasil, Século 20, Parte 1*, ed. Adolfo Crippa (São Paulo: Ed. Convívio, 1978), 11.

10. See Paim, ibid. and J. Cruz Costa, *Contribuição à história das idéias no Brasil* [Contribution to the history of ideas in Brazil] (Rio de Janeiro: Editora Jose Olympio, 1956). However, Newton Sucupira, "Tobias Barreto e o kantismo" (Tobias Barreto and Kantianism), *Revista Brasileira de Filosofia* 32, no. 135 (1982): 163, also mentions the contributions of this translator, reader, and critic from Sergipe. Sucupira accuses the writer of forgetting the names of those he cites, and he proves this by transcribing large excerpts along with the translation made by Tobias Barreto; all of this weakens the supposed originality of the work. We, however, strangers to this copyright debate, must wonder to what degree citing the name of the owner of an idea really would have changed the originality of opinions and of the work of someone who, under the influence of German Idealism, edited a newspaper in German in the picturesque city of Escada.

11. This book was recently reedited: Januário Lucas Gaffrée, *Teoria do conhecimento de Kant* [Kant's theory of knowledge], Prefácio de Valério Rohden (Porto Alegre: Editora da Pontifícia Universidade Católica de Rio Grande do Sul, Coleção de Pensadores Gaúchos, 2000).

12. Paim, "A corrente culturalista," 11.

13. The journal *Kriterion*, founded in 1947, is the oldest philosophy journal in Brazil; it is earlier than the *Revista Brasileira de Filosofia* (1951) and the *Sintese Política Económica e Social* (1959), which disappeared in 1968 and was refounded in 1974 with the name *Sintese-Nova Fase*. These three are the oldest.

14. São Paulo, Editora Ática.

15. *Kant*, ed. Manfredo Araújo de Oliveira et al. (Brazil: UnB, 1984).

16. *Filosofia e Política* 4 (1987): 49–65.

17. The Founding Charter with a list of the founding members and the statute of the Sociedade Kant Brasileira can be found online on the Campinas affiliates website: http://www.cle.unicamp.br/kant_campinas/estatutoi.htm.

18. All of the researchers in Brazil have their curriculum vitae available through Lattes do CNPq (Conselho Nacional de Desenvolvimento Científico e Tecnológico). It is possible to search by name at http://lattes.cnpq.br/index.htm to see the work of every one of them.

2

Self-Consciousness and Objective Knowledge in the Transcendental Deduction of the *Critique of Pure Reason*

Guido Antônio de Almeida

The work presented here proposes to investigate the question *whether* and in *what sense* epistemic self-consciousness constitutes for Kant a principle for explaining and establishing the possibility of knowledge.

Given Kant's explicit declarations, the question *whether* self-consciousness constitutes such a principle may undoubtedly appear remarkable. Did not Kant affirm this textually? Certainly, but if we read the texts with attention, we see that they are far from being clear and decisive to the extent that one would initially think. I wish to make two preliminary observations to this point. In the first place, it is convenient to observe that what is actually elevated into a principle of knowledge is not always simply self-consciousness, but also the "unity of self-consciousness." A modification of little importance? Merely a qualification of the aspect of self-consciousness that makes it a principle? By no means, I'd say. By the "unity of self-consciousness" Kant understands the unity of intuitions synthesized according to concepts of objects,[1] in other words, the objective unity that is produced when the synthesized intuitions are submitted *in judgment* to a concept of an object. But this would seem to mean that the unity of self-consciousness is nothing other than the conformity of intuitions to the concept of objects in judgment. This said, it is easy to understand why the unity of self-consciousness thus understood can be declared the selfsame principle of knowledge. One might indeed say that a proposition stating that "intuition necessarily conforms to concepts of objects" expresses in an abstract manner the form of all particular cognitive judgments; and proving that

This is a revised but not substantially modified translation of an article published as "Consciência de si e conhecimento objetivo na dedução transcendental de I. Kant," in *Analytica* 1 (1994): 187–219. Translated by the author.

this proposition is valid is to prove a priori, that is, in principle, the possibility of making cognitive judgments.

To be sure, the principle is formulated, not as a simple principle of the unity of intuitions (or of its conformity to concepts), but rather as a principle of the unity of intuitions *in* or *for self-consciousness*. The italicized expression indicates the condition under which it is possible to affirm the validity of the principle of the unity of intuitions. Does this not signify, however, that self-consciousness is the condition in which knowledge is possible? And is it not the same thing to say that self-consciousness is the condition, the foundation, or the ultimate principle of knowledge?

In order to be clear about this, it is necessary to consider what Kant actually intends to prove and how he goes about it. I propose that Kant's ultimate aim in the positive part of *Critique of Pure Reason* is to prove the possibility of objective knowledge in general. Since Kant's concept of knowledge requires subsuming sense intuitions under concepts of object, one can say that the ultimate aim is to prove the principle that all our sense intuitions are such that they can in principle be subsumed under concepts of objects, in other words: that our sense intuitions necessarily conform to concepts of objects. And since the application of concepts of objects presupposes thinking objects as such by means of nonempirical, "pure" concepts of objects in general, that is, categories that constitute the universal form of particular concepts of objects, Kant's ultimate aim may be said to be that of proving the necessary conformity of intuitions to categories, which is in fact the avowed aim of the Transcendental Deduction of the Categories (as explained in §13).

Now, it is possible to *have intuitions* without it being necessary ipso facto to *think them* by means of concepts, or in other words, without it being necessary to identify and characterize conceptually (as intuitions of this or that object) the selfsame content of our intuitions—so much so that we may attribute the capacity of perceiving the world around them to animals and beings incapable of thinking and expressing conceptually what they perceive. The conformity to concepts of objects is not, then, a condition of having intuitions, and we can say that there is nothing in intuitions as such that relate them by themselves alone to a concept of an object.[2] From this it follows, however, that it is not possible to prove the possibility of knowledge by merely clarifying the conditions under which it is possible to have intuitions. All difficulty of proving the possibility of knowledge, one might say, resides in this. But neither can we, as some propose, be released from the necessity of finding a solution, alleging that the question was inadequately formulated and that the problem is a false one. Furthermore, if we accept the analysis given of the concept of knowledge, the proposition that intuitions in principle conform to concepts of objects is a synthetic one, therefore a proposition contingently true, that may be denied without contradiction and whose assertion requires, therefore, a justification that extends beyond simple elucidation of the meaning of its terms.

The argument that Kant devised in order to establish the principle of the possibility of knowledge is based on the hypothesis that it is possible to prove the necessary conformity of the intuitions to concepts of objects for any subject that not only has intuitions but also knows that it has them, that is, has self-consciousness as well as intuitions.

Self-consciousness thus provides the tertium quid capable of establishing a relationship between intuitions and concepts of objects. The question however is: in what way? To my understanding, in only two ways: either self-consciousness is seen as a condition of the conformity of intuitions to concepts of objects, and this conformity to concepts is produced by the fact that we become aware of our intuitions, or conformity of intuitions to concepts of objects is taken to be a condition for the existence of a subject endowed with self-consciousness (its *ratio essendi*), and self-consciousness is then a condition, not of the conformity of intuitions to concepts of objects, but rather of the *discernment* of its possibility (its *ratio cognoscendi*). This is why I said that it is necessary to ask in what sense self-consciousness is interpreted as providing Kant with a principle for establishing the possibility of knowledge. In one sense, it is taken to be the very basis of the possibility of knowledge; on the other, it is considered as being only a perspective that permits us to discern the possibility of objective knowledge.

In which of these senses, therefore, must we understand the Kantian affirmation that consciousness provides a principle for establishing the possibility of knowledge? In order to reply to this question, I propose to return to the argument by which Kant purports to prove, in the two versions of the Transcendental Deduction, that our intuitions in principle conform to the categories, thus to concepts of objects in general.

My investigation is based on a hypothesis that I do not intend to discuss here, but that I hope can be accepted as having some plausibility. This hypothesis is that the argument in the Deduction, that it is to say, the argument for proving the necessary conformity of our intuitions to concepts of objects and, in consequence, to the categories, can be reconstructed as an argument directed against the skeptic who doubts the necessity for our intuitions to be in conformity to concepts of objects, but who doesn't doubt that it is possible to have consciousness of these intuitions as something that takes place within us.

I will attempt here to demonstrate two general theses. The first is that the Deduction consists in the proof that consciousness of intuitions, admitted by the skeptic who doubts the possibility of determining them according to concepts of objects, has as its condition self-consciousness (of the subject that has consciousness of its intuitions) as a numerically identical subject and that this consciousness of itself implies in its turn a consciousness of objects, that is to say, the capacity to determine given intuitions by means of concepts of objects.

The second general thesis is that the two versions of the Deduction diverge with regard to the nature of this implication. The first version tries to prove, if my interpretation is correct, that the possibility of thinking intuitions by means of concepts of objects is a consequence of self-consciousness, more precisely, of the fact that the manifold of intuitions is synthesized by a subject conscious of itself, and in consequence, of what it does. Self-consciousness appears here, then, one can say, as a *ratio essendi* of the thinking of objects and, in consequence, as a "source" of the categories or the principle that permits explanation of its genesis. In the second version, on the contrary, self-consciousness (the "I think" that is described in §16 as an "analytical unity of apperception") appears as having as its condition the power of making objectively valid judgments (and that corresponds to the "synthetic unity" that is necessary for self-consciousness). This further act plays the role of a premise in the argument against the skeptic, but now no longer as an explicative principle of the genesis of the categories, but rather uniquely as a premise permitting an explanation of the necessity of admitting the necessary conformity of our intuitions to the conception of objects. The argument is, therefore, in summary, that I cannot be conscious of myself, as would admit the skeptic, if I am not capable of judging objectively, since the power of judgment is a necessary condition for self-consciousness.

The Argument of the Deduction: From Consciousness to Self-consciousness

The Argument in the 1781 Edition (A)

We find the best and most succinct outline of the argument in the first version of the Deduction in the paragraph on the "Provisory Explanation of the Possibility of Categories as *a priori* Cognitions." Here Kant states:

> However, the possibility, indeed even the necessity of these categories rests on the relation that the entire sensibility, and with it also all possible appearances, have to the original apperception, in which everything is necessarily in agreement with the conditions of the thoroughgoing unity of self-consciousness, i.e., must stand under universal functions of synthesis, namely of the synthesis in accordance with concepts, as that in which alone apperception can demonstrate a priori its thoroughgoing and necessary identity. Thus the concept of a cause is nothing other than a synthesis (of that which follows in the temporal series with other appearances) in accordance with concepts; and without that sort of unity, which has its rule a priori, and which subjects the

> appearances to itself, thoroughgoing and universal, hence necessary unity of consciousness would not be encountered in the manifold perceptions. (*Pure Reason*, A111–12)

As obscure as it may be, this passage makes reasonably clear at least the point according to which the proof of the objective validity of the categories rests; in short, on two basic premises: (1) the relation of our intuitions, which are sensitive, to self-consciousness, and (2) the relation of self-consciousness, or rather, of "the unity of self-consciousness," to the "functions" of the synthesis of the intuitions in conformity to concepts. It is true that the passage does not make clear the exact nature of these relationships and, above all, does not indicate the kind of reasons on which Kant might have established the premises themselves. In order to clarify this, it is necessary to find in the Deduction those passages in which Kant explains his argument in full.

Kant's reasons for affirming the first premise are indicated in six different passages, but very summarily in each one. In A107 the unity of consciousness (identified with "transcendental apperception" in the next sentence) is presented as a condition of the occurrence within us of "cognitions" (*Erkenntnisse*),[3] as well as of its connection and unity.[4] In A113, self-consciousness is presented as a condition of all possible appearances as representations.[5] In A116, the apprehension (*Aufnahme*) of intuitions in consciousness is presented as a condition that intuitions must fulfill in order to "concern us" or to be something to us. In the sentence that follows, consciousness of the identity of the self is presented as a condition of the "possibility of all representations," because, Kant argues, representations represent something in me only if they belong together to a consciousness in which they can be connected.[6] In the famous note on A117 on "empirical consciousness," the possibility of empirical consciousness is presented as a condition of the existence of representations, and transcendental consciousness, in turn, as a condition of empirical consciousness.[7] In A120, consciousness is presented as a condition, not of appearance, but of appearance's being "an object of knowledge" and thus of its existing for us—and further, of its simply being some thing, since it only exists in cognitions.[8] Finally, in A123–24, the "I" of the "apperception" is a condition of consciousness of our representations.[9]

This is all we have to help us understand what Kant wants to say. Let us admit that it is little and that Kant's explanations appear as an attempt to remedy lack of clarity with larger obscurity. From the passages cited we can extract, however, at least two conclusions: (1) Kant did not intend to prove the necessary relationship of intuitions to self-consciousness directly, but rather in two steps, by proving first that all intuitions are related to a possible empirical consciousness and, subsequently, that self-consciousness is a condition of empirical consciousness, hence of intuitions themselves. (2)

The proof that all intuition is necessarily linked to consciousness is based on the assertion that otherwise it would not exist for us, or purely and simply would not exist as a representation.

But these indications still leave numerous doubts. It is true that the connection between the concept of consciousness and that of self-consciousness has a certain initial plausibility, which is due to the fact that we think of intuitions as mental events or subjective states (as expressed by sentences of the type "I know that I φ," where φ stands for a psychological, or mental, predicate such as: "I am seeing," "I am hearing," etc.). But it is not enough to ascertain that ordinarily we express the consciousness that we have of our intuitions as subjective states (that is, states of a subject that refers to itself as something distinct from the states that it has). Above and beyond that, it is important to explain why it should be so.

Our difficulties are even greater with regard to the relationship between consciousness and intuitions. Here, the assertion that, in order *to have intuitions*, it is necessary to *have consciousness* of these intuitions is not only implausible in itself, because it contradicts the statement that representations in general can be unconscious (A320), but also contradicts the doctrine of transcendental aesthetics regarding the conditions of intuition, according to which space and time are the only (formal) conditions of intuition.

I believe that these difficulties derive from a certain ambiguity in the use of the word "consciousness." As a matter of fact, we do use it in two different senses that I would like to term the *propositional* and the *nonpropositional* sense of "consciousness." In its propositional sense, "being conscious (or being aware) of something" is equivalent to "knowing that *p*" and involves the application of concepts. So, when we say, for example: "The religious man is conscious of God's presence in the world," we may rephrase what we mean by saying: "The religious man *knows that* God is present in the world" and by attributing thus to the religious man the capacity to conceive the notion of God and to think that God is present in the world. We can, however, speak of being conscious (or being aware) of something in relation to mental states that do not require the application of concepts, much less the understanding of propositions describing the state one is in, in order to be in it. So, when we say: "The dog is aware of his master's presence," we do of course attribute to the dog some sort of knowledge, which we might describe as *knowing how* to perform certain acts, such as turning its eyes in a certain direction and locating a certain person in space, but not the intellectual capacity of thinking that such and such proposition is the case.

Now, if we take the word "consciousness" in the propositional sense, we cannot say that consciousness is a condition of having intuitions (or even of having representations in a general sense, comprising concepts and propositions), since, in the propositional sense, "to have consciousness" includes the application of concepts, and "to have intuitions" by definition does not involve the application of concepts. This is why Kant has to admit the possibility of there being *unconscious* intuitions and even other classes of *unconscious* representations.[10]

If we take the word "consciousness" in the nonpropositional sense, we can say that consciousness is a condition of having intuitions, but in this case "to have consciousness" cannot signify anything but the capacity to distinguish that which is given, be it externally according to spatial relations, be it internally according to temporal relations. Given the synonymy between "to be conscious of" and "to know," as well as the possibility of speaking of a kind of nonpropositional knowing, the assertion that consciousness is a condition of having intuitions is always possible and explains why we can attribute some kind of consciousness to animal beings. In fact, we say of animals and infants that they are conscious or, on the contrary, that they lose consciousness, when they have or lose the capacity of distinguishing external objects, as well as the capacity of feeling (having sensations and feelings). In Kant and in the philosophical tradition in general we do not find the notion of consciousness as applied to the *external* sense, although there would be nothing to prevent this use of the term.[11] On the other hand, we find the notion of the internal sense assimilated to the notion of consciousness.

If, however, we take the word "consciousness" in a nonpropositional sense, and in consequence, as a synonym of "internal sense" in Kant, it will not be possible to derive here any of the consequences that Kant wishes to extract from the thesis that having (or at least being able to have) consciousness of our intuitions is a condition of having intuitions, namely: (1) that all intuition is necessarily related to a *possible* consciousness, and (2) that all consciousness of an intuition is related to self-consciousness.

Let us see, however, how far we can go if we interpret the passages in question with the aid of the *nonpropositional* concept of consciousness. We will say, then, that Kant's thesis is that consciousness understood as the internal sense, which is the capacity of discriminating in time what is internally given, is a condition of our having intuitions qua representations, that is, as something that exists in us and can only exist in us. And, given the fact that all external intuition is linked to something in us (sense affection, sensation), we can say that consciousness is also the condition of external intuitions to the extent that they also are linked to internal occurrences. This effectively allows us to arrive at the first conclusion that Kant wishes to draw, that is, that all intuitions are linked to consciousness (which we have accepted to assimilate to the internal sense).

The first difficulty with this interpretation is that it arrives at a much stronger conclusion than that extracted by Kant since it follows from it that a condition of having intuitions, considered as representations, or mental events, is being *actually* conscious of it. Indeed, one cannot have external intuition that is not at the same time apprehended in time as an internal representation, of which we are, therefore, actually aware in the nonpropositional sense. But this fits poorly with the thesis's restriction to the *possibility* of having consciousness. In any case, since whoever would prove the most would thereby also prove the least and since whatever is real is also possible, one could always contend that the objection is not decisive.

More decisive is a second objection based on the difficulty in linking our (nonpropositional) awareness of intuitions in us with (propositional) self-consciousness. In point of fact, it could be objected against Kant that nothing concerning self-consciousness follows from the mere fact that we are immediately aware of our intuitions in the inner sense, since self-consciousness involves thinking and has a propositional content whereas the inner sense as such does not involve thinking and therefore cannot have a propositional content.

Let us see, therefore, how far we can go with the propositional concept of "consciousness." According to this concept, as we have seen, to be conscious of an intuition of *x* consists in knowing that one has an intuition of *x* and implies, therefore, the capacity to use predicates by which we characterize our intuition as such, namely, as a representation *in us* through which we intuit something *outside* of, or different from, us.[12] Is this the concept of consciousness that Kant has in mind in the passages cited? On A106, consciousness[13] is presented as a condition of the *occurrence in us* of "cognitions," that is to say, of "intuitions."[14] On A113, consciousness[15] is presented as a condition of representations, which we can interpret as a condition of the existence of something in us which presents to us something outside of us, and, finally, on A120, consciousness is presented as a condition by which appearances would be for us an object of knowledge, which we can interpret in the sense that we can only know that appearances exist in us as representations if we have consciousness of them.

There is no doubt, therefore, that in all of these passages we are dealing with the recognition of intuitions as representations—in Cartesian terms: with the knowledge of intuitions in their *formal reality* qua representations in us as opposed to their *objective reality* qua representations of something else. The difficulty that remains is that Kant would seem to be expressing a tautology when he asserts that consciousness is a condition for intuitions (appearances, cognitions) to exist for us, or to constitute an object of knowledge for us. Indeed, what else can the expressions "to exist for us" or "to be an object of knowledge for us" mean if not "to be something of which we have consciousness"? Kant would have been saying therefore that we cannot have consciousness of our intuitions as our representations if we do not have consciousness of them. However, what we would expect Kant to do is to stipulate for the consciousness of intuitions a condition distinct from the simple fact of having consciousness of intuitions.

Let us consider again the propositional concept of the word "consciousness." This involves, as we have seen, the characterization of intuitions in us as representations, therefore by means of predicates of representations. But, if this is so, we can say (in order to avoid interpreting Kant's thesis as a tautology) that his claim is that consciousness of having intuitions depends on the possibility of thinking them by means of concepts, with which we specify them, not relatively to what is represented in them, but rather relatively to the fact of their being representations in us. To put it briefly, if Kant's initial thesis is not a simple tautology, it must be the thesis that consciousness of having intuitions is precisely consciousness in the propositional sense, and this means that we can only say that we have consciousness of our intuitions if we can think them (characterize them) as such, that is, as representations within us of something distinct from ourselves.

To be sure, we do not have to employ predicates such as "intuition" or "representation" in order to become conscious of our intuitions as representations.[16] These are second order (formal) concepts with which the philosopher makes explicit the first order (material) concepts with which we characterize prephilosophically our intuitions as representations (namely, predicates such as "see," "hear," "feel," etc.). It is precisely this class of predicates that is necessary to employ in order to know that one has intuitions. We have to say, therefore, that we only have consciousness of our intuitions insofar as we think or enunciate propositions of the form: "I am seeing, hearing, feeling, etc.," that is, when we can make those enunciations that, in the *Prolegomena*, Kant terms "judgments of perception."

Yet this is not enough to account for all that is said in the texts: more precisely, it is not enough to explain why Kant states[17] that consciousness is a condition of representations not only existing for us, but also purely and simply of there being representations at all. However, this assertion is incompatible with the admission of the existence of unconscious representations and does not follow from the assertion of the propositional character of the consciousness of having intuitions.

We can observe once more, however, that, on A117 note, Kant qualifies his assertion: it is the *possibility* of having an empirical consciousness, not an *actual* empirical consciousness, that is here presented as a condition of the existence of representations. What is necessary, then, in order to have representations (or, for that matter, intuitions) is that it should be *possible* for one to have, not that one must actually have, consciousness of having representations. So Kant's claim about empirical consciousness is, not that we *do in fact*, but rather that we *can in principle* have an empirical consciousness of each representation in us (or, more specifically, of each of our intuitions as a representation in us. Can this assertion be derived from the thesis about the propositional character of the consciousness of having representations?

What can be argued to this effect is, in my view, the following. In order to have consciousness of having representations (or, more specifically, of having intuitions as representations in us) it is necessary, as we have seen, to know how to characterize them as representations. Let us suppose, however, that one wishes to deny that our intuitions can be conceived of as representations and that this impossibility should be understood as an impossibility in principle, thus as something to be explained not by some factual hindrance (e.g., a psychological mechanism of repression), but rather by the logic of the concept of representation. In this case, we could bring forward two arguments: (1) the concept is self-contradictory and describes something that is as impossible as a circular square; and (2) the concept is not self-contradictory, but rather problematic, because we cannot indicate precise criteria for using it and, in this case, the concept will not designate anything that is impossible to think in itself, but rather impossible to be known.

Kant's claim about empirical consciousness can be argued for by discarding beforehand all kinds of reasons that could be alleged for rejecting it. Indeed, starting from the observation that these have to be either factual or conceptual, one can purport to show that neither can be accepted as a sufficient ground for discarding it. Since Kant's point is a conceptual one, it cannot be rejected by factual arguments, that is, based on the discovery of facts that hinder consciousness or make it impossible (such as psychological mechanisms of repression as those investigated by psychoanalysis). As seen, Kant claims only the *possibility* in principle of becoming conscious of any particular mental content (especially intuitions), and the discovery of facts hindering consciousness presupposes this very claim, since it only shows that there is something that prevents making actual what is any way possible in principle.

If at all, Kant's thesis can only be refuted, then, by conceptual reasons, and that means by claiming that the concept of empirical consciousness is either self-contradictory or vacuous. Now, claiming that the concept of empirical consciousness is self-contradictory would amount to saying that describing a particular mental event as an intuition (therefore all judgments of the form: I know that I intuit, see, hear, feel, etc., something) involves a contradiction. But why should it be so, unless by arbitrary stipulation? To be sure, intuitions are in Kant's conception mental events that one can have without thinking that one has them, but this means that they are mental events that thinking beings cannot be conscious of, if they have them, unless we define them so by arbitrary convention. Arbitrary conventions, however, may be discarded offhand, and so there is no reason to accept the suggestion that Kant's concept might involve a self-contradiction.

On the other hand, claiming that the concept of empirical consciousness is vacuous and therefore problematic (in Kant's sense) amounts to saying that the marks that make up the content of this concept do not provide any criteria for applying it to any given object. This not only entails rejecting Kant's concept of consciousness as a philosophical construction without any reality, but also all judgments of perception, namely, all usual judgments about what we see, hear, feel etc., that is, describing in mental terms the intuitions we have. Now, it certainly is a good rule of critical thinking to admit that any philosophical concept might in principle be a baseless construction, but we cannot treat in the same way those concepts that constitute the data of the problems that philosophical theories propose to explain and therefore have to presuppose.

So, if the concept of empirical consciousness (judgmental consciousness of intuitions that we characterize with mental predicates) is neither self-contradictory nor vacuous, Kant's point about the possibility of having empirical consciousness of any intuition one might have seems well taken.

We can now summarize the initial part of the argument. Kant starts from the fact, so to speak, that *we have consciousness of our intuitions*, that is, that we can say we have intuitions, even though by hypothesis we do not know whether they are intuitions of anything existing independently of being intuited. Indeed, to say that we are conscious of having intuitions is part of the hypothesis that our intuitions are not intuitions of objects that are distinct from them. For this reason, it is not strictly correct to say that Kant starts from the premise that we are aware of our intuitions taken as an empirical statement of fact. What was here called a fact is, rather, a presupposition of the question (whether intuitions conform to concepts of objects), and it is only for this reason that we can from the start assume it as if it were a fact.

This said, Kant can be read as proving, first, that consciousness of intuitions has a propositional character and depends on the possibility of characterizing our intuitions conceptually, not in relation to what is intuited in them, but rather relative to their existence in our minds as representations. (Finally, based on this analysis according to which consciousness of intuitions implies being able to think our intuitions as mental items in us, more specifically, as representations, Kant goes on to show that there can be in us no intuition that could escape consciousness in principle.) Indeed, so runs Kant's argument, holding that the contrary would commit us to the indefensible assertion that conceptual characterizations of our intuitions as representations in us would be either self-contradictory (which they are not except by stipulation) or empty (which they are not, for referring to our intuitions as representations is necessary in order to formulate the problem that makes a deduction necessary).

So far we have described only the first step toward establishing the first premise of the Deduction. The second step consists of proving the necessary relationship between "having consciousness of an intuition" and "having consciousness of oneself." The necessity of establishing the existence of this relationship remains obscured by the fact that from the outset we have characterized consciousness as a judgment of the form: "I know that I φ," where "φ" is that which we call "predicate of representations" (as in the "judgments of perception," of which Kant speaks in the *Prolegomena.*) But, strictly speaking, we still do not have any reason for claiming that the subject of these assertions is a subject capable of referring *to itself* by the pronoun "I" and, as much as one can know, the judgments of perception could have been of the form: "I know that I φ" ("I know that *I* am seeing, hearing . . . ," etc.), as much as of the form "I know that *it* φs." It is clear that the nonsubjective formulation of these assertions is odd, but this is so because it is already clear for us, before any philosophical analysis, that predicates of representation apply to a subject capable of referring to himself. But the philosophical question is, precisely, that of knowing why exactly it has to be so.

Let us see, once again, what Kant has to say concerning this in the six passages quoted above. Only two of these passages contain something that still waits for an explanation and that may serve, as it is reasonable to expect, as an argument for establishing the relationship between consciousness of intuitions and self-consciousness. I refer to A107, where "transcendental apperception" is presented as a condition of the "unity and connection" of the cognitions that occur in us, and to A116, where Kant's thesis is expressly established by the assertion that "representations only represent something in me" if they pertain to and "can be connected to a unique and same consciousness." All the rest are unproven assertions (A117 note and A123–24), or can be explained in terms of the relation between intuition and a possible consciousness.

Self-consciousness is presented, in short, as necessary for the unity and connection of cognitions as representations of something in me. Now, in the previous argument it was not necessary to mention the connection and unity of intuitions in order to make clear the relationship between the fact of having intuitions and the possibility of having consciousness of them. Thus, if Kant wants to establish now that self-consciousness is necessary in order to have intuitions by claiming that it is a condition of their unity and connection, it is first of all necessary to assume that consciousness of intuitions includes a consciousness of its unity and connection. But this is far from obvious. In the first place, although Kant talks of intuitions (cognitions, appearances) in the plural, nothing indicates that he had in mind intuitions in the collective sense, when he says that self-consciousness is a condition of the possibility of the empirical consciousness of having intuitions. On the contrary, it is reasonable to suppose that intuitions are to be considered here separately, since Kant's claim is that no intuition (and not: no manifold of intuitions) is of such a nature that it is in principle impossible to have consciousness of it.[18]

Here again consideration of the propositional character of our consciousness of intuitions helps us toward understanding Kant's argument. At first glance, before analyzing the concept of consciousness, it would seem that we might intelligibly talk about having consciousness of isolated intuitions. But we see that this assumption must be discarded the moment we attribute a propositional content to consciousness and analyze it as implying the capacity of characterizing conceptually that of which one is conscious. In effect, concepts are, in Kant's terminology, "representations by common marks" that serve to compare and distinguish intuitions from one another.[19] For this reason, whenever a concept is applied to an intuition, as something singular, this intuition is seen at the same time compared to and distinguished from other possible intuitions.

It is reasonable to suppose, then, that the unity and connection of intuitions as representations in us is the conceptual unity of the intuitions when characterized as representations. By the same token it becomes clear why self-consciousness is a condition of the unity of the representations in us. Indeed, application of concepts involves comparison and distinction of intuitions from one another, and this would not be possible if the subject making this comparison and distinction (the subject that designates itself by "I") were not the same relative to each one of the compared and distinguished intuitions (and because of this might express his or her consciousness by saying: "I know that *I* φ") In consequence, it is necessary to have consciousness of the intuitions considered collectively as existing for one and the same subject in order that it would be possible to think each intuition. That is why Kant characterizes, on A123–24, self-consciousness as *durchgängig*, that is, thoroughgoing, or present in, all consciousness of intuitions as its condition, and holds the identity of the "I" that knows that he has in such and such intuitions a "correlate of all our representations," that is, of all our intuitions insofar as we have consciousness of them. It is in the same sense that Kant refers indifferently to "the (transcendental) unity of apperception," or to "self-consciousness," be it to the consciousness of the identity of oneself or as a condition of the consciousness of intuitions.

The Argument in the 1787 Edition (B)

Having completed the exposition of the argument in A, it is now necessary to investigate how far-reaching the changes made in the second edition of 1787 are. We find the substance of Kant's revised theory in §16. In this new version, the first step still consists in stating the relationship between the manifold of intuitions and self-consciousness. Kant's argument in order to support his contention is presented immediately in the first lines of §16. In Kant's own words:

> The I think must be able to accompany all my representations; for otherwise something would be represented in me that could not be thought at all, which is as much to say that the representation would either be impossible or else at least would be nothing for me. That representation that can be given prior to all thinking is called intuition. Thus all manifold of intuition has a necessary relation to the I think in the same subject in which this manifold is to be encountered. (*Pure Reason*, B131–32)

If we had begun our interpretation with the text of edition B, we would have had to go through again all considerations that we made in connection with edition A, regarding the (propositional or nonpropositional) sense in which one can say that consciousness is a condition of the existence of representations in us. I presuppose all these considerations and, based on the explanations given, propose to recast Kant's argument in the following manner.

As in A, the starting point of the Deduction is the supposition that we are conscious of having intuitions even though we may not assert without proof that our intuitions are such that they may be thought in accordance with concepts of objects, that is, as representing something distinct from us. Indeed, without this supposition the problem the Deduction is expected to solve could not be stated, and therefore can be taken as a premise that must be accepted by whoever demands proof of the conformity of our intuitions to concepts of objects in general. This said, Kant's initial statement ("The **I think** must **be able** to accompany all my representations") can be taken as a statement of the condition under which we can have consciousness of something in us such as intuitions, namely, that we think, or characterize them as representations (more specifically, as instances of intuitive representations such as seeing, hearing, feeling, etc.).

The argument, then, for this thesis runs as follows. To deny that I can think the representations of which, by hypothesis, I have consciousness is equivalent to saying that the concept by which I think them are either self-contradictory (that is, that it is logically impossible to say that I have representations, and by extension that I see, hear, etc.) or problematic (that is, that I cannot know if something in me corresponds to the concept of representation, which would then be "nothing for me"). Kant must have thought this last contention to be quite obvious, since he does not bother to give a justification for it. This can indeed be easily supplied since one must by hypothesis (in order to formulate the problem that makes a deduction necessary) admit that one has representations. To put it briefly, it is not possible to deny that one can *think* one's representations as such, if it is admitted beforehand that one is aware, or knows, that one has representations.

If this interpretation is correct, to say that it must be possible for the "I think" to accompany all my representations boils down, then, to saying that one is not able to know that one has representations, if one is not able to think them as such. We can say therefore that, in Kant's understanding, this conceptual consciousness of representations expresses itself linguistically in sentences of the form: "I know that φ," where "φ" stands for predicate characterizing representations.

So far it is still to be demonstrated that consciousness of representations is, at the same time, consciousness of oneself as a subject that is distinct from the representations of which it is conscious and numerically identical in relation to them. What can be known at this stage of Kant's argument is that the "I think" could be a condition of each representation considered in isolation, therefore in such a way that the reference of the personal pronoun "I" could be different in each case. Nevertheless, the conclusion of Kant's argument is that the manifold of the intuitions has a necessary relationship with the "I think" in one and the same subject and from here it follows that the "I think" that accompanies the manifold of the representations is "one and the same," as Kant says in the same paragraph.[20] This conclusion must result, in consequence, merely from the fact that it is possible in principle to think by means of concepts all the representations of which I am conscious. Why this is so can be easily understood if we take into account (as in the interpretation of the corresponding passage in edition A) that what we think by means of a concept is the unity of a given manifold, and that this would not possible if the "I think" were different for each element of the manifold.

Kant's argument in B is not, therefore, substantially different from the argument in A respecting the first premise. In both, Kant's concern is establishing the necessity of self-consciousness relative to the manifold of intuitions of which we have, by hypothesis, consciousness, and the basis of the proof is the necessity of recognizing that, in order to have consciousness, we must be capable of thinking the unity of the manifold of intuitions by means of concepts of representations.[21]

From Self-Consciousness to Objective Knowledge

The Argument in the 1781 Edition (A)

Let us proceed now to the second premise of the Deduction, which is, as we have seen, the thesis of the necessary relationship of self-consciousness with the synthesis of intuitions according to concepts of objects, that is to say, with the condition of the possibility of objective knowledge. As self-consciousness was declared in the first premise to be a condition of the consciousness of intuitions, it is to be expected that the synthetic unity of intuitions would now be shown as a condition of self-consciousness. If this is to be so, it will be possible to set forth Kant's doctrine as a chain of inferences that, proceeding from the consciousness of intuitions as initial premise, successively establishes by a regressive argument the conditions and the conditions of the conditions of this premise. We can say, therefore, that Kant's argument unfolds in reply to the following question: what conditions must be satisfied in order that a subject may have consciousness of itself and of intuitions as its own intuitions? What we expect, therefore, is a proof that conformity of the synthesis of intuitions to concepts of objects must be regarded as being precisely this condition.

This expectation seems to find a most satisfactory confirmation in the following passage: In accordance with this principle [namely, "the principle of the unity of apperception"—GAA] all appearances whatever must come into the mind or be apprehended in such a way that they are in agreement with the unity of apperception that would be impossible *without synthetic unity in their connection*, which is thus also *objectively necessary*" (*Pure Reason*, A122; my italics).[22] However, Kant's formulation leaves open the question: of what precisely is the objective unity of the intuitions a condition? Is it a condition of the unity of apperception as a whole, including self-consciousness and consciousness of intuitions as its own, or is it a condition of only the latter (self-consciousness depending on other conditions, or being given in whatever other manner)?

It is true that, in other passages, the unity of consciousness is expressly identified with self-consciousness and considered impossible without the synthetic unity of the intuitions. So, on A108, the "identity of consciousness" is expressly identified with the "consciousness of the identity of oneself," and this Kant says would be impossible "if it did not have before its eyes the identity of its action [namely, of synthesis—GAA]."[23]

It is not immediately clear what Kant's exact meaning is and how he purports to justify his contention. Whatever the explanation may be, it is clear however from the start that it must provide a condition for the unity of apperception that may be taken as being both *sufficient* and *necessary*. Now, in order to prove that synthesis of intuitions (or the identity of the act of synthesis) is a *sufficient* condition of the unity of apperception, the explanation will have to establish what exactly, in the act of synthesis, makes it possible; in other words, it will have to show why the capacity to perform the act of synthesis (namely, of intuitions according to concepts) endows its subject with the power of becoming aware of himself and of his representations. In order to prove that this is a *necessary* condition, it will have to show further that unity of apperception is possible only under this condition, that is to say, that there is no possible alternative to it.

The only reason that Kant gives for his assertion that synthetic unity of the intuitions is a condition of the unity of apperception consists in the observation that this concept involves the concept of identity and that nothing that must be thought as identical can be represented as such by empirical intuition. "That which should **necessarily** be represented as numerically identical cannot be thought of as such through empirical data" (*Pure Reason*, A107).[24] But from here it follows merely that what must be represented as a subject (as well as that which must be thought as an object) can only be represented as such in thought, and the question now is: when, or under what condition, do we think of ourselves as subjects, more precisely as a subject that knows that it has a manifold of intuitions?

If we abstract from the practical, and restrict ourselves to the epistemic subject, and if we exclude recourse to intuition as a possible basis for epistemic self-consciousness, this must be sought in the performance of cognitive operations other than mere intuition. If we exclude once more complex cognitive operations (because of their dependence on those that are elementary), the only possible basis for the unity of apperception must be sought in what Kant calls the "synthesis" (of a given manifold) "according to concepts" (of objects). That is why Kant asserts, in an already quoted passage, that "synthesis according to concepts" is the place "in which alone apperception can demonstrate *a priori* its thoroughgoing (*durchgängig*) and necessary identity" (*Pure Reason*, A112).

This said, our question becomes: what is it that belongs to the performance of an act of synthesis according to concepts of objects and that makes it possible for whomever does this to become conscious *of himself* and of the given intuitions as *his* representations? To what precisely do we owe the unity of apperception? To the performance of an act, which happens to be an act of synthesis, but yet could be any other act? Or to the performance of an act of *synthesis*? Or, rather, to the fact that the synthesis is *subsumed under concepts*?

The first hypothesis suffers from such obvious difficulties that it is hardly worth considering. Indeed it is clear that, although actions do always presuppose an agent, that is, a *subject* that acts, from here it does not follow that all actions must be actions of a *self-conscious* subject—at least in the propositional sense of consciousness, which alone is, as we have seen, relevant for our discussion. The arguments presented above in order to show that consciousness, in the propositional sense, is not a condition for having representations, are equally valid for our actions. Just as a subject does not have to be able to say (or think) what he intuits in order to have intuitions, neither does he need be able to say (or think) what he does in order to act.[25] We will not lose time, therefore, with this first hypothesis.

At first sight, the second hypothesis does not appear to fare any better, since what is valid for action in general (the possibility of acting unconsciously) might be also valid for acts of synthesis in particular. That is the reasoning behind our attribution of sense perception to beings incapable of thinking, such as animals and infants, insofar as sense perception involves nonconceptual discrimination of objects in space and time, and therefore the capacity of making syntheses. As a matter of fact, this seems to be an inevitable consequence of Kant's notion of synthesis, and its attribution to imagination. To be sure, Kant's notion is not quite clear and has been a subject of some controversy, especially in connection with the question whether acts of synthesis in general depend on conceptual guidance and thereby on the understanding, or on imagination alone, conceived of as an autonomous cognitive power.

I will take, however, as Kant's official view, at least in the A edition, the idea that synthesis is an act whereby imagination (contrasted with the understanding and conceived of as an autonomous cognitive power) provides the manifold that is given in sense intuition with the connection that is required by *intuitive* representations (as contrasted with conceptual representations), in order to serve as a representation of what Kant calls an "appearance" (the conceptually indeterminate object of empirical intuition, as defined in A20/B34, and which we may identify with the spatial-temporal configuration, or image, of single objects).

That this is really Kant's view is more or less clearly indicated in the so-called Metaphysical Deduction (§10), which is an authoritative passage since it introduces the concept of "synthesis" for the first time. It is true that the text does not explicitly correlate synthesis with intuitive, nonconceptual representations, but only with cognitions (unspecified which). "By **synthesis** in the most general sense," so runs the text, "I understand the action of putting different representations together with each other and comprehending their manifoldness in one cognition" (A77/B103). "Cognition," of course, is a general term covering both intuitions and concepts (A320/B377), and taken in isolation this sentence could be read as implying that syntheses combine the manifold given in intuition according to the concept of a determinate object. However, that the kind of cognitions made possible by syntheses are to be taken as conceptually indeterminate representations of single objects, that is to say, intuitions, is made clear by the ascription of syntheses to imagination in contrast with the proper function of the understanding, which Kant describes here as that of "bringing the synthesis to concepts" (A78/B103). This explains why the imagination is described in the same passage not only as a "blind though indispensable function of the soul" but also as a function "of which we are seldom even conscious." In fact, for Kant, as we may recall, "intuitions without concepts" are blind (A51/B75), and so imagination is in the same sense said to be blind, since it is not guided (or, at least, need not to be guided) by concepts in the production of syntheses.

And since syntheses need not to be accompanied by thought in order to be accomplished, they may to this extent be performed unconsciously.

This analysis seems to leave no room for synthesis in the explanation of self-consciousness as involving unity of apperception. If there is no necessary connection between the capacity to perform synthesis and consciousness, why should the unity of apperception be connected with the performance of acts of synthesis according to concepts? To be sure, self-consciousness is neither a necessary condition of acts of synthesis nor a consequence of it. This does not imply, however, that synthesis is irrelevant for self-consciousness and the unity of apperception. That self-consciousness does not follow as a consequence upon the performance of syntheses means only that synthesis is not a *sufficient* condition of the unity of apperception, it does not mean that it is not a *necessary* condition. Now, if synthesis is, as it in fact is for Kant, a condition for concept application, and consciousness of one's representations involves conceptual characterizations of one's representations, it can be easily admitted that synthesis is presupposed as a necessary, although not sufficient, condition by the unity of apperception.[26]

We can, therefore, take the initial assertion that "consciousness of identity of oneself" depends on the "identity" or the "unity of synthesis of the appearances according to concepts" (on A108) as purporting to say that we can only have consciousness of ourselves if, beforehand, we can give to our intuitions, in one and same act of synthesis, the connection that is necessary for them to be able to be apprehended *collectively* as intuitions of one and same subject. In this sense, the performance (or the capacity to perform syntheses) is merely a negative condition, a *conditio sine qua non* (necessary, but not sufficient) of the unity of apperception. Kant's claim, one might also say, is that the capacity of becoming aware of oneself would remain a mere undeveloped potentiality in us,[27] were it not actualized by the capacity of performing syntheses.

This explanation provides, however, only a partial reply to the initial question about what it is precisely, in the realization of syntheses according to concepts, that makes possible unity of apperception. It leaves open two questions: *First*, naturally, since synthesis is only a necessary, not a sufficient condition of self-consciousness, the question about what it is, in the activity of conforming synthesis to concepts, that makes possible, or is in any way necessarily connected with, self-consciousness. In the *second* place, the question concerning the possibility of the *objective unity* of intuitions (which is the question the Deduction is meant to solve) also remains unanswered. In what way does consideration of the necessary connection between self-consciousness and the performance of syntheses according to concepts give us a reason to assert the necessary conformity of intuitions (synthesized by imagination) and concepts of objects?

Even though the function of synthesis does not constitute a sufficient condition of the unity of apperception, Kant's argument, in order to prove that the *objective* unity of the intuitions is a condition of the unity of apperception, is not doomed to fail, if we accept two points. The first one is that self-consciousness can be taken as simply given, in point of fact as an original and independent power of our mind, whose possibility cannot and needs not to be further investigated. The power to perform syntheses, on the other hand, can be presented as a condition, not, of course, of self-consciousness as such, but rather of self-attribution of representations (consciousness of representations as belonging to us). It would be possible to claim, then, that the objective unity of synthesis, or its conformity to concepts of objects, would result from the addition of these two complementary conditions: self-consciousness and the power to realize syntheses. The argument would be that, although syntheses do not need to be thought (according to concepts of objects) in order to be performed, they are necessarily found to be thought (according to concepts of objects) when made by a subject that happens to be self-conscious, and, for that very reason, capable of thinking (according to concepts of objects).

As a matter of fact, this would seem to be the explanation given by Kant in edition A. In two passages (quoted above) of the section containing an outline of the Deduction (A110 and A113), we have already seen that, in at least in one of them, the categorical unity of the intuitions would seem to be inferred, not as a condition of self-consciousness, but rather as a consequence of a premise according to which self-consciousness must be present in all synthesis. To recall: "Now since this identity [namely, the identity of self-consciousness—GAA] must necessarily enter into the synthesis of all the manifold of appearances insofar as they are to become empirical cognition, the appearances are thus subject to *a priori* conditions with which their synthesis (of apprehension) must be in thoroughgoing accord" (*Pure Reason*, A113). These conditions are, according to the sentence that follows, the "necessary laws" of the "transcendental affinity" of appearances, that is to say, the synthetic unity according to categories. If we accept that self-consciousness "enters" into the synthesis when this is realized by a self-conscious subject, then this passage would seem to assert that the conformity of the synthesis to the categories is a consequence of the fact that the synthesis is realized in a conscious manner.

We find a clearer statement of the same argument in the so-called definitive explanation (third section of the Deduction). On A119, understanding and, therefore, the concepts by means of which the unity of synthesis is thought, are presented as the product of the relationship of apperception to the synthesis of the imagination.[28] On A124, Kant explains that, since synthesis is itself "sensible," it is incapable of ensuring by itself the unity of intuitions according to concepts of objects. In order to secure this, it is necessary that it be "intellectualized," which occurs precisely when apperception is "added" to imagination, and it is to this addition of apperception to the manifold synthesized by imagination that we owe the emergence of concepts of objects.

The doctrine that emerges from these explanations is relatively clear or, at least, it is reasonably clear what Kant *means to say*. The ability to make syntheses and self-consciousness are presented as independent but related powers. The relationship between these powers, that is, the fact that syntheses are performed by a self-conscious subject, has two consequences. One of them is the possibility of apprehending the manifold of intuitions as having the subjective unity that they have insofar as they are *my representations*. The other is the possibility of apprehending the manifold of intuitions as presenting the objective unity that they have insofar as they are *representations of* objects distinct from the intuitions in which they are given to us. In the first case, it is the ability to perform synthesis that makes possible the subjective unity of the intuitions as my representations, for without the possibility of combining the intuitions with each other, apperception, or the power to become conscious of oneself, would exist in the subject only in a virtual manner. In the second case, it is self-consciousness, aroused in the subject by the performance of syntheses, that makes it possible to *think*, or to reflect on what is presented by the synthesized intuitions and determine which kind of object is intuited.

This view still leaves two questions open. The first, already mentioned above, is the question: what makes self-consciousness (and not just self-ascription of representations) possible? The second is: what is precisely the reason why categories, and with them concepts of objects, arise at all from the addition of self-consciousness to the activity of synthesis?

The fact that the first question remains open does not seem to entail any serious damage for the theory, since, as already noted, one can take consciousness simply as a fact whose possibility perhaps *can*, but in any case *need* not be investigated in order to accomplish the task of the Deduction, which is, as we know, to prove the conformity of our intuitions to categories. Certainly, that does not seem to square perfectly with those passages in which Kant refers to synthesis as the condition of (the identity of) self-consciousness. But that can be easily taken care of either by interpreting synthesis as a condition, not of possessing the power of self-consciousness but of making use of this power and, so speak, of actualizing it, or by taking synthesis to be the condition of the unity of representations in self-consciousness, or by doing both.

But the second question cannot remain unanswered, because the plausibility of the doctrine depends on it. It is essential, therefore, to explain why, after all, the intellectualization of the synthesis, or the subordination of the synthesized intuitions to concept of objects, can be taken as deriving from the mere addition of self-consciousness to the power of performing syntheses.

This manner of saying (that self-consciousness adds to, or relates to, the power of performing syntheses) must manifestly be understood in the sense that the power of synthesis and the actually performed syntheses become conscious themselves. What Kant means, therefore, can be presented in the following way: when syntheses, which in themselves can be carried out in an unconscious or unthought-of manner, come to be performed by a subject conscious of itself, they become ipso facto conscious for the subject that realizes them. From this, however, it still does not follow that the categories are produced when the subject becomes conscious and proceeds to think the syntheses that it effects—unless we accept an identification of the categories with abstract formulations of rules of synthesis. But this identification does not seem to be permissible. Categories are rules for the *identification* of *objects* of our intuitions.[29] Rules of synthesis, on the contrary, are rules for the *spatial-temporal discrimination* of *intuitions*.

For this reason, we can accept this transformation of the rules of synthesis into conceptual rules only if we can assume that a self-conscious subject already has at his disposal, independently of his power do perform syntheses, at least the concept of an object in general.[30] If we are ready to concede this, then it will be possible to explain the diversity of categories as arising from the diversity of ways in which the object thought by a self-conscious subject can be given in sensible intuition. Considered abstractly, the ways that an object can be given in intuition are what Kant names "schemata" of the imagination. No doubt, the idea that the diversity of categories might be explained as resulting from the schematization of a concept of an object in general is a very suggestive hypothesis. But what allows us to suppose that such a concept is given beforehand to any self-conscious subject by the simple fact that he is self-conscious? If this supposition is not to be rated as a mere postulate, introduced as a deus ex machina in order to save a theory in distress, it would be necessary to show how a self-conscious subject can have at his disposal beforehand, by the simple fact of being self-conscious, this concept of object. In a word: it would be necessary to show why the concept of self-consciousness implies the concept of an object in general.

Kant does not do this, at least in the A edition. But it is easy to see that he would only be able to do this in one of the two following ways: (1) deriving the concept of object from the concept of the subject, as suggested in a manuscript remark, where he conjectures that the object would not be anything other than "the subjective representation of the subject itself, but made general, for I am the original of all objects" (*R*4674, 17:646); or (2) presenting the concept of object (the capacity to use this concept or to perform some operation involving the ability to use this concept) as a presupposition or as preliminary condition prior of self-consciousness.

The difficulty with the first alternative is that it does not explain why the synthesized intuitions must be referred to an object *distinct* from the subject. Indeed, even if we admit that the self-conscious subject thinks of itself as *an* object, it still does not follow from this supposition that there are other objects (conceived of in conformity to its subjective original) to which it would be necessary to refer our intuitions. No wonder, therefore, that this alternative was not further explored by Kant. The second alternative requires that the question referring to the conditions of the possibility of self-consciousness be reopened. But, if we accept this, we will have to abandon the initial supposition that we can take self-consciousness as a fact that does not need to be further explained.

In the later version of 1787, one of the most salient modifications of Kant's argument is the role attributed to judgment, instead of synthesis, in the elucidation of the concept of the "objective unity of apperception." Now, judgment is precisely the operation through which intuitions are subsumed under concepts of objects. My hypothesis is that, in the reformulated argument of the second edition, mastery of the power of judgment is the condition, not only of the self-attribution of representations (or of the unity of representations in a self-conscious subject), but also of self-consciousness itself. In other words, my hypothesis is that, in the second edition, Kant tried to explore the third alternative outlined above.[31]

Self-Consciousness and Objective Knowledge in the 1787 Edition (B)

Let's try to see, therefore, what new information can be gleaned from the completely recast text of 1787 concerning the relation between self-consciousness and the possibility of objective knowledge. One of the most salient new features, as already indicated, is the emphasis given to judgment in the explanation of the consciousness of that objective unity that was found necessary for self-consciousness. To be sure, it would not be correct to say that the notion of judgment is absent from the A-Deduction, even if it is not mentioned by name, since the result of the intellectualization of the synthesis is precisely judgment. What we have to investigate now is whether judgment continues to be thought in the same manner in B, or if, on the contrary, it is introduced as a condition of self-consciousness.

The new argument begins with considerations that are already familiar to us on the relationship of the consciousness one has of one's intuitions (and which always changes with new intuitions) to the consciousness one has of oneself as the subject of these intuitions (and which always remain the same). What is necessary to explain, now, is the identity of self-consciousness, that is, the fact that, in the consciousness of each one of my intuitions, I relate to myself as being the same subject of a manifold of intuitions.

The first step toward this explanation is, to put it very briefly, the consideration that self-consciousness, since it cannot be based on an intellectual intuition of oneself,[32] can only be founded in the act that combines the intuitions of the same consciousness to one another, that is to say, consciousness one has of any object. The synthetic unity of intuitions (or, rather, the unity of the act that represents it to us) is, therefore, the basis of the identity of self-consciousness.[33] Now, the act that represents the synthetic unity of the intuitions is judgment (since unity itself cannot be represented in sense intuition, or by the imagination), and, so, one may claim that it is only in judgment, better: in the activity of making judgments about the objective unity of intuitions, that one can find that unity that is necessary for self-consciousness.

Kant gives then a very brief formulation of his theory:

> I find that a judgment is nothing other than the way to bring given cognitions to the objective unity of apperception. That is the aim of the copula is in them: to distinguish the objective unity of given representations from the subjective. For this word designates the relation of the representations to the original apperception and its necessary unity. (*Pure Reason*, B141–42)

The thesis to be proved, then, is the assertion that judgment expresses the objective unity that is the condition of apperception. Kant speaks, it is true, of *the objective unity of apperception*, but, since this unity is presented as a ground (*Grund*), or condition, of the identity of apperception,[34] the paraphrase that I made (the objective unity that is the condition of self-consciousness) seems to be admissible. Kant's thesis, then, is a twofold one: that judgment expresses objective unity of the representations and that the unity expressed through judgment is a condition required by self-consciousness.

The argument in favor of the first part of the thesis is, in brief, that judgment expresses the assertion of the objectivity of a connection of given cognitions, what can be clearly seen if one takes into consideration the function of the word "is," taken to be implicit in all judgments. Although Kant uses the expression "copula" (*Verhältniswörtchen*), the context leaves no doubt that he is not thinking only of predicative judgments. In effect, Kant begins §19 on judgment criticizing precisely the traditional definition that only considers categorical judgment. It is convenient, therefore, to understand the verb "is" in the sense, not of the predicate-subject relationship, but in the sense of an operator ("it is true that") that transforms connections of representations (in this case, propositions) into assertions.

The argument for the second part of the thesis is the consideration that the word (the operator) "is" serves to distinguish the objective unity of the given representations from its subjective unity. But what exactly is meant by this? We could have thought that Kant wished to say that the expressions "objective" and "subjective" are correlate terms and that, as a consequence, one cannot be understood without understanding the other. Thus, the assertion of the objective unity of representations would only be possible if the objective unity were to be contrasted with the subjective unity of representations. Yet how is it possible to talk of the subjective unity or representations without referring to the consciousness that we have of them as our representations? The reference to the subjective unity of representations in opposition to the objective unity presupposes, then, self-consciousness. Now, the question raised was precisely a question about the condition of possibility of this consciousness. Therefore, we would be going in circles if we wanted to explain the possibility of the consciousness of the subjective unity by contrast with the consciousness of objective unity.

If judgment effectively allows an explanation of the identity of self-consciousness, as Kant asserts, the notion of judgment cannot *presuppose* but must have the distinction between the subjective and the objective as a consequence. In other words, the notion of judgment cannot depend on the notion of self-consciousness, but must explain, on the contrary, how one can come to be aware of oneself by the simple fact of being capable of judging. Let us see, therefore, what can be done in this sense.

If the analysis proposed by Kant is correct, one could say that the form of all judgments is "it is true that *p*," where *p* designates a proposition (Kant would say: a "connection of cognitions" or of "representations"). But what the operator "it is true that" expresses, as we saw, is precisely the claim that a proposition is true. Now, since this assertion can be negated and found to be unwarranted, it becomes possible to make a distinction between what is true and what is false, and it is at this moment only that one can make the distinction between what was considered to be true, but is found to be false, on the one hand, and what was said to be true and is confirmed to be effectively true, on the other hand—in one word: the distinction between the real and the apparent. Thus it is only now, finally, that one can make the distinction between what is really true (*objective*) and what only seems, to *me*, to be true (*subjective*).

Now, the possibility of distinguishing the *objective* unity of representations (as representations *of an object*) from their *subjective* unity (as representations *in me*), gives one the ability to do two other things: one is to express the subjective unity of the representations of which one is conscious (that is, Kant's "empirical consciousness"). The other is to refer to oneself as the subject that is from now on conscious of the subjective unity of one's representations and, thereby, to express one's own self-consciousness as something that is present in all empirical consciousness (Kant's numerically identical self-consciousness). In other words, the capacity to make objective judgments, that Kant explains as the capacity to use the copula "is" (that is, the assertoric operator: "it is true that"), also enables its subject with the capacity to make subjective judgments, that is to say, judgments: (1) in which one characterizes the subjective unity of one's representations by mental predicates; and (2) in which one refers to oneself by means of the word "I" as the subject of these representations, therefore in judgments of the form: "I know that I φ," where "know" expresses awareness of oneself as a numerically identical subject of different representations, and "I φ" expresses the awareness one has of these diverse representations as one's own.

The interpretation that I submitted is based on the supposition that it is possible to judge without referring to oneself as the author of the judgment and without having to describe what is done as an act of judgment. I tried to explain this by showing: (1) that the act of judging, in Kant's theory, can be explained the use of the operator "is true that"; and (2) that the reference to oneself is an element of judgments of perception only, that is, of judgments expressing the subjective unity of representations and deriving from the negation of objective judgments. But does this entail that we can make judgments without being conscious of it?

Two considerations can be made. The first is a philological one, based on what Kant actually says. So, in the very same passage I commented on, Kant asserts that judgment brings intuitions to the identity of apperception *and* to objective unity. The second is a more substantive one: there are many things that we cannot do without knowing what we are doing, for example promises and engagements in general, which are such that they cannot be performed unless one refers to oneself as performing the act in question. Why should judgment be excluded from this class of things?

The last question is the easier one, so I will start with it. If we admit that acts of judging (more precisely: making objective judgments) involve self-consciousness in the same sense as, for example, promises, that is, in the sense implying self-reference and description of the act one is doing, then it follows that acts of judging will be of the form "I judge that (it is true) that *p*," in the same way as promises are of the form "I promise that *p*." However, it is easy to see that saying that I judge is very different from saying that I promise (not only in content, but also in what concerns self-reference and description of the performed act), because I do not judge that *p* when I say "I judge that *p*," whereas I do make the promise that *p* when I say "I promise that *p*." Indeed, I only judge that *p*, when I simply say "*p*" (or, more explicitly, "it is true that *p*"), and if I say "I judge that (it is true) that *p*," instead of making an objective judgment, or an assertion that may be true or false. I *either* express an opinion (make a subjective judgment)—and in this case it is a different act that I realize when I say that I judge—*or* I express the reflexive consciousness of making an objective judgment—and what I mean then is: I know that I am judging (and not: "it is true that *p*").

The first consideration might seem to be more difficult to handle, since Kant's statement that what is expressed in objective judgments is not only the objective unity of synthesized intuitions but also self-consciousness ("identity of apperceptions"), might be taken as a basis for objecting to the idea that self-consciousness is more a consequence than a condition of making objective judgments. What Kant actually says, however, is that judgment brings intuitions to the unity of self-consciousness (the "identity of apperception"), besides bringing them to an objective unity, and this is perfectly compatible with the idea that, by making an assertion about the objective unity of intuitions, judgment makes possible distinguishing appearance and reality and, insofar, making subjective judgments that express our consciousness of the related intuitions as representations in us.

Notes

1. See *Pure Reason*, B136–37.

2. See *Pure Reason*, A89–90/B122–23; *Jäsche Logic*, 9:33.

3. In the original article, *das Erkenntnis* (neuter) was translated in Portuguese as *cognição* (cognition) and *die Erkenntnis* (feminine) by *conhecimento* (knowledge), in the supposition that the first term designates (for at least the majority of cases) the elements into which one can break down the complete act of knowledge that only takes place in judgment. Thus, intuition and concept are cognitions while (objective) judgment is knowledge. In this article I generally use the terms "cognition" and "knowledge" to make the same distinction in English. Since "knowledge" (differently from *Erkenntnis* and *conhecimento*) does not admit of a plural, this distinction cannot be maintained throughout.

4. "Now no cognitions can occur in us, no connection and unity among them, without that unity of consciousness that precedes all data of the intuitions, and in relation to which all representation of objects is alone possible" (*Pure Reason*, A107).

5. "All possible appearances belong, as representations, to the whole possible self-consciousness. But from this, as a transcendental representation, numerical identity is inseparable, and certain *a priori*, because nothing can come to cognition (*in das Erkenntnis kommen*) except by means of this original apperception" (*Pure Reason*, A113).

6. "All intuitions are nothing for us and do not in the least concern us if they cannot be taken up into consciousness, whether they influence it directly or indirectly, and through this alone is cognition possible. We are conscious *a priori* of the thoroughgoing identity of ourselves with regard to all representations that can ever belong to our cognition (*unserem Erkentnis*), as a necessary condition of the possibility of all representations (since the latter represent something in me only insofar as they belong with all the others to one consciousness, hence they must at least be capable of being connected in it" (*Pure Reason*, A116).

7. "All representations have a necessary relation to a **possible** empirical consciousness: for if they did not have this, and if it were entirely impossible to become conscious of them, that would be as much as to say that they did not exist at all. All empirical consciousness, however, has a necessary relation to a transcendental consciousness (preceding all particular experience), namely the consciousness of myself, as original apperception" (*Pure Reason*, A117).

8. "The first thing that is given to us is appearance, which, if it is combined with consciousness, is called perception (without the relation to an at least possible consciousness appearances could never become an object of knowledge (*der Erkenntnis*) for us, and would therefore be nothing to us; and since it has no objective reality in itself and exists only in cognition (*im Erkenntnisse*) it would be nothing at all)" (*Pure Reason*, A120).

9. "For the standing and lasting I (of pure apperception) constitutes the correlate of all of our representations, so far as it is merely possible to become conscious of them, and all consciousness belongs to an all-embracing pure apperception just as all sensible intuition as representation belongs to a pure inner intuition, namely that of time" (*Pure Reason*, A123–34).

10. In order to have and apply a concept, it is not necessary to be capable of characterizing it as such by means of a concept of concepts. Thus, in order to have the concept of "man" and apply it in the judgment "Socrates is a man," it is not necessary to have a formal-semantic concept of "object," or the syntactic concept of "predicate," or whatever higher concept with which we might characterize it as concept. It is true that in saying "Socrates is a man" I necessarily know what I am doing (judging that Socrates is a man), but not (unless I am a philosopher or a logician) that I am *judging* or *applying a concept.*

11. One exception is that Tugendhat uses the expression "consciousness of space." Ernst Tugendhat, *Vorlesungen zur Einführung in die sprachanalytische Philosophie* (Frankfurt: Suhrkamp, 1976), 83.

12. In this respect see Konrad Cramer, "Über Kants Satz: Das: Ich denke, muss alle meine Vorstellungen begleiten können," in *Theorie der Subjektivität*, ed. Konrad Cramer, et al. (Frankfurt: Suhrkamp, 1990). Although in fact Cramer interprets a passage of the B edition, I believe that much of what he says here can be used in interpreting the first version of the Deduction, and I have done so throughout.

13. As a matter of fact, Kant refers here to the "unity of consciousness," identified in the following sentence with "transcendental apperception." But Kant later distinguishes self-consciousness, as a condition of the consciousness of intuitions, and consciousness (or, rather, the possibility of consciousness), as a condition for the occurrence within us of intuitions qua representations. Taking this into account and the fact that Kant talks here of the condition of "cognitions," one may conclude that Kant is referring at this point directly to the consciousness of intuitions, and only indirectly to self-consciousness, insofar as it is a condition of the first.

14. Intuitions and concepts are two subclasses of the class of cognitions, according to A320. Obviously, Kant cannot be talking here of the consciousness of concepts. Because of this, we may substitute the term "cognitions" for "intuitions."

15. Textually, self-consciousness. But what is here attributed to self-consciousness fits self-consciousness only because it also fits consciousness of intuitions. See note 13 above.

16. Neither do we need to employ here concepts such as "object" or "phenomenon" in order to know what we intuit.

17. See A116, 120, and, implicitly, on A123–24.

18. See in this respect, Cramer, "Über Kants Satz," 168.

19. See *Jäsche Logic*, §§1 and 6 (9:91 and 9:94–95).

20. "I call it [namely, the spontaneity to which we owe the "I think"—GAA] the **pure apperception**, in order to distinguish it from the **empirical** one, or also **original apperception**, since it is that self-consciousness which, because it produces the representation **I think**, which must be able to accompany all others and which in all consciousness is one and the same, cannot be accompanied by any further representation" (*Pure Reason*, B132).

21. Cf. the recapitulation of the first premise of the deduction in B: "The manifold that is given in a sensible intuition necessarily belongs under the original synthetic unity of apperception, since through this alone is the **unity** of the intuition possible" (*Pure Reason*, B143), as well as the additional commentary in the footnote: "The ground of proof rests on the represented **unity of intuition** through which an object is given, which always includes a synthesis of the manifold that is given for an intuition, and already contains the relation of the latter to the unity of apperception" (B144 note).

22. The same thesis is repeated in different formulations on A108, A111–12, A113, and A117 note.

23. Yet the explanation that will later be given for the necessity to subsume synthesized intuitions under categories seems to be based on a different doctrine, according to which synthesis (together with self-consciousness) is a condition of the consciousness of intuitions as mine, and self-consciousness by itself a condition of the conformity of synthesized intuitions to concepts. We will discuss this later.

24. In other passages, Kant qualifies his assertion in two ways. On A108, it is the *identity* of the function or act of synthesis that is presented as a condition of the "identity of consciousness of oneself." It appears to me that with this Kant wishes to say that the representations must be apprehended by the same act by which they can be thought and combined in the "unity of apperception." See in this respect B137. In the second edition, it is not the actual performance of an act of synthesis, but the consciousness of being able to combine representations that is the condition for the unity of apperception.

25. That, of course, does not apply to intentional and imputable actions, which presuppose a propositional consciousness of the act.

26. Thus, we read: "This synthetic unity, however, presupposes a synthesis, or includes it, and if the former is to be necessary *a priori* then the latter must also be a synthesis *a priori*. Thus the transcendental unity of apperception is related to the pure synthesis of imagination, as an *a priori* condition of the possibility of all composition of the manifold in a cognition" (*Pure Reason*, A118).

27. "Hidden in the interior of the mind, like a dead and to us unknown faculty" (to extrapolate an expression that is used by Kant to characterize something else, namely, imagination, not self-consciousness). See A100.

28. "**The unity of apperception in relation to the synthesis of the imagination** is the **understanding**, and this very same unity, in relation to **the transcendental synthesis**

of the imagination, is the **pure understanding**. In the understanding there are therefore pure *a priori* cognitions that contain the necessary unity of the pure synthesis of the imagination in regard to all possible appearances. These, however, are the **categories**, i.e., pure concepts of understanding" (*Pure Reason*, A119).

29. Rules of identification are, strictly speaking, only the concepts of particular objects, which we currently call (according to the terminology introduced by Strawson) "sortal predicates," as, for example, "book," "tree," "pyramid," etc. Categories are formal concepts of objects in general and express in an abstract and general manner the conditions in which we can identify the object of any manifold of intuitions. They can be best defined, to adopt Wolff's well-known suggestion, as rules or concepts for the formation of rules or concepts of objects.

30. It is this that inspires Kant's reference to the concept of the object, more precisely, to the "transcendental object" to which we refer the intuitions, "that can serve only as a correlate of the unity of apperception for the unity of the manifold in sensible intuition" (*Pure Reason*, A250).

31. Namely, that the "unity of apperception" is to be explained by the subsumption of the synthesis under concepts.

32. Kant's point, spelled out in full, should be that self-consciousness can neither be based on empirical intuition, since sameness or identity is something that cannot be given through sense-impressions and can only be thought by means of pure concepts of the understanding, nor on intellectual intuition, since intellectual intuitions are not available for finite beings like us, for whom objects must be given in sense-intuition.

33. See B134.

34. Ibid.

3

Intuitive Knowledge and *De Re* Thought

João Carlos Brum Torres

Kant's Intuitions as a Variant of Contemporay *De Re* Thought

This text aims to explore the exegetical hypothesis that the Kantian conception of empirical intuition can be interpreted as a variant—obviously a variant *avant la lettre*—of the contemporary theory of *de re* thoughts.

An elementary and minimal presentation of this theory will suffice for this purpose: *de re* thoughts are *object-dependent* thoughts, thoughts whose individuation derives not from conceptual conditions to be satisfied by the properties of their objects, but rather from the immediate relations of the subject of these thoughts to the objects of which they are thoughts. This is also to say that these thoughts are intrinsic and constitutively *relational*, perception being the paradigmatic illustration of them. This idea is clearly presented by Kent Bach:

> When we perceive something, we can think about it in a fundamentally different way than if we thought of it merely by description. To think of something by description is just to think of whatever happens to have the properties expressed by the description. But to perceive something is to be in a real relation to it, to be in a position to think of that object in particular, no matter what its properties. While attending to it, somehow . . . we can think of it as "that," not merely, under some individual concept, as "the F." Our thoughts about it are not DESCRIPTIVE but *DE RE*. Thoughts about objects of perception make up the basic . . . kind of *de re* thought.[1]

This text is a revised version of the paper "Cognição intuitiva e pensamento de re" that I presented in Poços de Caldas, Minas Gerais, Brazil, on October 6, 2000, at a roundtable discussion of the Study Group on Kant, which was part of the program of the Ninth National Postgraduate Philosophy Association Congress—ANPOF. The text was later published in *Analytica* 4 (1999): 33–63. Translated by the author.

Another good illustration of this thesis can be found in François Recanati, *Direct Reference*:

> A *de re* thought . . . is empirically related to what it is about. The apple causes the perception of the apple, and this must be so for there to be a perception of the apple, and this must be so such empirical relation between descriptive modes of presentation and the reference: there need be no casual connection between the strongest man in the world and my thoughts about the strongest man in the world.[2]

So, considering the analyses of the Transcendental Aesthetic, and in light of several other formal declarations by Kant, it seems almost obvious that the Kantian conception of intuitive cognition can be considered as a precursory variant of the theories of *de re* thought. In fact the opening statement of the Aesthetic says:

> In whatever way and through whatever means a cognition may relate to objects, that through which it relates immediately to them, and at which all thought as a means is directed as an end, is intuition. This, however, takes place only insofar as the object is given to us; but this in turn, is possible only if it **affects** the mind in a certain way. The capacity (receptivity) to acquire representations through the way in which we are affected by objects is called sensibility. Objects are therefore given to us by means of sensibility, and it alone affords us intuitions. . . . That intuition which is related to the object through sensation is called **empirical**. (*Pure Reason*, A19–20/B33–34)

Much later, at the start of the first book of the Transcendental Dialectic, in what is known as the classification passage, Kant reiterates this same thesis:

> A **perception that** refers to the subject as a modification of its state is a **sensation** (*sensatio*); an objective perception is a **cognition** (*cognitio*). The latter is either an **intuition** or a **concept** (*intuitus vel conceptus*). The former is immediately related to the object and is singular; the latter is mediated, by means of a mark, which can be common to several things. (*Pure Reason*, A320/B376–77)

We also find expression of this same point in the *Logic* courses. The opening paragraph of the *Jäsche Logic*, for example, says: "All cognitions, that is, all representations related with consciousness to an object, are either **intuitions** or **concepts**" (9:91). In the same sense, we can read in the *Vienna Logic*: "To cognize, *percipere*, is to represent something in comparison with others and to have insight into its identity or diversity from them. Thus to cognize something with consciousness" (24: 845–46). Therefore, the texts very clearly demonstrate the following of Kant's convictions:

- The first and fundamental characteristic of intuitive cognition is that of referring *immediately* to *objects*.
- The objects to which cognition immediately relates are *singular*.
- The immediate reference to these singular objects is dependent upon our sensibility being affected by these objects.
- The result of this affection of our capacity to acquire representations by contact with the objects is *sensation*, which, when it is, as explained in §3 of the *Critique of the Power of Judgment*, *referred to the object* and not to the subject, *gives* us these objects and is a form of cognition.[3]
- As a form of cognition, intuition allows us to *identify* and *consciously discriminate the objects*; to the effect of these discriminatory acts we can attribute a specific clarification called *aesthetic* clarity,[4] which, according to the *Jäsche Logic*,[5] should be restrictively applied only to the cognition of *individuals* and which needs to be contrasted with "*logical clarity*," only attainable when cognition occurs "*through concepts*."

It therefore seems to be without doubt that these characteristics make empirical intuition a form of *de re* thought and, therefore, a paradigmatic case of object-dependent thought.[6] In fact, to assert that intuition is a form of *immediate* and *singular* cognition is to say that it is a direct cognition of an object, not cognition through conceptual marks and not cognition of conceptual relations; and that it is a cognition that is performed by means of the sensible presence of an actual object to the subject of the cognition.[7]

Beck's Objections to Kant's Objects of Intuitions

However, calling up the ABC of Kantianism is enough to challenge the apparent soundness of this analysis and place the hypothesis of a clear equivalence between Kant's doctrine of intuitive cognition and the theories of *de re* thought under suspicion.

First, and very generally, it can be seen that, however sensible *affection* may be a *necessary* condition of empirical cognition, it can in no way be considered as a *sufficient* condition, since in order for us to have a representation of an external object it is essential that we represent it in space, which—this is the first and most elementary teaching of Kantianism—can only be achieved to the extent that, a priori, we have space as a *form of intuition*. Thus, the forms of intuition, far from being extracted from empirical impressions, are necessarily presupposed by them.[8]

Furthermore, it is a central and at the same time elementary tenet of the Transcendental Deduction that all cognition of objects involves the synthesis of a given manifold, such that, in the strict sense, our cognition of objects *is never immediate*. Thus, to give just one of many possible examples, the following can be read in §20:

> The manifold that is given in a sensible intuition necessarily belongs under original synthetic unity of apperception, since through this alone is the **unity** of the intuition possible (§17). That action of the understanding, however, through which the manifold of given representations (whether they be intuitions or concepts) is brought under an apperception in general, is the logical function of judgments (§19). Therefore all manifold, insofar as it is given in **one** empirical intuition, is **determined** in regard to one of the functions of the logical functions of the judgment, by means of which, namely, it is brought to consciousness in general (*Pure Reason*, B143).[9]

From this and several other parallel texts it therefore seems that the following applies:

- Intuitions give us *not objects*, but a *manifold*, or rather a group of data or sensory information.
- Only through the unification of this manifold by the action of understanding, according to the logical functions of judgments, does the awareness and experience of objects become possible.
- This unification of the sensory manifold, according to the explanation in §24 of the Transcendental Deduction, is performed by the imagination in what is known as *figured synthesis*, which is made according to and guided by the rules provided by pure concepts of understanding.

Moreover, it is a well-founded principle of Kantianism—as can be seen, for example, in the letter to Beck of July 3, 1792, that "nothing composite can **as such** be given to us" (11:347).[10]

So, from these points it seems to follow that not only is the claim revoked that through intuitions we have an immediate cognitive access to singulars, but also that the hypothesis we started from is unsustainable, namely, that Kant's intuitions can be considered as a kind of a *de re* thought.

In fact the consequences implied by the points raised so far are even more serious since they suggest there is a profound incoherence in the Transcendental Doctrine of the Elements, which unfolds as if the second part had been written to challenge and contradict the first.

Our confusion and perplexity further increase when we realize that in the history of critical philosophy this difficulty had already been raised by the first generation of Kantians and presented in the most clear and formal way to Kant himself, without, however, this inquiry having motivated him to make any kind of correction or amendment, if not of the central doctrine of the *Critique of Pure Reason*, then at least of how it is presented.

Indeed, J. S. Beck argued the following in a letter he wrote to Kant on November 11, 1791:

> The **Critique** calls "intuition" a representation that relates immediately to an object. But in fact, a representation does not become objective until is subsumed under the categories. Since intuition similarly acquires its objective character only by means of the application of the categories to it, I am in favor of leaving out that definition of "intuition" that refers to it as representation relating to objects. I find in intuition nothing more than a manifold accompanied of consciousness (or by the **unique** "I think"), and determined by consciousness, a manifold determined by the latter, in which there is as such no relation to an object. I would also like to reject the definition of "concept" as a representation mediately related to an object. Rather, I distinguish concepts from intuitions by the fact they are thoroughly determinate whereas intuitions are not thoroughly determinate. For both intuitions and concepts acquire objectivity only after the activity of judgment subsumes them under the pure concepts of the understanding. (11:311)

As can be seen, it is difficult to show the issue more precisely, honestly, and directly than the way Beck does. However, Kant turned a deaf ear and did not *directly* face the objection—either in the letter to Beck of January 20, 1792, or, as we shall see, later.[11] Come what may, almost seven months after his first interpellation, Beck, clearly uneasy, but also clearly convinced that the point he had raised was a central difficulty that could not be passed over, addressed himself to Kant again, reiterating his question and saying:

> I should like to know whether you agree with the following remarks. It seems to me that one ought not to define "intuition," in the Transcendental Aesthetic, as a representation immediately related to an object or as a representation that arises when the mind is affected by the object. For not until the Transcendental Logic can it be shown how we arrive at objective representations. The fact that there are pure intuitions also rules out such a definition. I really do not see where I err when I say: intuition is a thoroughly determinate representation in relation to a given manifold. In this way it also becomes clear to me that mathematics is a science dependent on the construction of concepts. . . .
>
> In my last letter I mentioned this point as one that seems to me obscure. Your silence, dearest sir, made me fear that I had uttered some nonsense in connection with this. Yet the more I turn the matter over my mind, the more I fail to find any error in asking you for instruction, and I beg you for it once more. (11:338–39)

Before examining the response that Kant is then compelled to give Beck, it is worth underscoring—in function of the analysis we will be developing next—that there are *two* problems to be elucidated here.

The first is the exegetic problem of understanding how the Transcendental Aesthetic and the Transcendental Analytic are articulated, or, speaking materially, the analysis of how sensibility and understanding are linked in our cognition of particulars. The second is the obscure and enigmatic question of the philosophical reasons that deeply prevented Kant from accepting Beck's corrections and that obliged him to maintain—although at the price of a very obscure, elliptical, and apparently contradictory expression—the claim that intuitions give us immediate access to time-space located singulars.

It will not be too much to note at this moment in our analysis that the reply to the second of these problems will be what keeps us on the trail we started on and that will return us to the discussion about the equivalence of the Kantian doctrine of intuition to contemporary theories of *de re* thought. It can be said that the standard way of dealing with the difficulties of the compatibility of the analyses of the Transcendental Aesthetic and those of the Transcendental Analytic consists of disqualifying cognitive intuition and reducing intuition to sensations. Thus, to give just one example, professor Henry Allison writes:

> The problem is that, according to Kant's theory of sensibility, sensible intuition provides the mind with only the raw data for conceptualization, not with the determinate knowledge of objects. Such knowledge requires not only that the data be given in intuition, but also that it be taken under some general description or "recognized in a concept." Only then can we speak of the "representation of an object."[12]

According to this line of analysis, it is denied that intuitions can be real cognitions of objects. Instead it is assumed, implicitly or explicitly, that they are equivalents of mere sensations, and, as Francois-Xavier Chenet has claimed in a recent commentary on the Aesthetic, the passages of the *Critique of Pure Reason* in which Kant speaks of intuition as a cognition of objects must be interpreted as no more than an inertial survival—equivocal and undesirable—of the Dissertation of 1770.[13]

However, it seems simply evident that the texts of the *Critique of Pure Reason* can be coherently read without needing to opt for this radical strategy of correction and amputation of Kant's text.

In fact, for the *Critique* to be understood differently, it is enough to admit that intuitions, *while remaining intuitions*, involve, in addition to the sensible material content resulting from affection, the determinations resulting from the *form of intuition* itself, and also the properties of *objective* cognition, which result from the submission of the sensible manifold to the synthetic unity of apperception.

The exegetic alternative we are considering here is as follows. Either one considers that the cognitive function Kant names *combination* or *synthesis* is entirely identified with the act of judging, in consequence of which perceptions must be considered as and reduced to a kind of judgment—occasionally not expressed linguistically, but no less certainly executed in thought—or one admits that the synthetic activities of understanding are exercised doubly, both for the combination of conceptual representations in judgment and for the unification of the sensible manifold in the synthesis of apprehension.

Only this second option is consistent with the essential texts of the Transcendental Deduction, such as the following passages from §26, for example:

> First of all I remark that by synthesis of apprehension I understand the composition of the manifold in an empirical intuition, through which perception, i.e., empirical consciousness of it (as appearance) becomes possible. . . .
>
> Consequently all synthesis, through which even perception itself becomes possible, stands under the categories, and since experience is cognition through connected perceptions, the categories are conditions of the possibility of experience, and are thus also valid a priori of all objects of experience. (*Pure Reason*, B160–61)

I believe Hoke Robinson clearly and persuasively presents what is implied in this option when he explains:

> The function of the understanding is to produce cognitions, by combining two (or more) representations into a judgment; all judgments arise in this way. Now logic tells us that there are a certain number of ways representations may be combined into judgments: this combination is made by the understanding. But these modes of judgment can be viewed as the specialized application to judgment of general modes of combination resident in the understanding: if it should turn out that there are other areas in addition to judgment in which the understanding can perform its combinatory activity, we would expect there to be a system of combination-forms corresponding to the forms of judgment. . . . But at this point in the exposition (the *Leitfaden*) there is no indication that there in fact exist, in addition to judgment, any further areas of specialization of the understanding's general functions of combination: we do not yet know what we will learn in the Deduction, namely that the categories apply, not only to judgment-formation, but to intuition-formation as well.[14]

Properly understood, this hermeneutic option implies, as Lorne Falkenstein says, that operations through which, in perception, we take our representations of the sensible manifold as representations of objects, are included among the operations of understanding.[15]

It is fundamental to consider, however, that if on the one side this line of interpretation makes it possible to overcome the apparent contradiction between the Aesthetic and the Analytic—and allows it to be resolved without amputation of the critical text or renouncing the idea that intuitions, even in the context of the Analytic, have to be understood as cognitions of singular objects—on the other side it leaves us with an even bigger difficulty: the problem of understanding how, despite its dependency of combination and synthesis, intuition of particulars can continue to be thought of as a form of immediate cognition.

Be that as it may, it must be noted that the preservation of the hypothesis we initially presented—that empirical intuitions can be equivalent to so-called *de re* thoughts—depends on the possibility of positively solving this enigma.

Kant's Replies to Beck: The Given Composite

To proceed in resolving this difficulty, however, requires a correct understanding of at least two obscure and important texts by Kant: the oft-analyzed note to §26 of the Transcendental Deduction, and Kant's reply to the aforementioned letters from Beck.

Yet before presenting what seems to be the solution to this difficult question, it is worth underlining that the difficulty lies in explaining how it is possible for perception, although resulting from a synthesis of understanding, to retain the character of direct relation to the objects.

This is also to say that the critical point lies in comprehending how the connection of synthetic representation to the object that was the origin of these components is *preserved*. An illustration of the difficulty in play here—though shown in another terminology and in a different context, which yet, despite being anachronistic, can be useful for clarifying the point that interests us—can be found in the following passage from Bertrand Russell:

> It will be observed that, according to the general principles which must govern any correspondence of real things with objects of perception, any principle which introduces diversity among objects of perception must introduce a corresponding diversity among real things. I am not now concerned to argue as to what grounds exist for assuming a correspondence, but, if there is such correspondence, it must be supposed that the diversity in the effects—i.e., the perceived objects—imply diversity in the causes—i.e., the real objects. Hence if I perceive two objects in the field of vision, we must suppose that at least two real objects are concerned in causing my perception.[16]

So, if the representation of objects necessarily results from a synthesis of the empirical manifold, it seems necessary to admit that there is necessarily a *suspension* of the dependence (i) of the *object represented through synthesis*, and (ii) *of the object that causes the sensible impressions*, since the founding element of this dependency, the *given* nature of the object, seems to be dissolved as a result of the view according to which *the given is the manifold*, not the *object* of intuition.[17]

The interpretive challenge here is not to explain how the given manifold can be synthesized, but rather to demonstrate how the *synthesized* multiple—what Kant calls the *composite*—can be *synthesized as given*.

Before trying to elucidate this point it is worth recalling, however, that Kant rejected the suggestion twice presented to him by Beck of leaving out "the definition of 'intuition' that refers to it as a representation relating to objects" (Beck letter to Kant, November 11, 1791, 11:311), or as "a representation immediately related to an object or as a representation that arises when the mind is affected by the object" (Beck letter to Kant, May 31, 1792, 11:338).

As we have seen, Kant did not directly present the reason behind his refusal, but instead showed it, in a kind of circumlocution, by refusing the suggestion of a new and alternative conceptualization of the *intuitions*. In fact, Beck had proposed a new definition of the term "intuition" when he said: "I really do not see where I err when I say: intuition is a thoroughly determinate representation in relation to a given manifold" (Beck letter to Kant, May 31, 1792, 11:338).

Kant's reply was a formal yet polite refusal of this suggestion:

> As for your definition of intuition as thoroughly **determinate** representation in respect to a given manifold, I would have nothing further to add except this: the thorough determination here must be understood as objective, not merely as existing in the subject (since it is impossible for us to know all determinations of the object of an empirical intuition). (Kant letter to Beck, July 3, 1792, 11:347)

This is almost to say that Beck's proposal is nonsense. Indeed, if, as Kant explains, it is impossible to define intuition, qua representation, as an entirely *determinate* representation simply because only the *object* itself can be completely *determinate*, we see that Beck's error is a kind of categorical quid pro quo, since his proposal is to attribute to the *cognitive* domain what is a *worldly* property.

Nevertheless, Kant's most important reply is yet to come, since while he says, as the text continues, that "nothing composite can *as such* be given to us" (11:347),[18] he nonetheless asserts that the synthesis of representations, "in order to be in accord with the object, *cannot be arbitrary*" (11:348, emphasis added).

If we seek now to elucidate the meaning of the term "arbitrary" based on Kant's analyses of concepts called *arbitrary*, be they in the *Critique of Pure Reason* or the logic courses, we will be led to conclude that Kant understands as *arbitrary* the concepts that are *not given* to us "either through the nature of the understanding or through experience," and which, on the contrary, are produced by an "arbitrary synthesis," as occurs in mathematics, where "through the explanation of the concept the object is originally given" (*Pure Reason*, A729–30/B757–58).[19]

It is thus implied that, if the synthesis of representations cannot be arbitrary, the *synthesized*—despite Kant's claim that "nothing composite can **as such** be given to us"—has, in a way, to be *given*, because, if not, we have no secure link between it and the objects of which it is sensed to be the representation.

The solution to this problem cannot be seen at first sight, since we seem caught in a formal contradiction. However, Heidegger, always a profound and witty reader of Kant, gives an indication of the way out of this impasse when he says:

> The expression "synthesis" is by itself not only ambiguous but it is also often used by Kant precisely when he does not mean a putting together and gathering together by the positing thetic spontaneity, but rather when he means a *putting* together which he understands more as an *intuiting* together [Zusammen-*schauen*], i.e., as letting-be-encountered. By such a *synthesis* he actually means a syn*opsis*,—as he admittedly says too seldom—and by that he means an original giving-together, i.e., to let the together be encountered out of a unity. This letting-be-encountered already in advance out of a unity holds together more originally than any subsequent holding together of what was previously scattered about.[20]

Heidegger's teaching, therefore, is that we should interpret synthesis as a *joint sight*, as an original unification, as it were. The exegetic challenge is clearly to go beyond Heidegger's metaphors and find an interpretation closer to Kant's text: an interpretation that effectively makes clear how the synthesis required for all cognition of objects can preserve the precedence of them regarding the objective content of the representation, or, as it can also be said, *a precedence that secures* the dependence of thoughts of the objects they are thoughts of.

The central textual base for such an interpretation is found in the aforementioned note to §26 of the Transcendental Deduction, which says:

> Space, represented as object (as is really required in geometry), contains more than the mere form of intuition, namely the **comprehension** of the manifold given in accordance with the form of sensibility in an **intuitive** representation, so that the **form of intuition** merely gives the manifold, but the **formal intuition** gives unity of the representation. In the Aesthetic I ascribed this unity merely to sensibility, only in order to note that it precedes all concepts, though to be sure it presupposes a synthesis, which does not belong to the senses but through which all concepts of space and time first become possible. For since through it (as the understanding determines the sensibility) space or time are first **given** as intuitions, the unity of this a priori intuition belongs to space

and time, and not to the concept of the understanding (§24). (*Pure Reason*, B160–61, note)

Without being able to comment *mot-à-mot* on this troubling and decisive text now, I wish to first and simply emphasize the statement according to which *space and time are given as intuitions through synthesis*. And this is because what simply seems impossible—the compatibility of the concepts of *synthesis* and the *given*—is expressively connected by Kant, and connected in such a way that *it is the given character of space and time which is dependent on synthesis*.

However, this textual support will be no more than a purely verbal solution while the strict conditions under which this enigmatic conjunction of *synthesis* and the nature of the *given* of intuitive representations can be understood are not clarified. It is essential to understand here that there can only be room for this happy conjunction if the manifold to be synthesized has a unique form compatible with this, which is: *the form of a singular a priori representation*—which is, as we know, just *the form of space or time*—and not, as the text sustains, the universal form of a common concept.

This is to hold that *only that which has the fundamental property of the form of intuition—a priori singularity—can preserve the form of individuation belonging to the entities that to pure intuition are as parts of it and as parts that, through being limitations of infinitely given space, are virtually always available, since space as the original form of intuition is* "an infinite **given** magnitude" (*Pure Reason*, B39).[21] Which is also to say that it is *this submission to intuition's form that guarantees the nonarbitrary character of the synthesis*, that is: a synthesis in which *the composite* is synthesized *as given*.[22]

This being so, it should be understood that, in terms of the example proposed in the note to §26, the formation of specific spatial representations—not of space and time as such, as some have misinterpreted,[23] but rather of spatial figures determined as a conical or spherical shape, according to the illustration in §38 of the *Prolegomena*—presupposes the structure of space. So it is space itself (to which we must attribute both formal properties, such as continuous character, divisibility, or three dimensionality, and the spatial regime of relation of parts/whole that is proper to it) that ensures the nonarbitrary character of synthesis, precisely inasmuch as its inner structure is what allows *the composite as such*, although *synthesized, to inherit and retain the "given" nature of its components*. This seems to me to be the very meaning of the final sentence of the note we are referring to, when Kant says that "the unity of this a priori intuition belongs to space and time, and not to the concept of the understanding" (*Pure Reason*, B161, note).[24]

I believe this analysis can be further clarified if, recalling the example from the Second Analogy, we recognize that having a representation of a house, we could go over aspects from its roof ridge to its foundations, or likewise the other way, without, however, being unable to recognize—and recognize immediately—the topologically *given* relations that prevent us from having the roof near the ground, or the foundations pointing at the stars, or the windows to the left of the door or on the right of it, and so on.[25] Another example, perhaps a little more eloquent, would be what obliges us to represent a glove as left- or right-handed, but not indifferently.

In fact Lorne Falkenstein gives us a more accurate explanation of this point when he says:

> Imagine a solid black triangle drawn on a sheet of white paper. Imagine that all points on the sheet are named by the triplet "x, y, b/w," where *x* and *y* refer to the Cartesian coordinates of the point on the sheet of paper, and *b* is selected if the point is black, *w* if it is white. Then imagine that each point of the sheet of paper is made the object of a distinct thought. The result would be an infinite list of thoughts, "(0, 0, b)," "(3, 7, w)," and so on. As long as each point on the sheet is the subject matter for a distinct thought, there is nowhere a thought of the appearance of the sheet of paper as a single whole, and there is therefore a sense in which the sheet has not been perceived. To be represented, this infinite multiplicity of information has to be somehow brought together into a single thought, the "sum" of what all the listed thoughts "add up to," as it were. The thought "triangle" does this. It captures an infinity of different representations in a single representation, and thereby brings many thoughts together in a single consciousness able to perceive the "sum" of what has been presented. But for this to happen, some process of "summation" has to occur. All the different thoughts of points on the sheet have to be put together or compounded.[26]

Of course, Falkenstein emphasizes the necessity for the conjunction or sum of points to be perceived serially, but it is obvious that the image of the sheet of paper makes it necessary to think that, in the kind of synthesis he is considering, the elements on which it is performed—the points—are taken as *points of the sheet of paper*. If so, we must recognize that the synthesized—the *total* of the points—is presupposed to be in a way antecedent to the act of conjunction from which, in another sense, it results.

I believe that another way of illustrating this thesis is to bear in mind the way we perceive a solid, nontransparent cube. We can basically say that we apprehend it in a succession of perceptual looks that can be schematically presented as follows (where "T_1" stands for "*Time 1*," and so on; "S_1" is "*Side 1*," and so on):

T_1: perception of S_1 and S_2;
T_2: perception of S_3 and S_4;
T_3: perception of S_5 and S_6.

As the three-dimensional nature is a constitutive property of the representation of space, it is clear that when *reaching* the until then unseen[27] faces of a solid object we have perceptively in front of us we will not be acquiring knowledge of anything *we did not already know*. Rather, we must first realize that the temporal distribution of the perception of the sides of the cube, while necessarily serial, seems negated by the already given three-dimensional nature of representation of space, which makes the sequencing of the views into a simply subjective movement of recognition of spatial properties that are accessed as always having been there. Which is to say that empirical intuition of a die is the *immediate* intuition of a three-dimensional object, with six faces, although the perceptive views cannot give us simultaneous access to them all. In this context we must note also that the mnemonic retention of S_1, S_2, S_3, and S_4 in T_3 has no epistemic privilege at all,[28] doing no more than ratifying what, at any of the times in question—in T_1 as much as T_2 or T_3—is already known.[29] Not only does this case clearly illustrate the sense in which the elements to be synthesized are *given* (in the example: S_1 and S_2; S_3 and S_4; S_5 and S_6), but also the sense in which the *composite*—let us say: the cube—is synthesized *as a given*.

Or to put it in a generalized way: this is the sense in which we can say that spatial figures are *given* to us through *synthesis*. Once this point has been correctly established, it also becomes easy to understand why, for the relation of synthesized composites to their objects not to be arbitrary, it is essential not just that the manifold to be synthesized has been given but also that the *synthesized* manifold—which in Kant's text is called *the composite*—be *synthesized as given*.

In fact this is a *basic point* of Kant's philosophy, already present in the actual determination of simultaneity as an essential feature of the concept of space in contrast to successiveness, which performs the same role in relation to the concept of time. This claim is very clearly expressed in the following passage from the Metaphysical Exposition of the Concept of Time: "different times are not simultaneous, but successive just as different spaces are not successive, but simultaneous" (*Pure Reason*, A31/B47).

This same point is made with spectacular clarity in *Reflection* 6314 where Kant says we must *apprehend, not merely think, the multiplicity as given simultaneously together in one representation*:

> We cannot represent any number except through successive enumeration in time and then grasping this multiplicity together in the unity of a number. This latter, however, cannot happen except by my placing them beside one another in space: for they must be conceived as given simultaneously, i.e., as taken together in one representation, otherwise this multitude does not constitute a magnitude (number); but it is not possible to cognize simultaneity except insofar as, beyond my action of grasping it together, I can **apprehend**

(not merely think) the multiplicity as given both forwards and backwards (*R*6314, 18:616).[30]

It is also worth noting that even if we vary the mental experiment and, taking a triangle as an example, we suppose not that it is given but rather that it is being drawn, the mathematical synthesis in pure intuition would still not be entirely free of constraints. This is what Falkenstein explains in the continuation of the text we have quoted above:

> But it is important to be clear about what I do and what I am constrained to do. When I draw a triangle on paper, there is a sense in which the "space" for my activity already exists. The paper is there; all its points are ordered in two dimensions, and all I do is mark off certain of these points (by coloring them black) one after another. While I have a certain freedom over how to carry out this procedure—I can mark any point I wish, and as I mark off one adjacent point after another I can change directions as I wish—the paper itself constrains me in other very important ways. The order of points is originally fixed by the paper, not by my own decisions about how to mark. Unless I cut and paste, I cannot mark (0, 0) immediately after (-3, 0)—not without leaving a gap in the line. (With paper I can at least cut and paste, but I cannot cut and paste parts of my visual field.) All I can do, in other words, is choose how to run through an order of points that is already given. I cannot create or define the order itself or, to put the point more technically, I cannot change its topology, or even its metric, as I please. There are aspects that are simply given and outside my control.[31]

So, I believe it is precisely these constraints *prior* to the construction of certain geometric spaces and their respective figures that lead Kant to reject the proposed renunciation of the thesis of the *Critique of Pure Reason* that we are *given objects* by intuition. And I believe that it is exactly this point that he seeks to explain in the letter addressed to Beck on July 3, 1792, where he says:

> Now, since nothing composite can **as such** be given to us[32]—rather, the **composition** of the manifold is something we ourselves must always **produce**—and since too the composition, if it is to conform to the object, cannot be arbitrary, it follows that even if a composite cannot be given, nevertheless the form, i.e., the only form in accordance with which the given manifold can be composed, must be given a priori. This form then is the merely subjective (sensible) aspect of intuition, which is indeed a priori but is not **thought** (for only **composition** as activity is a product of thinking); rather it must be **given** in us (space and time) and consequently it must be a **singular** representation and not a concept (a general representation, *repraesentatio communis*). (11: 347–48)

Which implies that we should also admit that this same analysis goes beyond the terrain of geometrical representations and must be applied to perception in the strict sense, to empirical intuition of real objects. This is a central and very explicit tenet from the *Critique of Pure Reason*. Thus we read in the Elucidation of the Postulates of Empirical Thought:

> Now that space is a formal a priori condition of outer experiences, that this very same formative synthesis by means of which we construct a figure in imagination is entirely identical with that which we exercise in the apprehension of an appearance in order to make a concept of experience of it—it is this alone that connects with the concept the representation of the possibility of such thing (*Pure Reason*, A224/B271).[33]

The same point is made, although reversely and in stronger and more obscure terms, in the proof of the principle of the Analogies, in a passage where Kant says that, on the occasion of an empirical intuition, the principle of the Axioms allows what is apprehended in the phenomenon to be constituted a priori. The text says: "Now the way in which something is apprehended in appearance can be determined a priori so that the rule of its synthesis at the same time yields this intuition a priori in every empirical example, i.e., can bring the former about from the latter" (*Pure Reason*, A178/B220–21).

If we now return to our starting point—the idea that the intervention of understanding in intuitive representation of objects prevents equating the Kantian doctrine of empirical intuitions with the contemporary theory of *de re* thought—I believe we will be comforted and strengthened by the understanding we now have, namely, that the composition of parts belonging to Kantian intuitions presupposes the topological and mereological structuring of intuited objects as *given* together with the *form of intuition*.

In this sense I want to believe that the fundamental requisites of so-called *de re* thoughts—the object dependency of representations—can be recognized as being preserved in, and thanks to, the Kantian doctrine of the a priori[34] conditions of empirical cognition.

Strawson's Analysis of Wholes and Parts

To conclude, it is also worth presenting a kind of counterproof, not of Kant's good exegesis, but rather of the heuristic strength, acuteness, and penetration of Kantian analyses of intuitive cognition, bringing into this present discussion the analyses to which Peter Strawson submitted two unexpected and apparently implausible objects: Betty and the Plough.

However, before presenting Strawson's examples, it is worth specifying that the word *counterproof* is used here both as a metaphor in the typographical sense of the term and in the more abstract sense of *verification*. The idea is that the analyses of Strawson we will be now presenting can be considered as a modern version of the Kantian doctrine of intuition. Second, we also want to hold that this *repetition*, done in the context of a logical-semantic analysis, is at the same time a kind of corroboration and confirmation of Kant's main claims.[35]

In the text I am considering, Strawson says the following:

> Well, it will be scarcely denied that "Betty" is typically used to designate a spatio-temporally continuous particular. And it will scarcely be denied that the meaning of "pretty" is such that it may be said to **group** such particulars in accordance with a certain kind of principle. The term may be said to group all those particulars whose designations may be coupled with it to yield true statements. Now in a certain sense "Betty" may be said to group particulars too: a particular arm, leg, face, even a particular action, might all be truthfully ascribed to Betty. But obviously the principle on which "Betty" groups particulars like arms and legs is quite a different sort of principle from the principle on which "pretty" groups particulars like Betty and Sally.[36]

The term "beautiful" groups particulars in clearly the same way as what Kant calls the external use of concepts does, that is, utilization of the characteristic notes to establish the identity or diversity of objects, the notes being employed as a *secundum quid* in relation to which the objects have to be seen as equal or different. This is the lesson gathered from the *Vienna Logic*, for example:

> A mark is a ground of cognition, principally, too, in the comparison of things. In comparison, I look to the identity or diversity of things. We need marks not merely to distinguish things, as our author holds, but also to discover their agreement. E.g., I do not want merely to distinguish a sheep from a goat, but also want to know wherein it agrees with another sheep. (*Vienna Logic*, 24:834)

It should be understood, however, that, although used for identification of objects, the characteristic notes allow them to establish only *qualitative* identity. This is to say that even when used for cognition of a particular, the concept functions by *discarding differences*, since its function is not to establish a certain conjunction of parts of a singular object, but rather to recognize an individual as being subsumable in a general term.[37]

I believe that this point becomes even clearer if we compare how (i) the term "Betty" groups particulars and how (ii) the concept "female body" groups particulars.

The term "Betty" groups the legs and arms, torso, face, and hair of Betty—not those of Gisele Bundchen or Ana Paula Arósio. While the concept "female body" *contains under it* the subordinate concepts of "female legs and arms," "female torso," "female face," "female hair," and allows grouping

Betty, Gisele Bundchen, and Ana Paula Arósio only to the extent that each of them can be considered as an instance of the concept "female body" and of the other subordinate concepts included within its sphere.

The term "Betty," however, groups particulars in a very different way because when we use the name with a determinate person in mind, a certain idiosyncratic configuration of sensible and iconically represented parts is either perceived or imagined, that is, the configuration given by Betty's unique physiognomy, her body profile, and what physically distinguishes her from other women. That is to say that the way the name "Betty" groups particulars is founded in the intuitive cognition of Betty and the way in which her parts *compose* her *figure*.

To understand that we are still at the heart of the same subject dealt with in the previous parts of this text, it is, however, fundamental to listen to what Strawson has to say about the term "the Plough" and the distinction between the way in which the terms "Betty" and "the Plough" group particulars. Strawson says:

> Not all particulars are spatio-temporally **continuous** as Betty is. But the contrast between principles of grouping is not in general dependent in such continuity, though it is seen most easily in cases characterized by continuity. The expression "The Plough" (used as a name of a constellation) designates a spatio-temporal particular, though not a continuous one; whereas even if it should come to pass that all the gold in the universe formed one continuous mass, this would not turn "gold" into the designation of a spatio-temporal particular. What makes it correct to count a star as a bit of the Plough or an arm as a bit of Betty has at least to do with their spatio-temporal relation to other bits of the Plough or of Betty in a way in which what makes it correct to count something as an instance of gold has nothing to do with its spatio-temporal relations to other instances of gold. The distinction between being **a particular part of** (or **element** in, etc.) and **being a particular instance of** remains bright enough here, even though spatial continuity is gone.[38]

It is therefore very clear that the way in which the terms "Betty" and "the Plough" group particulars is quite distinct, since while "Betty" defines genuine limits, based on relations of internal spatial continuity-discontinuity and in discrimination of heterogeneities of form, color, and movement of the grouping particulars, "the Plough" defines limits with a degree of higher arbitrariness, as it takes a multiplicity of spatially disconnected objects as a unity, although taking into account certain relationships of proximity and symmetry between them. Making use of the contemporaneously proposed terminology of Barry Smith and Archille Varzi, we can say, therefore, that the terms "Betty" and "the Plough" are paradigmatic examples of bona fide *objects* and *agglomerations*, respectively.[39]

Despite this difference, however, Strawson's observation remains true that the way in which the names "Betty" and "the Plough" group particulars is categorically distinct from the way concepts or classes do, since in the former case the basis or criteria for grouping are not constituted by characteristic notes as they are in this latter case, but rather by direct and constitutively iconic representations; or to use Kant's term, representations that are hypotyposis, that is, presentations of external objects given perceptively and *meaningfully* structured by mereological and topological relations.[40]

That the cognitive access to such objects primarily depends on the direct relation with them seems, therefore, beyond doubt. Consequently, our initial conjecture that the Kantian doctrine of empirical intuition can be considered as a precocious variant of the contemporary theory of *de re* thought also proves to be fully justified.

Notes

1. Kent Bach, *Thought and Reference* (Oxford: Oxford University Press, 1987), 11.

2. François Recanati, *Direct Reference* (Oxford: Blackwell, 1997), 103.

3. It can also be read at the start of the *Critique of Pure Reason* that "Objects are therefore given to us by means of sensibility, and it alone affords us intuitions. . . . That intuition which is related to the object through sensation is called **empirical**" (*Pure Reason*, A19–20/B33–34).

4. In §6 of the *Anthropology* Kant defines the word "clarity" as follows: "Consciousness of one's representation that suffices for the **distinction** of one object from another is **clarity**. But that consciousness by means of which the **composition** of representations also becomes clear is called **distinctness**" (7:137–38).

5. See *Jäsche Logic*, 9:62. See also §15, note (*Jäsche Logic*, 9:99).

6. And even more so when we recall that Kant used to accompany the aforementioned characterization with the emphatic contrast of cognition by concepts, which is always called *indirect*, or *mediate*, depending on characteristic notes and directed at discrimination of what is common to various things. See *Pure Reason*, B33–34 and A19; see also *Jäsche Logic*, §1, note 1.

7. It should also be underlined that this capacity of the empirical objects to be present belongs to the *senses* in the strict acceptance of the term, in contrast to the imagination. In fact, according to Kant's analysis, the senses comprise the first element of the *sensible faculty*, which is characterized as the *faculty of intuition with* the presence of the object, contrasting with the faculty of intuitions *without* the presence of objects, the *imagination*. The following passage conveys the point very clearly: "Sensible cognition arises either entirely from the impression of the object, and then this sensible cognition is a representation of the senses themselves, or sensible cognition arises from the mind, but under the condition under which the mind is affected by objects, and then sensible cognition is an imitated representation of the senses. E.g., the representation of that which I see. . . . But if I make present to myself a house that I saw earlier, then the representation arises now from the mind, but still

under the condition that the senses were previously affected by this object. Such sensible cognitions which arise from the spontaneity of the mind are called: **cognitions of the formative power**; and the cognitions which arise through the impression of the object are called: **representations of the senses themselves**" (*Metaphysics* L_1, 28:230).

8. See A23/B38.

9. In the same sense, and perhaps even more clearly, Kant writes to Marcus Herz on May 26, 1789: "In other words I ascribe to the understanding the synthetic unity of apperception, through which alone the manifold of the intuition (of whose **every feature** I may nevertheless be **particularly** conscious), in a unified consciousness, is brought to the representation of an object in general (whose concept is then determined by means of that manifold) . . . consequently, the form in which they are given depends on us,—on the one hand, on its subjective aspect, [objects are] dependent on the specific character of our intuition; on the other hand, they are dependent on the uniting of the manifold in a consciousness, that is, on what is required for the thinking and cognizing of objects by our understanding. Only under these conditions, therefore, can we have experiences of those objects; and consequently, if intuition (of objects of appearance) did not agree with these conditions, those objects would be nothing for us, that is, not objects of **cognition** at all; neither cognition of ourselves nor of other things" (11: 50–51).

10. The same thesis expressed in slightly different terms is presented in the letter to Tieftrunk, of December 11, 1797: "For that which is composed cannot as such be **intuited**" (12:222).

11. It is true that, *in pectore*, Kant immediately rejected Beck's suggestion, since in the margin of the letter he wrote: "To make [*Bestimmung*] a concept, by means of intuition, into a cognition of an object, is indeed the work of judgment; but the reference of intuition to an object in general is not. For the latter is merely the logical use of representation insofar as a representation is thought as being a cognition. When, on the other hand, a single representation is referred only to the subject, the use is aesthetic (feeling), in which case the representation cannot become a piece of knowledge" (11:311).

12. See Henry E. Allison, *Kant's Transcendental Idealism* (New Haven: Yale University Press, 1982), 67. W. H. Walsh's position is no different; he says, more explicitly: "According to the theory stated above, intuitions need to be brought under concepts in order to be comprehended; if they are particulars they already stand under concepts. The only way I can see out of this is to say that sensation is not strictly a form of awareness, since it has no true objects, but a mode of experience which is *sui generis*; without it experience of particulars would be impossible, though it is false to describe it as presenting particulars for description. Sensory content—'intuitions,' as Kant calls them—are not objects of any sort, public or private." See W. H. Walsh, *Kant's Criticism of Metaphysics* (Edinburgh: Ediburgh University Press, 1975), 13–14.

13. See François-Xavier Chenet, *L'assise de l'ontologie critique—L'esthétique transcendentale* (Lille: Presses Universitaires de Lille, 1994), 287.

14. Hoke Robinson, "The Transcendental Deduction from A to B: Combination in the Threefold Synthesis and the Representation of a Whole," *Southern Journal of*

Philosophy 25 Suppl. (1986): 47–48. This interpretation can be supported by many texts. In B130, for example, one can read that "all combination, whether we are conscious of it or not, whether it is a combination of the manifold of intuition or of several concepts, and in the first case either of sensible or non-sensible intuition, is an action of the understanding, which we would designate with the general title of **synthesis** in order at the same time to draw attention to the fact that we can represent nothing as combined in the object without having previously combined it ourselves." Cf. B162, note.

15. The following text explains this very clearly: "In this sense, indeed, concepts are only one among the products of intellectual synthesis; there are also perceptions. Paralleling this second choice, we might also take 'intuition' to mean singular representation or perception. But if we define 'intuition' in this way, then we must recognize that 'intuitions' are not distinct from intellectual representations, but are a subset of intellectual representations: namely, products of the intellectual process of combination or figurative synthesis." Lorne Falkenstein, *Kant's Intuitionism: A Commentary on the Transcendental Aesthetic* (Toronto: University of Toronto Press, 1995), 69–70. Wilfrid Sellars had expressed the same point when he said: "It is essential to see that intuition is a species of thought, for any sense-datum like approach makes essential features of Kant's theory of knowledge unintelligible, e.g., the Schematism. Thus the categories apply to intuitions, because, although the content of sensations does not contain the categories, the content of intuitions (of manifolds) does. This is the point of Kant's problem about homogeneity and of his solution." See Wilfrid Sellars, "Transcendental Idealism," §11, http://www.ditext.com/sellars/kti.html; originally published in *Collections of Philosophy* 6 (1976): 165–81.

16. See Bertrand Russell, "On the Relations of Universals and Particulars," in *Logic and Knowledge: Essays, 1901–1950*, ed. Robert Charles Marsh (London: George Allen & Unwin, 1956), 121.

17. If this were the case one would have to admit the possibility that from the manifold originating from the senses being affected by a *single* object we would be *free* and *able* to *perceptually* represent one, two, three, or more objects!

18. Arnulf Zweig changes his translation of this passage in the Cambridge edition of Kant's correspondence as follows: "nothing composite can **as composite** be given to us," but his former option to translate the German *als ein solches* as *as such* seems preferable. See Immanuel Kant, *Philosophical Correspondence 1759–1799*, ed. and trans. Arnulf Zweig (Chicago: The University of Chicago Press, 1986), 193.

19. See *Lectures on Logic* (24:918–19).

20. Martin Heidegger, *Phenomenological Interpretation of Kant's Critique of Pure Reason*, trans. Parvis Emad and Kenneth Maly (Bloomington: Indiana University Press, 1997), 93.

21. This is exactly the idea presented at *Pure Reason*, A438/B466 when Kant says: "Properly speaking, one should call space not a *compositum* but a *totum*, because its parts are possible only on the whole, and not the whole through the parts. In any case, it could be called a *compositum ideale* but not *a compositum reale*."

22. Kant also says: "For in the appearance the objects, indeed even properties that we attribute to them, are always regarded as something really given" (*Pure Reason*, B69–70).

23. Michel Fichant points to an alleged error in Longuenesse's reading of this text. See "*L'espace est représenté comme une grandeur infinie donnée: La radicalité de l'esthétique*," in *Philosophie* 56 (December 1997): 35. Fichant is considering the interpretation of the Transcendental Aesthetic proposed by Longuenesse on page 236 and after, in *Kant et le pouvoir de juger* (Paris: Epiméthé, PUF, 1993). Long before this French debate, Arthur Melnick, commenting on the apparent conflict between the Aesthetic and the Axioms of Intuition raised by Vahinger and Robert Paul Wolff, analyzed this same question and wrote with remarkable precision: "The conflict rests on the fact that Kant seems to be saying in the Axioms that the intuition of space and time (space and time as purely intuited) requires construction. And yet the Axioms are concerned with the construction of figures in space (the construction of determinate spaces) and not with the construction of the space itself within which figures are constructed. Kant says, 'I cannot represent to myself a line, however small, without drawing it in thought, that is generating from a point all its parts one after another' [*Pure Reason*, A163/B203]. I can only draw a line in (against the background of) space. If space were not already given to me (imagined by me), I could not generate the line **from a point**. 'Points and instants are only limits, that is, mere positions that limit space and time. **But positions always presuppose the intuitions which they limit or are intended to limit**' [*Pure Reason*, A169/B211]." Arthur Melnick, *Kant's Analogies of Experience* (Chicago: University of Chicago Press, 1973), 18, quoting Kant as noted.

24. I believe a thesis very similar to this is found in *Pure Reason*, A284/B340: "But since something is contained in the intuition that does not lie at all in the mere concept of a thing in general, and this yields the substratum that cannot be cognized through mere concepts, namely a space that, along with everything that it contains, consists of purely formal or also real relations."

25. It seems to me that this is exactly the point, although expressed in a rather obscure manner, that Kant is considering when he says: "Thus if, e.g., I make the empirical intuition of a house into perception through apprehension of its manifold, my ground is the **necessary unity** of space and of outer sensible intuition in general, and I as it were draw its shape in agreement with this synthetic unity of the manifold in space" (in §26, *Pure Reason*, B162).

26. See Falkenstein, *Kant's Intuitionism*, 246–47.

27. Due, of course, to the point of view we have each time.

28. It is important to note that denying the epistemic privilege of "reproduction" is not to deny the psychological and logical transcendental necessity—so clearly and emphatically stated in A102—of the sequence of perceptions, but rather is to simply say that the retention of the perceived in T_1 and T_2 in T_3 is symmetrical to the function performed by the imagination at T_1, in anticipating the intuitive cognition of the sides that can only be seen at T_2 and T_3. About the anticipatory function of the imagination, see *Anthropology*, 7:182 and *Metaphysic* $L_{1,}$ 28: 236–37.

29. We are considering the *formal* properties of objects intuited spatially here. Which is to say that if, on seeing an orange, I know immediately that it has a part behind that I cannot see, in no way will I be able to know, a priori, if that part is rotten or not. (Fabian Scholze alerted me to the importance of making this point in one of my classes at the Federal University of Rio Grande do Sul.) Furthermore,

Kant deals with this point formally in the Discipline of Pure Reason in Its Dogmatic Employment, when he says: "For only the concept of magnitudes can be constructed, i.e., exhibited a priori in the intuition, while qualities cannot be exhibited in anything but in empirical intuition. . . . The shape of a cone can be made intuitive without any empirical assistance, merely in accordance with the concept, but the color of this cone must first be given in one experience or another" (*Pure Reason*, A714–15/B742–43). On the other hand, it is also worth observing that if, on intuiting, I make use of the *concept* of the intuited thing, I can then anticipate its *essential* characteristics or material properties, even if I do not perceive them directly. This is what Kant explains in §5 of the *Anthropology* when he tells us: "When I am conscious of seeing a human being far from me in a meadow, even though I am not conscious of seeing his eyes, nose, mouth, etc." I have to admit that these traces, in a way—or more exactly, *through the mode of inference*—are included in the intuitive representation, because if not, I would also not be able to say that I see a human being, "since the representation of the whole (of the head or of the human being) is composed of these partial ideas" (*Anthropology*, 7:135).

One can go on to think that anticipation of the three-dimensional nature of the given object in perception—the anticipation that the observer will have of the part behind or below, whose view, in the strict sense, will depend on the sequence of perceptive acts—can be reduced to the same terms of this example, assuming that there is an *inference* here as well as there. I think the difference between the two cases becomes clear, however, when we recall the distinction Kant establishes between *error* and *illusion*. Illusion, unlike error—be it sensible illusion, or transcendental illusion—is not a fault in the inferential chain and therefore does not fail to produce its effects when corrected: it is a primary disorder, immanent and necessary from the use of the cognitive faculties. Moreover, in the case of *intuitive* illusion, it is an *immediate* disorder. Kant makes this clear in *Pure Reason*, A297/B354, which says: "This is an **illusion** that cannot be avoided at all, just as little as we can avoid it that the sea appears higher in the middle than at the shores, since we see the former through higher rays of the light than the latter, or even better, just as little as the astronomer can prevent the rising of the moon from appearing larger to him, even when he is not deceived by this illusion." Therefore, the impression of three dimensionality Kant speaks about when evoking the example of the painting of a staircase in Amsterdam Town Hall, which is introduced as "the painted steps with a half-opened door . . . where one is induced to climb up them" (*Anthropology* 7:150), is a case of illusion, not of inferential error, and if it is considered, *a contrario*, we can recognize in it the immediate, not illative, character of the cognition of the possible three dimensionality of given objects in space.

It is, by the way, recorded that if, in terms of the example mentioned above, it should happen that the *die* that we perceive is not a *die* but a three-dimensional model produced by an industrial designer to show to a company director the final appearance of the dice to be manufactured, in which model two sides were missing, the error in taking this proof as a die would be an error of illation, because in this hypothesis we would be taking the view of four sides as the basis of inference for believing that the object in question has two other sides not yet seen. By contrast, in the case of taking a perspective drawing as evidence of depth, the error does not derive from the faulty inference that carries seen material properties to unseen *material* properties, but rather happens beforehand, from a distortion directly caused by *sight*, through a kind of structuring of what is completely manifest, directly presented to the eyes. The error in the first case lies not in the supposition of the three dimensionality of the perceived object, but rather in the mistaken anticipation, based on the *concept* of *dice*, that the model would be complete and would materially have six sides. While in the case of the Amsterdam door, the error is a consequence of a certain manipulation of perspective that makes us unduly actualize in the pure intuition (as if our intuitive faculties had been triggered by such manipulation) the a priori presupposition of the three dimensionality of space, which is inherent to the form of intuition.

Before concluding, it is also worth observing that the statement in B154 that "we cannot represent the three dimensions of space at all without **placing** three lines perpendicular to each other at the same point" seems to frontally contradict the line of reading we are proposing. However, I believe it is enough to properly understand the meaning of "to represent" in this context not to underestimate the force to be attributed to "placing": *represent* here means *to form the image*, it is *figuration* of three dimensionality such that what is *placed* is not the three dimensionality of space, but rather its depiction; "placing" here is in turn what is only possible if space is supposed as a form of intuition. Commenting on this same text, Arthur Melnick wrote: "I can only draw a line in (against the background of) space. If space were not already given to me (imagined by me), I could not generate the line **from a point.**" Melnick, *Kant's Analogies*, 18.

30. See Paul Guyer, *Kant and the Claims of Knowledge* (Cambridge: Cambridge University Press, 1987), 298. In B134 one can also read: "Synthetic unity of the manifold of intuition, as given a priori, is thus the ground of the identity of apperception itself, which precedes a priori all **my** determinate thinking." Finally in §26 of the *Critique of the Power of Judgement* Kant expands this point, so to speak, when he states: "But now the mind hears in itself the voice of reason, which requires totality for all given magnitudes, even for those that can never be entirely apprehended although they are (in the sensible representation) judged as entirely given, hence comprehension in **one** intuition, and it demands a **presentation** for all members of a progressively increasing numerical series, and does not exempt from this requirement even the infinite (space and past time), but rather makes it unavoidable for us to think of it (in the judgment of common reason) as **given entirely** (in its totality)" (*Judgment*, 5:254). I believe this point is also implied in the introduction of the concept of synthesis of apprehension, as it appears in A99. See also the commentary by Richard Aquila in *Matter in Mind* (Bloomington: Indiana University Press, 1989), 73. And the point is returned to with the right clarity and vigor in A120–21, when Kant says that the *synthesizing* action of the imagination is *apprehension* (*Pure Reason*, A120).

31. Falkenstein, *Kant's Intuitionism*, 246–47.

32. See note 18.

33. This is also the very explicit lesson of A165/B206 that, notably, says the following: "Empirical intuition is possible only through the pure intuition (of space and time); what geometry says about the latter is therefore undeniably valid of the former, and evasions, as if objects of the senses did not have to be in agreement with

the rules of construction in space (e.g., the rules of divisibility of lines and angles), must cease. For one would thereby deny all objective validity to space, and with it at the same time to all mathematics, and would no longer know why and how far they are to be applied to appearances. The synthesis of spaces and times, as the essential form of all intuition, is that which at the same time makes possible the apprehension of the appearance, thus every outer experience, consequently also all cognition of its objects, and what mathematics in its pure use proves about the former is also necessarily valid for the latter."

34. A priori, yes! Well, this is true if *object-dependent* thoughts are also *a priori-dependent*, which is, after all, the best illustration of the combination of *transcendental idealism* and *empirical realism* that characterizes Kantianism.

35. Which suggests that Strawson's analysis considered in sequence is a kind of semantic mirror of the logical and epistemological analyses—or, if preferred, logico-transcendental analyses—of Kant. It should also be noted that it is obvious that the expression "to group particulars" used by Strawson can be placed alongside the combination or synthesis of Kant.

36. Peter F. Strawson, "Singular Terms and Predication," in D. Davidson and J. Hintikka, *Words and Objections: Essays on the Work of W. V. Quine* (Dordrecht: D. Reidel, 1969), 110.

37. Robert Wolff expresses this thinking well when he says that the concept is found "always at least at a single remove from its object." Robert Paul Wolff, *Kant's Theory of Mental Activity* (Cambridge: Harvard University Press, 1963), 63.

38. Strawson, *Singular Terms*, 117.

39. See Barry Smith and Achille C. Varzi, "The Formal Ontology of Boundaries," *Electronic Journal of Analytic Philosophy* 5, no. 5 (1997), no pagination, http://ejap.louisiana.edu/EJAP/1997.spring/smithvarzi976.html. Smith and Varzi note, for example: "Examples of bona fide objects are: all geographical entities demarcated in ways which do not respect qualitative differentiations or spatio-temporal discontinuities in the underlying territory." It is clear that the term "Betty" *is bona fide* in this sense. While the term "the Plough" should not be considered as an object but as a *bona fide agglomeration*, understood as "agglomerations which are, in their own right, genuine parts of the causal order of what happens," as, for example, "colonies of single-celled organisms or to shoals of fish," and which can be characterized as "agglomerations which exist independently of all human cognition"—in contrast to *agglomerations fiat*, whose characteristic is to be "discriminated from their surroundings as a result of human decision or convention." See Barry Smith, "Agglomerations," in *Spatial Information Theory: Cognitive and Computational Foundations of Geographic Information Science: International Conference* COSIT '99, *Stade, Germany, August 1999: Proceedings*, ed. Christian Freksa and David M. Mark (New York: Springer, 1999), 278. It can also be said that the term "the Plough," despite being formed of topologically separate parts, is, however, a mereo-topologically structured whole, not just because of the neighboring and symmetrical relationships between its parts, but also because these move as if they were a single object. See Roberto Casati and Achille C. Varzi, *Parts and Places* (Cambridge: MIT Press, 1999), 14.

40. This is the point Strawson makes when he says of geometry that its axioms are true in function **"of the meanings attached to the expressions they contain,"**

meanings which are "**essentially picturable.**" The text I am referring to says the following: "Consider the proposition that not more than one straight line can be drawn between any two points. . . . The natural way to satisfy ourselves of the truth of this axiom of phenomenal geometry is to consider an actual or imagined figure. When we do this, it becomes evident that we cannot, either in imagination or on paper, give ourselves a picture such that we are prepared to say of it both that it shows two straight distinct lines and that it shows both these lines as drawn through the same two points. Such an impossibility used to be expressed by saying that such axioms are necessarily true because they are self-evident. This left the character of the necessity, or the impossibility, insufficiently explained. We can explain it by saying that the axioms are true solely in virtue of the meanings attached to the expressions they contain, but these meanings are essentially phenomenal, visual meanings, are essentially picturable meanings." Peter F. Strawson, *The Bounds of Sense* (London: Methuen, 1966), 283.

4

Predicative Judgments and Existential Judgments

Apropos Kant's Critique of the Cartesian Ontological Argument

Raúl Landim

Introduction

Considered in schematic form, the Cartesian a priori proof of the existence of God—defined by Kant as an ontological argument—contains two main stages: (a) the first derives knowledge of the reality of God's essence from the innate, clear, and distinct idea of God; while (b) the second derives knowledge of God's existence from knowledge of His essence.

In the second stage of the proof, the predicative proposition "God is existent" is deduced from the proposition "God is a supremely perfect being" and the supposition that existence is a perfection or a real predicate (a supposition explicitly admitted by Descartes in the *Fifth Set of Replies*),[1] in the same way that the predicative proposition "God is omnipotent" could be deduced. But since the proposition "God is existent" means that *God exists*, the conclusion of the ontological argument is therefore an existential proposition.[2]

Kant's refutation of Descartes' version of the ontological argument is based on the thesis that existence is not a real predicate.[3] This thesis in turn leads to the argument that existential judgments cannot be assimilated to categorical judgments (predicative judgments),[4] since categorical judgments represent an object with its properties, connecting different conceptual representations by means of the copula, while existential judgments signify that objects are actual instances of concepts.

This is a revised but not substantially modified translation of an article published as "Juízos predicativos e juízos de existência: A propósito da crítica kantiana ao argument ontológico cartesiano," in *Analytica* 5 (2000): 83–108. Translated by David Rodgers.

Focusing on Kant's characterization of *categorical judgments*, formulated in his texts on logic,[5] and *existential judgments*, formulated in the work *The Only Possible Argument in Support of a Demonstration of the Existence of God* and resumed in the *Critique of Pure Reason* (*Pure Reason*, A592/B620) in the section On the Impossibility of an Ontological Proof of God's Existence, I shall examine the Kantian critique of Descartes' ontological argument, looking to analyze the connections between the thesis that *existence* is not a real predicate and the relations between categorical judgments (whether analytic or synthetic) and existential judgments, whose logical form is not recognized in Kant's texts on logic.[6]

However, in reconstructing this critique, I shall not use the results of the Analytic of Principles (*Pure Reason*, A137–292/B176–349),[7] since these eliminate a priori proofs of existence from the outset, rendering them meaningless.

Indeed, the intention of the Cartesian version of the ontological argument is to show that, by reason of the characteristics of a specific idea or concept, namely, the concept of the supremely perfect being, the latter concept has an actual instance—that is, it cannot be empty.

But, if the meaning of the term "existence" is expressed by the schematized category of existence,[8] and if the proof that something exists effectively demands, as the Second Postulate of Empirical Thinking states, the connection through rules of this something with sensible perception—that is, with sensation—then obviously every proof of existence must be a posteriori. Consequently, a priori proofs of existence (whether analytic or synthetic) are excluded from the outset. Thus, the results of the Analytic of Principles render the refutation of the ontological argument trivial.

Now, the thesis that existence is not a real predicate is a precritical thesis, reasserted in the Transcendental Dialectic, and seems to be sufficient for the refutation of the Cartesian version of the ontological argument.[9] Obviously it does not depend on theses demonstrated in the Analytic of Principles, although, in developing his explanation, Kant makes use of notions expounded in this part of the *Critique of Pure Reason*, such as judgment, concept, predicate, object, and so on.

Categorical Judgments and Existential Judgments

Kant defines the logical function of judgments as that of unifying the manifold of given representations (intuitions or concepts) in the unity of apperception (*Pure Reason*, B143, §20).[10]

In the section On the Logical Use of the Understanding in General of the *Critique of Pure Reason* (A67–70/B92–94), Kant analyzes the function of concept and judgment, taking as his model the affirmative categorical judgment.

Judgment is initially characterized as a function of unity, a "kind" of complex concept, a representation of representations ("All judgments are accordingly functions of unity among our representations. . .").[11] Indeed, in the (affirmative) judgment, a conceptual unification is effected through a relation of subordination: a *higher* representation subordinates *under itself* various other conceptual representations ("since instead of an immediate representation a higher one, which comprehends this and other representations under itself . . ."). Accordingly, concepts are connected in the affirmative judgment by the relation of subordination. By subordinating concepts, though, judgments subsume a manifold of intuitive representations through the subject concept: "In every judgment there is a concept that holds of many, and that among this many also comprehends a given representation, which is then related immediately to the object" (*Pure Reason*, A68/B93).

Paragraph §19 of the Transcendental Deduction section of the *Critique of Pure Reason* complements the analysis of the function of the judgment. This text introduces the *objective unity of apperception* as a notion constitutive of every judgment. The latter have an objective unity; in other words, they have a necessary relation to objects insofar as they satisfy, in addition to the relation of subordination and subsumption, the necessary rules of the understanding. Only thus do they have an objective validity—that is, they may or may not agree with the object represented in the judgment.

By connecting the subject concept with the predicate concept through the copula in an affirmative categorical judgment, a synthetic unity of different representations is formed. This unity ought to be able to represent, at least in the categorical judgment, the unity of the object that, with its manifold determinations, is distinct from and opposed to the judgment's representations (*Pure Reason*, A104–5).

From the point of view of relation, judgments are classified into categorical, hypothetical, and disjunctive. (Affirmative) categorical judgments are connections of concepts taking the form *S is P*. They signify that everything to which the subject concept *S* agrees, the predicate concept *P* also agrees.[12]

In criticizing the classical definition of a judgment as a relation between concepts (*Pure Reason*, B140–41, §19), Kant also suggests that this definition applies only to categorical judgments. Indeed, the matter of these judgments consists of the subject and the predicate, while their form consists of the copula connecting the predicate to the subject (*Jäsche Logic*, 9:105, §24). Since subject and predicate are concepts, whether simple or complex, the matter of categorical judgments is the subject concept and the predicate concept. This, at least, is the claim made by Kant in the *Vienna Logic*: "The matter of a categorical judgment consists of two concepts, the form in the relation in which the one concerns the subject, the other the predicate" (24:932–33).[13] The matter of hypothetical and disjunctive judgments consists of other judgments,[14] which lends plausibility to the thesis that categorical judgments, which break down into concepts, can be defined as connections of concepts, while hypothetical or disjunctive judgments, which break down into judgments, are connections of judgments.

Although Kant's logic does not present a method for breaking complex judgments down into simple ones, it seems clear that categorical judgments—insofar as they are not decomposed into other judgments, but only into concepts—comprise the simple (elementary) judgments of Kantian logic. Obviously the term "simple" here does not mean atomic, since the judgment "all men are white" is a categorical judgment and also a simple judgment given that it cannot be broken down into other judgments. Indeed, it is a judgment of the subject-predicate form, where the subject concept has been taken to be universal. It is not, however, an atomic judgment, given the occurrence of the syncategorematic expression "all." It is perfectly true that hypothetical or disjunctive judgments have a different logical form to categorical judgments and cannot be reduced to the latter, as Kant repeatedly argues in his texts on logic. However, this does not refute the thesis that categorical judgments are the constitutive elements of hypothetical or disjunctive judgments. Categorical judgments connect the subject concept to the predicate concept by means of the copula. They are connections of concepts. Hypothetical or disjunctive judgments are connections of judgments.

Since categorical judgments cannot be broken down into other judgments and since they are the constitutive elements of hypothetical or disjunctive judgments, either they have an existential function, and judgments composed by them can also exercise this function, or they lack this function, meaning it cannot be found in any of these other judgments. Thus the question concerning the existential function of complex, hypothetical, or disjunctive functions can be answered by the analysis of the function of categorical judgments.

Kant does not expound on the form of existential judgments in his texts on logic. This kind of judgment is not included in the Table of Judgments in the *Critique of Pure Reason*, nor is it considered a judgment with a specific form in any of Kant's various texts on logic. It is only in the context of the critique of the ontological argument, whether as formulated in *Only Possible Argument* or in the Transcendental Dialectic section of the *Critique of Pure Reason*, that Kant appears to recognize the specificity of the form of existential judgments.

In the work *The Only Possible Argument in Support of a Demonstration of the Existence of God*, Kant characterizes the existential judgment in the following way:

> If I say "God is an existent thing" it looks as if I am expressing the relation of a predicate to a subject. But there is an impropriety in this expression. Strictly speaking, the matter ought to be formulated like this: "Something existent is God." In other words, there belongs to an existent thing those predicates which, taken together, we designate by means of the expression "God." These predicates are posited relative to the subject, whereas the thing itself, together with all its predicates, is posited absolutely. (*Only Possible Argument*, 2:74)

Accordingly, existential judgments seem to have a different function from that of categorical judgments, which are connections of concepts. An existential judgment expresses that an actually existing object satisfies the characteristic marks contained in the concept exercising the subject function in this kind of judgment. The term "existence" in an existential judgment indicates the actual satisfaction, by actual objects, of the marks (properties) contained in the subject concept. A categorical judgment expresses that what is thought according to the characteristic marks of the subject concept has the properties signified by the predicate concept.

The distinction between categorical judgments and existential judgments can be illustrated by the analysis of the judgments "God is omnipotent" and "God is."[15] The term "is" in the judgment "God is omnipotent" relates two concepts, expressing finally that the object thought by the concept God has the properties expressed by the concept "omnipotent."

Thus, if the judgment "God is omnipotent" is true, an object that satisfies the concept "God" will satisfy the concept "omnipotent." However, the judgment "God is" (or "God exists") does not relate concepts, but rather indicates that the concept "God" is satisfied by an actually existing object that contains all the properties expressed by the concept "God."

It is perfectly true that the difference in the function of categorical judgments and existential judgments does not exclude the possibility that certain categorical judgments may have an existential function. Indeed, the categorical judgments, like any judgment, signify objects.[16] May they not then also exercise an existential function, at least implicitly?

In categorical judgments, considered independently of other logical forms of judgments, the modality, expressed by the copula, of the attribution of the predicate to the objects signified by the subject concept remains indeterminate. Thus categorical judgments can be used without an assertoric function (as antecedents, for example, of hypothetical judgments). If the connection of the subject concept with the predicate concept by means of the copula expresses only the compatibility between the characteristic marks of the subject concept with the properties signified by the predicate concept, then the judgment expresses no more than a logical possibility:[17] that which is thought by the marks of the subject concept *may* have the properties expressed by the predicate concept. This judgment is considered neither determinedly true nor determinedly false, although other judgments may be inferred from it. This is denominated the problematic judgment.[18] But categorical judgments can also be assertoric. If the connection between the subject concept and the predicate concept is considered to be *actual*—that is, if what is thought by the subject concept is thought to contain *actually* the properties expressed by the predicate concept—then the judgment has a truth value and is denominated an assertoric judgment. If the judgment is always true, it is denominated an apodictic judgment.

Assertoric categorical judgments express an objective unity, since they are based on necessary rules (*Pure Reason*, B141–42, §19) and have a truth value. In certain cases, they have a truth value by reason of expressing necessary rules. This is what occurs with certain propositions of a philosophical nature. In other cases, the conceptual unity expressed by the judgment agrees with the effective unity of the object. In these cases, it would not be implausible to interpret these true categorical propositions as presupposing an existential proposition or as asserting the actual existence of an object.[19] Indeed, it is necessary to distinguish what judgments *presuppose* from what they *assert*. Presupposing existence is not the same as asserting it.

Are categorical propositions—which presuppose or assert the existence of something—authentic hypothetical judgments, whose antecedent would be an existential proposition and whose consequent would be the categorical proposition itself?

Categorical judgments are the simplest judgments of classical logic. Were assertoric categorical judgments to have the form of hypothetical judgments, it would be impossible to determine the truth of propositions, since hypothetical judgments are constituted by categorical judgments and their truth depends on the truth of categorical judgments. But the latter, for their part, would be hypothetical judgments, whose truth would depend on that of the categorical judgments, and so on indefinitely. A categorical judgment cannot, therefore, be interpreted as a hypothetical judgment. However, this does not prevent us from treating certain true categorical propositions as if they presume the truth of an existential proposition. Kant did not formulate a theory of supposition in his Logic, but Strawson's analyses on supposition are far from being incompatible with the Kantian theses on General (Formal) Logic.

Would the thesis that existence is not a real predicate exclude the possibility that assertoric categorical judgments could have an existential function, that is, they could *assert* the actual existence of an object?

Kant's Critique of the Cartesian Version of the Ontological Argument

Kant recognizes that the Cartesian proof would be conclusive were the term "existence" to designate a real predicate: "If existence could also be counted as one of the various predicates that may be counted as belonging to a thing, then certainly no proof that would be more conclusive and at the same time more intelligible than the Cartesian one could be demanded for demonstrating the existence of God" (*R*3706, 17:240).

The Cartesian ontological argument is reconstructed by Kant in various stages (*Pure Reason*, A596–97/B624–25). The initial stage consists of the admission of a supposition considered self-evident by Descartes but later developed by Leibniz. For the sake of argument, it is accepted that the concept "a most perfect being"[20] is not logically contradictory. Then, as the logical possibility of a concept implies the (analytic) possibility of the object of this concept,[21] it is assumed that a most perfect being is possible. Obviously, in Kantian theory, the logical possibility of an object (noncontradiction of the concept) does not imply the real possibility of the object (possibility of the object in experience), since the distinction between the logical meaning and transcendental meaning of possibility prevents such an implication.[22]

Having admitted these suppositions, the Kantian reconstruction of the Cartesian proof seeks to demonstrate that, given the (noncontradictory) concept of a most perfect being, it follows that this concept is not empty, since the suppression of the actual (rather than merely possible) existence of the object of this concept would imply a contradiction. If the concept of a most perfect being is not contradictory, its object is possible; in other words, a most perfect being is a possible entity. If it is possible, then it exists and exists necessarily.

What would authorize these latter affirmations?

It was admitted that the concept of a most perfect being—that is, the concept of an entity that contains all the perfections—is not contradictory. Thus all the properties that express perfections are contained in the marks of this concept. It was also admitted that a most perfect being, with all its perfections, is a possible entity. If existence is a perfection—that is, if existence is a mark contained in the (logically possible) concept of a most perfect being—then denying the existence of this entity implies denying one of its perfections. In other words, it implies denying that a most perfect being contains all the perfections, which is equivalent to *denying*: (a) that the notion of a most perfect being is being analyzed (since the entity being analyzed does not contain all the perfections); or (b) that a most perfect being is possible (since perhaps the concept of an entity with all the perfections is contradictory). In the first alternative (a), there is nothing to contrapose, since the notion of a most perfect being is not being analyzed. In the second alternative (b), given that the possibility of a most perfect being was admitted, denying one of its perfections, namely, existence, and admitting at the same that a most perfect being is possible and, consequently, possesses all the perfections is contradictory. Now, as it is impossible to deny that a most perfect being exists, then it necessarily exists.

Having admitted the hypothesis of the noncontradiction of the concept of a most perfect being and consequently admitted the possibility of its object, the decisive and problematic supposition of the proof is that *existence* is a mark of the concept of this entity and that, therefore, as a possible object, a most perfect being contains what this note expresses as a property. Since existence is a property, a (predicative) categorical proposition that connects the concept of a most perfect being to the concept of existence would have an existential function.

So what is the meaning of this supposed existential proposition?

Kant replies to this question by analyzing the meaning of the concept of existence involved in the proof. As the argument extracts from the premise "a most perfect being is possible" the categorical proposition "a most perfect being exists," this proposition, by connecting the concepts "a most perfect being" and "existence," makes explicit what is implicitly supposed in the concept of a most perfect being. Likewise, the proposition "a most perfect being is omnipotent," connecting the concepts "a most perfect being" and "omnipotence," also makes explicit what is thought when the subject concept "a most perfect being" is thought. Thus, the conclusion of the argument is a proposition that makes explicit the *meaning* of the concept "a most perfect being."

Obviously, the ontological argument is not intended to explain the meaning of the concept "a most perfect being," but to prove that it actually exists. In the conclusion of the argument, it is actual existence that ought to be signified by the concept of existence. In this case, Kant argues (*Pure Reason*, A597–98/B625–26), the proof would not only be analytic,[23] but also a mere tautology, since it would repeat in the conclusion what had already been assumed in the premise. In fact, supposing that a most perfect being is possible is equivalent to supposing that it has all the perfections; as it was also supposed that actual existence is a perfection, supposing that a most perfect being is possible is equivalent to supposing that a most perfect being effectively exists. Kant shows by this argument that, if existence is a real predicate and "existence" signifies actual existence, then the concept of a most perfect being implies that logical possibility (absence of contradiction in the concept) and actual existence are equivalent notions. From this it follows that a most perfect being can only be considered as a possible entity insofar as it actually exists. Therefore, if the proof assumes as a premise that a most real being is possible, it also assumes as a premise that the most real entity actually exists.

Hence, following the Kantian argument, the conclusion of the ontological argument appears to be an existential proposition, but is in fact an analytic categorical proposition[24] that makes explicit the meaning of the concept a most perfect being. But, if the conclusion of the ontological argument were an existential proposition, once the proof is constituted by analytic premises, the existential conclusion must have been assumed in one of the premises of the proof, rendering the argument tautological,[25] since analytic propositions are not sufficient grounds for justifying an existential assertion. Hence the dilemma formulated by Kant puts in question the Cartesian version of the ontological proof: (a) if existence is a *characteristic mark* of the subject concept of a judgment that connects concepts, the conclusion of the argument is not existential, but rather simply makes explicit the meaning of the subject concept; and (b) if existence is assumed as a real predicate and signifies actual existence, the conclusion of the argument appears to be existential, but the proof would be a mere tautology.

This dilemma supposes that the premises of the ontological argument are analytic propositions and the conclusion purports to be an existential proposition. In fact, the dilemma is based on the theses that analytic propositions do not have an existential function and that existential propositions cannot be extracted from them. What would justify this assertion?

Kant's analyses of the meaning of the term "existence" (*Dasein*, *Existenz*) afford a better comprehension of what an existential judgment would be in opposition to the analytic categorical judgment.[26] To determine the meaning of "existence," the meaning of a more general term is analyzed, namely, the meaning of the term "being" (*Sein*), which comprehends the meaning of "existence." The key to explaining the verb "to be" ("being") is the analysis of its function in the structure of the act of judgment. In a judgment, *being* performs the function of a copula and/or indicates the existential dimension of the judgment. As a copula, "being" expresses the connection between concepts: the determination expressed by the predicate concept is posited in relation to the objects signified by the subject concept. Hence categorical judgments appear to provide the paradigmatic expression of "being" as a copula: connecting the predicative determination to the subject concept, the conceptual unity constituted by the copula of this kind of judgment expresses the complex unity of the object: "Now, something can be thought as posited merely relatively, or, to express the matter better, it can be thought merely as the relation (*respectus logicus*) of something as a characteristic mark of a thing. In this case, being (*Sein*), that is to say, the positing of this relation, is nothing other than copula (*Verbindungsbegriff*) in a judgment."[27]

But "being" (*Sein*) may also signify an absolute position. What is the meaning of this expression "an absolute position"? Obviously it is opposed to "a relative position." Hence, the judgment expressing the notion of an absolute position cannot have the form of a categorical judgment, which is characterized by establishing a relation between concepts and by expressing, therefore, a relation between different meanings of a concept. "Being" as an absolute position signifies the actual realization of properties by objects.

Thus the judgment that expresses this notion must show that the determinations signified by the concepts that it contains are effectively realized in an object and not only connected with other concepts. It designates the position of a thing—that is, it indicates that the determinations or properties expressed by the subject concept are actually realized in the thing or that its subject concept is not empty.

The two meanings of "being," as a relative position and an absolute position, seem to express two ways of conceiving the form of an act of judgment. "Being" as a relative position has the categorical judgment as a model: the determinations expressed by the predicate concept, thanks to the copula, are posited in what is signified by the subject concept. What is posited is not the object in itself, but the attribution of properties, expressed by the predicate, to the objects signified by the subject concept. "Being" as an absolute position has the existential judgment as a model: the determinations contained in the subject concept are asserted as actually satisfied by the objects signified by the concept.

The argument proving that an analytic proposition lacks an existential function is based on two kinds of reasons: reasons that concern the verification of the truth value of a proposition and those concerning the logical form of propositions. From the point of view of the logical form, a categorical proposition is a connection of concepts; an analytic categorical proposition is a proposition in which the predicate concept is a characteristic mark of the subject concept. An existential proposition supposes the existence of the object signified by the subject concept and states that the object satisfies the properties expressed by the characteristic marks contained in the subject concept. From the point of view of the truth conditions, the truth of an analytic categorical proposition is established by a mere conceptual dismemberment of the subject concept, while the truth of an existential proposition demands *going beyond the concept* and verifying whether the object is an actual instance of the subject concept.

If this analysis is correct, an existential judgment is not a categorical judgment; in other words, it is not a connection of concepts. A categorical judgment may presuppose an existential judgment. A connection of concepts does not express, though, *the absolute position of a thing*. This is the function of the existential judgment, which performs this function insofar as it does not relate concepts but *posits* the object with its own determinations. Hence, the term "existence" in an existential judgment does not have an attributive function; that is, it does not add a new determination to the objects signified by the subject concept.

This critique of the ontological argument disallows a proof whose conclusion is existential from being reduced to an exclusively conceptual proof, that is, to a proof constituted by analytic propositions alone.

However, the Transcendental Logic classifies judgments into analytic or synthetic. Synthetic categorical propositions, as categorical judgments, are connections of concepts. But the reason that justifies this connection involves something nonconceptual. Thus those arguments that exclude proofs with an existential conclusion from being merely conceptual proofs do not exclude the possibility that synthetic categorical propositions may have an existential function and that, therefore, they may be conclusions of proofs that have premises consisting of synthetic propositions. But can synthetic categorical propositions have an existential function?

Synthetic propositions certainly always involve intuitions; hence, *they go beyond the concept* and refer to objects mediately. However, a priori synthetic propositions express either a rational knowledge based on the construction of concepts or a rational discursive knowledge based on concepts (*Pure Reason*, A713–14/B741–42). A discursive knowledge based on concepts is a knowledge of the rules necessary to the constitution of objects (*Pure Reason*, A720–22/B748–50). A knowledge based on the construction of concepts exhibits an object in the pure intuition of space and time. Hence, at least from the viewpoint of theoretical reason, a priori synthetic propositions refer to the form of sensible objects (in the case of rational knowledge based on the construction of concepts) or to rules of constituting objects (in the case of rational knowledge based on concepts). But in both cases, neither of these forms of knowledge expressed by a priori synthetic judgments concerns the actual existence of objects.

Do categorical a posteriori synthetic judgments perform an existential function that neither a priori analytic judgments nor a priori synthetic judgments can perform?

Categorical a posteriori synthetic judgments may "agree" with the objects given factually in experience. Consequently, these judgments seem to perform an existential function. So what is the relation between categorical a posteriori synthetic judgments and existential propositions?

Clearer insight into this question can be acquired by distinguishing what a proposition presupposes from what it asserts.

Aristotelian logic, analyzing the relations between the forms of universal, particular, affirmative, and negative propositions, posited that the validity of certain logical relations depends on the supposition that certain general terms, which occur in the propositions exemplifying these forms, are not empty. The requirement that certain general terms must have instances in order for certain immediate inferences to be considered valid was denominated an *existential import*, since the assertion that a general term has at least one instance would mean that the instance of the general term exists.

Kant's General Logic assumes as valid the Aristotelian immediate inferences denominated *per judicia subalternata*'[28] *conversio per accidens*,[29] and *per judicia contrarie opposita*[30] inferences—inferences that are only valid by reason of the supposition of the existence of certain terms occurring in them. Consequently, the Kantian General Logic, like almost all the pre-Fregean forms of logic, has an *existential import.*

There is no space here to examine the diverse interpretations concerning the presupposition of existence in Kant's General Logic. However, Peter Strawson in one of his books,[31] returning to an interpretation of the Thomist logician and philosopher of the seventeenth century, John of St. Thomas, reformulated the earlier theory of the medieval supposition in contemporary terms and applied it to Kant's Classical Logic and, in particular, the Kantian logic. The *existence* of at least one member of the extension of the subject concept[32] of the propositions that take one of the forms described by the Aristotelian logical square would therefore be *presupposed* and the *truth* of existential statements, which take as a subject these nonempty concepts that occur in those propositions that belong to the logical square, would be a necessary condition, not for the predicative proposition (which would exemplify one of these forms) to be considered true, but rather for it to be able to be attributed with a truth value (either true or false). Thus the affirmative categorical propositions that take the form "A is B" would presuppose the truth of existential statements of the form "A exists." Consequently, the immediate inferences deriving from the Aristotelian logical square may be considered valid.

But supposing is not equivalent to affirming existence.

Existential statements, which are presupposed by predicative propositions, cannot belong to the logical system that analyzes the relations of inference of predicative propositions. Were they to belong, they would imply the following absurdity: in order to a have a false truth value, an existential proposition would have to be true.

What needs explaining, therefore, is how synthetic assertoric categorical judgments in the Kantian logic can perform the same function performed in other systems by the assertion of existential judgments.

It is the Transcendental Logic that, through the second postulate of empirical thinking, determines the conditions that an a posteriori synthetic judgment must satisfy in order to be true. (*Pure Reason*, B272–74). Consequently, from the viewpoint of the General Logic, judgments can have presuppositions of existence. But from the viewpoint of the Transcendental Logic, over and beyond the presuppositions of existence, certain a posteriori synthetic assertoric categorical judgments can assert the actual existence of the objects given in experience. However the satisfaction of the second postulate of empirical thinking implies that a posteriori synthetic judgments are contingent judgments, and not necessarily true as the conclusion of the ontological argument claims to be. Furthermore, a posteriori synthetic assertoric categorical judgments do not attribute existence to a thing, but rather assert that the properties of an actually existing thing are expressed by the judgment. Thus, in these judgments existence does not have an attributive function, that is, it does not add a new determination relative to the objects signified by the subject concept. Accordingly, existence in these judgments cannot be considered a real predicate.

A posteriori synthetic judgments perform a particular function in the Kantian explanation of the knowledge of objects: as categorical judgments, they are connections of concepts and can have presupposition of existence. The fact that they can express knowledge of existing objects is not due to being categorical judgments, that is, connecting concepts through a relation of subordination. Rather, it is due to their subject concept *subsuming* empirical intuitions in accordance with necessary rules. Thus, while from the viewpoint of the General Logic it is plausible to claim that categorical judgments have an existential presupposition, from the viewpoint of the Transcendental Logic only a posteriori synthetic assertoric categorical judgments seem to perform a function that in other contexts is attributed to judgments of existence.

Conclusion

The analysis of the function of judgments, assertoric categorical judgments, and the function of existential judgments in the Kantian perspective, accompanied by a reflection on the classification of judgments from the viewpoint of the Transcendental Logic, has allowed me to explain in this article the reasons for Kant's rejection of the Cartesian ontological argument and the thesis that existence is a real predicate.

The ontological argument purports to show that, given the specific characteristics of a single concept, it is necessary to affirm that this concept is not empty, since, were the opposite the case, a contradiction would occur. Kant summarizes this thesis in an imaginary dialogue with the defender of the ontological argument: "you challenge me with one case that you set up as a proof through the fact that there is one and indeed only this one concept where the non-being or the cancelling of its object is contradictory within itself, and this is the concept of the most real thing" (*Pure Reason*, A596/B624).

Indeed, Descartes aimed to extract analytically the existential proposition "God exists" from the concept of a supremely perfect being (or a most real thing). In so doing, he constructed a proof in which only analytic propositions occur, save for the proof's conclusion that amounts to an existential proposition. The validity of this demonstration is based on the thesis that existence is a real predicate, since a supremely perfect being should contain all the perfections, including the perfection of existence, which is one of the properties supposedly characterizing this entity.

Focusing on the Kantian logico-semantic analyses of the notion of judgment, it has been possible to criticize the Cartesian argument showing that (a) no existential proposition can be inferred from an analytic (assertoric categorical) proposition; (b) a priori synthetic (assertoric categorical) propositions do not involve an assertion of existence; and finally (c) although a posteriori synthetic propositions can exercise an existential function, existence does not perform any attributive function in them, meaning it cannot be considered a real predicate. Accordingly, the foundations of the Cartesian proof were put in question.

Notes

1. Rene Descartes, *Oeuvres de Descartes*, vol. 7, (AT) *Meditationes de Prima Philosophia, Quintae Responsiones*, ed. C. Adam and P. Tannery (Paris: Vrin, 1973), 382–83.

2. In the Port Royal Logic, the existential judgment *x exists* has the same meaning as the judgment *x is existent*. See A. Arnauld and P. Nicole, *La logique, ou l' art de penser* (Paris: Vrin, 1993), 114.

3. A "Real Predicate," according to Kant is "*the determination of a thing. . . . But the determination is a predicate, which goes beyond the concept of subject and enlarges it*" (*Pure Reason*, A598/B626).

4. In this article I shall use the terminology that Kant employs in his texts on logic: a *proposition* is an assertoric judgment; that is, a judgment possessing a determinate truth value. Predicative propositions are assertoric categorical judgments.

5. See, for example, *Vienna Logic*, Of Judgments (24:932–33); and *Jäsche Logic*, Of Judgments, §24 (9:105).

6. Kant does not introduce the notion of a judgment of existence in either his classification of the judgments (*Pure Reason*, A70/B95), which aims to be a complete classification, or in his various texts on logic. *Existence* (*Dasein*) is a category extracted from assertoric judgments, while *actuality* (*Wirklichkeit*) is the schematized category of existence (*Pure Reason*, A774–76/B99–101).

7. To explain the meaning of *a posteriori* synthetic judgments, I shall naturally make use of the "Second Postulate of Empirical Thinking" from the Analytic of Principles.

8. *Pure Reason*, A145/B184: "*The schema of actuality (Wirklichkeit) is existence (Dasein) at a determinate time*."

9. See *Only Possible Argument*, 2:156–57.

10. Kant formulates various definitions of the judgments in his texts on logic and in the *Critique of Pure Reason*. See B. Longuenesse, *Kant and the Capacity to Judge* (Princeton: Princeton University Press, 1998), chapter 4, "Logical Definitions of Judgments," 81–106. See too R. Stuhlmann-Laeisz, *Kants Logik* (Berlin: Walter de Gruyter, 1976), chapter 3, "Kants Definitionen eines Urteils," 55–59.

11. "All judgments are accordingly functions of unity among our representations, since instead of an immediate representation a higher one, which comprehends this and other representations under itself, is used for the cognition of the object, and many possible cognitions are thereby drawn together into one" (*Pure Reason*, A69/B94).

12. This characterization of categorical judgments implicitly assumes one of the different definitions of judgment formulated by Kant: judgments are subordinations of concepts. Thus, for example, in the *Dohna-Wundlacken Logic*, Judgments (24:762–63), Kant defines the judgment as "the representation of the unity of given concepts, insofar as one is subordinated to the other or excluded from it." Categorical judgments can also be defined on the basis of conditions that would justify the attribution of the predicate to the subject: if it is the subject concept itself that allows the attribution of the predicate to the judgment's subject, then the judgment is said to be categorical. (See *Jäsche Logic*, §25). Thus, in the categorical judgment "there is no settled condition" (*Vienna Logic*, 24:932–33). The definition of categorical judgments presented in this article shows that these judgments subordinate concepts insofar as they are considered as connections of concepts. It may also be noted that categorical judgments, like all other judgments, have a modality—that is, they are either problematic or assertoric or apodictic judgments. This means, according to Kant's expression, that "*the value of the copula*" of the categorical judgment does not belong to its definition.

13. Also see on on the same pages the following assertion: "The matter of all categorical judgments consists of a concept, in which the concept of the subject belongs to the concept of the predicate."

14. "Categorical judgments constitute the basis of all remaining ones" (*Vienna Logic*, 24:932–33). "Categorical judgments constitute the matter of the remaining judgments" (*Jäsche Logic*, 9:105).

15. "If I say 'God is omnipotent' all that is being thought is the logical relation between God and omnipotence, for the latter is a characteristic mark of the former. Nothing further is being posited here. Whether God is, that is to say, whether God is posited absolutely or exists, is not contained in the original assertion at all" (*Only Possible Argument*, 2:74).

16. In various passages of her book *Kant and the Capacity to Judge* (see, for instance, 108–11), Longuenesse asserts that the logical form of the judgment includes the indication of the nondiscursive, intuitive element (x) that signifies the judgment's object. Hence, every judgment of the form "S is P" states: if the concept S belongs to the object x, then the concept P also belongs. What is the substitutional instance of the variable x that belongs to the logical form of the judgment? How to introduce, from the viewpoint of the General Logic, the notion of object into the formal definition of judgment? On one hand, no determinate content, no object with a numerical identity, belongs to the logical form of the judgment. On the other hand, if the subsumption of intuitions by concepts is a necessary condition of the judgment, it follows that the judgment necessarily involves a relation with something nonconceptual. As the given of sensible intuition and what is organized by the imagination, independently of the necessary rules of the understanding, cannot be considered as objects, the reference to something nonconceptual in the logical form of the judgment is a reference to something indeterminate. Very often Kant represents this indeterminate, which belongs to the logical form of the judgment, by means of a variable. For example, in the *Jäsche Logic*, §36, the form of the analytic proposition is explained as follows: "To everything x, to which the concept body ($a + b$) belongs, belongs also extension (b)." Hence, even in analytic judgments, the subject concept,

which represents the logical subject of the judgment, mentions an object (any *x*). Henry Allison interprets this thesis in the following manner: "Analytic Judgments are, therefore, 'about' an object; they have a logical subject and, as Kant's example shows, they can also have a real subject. Nevertheless, since the truth or falsity of the judgment is determined merely by analyzing the concept of the subject, the reference to the object *x* is otiose." Henry Allison, *Kant's Transcendental Idealism*, rev. and enlarged ed. (New Haven: Yale University Press, 2004), 91. Obviously, introducing the notion of object into the logical definition of judgment does not mean assuming, for example, that judgments—especially, categorical judgments—by mentioning something indeterminate given by sensible intuition, make some type of supposition of existence. It just means showing that the act of judgment, realized by the understanding, necessarily involves a relation with nonintellectual functions.

17. ". . . problematic judgments, contain logical possibility" (*Dohna-Wundlacken Logic*, 24:766). See too *Critique of Pure Reason*, A75/B101: "**Problematic** judgments are those in which one regards the assertion or denial as merely **possible** (arbitrary)."

18. In the *Jäsche Logic*, §25, Kant appears to assimilate categorical judgments with assertoric judgments: "In categorical judgment nothing is problematic, rather everything is assertoric, but in hypotheticals only the *consequentia* is assertoric." It should be noted that Kant seems to introduce the notion of problematic judgment to explain the notion of a hypothetical judgment or disjunctive judgment. Hence, the problematic judgment would be a judgment that constituted a complex, hypothetical, or disjunctive judgment. But, from the point of view of the relation, what would be the form of this problematic judgment? Since disjunctive or hypothetical judgments are broken down into categorical judgments, a problematic judgment that is not a complex judgment (hypothetical or disjunctive) should have the form of a categorical judgment. What cannot be overlooked is that an act of judgment takes place, even in a problematic judgment: the predicate is connected via the copula to the subject concept; it is, therefore, posited relative to the objects signified by the subject concept.

19. Interpreting the suppositions of existence of the four modes of categorical judgments of classical logic, Strawson, in *Introduction to Logical Theory* (London: Methuen, 1971), 175, and in other articles, provides a precise definition of the notion of presupposition: the statement "S presupposes S′," if S is only true or false in the case S′ is true. The *truth* of S′ would therefore be a condition of the truth value of S. For example, the statement "this cake is bitter" would presuppose the statement "this cake exists," since if "this cake exists" were false, there would be no sense in presuming that the statement "this cake is bitter" has a truth value.

20. Kant uses a variety of expressions as synonyms of the term "God": "a most real being," "the absolutely necessary being," "a most perfect being," "a highest being," etc.

21. The concept "a most perfect being" is not a *nihil negativum* (*Pure Reason*, A292/B348–49), that is, it is not a logically contradictory concept, therefore, without an object. In the *Critique of Pure Reason* Kant states: "The analytic mark of possibility, which consists in the fact that mere positings (realities) do not generate a contradiction, of course, cannot be denied of this concept [a highest being]" (*Pure Reason*, A602/B630).

22. See *Critique of Pure Reason*, B100; B184; B265–72; B624 note; B629–30.

23. Kant does not use the expression "analytic proof." But, taking a slight liberty with his language, we could say that an analytic proof is a proof constituted by analytic propositions only.

24. Contemporary philosophical analyses show the difficulty in producing a precise characterization of the notion of analyticity. Kant, whether in his texts on logic, or in his texts on theoretical reason, characterizes an analytic judgment as the mere explanation or elucidation of the judgment's subject concept by the predicate concept (*Pure Reason*, Introduction, A6–7/B10–11). In order to verify the truth value of analytic propositions, therefore, it suffices to examine the characteristic marks or partial concepts that compose its subject concept. The *Jäsche Logic*, §36, for instance, defines analytic propositions as those "whose certainty rests on **identity** of concepts (of the predicate with the notion of the subject). . . ." For this reason, the supreme principle of analytic propositions is the principle of contradiction (*Pure Reason*, A150–54/B189–94). Hence, it is a consequence of the analyticity of a proposition that its truth value can be determined simply by the analysis of the partial concepts that compose the subject concept. Note that according to this characterization of analytic propositions only categorical propositions can be analytic, since only they connect concepts. Neither disjunctive propositions, nor hypothetical propositions, nor the tautological propositions of contemporary logic would be considered analytic propositions. However, in the section On the Supreme Principle of all Analytic Judgments (*Pure Reason*, A150/B189) Kant formulates a more inclusive criterion for analytic propositions than the definition stated in the Introduction to the *Critique of Pure Reason*: here, analytic propositions are those whose truth is based exclusively on the principle of contradiction. Thus, certain hypothetical and disjunctive propositions can also be classified as analytic propositions.

25. According to Kant, a tautological proposition is an analytic proposition in which an express identity of the concepts constituting the proposition occurs (*Jäsche Logic*, §37; and *Hechsel Logic* in *Lectures on Logic*, 381).

26. See *Only Possible Argument*, 2:119–22; and *Pure Reason*, A598–600/B626–28.

27. *Only Possible Argument*, 2:119. Also see *Pure Reason*, A598–99/B626–27.

28. See *Jäsche Logic*, §46.

29. See *Jäsche Logic*, §52 and §53.

30. See *Jäsche Logic*, §49.

31. *Introduction to Logic Theory* (London: Methuen, repr. 1971), chapter 6, "Subjects, Predicates, and Existence," 152–94.

32. In certain cases, the predicate concept must also not be empty.

5

An Experiment with Practical Reason

Valerio Rohden

This is the second part of a study on the handwritten corrections that I found in the original copy of the *Kritik der praktischen Vernunft* at the University of Erlangen-Nürnberg Library.[1] Whereas the first part of that research resulted in a predominantly philological and historical investigation on those corrections taken as a whole, in this paper I focus on the philosophical meaning of a single correction, namely, the one on line 11 of page A166 of the original edition (*Practical Reason*, 5:93). There the word *nur* (only) was changed to *nun* (now), apparently with the intent of expressing more adequately the experiment with practical reason that Kant discusses in the passage.

With the help of Erlangen professors Jens Kulenkampf and Severin Koster (classical philologist), I obtained corroboration for a hypothetical dating of this particular change and others. Up until then the author of those corrections was unknown, and it was presumed that they had been made in the late eighteenth or early nineteenth century. The book, however, is signed by two previous owners, and the assumption was that their signatures were written down only much later, at the beginning of the twentieth century. Professor Koster was right about the first hypothesis, but not about the second. I found out that the signatures belonged to people who were Kant's contemporaries and belonged to his circle of relationships. I also found out that one of them, Paul Joachim Sigmund Vogel (1753–1834), was responsible for the corrections and had exchanged some correspondence with Kant. In 1797 he took up the chair for Kantian philosophy at the University of Altdorf, which preceded the University of Erlangen. In 1808 he became full professor at the Faculty of Theology at the University of Erlangen, to whose library he allegedly donated his personal copy of the *Critique of Practical Reason*.[2] This

This is a revised but not substantially modified translation of a paper originally delivered at a 2002 conference in Caracas, and published in its proceedings: "Un experimento con la razón práctica," in *Memórias del Quinto Congresso Sudamericano de Filosofia*, ed. Marta de la Veja Visbal (Caracas: Universidad Simon Bolívar, 2004), 129–40. Translated by Rogério Passos Severo with a revision by A. Blom.

library would then have passed it on to the recently created Central Library of the University of Erlangen, since the rubber stamp on the copy dates from the period 1808–18. The discovery of the authorship and authenticity of the corrections was achieved by a comparison of the corrections and Vogel's signature on the volume with his manuscript letters, which now belong to the manuscript section of that same library.

The correction in point, on A166 (*Practical Reason*, 5:93), differs from other corrections of the *Critique of Practical Reason* in that it was uniquely recorded by Vogel. It was ignored by Grillo (1796), Hartenstein (1838, 1867), and Rosenkranz (1838), and by all others who corrected the text of the *Critique of Practical Reason*. Hence, Vogel is its author. The fact that the passage remained unnoticed by others does not mean that it is irrelevant. Analyzing Vogel's philosophical works on Kant's ethics, one sees that he had the competence to make it, and anticipated all others in several other corrections, which by mistake have not been attributed to him but rather to people who succeeded him, especially Hartenstein.

May this suffice as an informative introduction on the origins of this paper, which was motivated by a translation of the *Critique of Practical Reason* into Portuguese, a comparative study of its variants, and a research project at the University of Erlangen in 2001 in collaboration with Professor J. Kulenkampf.

Theoretical Context of an Experiment with Practical Reason

We shall look at the theoretical context of the correction mentioned above so as to assess its authenticity. The correction is located within the context of what Kant called "an experiment with practical reason." The experiment aims at proving, by means of an analysis of an example, that practical reason and personal advantage do not mingle, analogously to chemical elements that when mixed turn out to be incompatible. Rather, practical reason and personal advantage repel each other in the moral consciousness of the ordinary man.

The passage is part of the Critical Elucidation of the Analytic of Pure Practical Reason, which establishes a systematic difference between theoretical and practical reason from a cognitive perspective by means of a comparison that is at first formal but later also material. The first paragraph of the Elucidation mentions a key element that connects the two cognitive forms of reason: both are pure. The Elucidation, however, is concerned with comparing and justifying the form and matter that are specific to the ways reason presents itself. From a formal standpoint, it is shown that theoretical reason begins with what is given, whereas practical reason begins with a priori practical principles, and proceeds from these to the determination of objects and motives. This is so because the will does not have any prior objects, but attains them from the representation of what it wants.

The experiment lies in the part concerning the difference in cognitive content of each mode of reason. In the case of theoretical reason, the examples from the sciences "easily and evidently" (A163; *Practical Reason*, 5:91) prove that pure rational knowledge exists. There is no need to fear a "secret mixture of empirical grounds of cognition" (A163; *Practical Reason*, 5:91). On the other hand, the fear is stronger in regard to common practical knowledge.[3] Kant wants to prove with his experiment with practical reason that, in its common practical use, pure reason can recognize the moral law as the supreme law of its own will: "that pure reason, without the admixture of any empirical determining ground, is practical of itself alone: this one had to be able to show from the *most common practical use of reason*" (A163; *Practical Reason*, 5:91). Therefore, the experiment with practical reason will involve this proof from the common use of reason. Kant purports to prove that reason distinguishes sharply pure practical reason and empirical practical reason, or reason and personal advantage. A proof of this distinction is the fact that the transgressor feels the need to hide when contemplating the moral law (see A142; *Practical Reason*, 5: 79–80).

Kant puts forth another argument for the purity of the supreme practical principle in judgments by common reason. The elusive presence of empirical elements in our maxims purporting to ground our will is immediately detected by the feelings of pleasure and displeasure and by the desire that necessarily emerges, whereas a practical lawgiving reason resists all admixture of inclinations. The presence of an autonomous reason within common reason is shown by the peculiar feeling that it brings about, that of respect. This respect is not felt as an inclination, but only as the presence of the moral law (see A164; *Practical Reason*, 5:92). Therefore, the difference between two opposing types of determining grounds of the will is detected by the different types of feeling that one has: sensory pleasure *versus* feeling of respect. So the way to experience the effective presence of a lawgiving reason within common reason is shown through an example in which one observes what type of feeling it produces in relation to someone's actual practice.

Analogy with the Chemical Experiment

One can see the central importance of the experiment with practical reason for the *Critique of Practical Reason* by noticing that it lies at the crossroads where the difference between the doctrine of happiness and the doctrine of morality is established. Kant refers to that difference quite emphatically, and says that it is the most important task of an Analytic of pure practical reason (see A165; *Practical Reason*, 5:92). In the light of the significance of that distinction, whereby empirical principles are rejected as determining grounds for morality, Kant demands of the Analytic maximum rigor and attention to detail. The standards of the Analytic are to be the same as that of a geometer at his work. The absence of intuition as a foundation of the experiment is overcome by the fact that the moral philosopher can perform, with anyone's practical reason, an experiment almost identical to that of a chemist who tests the reaction of elements that when put together do not mix but rather repel one another.

Kant's comparison between his experiment with practical reason and a chemical experiment is not arbitrary. It stems from a close proximity of Kant's philosophy as a whole to the language of chemistry. According to a recent work by Pierre Kerzberg, the analogy between Kant's philosophy and chemistry is justified because the latter conceives of pure elements, which render chemical processes possible. These pure elements are involved in chemical combinations, which may then yield compounds that may or may not be incompatible with each other. The chemist breaks up heterogeneous elements in a compound body. After the Copernican revolution, knowledge is to be organized in the concepts of the understanding by the transcendental synthesis, whose combination of concepts conduces to the pure principles of the understanding. Kerzberg speaks of an experiment as a deduction. Beyond possible experience one can experiment with the same concepts and principles, having in mind their transcendental use. The power of transcendental synthesis, in analysis, separates and organizes the elements of reason. Attempting a reduction, understood here as the bringing together of things separated by analysis, reason works according to a technique similar to the one used in a chemical synthesis: reduction is a *fusion toujours manquée*, but always attempted yet again between the sensory and the suprasensory.[4] According to Stahl, who is mentioned by Kant in the Preface to the second edition of the *Critique of Pure Reason*, the chemist cannot isolate the original and specific elements of matter. These would only lend themselves to observation in compound and interacting bodies. Kerzberg says that "for Kant, whatever has been completed by nature, the chemist cannot destroy; he is no match against nature's achievements."[5] The comparison between chemical analysis and a critical interpretation is conducive to a better understanding of the latter. Just as chemistry is carried out on the less directly perceivable, aiming at the intelligibility of the phenomenon, a critical interpretation concerns the absolutely unperceivable influence of sensibility on understanding. To take objects that transgress the bounds of possible experience as phenomena is a source of transcendental illusions.

This criticism of transcendental illusion that has as its source the unperceived influence of sensibility on understanding somehow serves practical criticism, in which Kant seeks to show that there is a covert mixture of impure elements with pure motives. Although Kerzberg is aware of the passage that concerns us here, he did not dwell on the issue of chemistry in the *Critique of Practical Reason*. He gets closest to it when dealing with the issue of taste in the third *Critique*, which does not allow for a mixture of the a priori and empirical.

I finish up these remarks with a brief reference to an essay by Karen Gloy, "Kant's Philosophy and the Experiment."[6] According to this author, in principle the experiment involves a theoretical task in which one has to situate oneself so as to observe reality from a certain perspective, so that reason will only know what it produces from a certain plane and constructs objects from a certain point of view. In regard to objective knowledge, Kant says that transcendental philosophy takes up the features of an experimental method in which experiment is extended also to metaphysics:

> This method, imitated from the method of those who study nature, thus consists in this: to seek the elements of pure reason in that **which admits of being confirmed or refuted through an experiment**. Now the propositions of pure reason, especially when they venture beyond all boundaries of possible experience, admit of no test by experiment with their **objects** (as in natural science): thus to experiment will be feasible only with **concepts** and **principles** that we assume *a priori* by arranging the latter so that the same objects can be considered from two different sides, **on the one side** as objects of the senses and understanding for experience, and **on the other side** as objects that are merely thought at most for isolated reason striving beyond the bounds of experience. If we now find that there is agreement with the principle of pure reason when things are considered from this twofold standpoint, then the experiment decides for the correctness of that distinction. (*Pure Reason*, Bxviii–xix, note)

Just as interest in the hypotheses of theoretical reason aims at extending knowledge, practical reason is interested in its limitation. This is resolved by a twofold perspective on objects, and it is to decide between them that Kant introduces the experiment in the Preface to the second edition of the *Critique of Pure Reason*.

According to another author, Brigitte Falkenburg, at a theoretical level the experiment of reason consists in the exposition of the "conditions of possibility for objective knowledge as a constitutive presupposition for the knowledge of objects." But in neither case, she continues, does Kant explicitly take up "experiment of reason" as a topic: "The theory that we find as a ground for the experiments of reason, which does not refer to determinate things or events as in physical theory but to objects of knowledge in general, was not made explicit by Kant in all its features, and it did not even occur to him that this theory might be challenged."[7]

While interpreting the experiment of reason, these works leave aside its use in the practical domain.

The Dynamics of the Moral Experiment

According to the text, the difficulty posed by the absence of intuitions is compensated for by the fact that the moral philosopher can at any moment make an experiment with the practical reason of anyone, aimed at detecting in each person the presence of or the distinction between pure and empirical moral determining grounds. On the one hand, Kant uses here the chemical experiment as a model and applies it analogically to the observation of common practices; on the other hand, he uses this analysis of chemical similarities on examples of moral practice. In the case of the chemical experiment, by adding alkali (lithium, potassium, sodium bases, etc.) to a solution of calcium carbonate in muriatic or hydrochloric acid (formed by the combination of a hydrogen atom with a chlorine atom), the muriatic acid rejects the calcium carbonate and clings to the alkali, whereas the calcium carbonate drops to the bottom. This experiment serves as a comparison, allowing us to better understand what happens when we assess certain practices, such as the one in which someone decides to lie in order to gain advantage for him or herself. Kant places the example in the mind of a man up until then thought to be honest, who this time thinks of himself as an honest man and judges his action from a moral point of view. Confronting the moral law with his own practice of lying in order to gain advantage for himself, he recognizes himself as an undignified liar. But then what happens to his practical reason? When judging what should be done in this case, reason immediately backs away from seeking advantage and takes up veracity (as opposed to lying) as that which deserves respect, unlike the undignified behavior of the liar, which is despised. Then, the text says, advantage is set apart from reason. They can nevertheless come together, only not in those cases that contradict the moral law. We have left aside two aspects of the permanent link between reason and duty, or reason and the moral law. Even though this is true, we can still see that what the experiment intends to show is the dynamics of the conflict between reason and advantage: initially reason and advantage are not separate in an honest person; they come apart when someone decides to lie in order to gain advantage for him or herself, but can come together again when the relation between reason and advantage does not contradict the moral law.

This last point agrees with the remarks that follow in the Kant text, according to which the distinction between the principles of happiness and morality does not entail an immediate opposition between the two. An opposition happens when happiness overrules duty. Theoretically there is no opposition between matter and form of the maxim: "the matter of the maxim can indeed remain, but it must not be the condition of the maxim" (A60; *Practical Reason*, 5:34). In the next sentence, Kant adds: "Hence the mere form of a law, which limits the matter, must at the same time be a ground for adding this matter to the will but not for presupposing it" (A61; *Practical Reason*, 5:34). This means that man as a rational animal can, and sometimes even should, take in his animal nature. As in the quote above, the law that limits the matter is at the same time a ground for adding matter to the will. Seeking advantage is consistent with reason. Anyone can do it; each of us is an individual who sets for him or herself ends that do not interfere with the ends of others. But seeking those ends in an undignified way, causing damage to others, is to deceive others in order to attain a personal advantage at their expense. To deceive is to lie. While acting dishonestly one has to deceive or hide the end of one's action so as to render achievable one's own intent.

The passage concerning the experiment can be interpreted in two ways: (1) literally, as did all the editors and critics but Vogel; and (2) as modified by the latter, and unconsciously followed by all who adopted the 1984 Harald Fischer Verlag edition of the *Critique of Practical Reason*, without noticing Vogel's modification. They did not err in doing so, only they were unaware of having done it, and mistook Vogel's modification for the presumed Kantian text.

But Vogel's version is possibly better than Kant's, as it better agrees with the spirit of the text. The fact that Kant did not himself make that modification is contingent. The text was corrected at several other places, and Kant did not revise carefully his own copies, which contained numerous misprints. In the Handexemplar of the *Critique of Practical Reason* alone we find four corrections made by Kant himself, but these do not indicate a careful revision of the whole text. According to a letter by Kant dated January 1797, prior to the fourth edition he lost interest in such a revision, and ordered a reprint of the first edition.

Let us therefore look into Kant's experiment and see how adequate each of the two versions is. We know that Vogel's correction is on line 11 of page 166 of the original (A) edition (*Practical Reason*, 5:93), where *nur* (only, merely, solely) was changed to *nun* (now). In Kant's version we read (with my emphasis): "the advantage, after it has been separated and washed from every particle of duty (which is ALTOGETHER on the side of reason)."[8] In Vogel's version we read: "the advantage, after it has been separated and washed from every particle of duty (which is NOW wholly on the side of reason)."

Kant's version has going for it the fact that it agrees completely with another passage, at the end of that same paragraph: "the moral law, which reason *never abandons* but unites with most intimately" (italics added). In other words, reason is always on the side of duty and the moral law, intimately united with them. Reason and duty, or moral law, are never dissociated.

Let us now turn to Vogel's version: reason first unites with advantage in an allegedly honest man, but later, second, distances itself from it when he decides to lie in order to gain advantage for himself; then, third, reason unites with veracity, and concludes from these previous steps, fourth, that it is *now* wholly on the side of duty; fifth, reason draws as a second conclusion that it can in other cases be on the side of advantage, as long as it does not contradict the moral law; and sixth, a justification is stated: reason never abandons the moral law, but rather unites with it. The fact that reason is always on the side of duty and the moral law does not prevent the experiment from exhibiting a movement, which is proper to the experiment. The end sought is twofold: to show that reason does not mingle with dishonesty and that as soon as duty becomes an issue it separates itself from any advantage that seeks to become a maxim. But the experiment shows this dynamically, through the hypothetical representation of a movement of reason. If the version with *nur* (only) were the best, the previous step—in which reason unites with veracity—would make no sense, since according to the *nur* the movement would be a priori cancelled, and there would be no experiment to begin with.

The experiment is a mental fiction, purporting to show at which moment reason and advantage are indifferent to one another, namely, before analysis. Once the analysis is carried out, incompatible elements are separated and compatible ones are joined: that is, reason and advantage become incompatible in the case of dishonesty, just as alkali and calcium carbonate do not combine when under the effect of muriatic acid.

Concluding the *Critique of Practical Reason*, Kant takes up almost literally the model of the chemical experiment, which proves its centrality as a paradigm of moral judgments. Referring to the significance that the discovery connected to the observation of a stone falling had for physics and for the knowledge of the structure of the world, Kant states at the beginning of the last paragraph of the second *Critique*:

> This example can recommend that we take the same path in treating of the moral predispositions of our nature and can give us hope of a similarly good outcome. We have at hand examples of reason judging morally. We can analyze them into their elementary concepts and, in default of *mathematics*, adopt a procedure similar to that of *chemistry*—the *separation*, by repeated experiments on common human understanding, of the empirical from the rational that may be found in them—and come to know both of them *pure* and what each can accomplish of itself. (A291; *Practical Reason*, 5:163)

The "similarly good outcome" mentioned here reveals a concern that Kant already had in the previous experiment and throughout his concluding remarks on morality, namely, a concern that it be connected with science (not the reduction of morality to science), so that it will not fall into any sort of astrology, mysticism, or extravagances of genius. This connection reveals itself in the analytic judgment of moral examples as if they were chemical experiments. Just as the natural state in chemistry is that of a composite, so too the empirical and the rational can get along, and their union is natural to man and agrees with morality, so long as the empirical does not become a ground for it. It goes to the chemical experiment model the task of showing precisely how man's common reason can acknowledge perfectly the mixture and the compatibility or incompatibility of the elements of moral practice.

Perhaps the most touching example illustrating this capacity is the one Kant offers in which one asks "a ten-year-old boy for his appraisal . . . [of] the story of an honest man whom someone wants to induce to join the calumniators of an innocent but otherwise powerless person" (A277; *Practical Reason*, 5:155). According to the introduction of the paragraph,

> If one asks: What, then, really is *pure* morality, by which as a touchstone one must test the moral content of every action? I must admit that only philosophers can make the decision of this question doubtful, for it is long since decided in common human reason, not indeed by abstract general formulae but by habitual use, like the difference between the right and the left hand. (A277; *Practical Reason*, 5:155)

The conclusion of the analysis of the example emphasizes the chemical model: "All the admiration, and even the endeavor to resemble this character, here rests wholly on the purity of the moral principle, which can be clearly represented only if one removes from the incentive to action everything that people may reckon only to happiness" (*Practical Reason*, 5:156).

The examples are tools used in the experiment for the analysis of morality. They are primarily a didactic way of showing to the student the feasibility of moral practice. In the *Doctrine of Virtue*, we read that "The *experimental* (technical) means for cultivating virtue is the *good* example (*Beispiel*) on the part of the teacher" (6:479). Kant adds a few lines down, however, that the example (*Exempel*) "should not serve as a model, but only as a proof that it is really possible to act in conformity with duty." One must not compare oneself to other people, but with the idea (of humanity), with the law; it is this standard that the master should always point to when educating.[9]

Conclusion

In analyzing the practical reason experiment, I have set aside (for now) some theoretical remarks on the analogy with chemical experiment. I recommend, on this matter, a work by Annemarie Pieper.[10] The usefulness of the comparative value of the chemical experiment is evident: moral judgment must imitate the chemical procedure in order to detect the presence or absence of impure elements in the moral action. But the chemical model is useful also for teaching rigor in the philosophical procedure on moral practice. In the absence of mathematics and geometry, the chemical procedure seems adequate to moral analysis. Union with scientific procedures is something Kant demands throughout his philosophy, even in aesthetics.

If this is true, then hasn't Vogel's correction followed that rigor in interpreting Kant's text according to the dynamics that it requires, that is, that its spirit requires? I think we can concede to Vogel a rule of interpretation that Kant established in the *Critique of Pure Reason*: a later philosopher is better positioned to understand an earlier author than the author understood himself. Vogel was practically Kant's contemporary, but proceeded as someone who up until today understood him on his own, at least in regard to this experiment with practical reason, by proposing a correction to the text that deserves attention in future editions of the *Critique of Practical Reason*. If that should not happen, the least we can expect is for the 1984 Harald Fischer Verlag edition—which reproduces the corrected Erlangen text of the *Critique of Practical Reason*—to be challenged or abandoned, something that has not been done until now.

Notes

1. Original edition (A), of 1787: *Critik der praktischen Vernunft* (Riga: bey Johann Friedrich Hartknoch, 1788). A reprint can be found in Immanuel Kant, *Kritik der praktischen Vernunft: Kant im Original* (Erlangen: Harald Fischer Verlag, 1984). The first part of this study was presented in 2001 at the Third Brazilian Kant Congress in Itatiaia, and later published as "Die handschriftlichen Korrekturen im Erlanger Originalexemplar der *Kritik der praktischen Vernunft*," *Kant-Studien* 95 (2004): 135–45. Research was undertaken with the support of FAPERGS and DAAD.

2. The Faculty of Theology took on a theoretical outlook influenced by Hamann—a personal acquaintance of Kant. Several other theologians from there, such as Ammon and Seiler, corresponded with Kant, not to mention philosophers such as Abicht, whose books Kant owned.

3. A passage at the beginning of the second part of the *Groundwork* takes up the same kind of problem (*Groundwork*, 4:407). See also *Theory and Practice*, 8:284.

4. See Pierre Kerzberg, "La chemie chez Kant," in V. Gerhardt et al., *Kant und die Berliner Aufklärung*, Akten des IX. Internationalen Kant Kongresses, vol. 6 (Berlin: Walter de Gruyter, 2001), 575.

5. Ibid., 576.

6. In *Kant in der Diskussion der Moderne*, ed. G. Schönrich and Y. Kato (Frankfurt: Suhrkamp, 1996), 64–91.

7. Brigitte Falkenburg, *Die Form der Materie* (Frankfurt: Athäneum, 1987), chapter one, "Die Experimente der Vernunft," 105.

8. This is how Mary Gregor's English translation reads, in *Practical Philosophy*, The Cambridge Edition of the Works of Immanuel Kant (Cambridge: Cambridge University Press, 1996), 214. "Altogether" is her translation of *nur gänzlich*. In Vogel's corrected version, we read *nun gänzlich* (now wholly) instead.

9. I will not go into any detail here about the German and also Kantianism distinction between *Beispiel* and *Exempel*. That would certainly enrich this paper, but it would probably be an enhancement of little use, and unfeasible in Portuguese, where we have only the word "exemplo" (example) for both cases. I quote, however, an informative passage in which Kant's conception follows mostly Lessing and not Wolff: "*Beispiel*, a German word, is commonly used as synonymous with *Exempel*, but the two words really do not have the same meaning. To take something as an *Exampel* and to bring forward a *Beispiel* are altogether different concepts. An *Exempel* is a particular case of a *practical* rule, insofar as this rule represents an action as practicable or impracticable, whereas a *Beispiel* is only a particular (*concretum*) represented in accordance with concepts as contained under a universal (*abstractum*), and is a presentation of a concept merely for theory" (*Doctrine of Virtue*, 6:480). The English translation by Mary Gregor (in the Cambridge edition) translates *Exempel* as "example" and *Beispiel* as "instance" in this particular passage. But she uses "example" for *Beispiel* in the passage quoted above (*Doctrine of Virtue*, 6:479).

10. Annemarie Pieper, "Kant und die Methode der Analogie," in Schönrich, *Kant in der Diskussion*, 92–112.

6

On the *Faktum* of Reason

Darlei Dall'Agnol

Introduction

The problem of the existence of a pure reason capable of determining the will, that is, capable of being practical, is an issue for philosophy of action, which is paramount to ethics since any discussion on whether an action is good or bad or on what must be done has to presuppose that action is possible at all. To deny the existence of a pure practical reason seems to imply the denial of the very possibility of making an agent accountable for his or her actions and, therefore, the very purpose of philosophical matters such as ethics, political philosophy, philosophy of law, etc. At least, it seems to deny that it is possible to act under rules capable of being objective, that is, universally valid.

In the history of philosophy, there were antagonistic views on this question. For instance, Hume held that reason is only capable of distinguishing what is true from what is false and it is unable to determine the will. In his own words: "Reason is the discovery of truth or falsehood. . . . Reason is wholly inactive."[1] To the author of *A Treatise of Human Nature*, reason is a slave of passions, that is, the ends of actions are established by the will and reason is only capable of saying whether a means *x* is better or worse than another means *y* to reach the desired end. He wrote: "Reason is, and ought only to be the slave of the passions, and can never pretend to any other office than to serve and obey them."[2] Kant, on the contrary, tried to show against Hume that pure reason is capable of determining the will, of acting from the representation of universal laws. It was precisely to show that there is a pure reason that is practical that he wrote the *Critique of Practical Reason*: "its task is merely to show that there is a pure practical reason" (*Practical Reason*, 5:3). According to Kant, it is possible to prove that pure reason is practical, that it is capable of determining the will, by the *Faktum* of reason

This paper was first published as "Sobre o *faktum* da razão," in *Filosofia, lógica, e existência: Homenagem a Antonio Carlos Kroeff Soares*, ed. L. C. Bombassaro and J. Paviani (Caxias do Sul: Educs, 1997), 268–87. Translated by the author.

(*Practical Reason*, 5:6). To prove that pure reason is capable of determining the will is equivalent to showing the reality of freedom.

To understand this proof and, more than that, to discuss whether it is a good proof—of course under the assumption that it is well understood—is one of the most difficult problems of interpreting Kant's practical philosophy. There are many criticisms of the way Kant thought to show the reality of freedom. However, most of them do not reach the central point of Kant's argumentation for the simple reason that it is not well comprehended.

In this essay, I will try to clarify the meaning of the expression "*Faktum* of reason" (*Faktum der Vernunft*) and to determine the *place* it occupies in Kantian practical philosophy, showing that a good understanding of the *Faktum* of reason depends upon the reconstruction of the steps Kant gave to prove the reality (*Realität*) of freedom. Thus, the problem of the *Faktum* is connected to a specific kind of proof, and its correct understanding depends upon: (1) a clarification of what the expression "*Faktum* of reason" means, (2) the discussion of what a philosophical proof is, (3) the reconstruction of the steps Kant gives to prove the reality of freedom, and (4) finally, the assessment of the nature of this proof.

The essay is divided in three sections. In the first, I will extensively quote Kant's texts where the expression "*Faktum* of reason" appears, trying afterward to clarify its meaning. In the second section, I will reconstruct the steps given by Kant to prove the possibility that pure reason can determine the will or, what turns out to be the same, the reality of freedom. Finally, in the third section, I will discuss the nature of this proof, trying to establish whether it is a good proof or otherwise.

The expression *Faktum der Vernunft* has mainly been interpreted as referring to the moral law or to the consciousness of this law, which then gives a motive to pure reason to be practical, that is, to determine the will to action. Nevertheless, many questions arise, since the problem of the *Faktum* of reason could, generally speaking, be put in this way: I can do something if it is required that I should do it. For instance, if I must keep my promises, then I can do it even if I have to refrain from my inclinations or other influences, which are impelling me to do otherwise. This thesis, however, may to some look implausible. For instance, a physician must save lives, but that may not always be possible even if she or he desires to do so. Another example: I see a person sinking in the ocean, I must save her, but if I cannot swim, then I cannot save her. Furthermore, how to explain that evil is possible? If the moral law is a *Faktum* that makes pure reason determine the will, then either a bad action is not possible at all, since freedom and morality are coextensive, or evil is just the result of a heteronymous action. It follows that an agent is not accountable for its own actions because it would then only be involved in natural events causally determined.

Does the expression "*Faktum* of reason" refer exclusively to the moral law that then requires that pure reason determines the will? If this is the case, how to explain bad actions or evil? Is it possible to prove that pure reason is practical independently of the consciousness of the moral law? What does "*Faktum* of reason" mean after all? These are the main questions that I will try to answer in this paper.

The Meanings of "*Faktum* of Reason"

Kant uses the expression "*Faktum* of reason" in many different places in his works, but it is in the *Critique of Practical Reason* that it appears more frequently.[3] Apparently, there is no univocal meaning for this expression. However, it does not follow, as I will show, that the meaning is equivocal. Kant employs, in the second *Critique*, the expression "*Faktum* of reason" in eleven different contexts. I will now quote all of them and make some remarks in order to clarify the meanings of this expression:

(a) Now practical reason itself, without any collusion with the speculative, provides reality to a supersensible object of the category of causality, i.e., to freedom. This is a practical concept and as such is subject only to practical use; but what in the speculative critique could only be thought is now confirmed by fact. (*Practical Reason*, 5:6)

(b) The consciousness of this fundamental law may be called a fact of reason, since one cannot ferret it out from antecedent data of reason, such as the consciousness of freedom (for this is not antecedently given), and since it forces itself upon us as a synthetic proposition a priori based on no pure or empirical intuition. (*Practical Reason*, 5:31)

(c) In order to regard this law without any misinterpretation as given, one must note that it is not an empirical fact but the sole fact of pure reason, which by it proclaims itself as originating law (*sic volo, sic iubeo*). (*Practical Reason*, 5:31)

(d) This Analytic proves that pure reason can be practical, i.e., that of itself and independently of everything empirical it can determine the will. This it does through a fact wherein pure reason shows itself actually to be practical. This fact is autonomy in the principle of morality by which reason determines the will to action. (*Practical Reason*, 5:42)

(e) At the same time it shows this fact to be inextricably bound up with the consciousness of freedom of the will, and actually to be identical with it. (*Practical Reason*, 5:42)

(f) The fact just mentioned is undeniable. One need only analyze the sentence which men pass upon the lawfulness of their actions to see in every case that their reason, incorruptible and self-constrained, in every action holds up the maxim of the will to the pure will, i.e., to itself regarded as a priori practical; and this it does regardless of what inclination may say to the contrary. (*Practical Reason*, 5:32)

(g) On the other hand, the moral law, although it gives no such prospect, does provide a fact absolutely inexplicable from any data of the world of sense or from the whole compass of the theoretical use of reason, and this fact points to a pure intelligible world—indeed, it defines it positively and enable us to know something of it, namely, a law. (*Practical Reason*, 5:43)

(h) Moreover, the moral law is given, as an apodictically certain fact, as it were, of pure reason, a fact of which we are a priori conscious, even if it be granted that no example could be found in which it has been followed exactly. (*Practical Reason*, 5:47)

(i) The objective reality of a pure will or of a pure practical reason (they being the same) is given a priori in the moral law, as it were by a fact, for the latter term can be applied to a determination of the will which is inescapable, even though it does not rest on any empirical principles. (*Practical Reason*, 5:55)

(j) But that pure reason is of itself alone practical, without any admixture of any kind of empirical motives—one had to show this from the commonest practical use of reason by producing evidence that the highest practical principle is a principle recognized by every natural human reason as the supreme law of its will, as a law completely a priori and independent of any sensuous data. It was necessary first to establish and justify it, by proof of the purity of its origin, in the judgment of common reason, before science could take it in hand to make use of it, so to speak, as a fact which precedes all disputation about its possibility and all consequences which may be drawn from it. (*Practical Reason*, 5:91)

(k) Then it was only a question of whether this "can be" could be changed to an "is"; it was a question of whether in an actual case and, as it were, by a fact, one could prove that certain actions presupposed such an intellectual, sensibly unconditioned, causality, regardless of whether they are actual or only commanded, i.e., objectively and practically necessary. (*Practical Reason*, 5:104)

As can be realized, Kant seems to refer to different things when he uses the expression "*Faktum* of reason." Thus, three primary remarks need to be done before one can make a careful analysis of what he meant. The first is the following: Kant always uses the Germanized Latin word *Faktum* and never the typical German word to refer to a fact, namely, *Tatsache*. The reason for doing so is the following: whatever he meant, it is obviously not an empirical fact. This can clearly be seen in the quotation (c) above. That is to say, the *Faktum* of reason is not a phenomenon, which fulfills the conditions that the *Critique of Pure Reason* has shown to be necessary to consider something a fact. Therefore, it is important to recall that a phenomenon is real if and only if it satisfies the material conditions of experience, that is, of perception that is made of singular representations of external objects (intuitions) that must be subsumed under universal representations (categories). It is only then that it is possible to have knowledge of phenomena in space and time; only then can one speak of empirical reality. Ideas are not representations of objects that can be given in experience and, therefore, their reality is problematic. Among these ideas is precisely that of freedom. The *Faktum* of reason, whatever it means, cannot pretend to show the empirical reality of an idea, of freedom.[4] The *Faktum* of reason is not an empirical fact, not a phenomenon.

The second remark is also related to the usage of the word *Faktum*. The employment that one finds in Latin writers is synonymous of a deed, for instance in expressions such as *facta illustra et gloriosa* (glorious and beautiful actions). Considering the Latinized use of the expression, it is not without purpose to translate the whole expression *Faktum der Vernunft* as "the deed of reason." In this way, reason is wholly active, that is, capable of being the cause of action. That may be the meaning used by Kant in the quotation (d), where the *Faktum* is simply this: pure reason's self-determination to act. This is a possible connotation of the expression "*Faktum* of reason" that is important to keep in mind.

The third remark is related to the "numerical" question of this *Faktum*. Although Kant writes, in one of the above quotations (c), of the sole *Faktum* of reason, he says that the moral law can *also* (using the German word *auch*) be considered a *Faktum* (h), which makes it clear that he does not necessarily hold that there is only ONE *Faktum*. It is important to note that Kant holds that the moral law can *also* be considered a *Faktum* immediately after saying that pure reason *is* practical (*Practical Reason* 5:47). Furthermore, the expression *das einzige Faktum* may just mean the following: this *Faktum*, as many others, is unique. In this way, it is possible to hold that there is more than one *Faktum* of reason. Therefore, the analysis does not need to be guided by the prejudice that the concept is univocal. Perhaps it is important to remark that Kant employs also the term *Datis der Vernunft* (data of reason) and that this expression characterizes the "products" of reason, that is, ideas, in the same way that intuitions and categories are the results of sensibility and understanding. Thus, a *Faktum* may just be a data of reason.

The central question, however, is this: what is exactly Kant referring to when he uses the expression "*Faktum* of reason"? Lewis Beck, mentioning only four passages, quoted in (b), (c), (d), and (h) above, holds that there are three important meanings of the expression "*Faktum* of reason": (1) in (b), the *Faktum* refers to the consciousness of the moral law; (2) in (c) and (h), the reference is to the moral law itself; and (3) in (d), it refers to autonomy.[5] According to Beck, given that Kant identifies freedom, here understood as autonomy, with the moral law itself, then there are only two basic meanings of the expression: the consciousness of the moral law and the moral law itself. Beck thinks that the existence of these two meanings is a problem and tries to show that there is only *one* (the sole) *Faktum* of reason.

To solve this ambiguity of the expression—a duality that could bring no problem at all, since there are many words and expressions that have more than one meaning in the ordinary language and they still can signify something in a clear way—Beck makes a distinction between the fact of pure reason and the fact *for* pure reason. I quote: "'Fact of pure reason' may mean a fact known by pure reason as its object, *modo directo*. Or it may mean the fact that there is pure reason, known by reason reflexively. These may be distinguished as 'fact for pure reason' and 'fact of pure reason.'"[6] This distinction may be helpful in the attempt of finding an univocal meaning for the use of the expression "*Faktum* of reason" in all the different contexts, if this univocality is to be reached at all. Thus, the conclusion that Beck holds is that the moral law is the fact of reason:

> Only a law which is given by reason itself to reason itself could be known a priori by pure reason and be a fact for pure reason. The moral law expresses nothing else than the autonomy of reason . . . it is a fact for pure reason only inasmuch as it is the expression of the fact of pure reason, i.e., of the fact that pure reason can be practical. That is why the moral law is the sole fact of pure reason and for pure reason.[7]

The solution is indeed ingenuous, but it does not make sense of the all usages of the expression I am considering in Kant's works, as one can realize looking carefully at the quotations given above. However, the main reason for not accepting Beck's solution is the following: with the distinction between fact of reason and fact for reason it may not possible to explain why Kant considers the *Faktum* of reason a proof that pure reason can be practical. Only by reconstructing the context in which the *Faktum* is a step in a proof is it possible to understand what is the function of the expression in Kant's practical philosophy. I think that this is the central point around which the discussion should focus.

Another commentator of Kant's practical philosophy, Henry Allison, quoting eight passages from the *Critique of Practical Reason* (a, b, c, d, h, i, j, and k, mentioned above) and fostering the analysis given by Beck, holds that there are six different meanings of the expression *Faktum* of reason: (1) the consciousness of the moral law, (2) the consciousness of the freedom of the will, (3) the moral law, (4) autonomy as the supreme principle of morality, (5) the determination of the will by the moral law, and (6) a real case of an action presupposing an unconditional causality.[8] Allison holds that Kant identifies also the *Faktum* with (7) freedom, (8) the practical law of freedom, and (9) the categorical imperative making in this way the question more difficult. However, Allison accepts Beck's classification of the meanings of the expression "*Faktum* of reason" in two classes and then tries to find a focal meaning for it. The conclusion Allison reaches, after analyzing these different meanings, is the following: "Although the texts are far from unambiguous on this score, the bulk of the evidence suggests that the fact is best construed as the consciousness of standing under the moral law and the recognition of this law 'by every natural human reason as the supreme law of its will.'"[9]

Allison tries to unify the different meanings of the expression using the consciousness of the moral law as the basic meaning of "*Faktum* of reason." I believe, however, that there are some problems in Allison's view. What does the term "consciousness" mean here? If it means some kind of intuition that apprehends the moral law, then Allison may be wrong, since Kant denies that the moral law can be an object of an intuition as can be realized in (b) above. Furthermore, as Beck pointed out, the consciousness of something is not a sufficient condition to show its objectivity.[10] For instance, if I believe that there is a God and that duty is determined by God's will, and in fact there is no God, then it remains a fact that I feel the call of duty, but it is not a fact that duty obliges in an objective way.

Thus, the question, what does the expression "*Faktum* of reason" mean? remains without a satisfactory answer. I think that in order to find a solution, the first step is not to be overwhelmingly concerned about the unification of all the uses of the expression under a unique meaning. There is a good reason for thinking in this way: taking the meanings already pointed out by Beck and Allison, but without their attempt to reduce them to a single one, it is just reasonable to admit the plurality of the meanings of the expression, that is, that there are *Fakta* of reason.

To show this point, I would like to illustrate two of the usages Kant makes of the expression "*Faktum* of reason," sometimes referring to the *Faktum* of the moral law, sometimes to the *Faktum* that pure reason is itself practical. I leave aside for now any relationship between these two meanings. Later, I will analyze the mutual implication that may exist between them. That morality is a fact of reason, a *Faktum*, can be clearly seen in the *Groundwork of the Metaphysics of Morals* as well as in the *Critique of Practical Reason*, since Kant never tries to demonstrate that it exists. The transition from the common sense morality to the popular philosophical knowledge, and from this to the metaphysics of morals, has the presupposition that morality is just given in the same ways as other a priori synthetic judgments in mathematics and physics are given, and it is only necessary to explain how they are possible. In the same way, the categorical imperative is already given to the common moral sense—though not necessarily in an explicit way—and what is needed is to show how it is possible. Therefore, Kant never tries to prove that there is morality in the *Groundwork*. In the same way, in the *Critique of Practical Reason* there is no attempt to prove that there is morality. Here is Kant's good philosophical education:

> Thus the objective reality of the moral law can be proved through no deduction, through no exertion of the theoretical, speculative, or empirically supported reason; and, even if one were willing to renounce its apodictic certainty, it could not be confirmed by any experience and thus proved *a posteriori*. Nevertheless, it is firmly established of itself. (*Practical Reason*, 5:47)

It is exactly because it is impossible to demonstrate it and, at the same time, because morality is undeniable, that Kant uses the word *Faktum* to characterize the objective reality of the moral law. Thus, while the *Groundwork* argues from a conditional presupposition, namely, if there is morality, then its formula is the categorical imperative, the second *Critique* simply postulates that morality is something real. Morality is a *Faktum* of reason as the starry heavens above is a fact of the world.

Kant also speaks of the *Faktum* that pure reason is practical and this is not equivalent to the *Faktum* that there is moral law. This point can be realized in the *Critique of Practical Reason* (5:31) when its author considers reason to be practical by itself alone. Now I would like to present some arguments to make plausible this way of interpreting the *Faktum* that pure reason is practical for itself independently of the *Faktum* that morality exists, even if the latter is a privileged motive to postulate the existence of the pure practical reason. First, I would like to start from a well-known criticism of Kantian ethics, namely, if Kant simply identifies freedom with morality (this identification is known as the reciprocity thesis, since according to the *Groundwork* once freedom is given, then morality follows by analysis of its concept), then either moral evil would not be possible or it would be the result of the inclinations, and that means that an agent would not be accountable for its own actions. Thus, when Kant speaks of the radical evil in *Religion within the Boundaries of Mere Reason*, he would be contradicting his critical work. Now, given that the denial of freedom itself is not possible, but that moral evil may just be real, then it must also be possible for autonomy to exit. The condition for that is that freedom is real, even when acting in an amoral way, and that means that pure reason must be practical independently of the moral law. I believe that this is the strong motive for looking for a Kantian proof of the reality of freedom not only starting from the *Faktum* that there is moral law. Second, Kant seems to accept that even technical imperatives show that pure reason can determine the will to action, since even geometry has postulates, as practical propositions, which start from the assumption that one *can* do something if one *should* do it (see *Practical Reason*, 5:31). Finally, I believe that one has to minimize Kant's appeals to daily evidences, which supposedly confirm the order of concepts, namely, first to postulate duty and then show that one can do it.[11] Thus, I believe that Kant in fact identifies morality with one concept of freedom, namely, positive freedom or autonomy, but he does not consider morality and freedom simply as coextensive, though he is not always careful while using his terminology.

If this is correct, then I would like to stress that the central point in the right comprehension of what Kant intends to do when he is using the expression "*Faktum* of reason" depends upon the good understanding of what he is trying to prove or simply of what is left without demonstration and assumed as valid. It seems clear to me that it is exactly this second point that is important in order to understand the uses of the expression "*Faktum* of reason." Therefore, given that the central aim of the *Critique of Practical Reason* is just to prove, as it was already seen, that there is a pure practical reason (*Practical Reason* 5:3) and that the understanding of the *Faktum* is related to the context of proof that Kant is undertaking, I would like now to reconstruct the main steps that Kant gives to show the reality of freedom, that is, that pure reason can effectively determine the will.

Kant's Proof of the Reality of Freedom

I have here to leave aside the analysis of each of the possible references of the expression "*Faktum* of reason" since it goes far beyond the limits of this paper. Instead, from now on, I will focus on the use of this expression as a way of proving that pure reason is practical. I will maintain that there are three main steps in the proof of the reality of freedom: (1) the first is taken in the *Critique of Pure Reason* where Kant shows that natural causality and freedom are compatible, that is, that freedom is just possible; (2) a step forward is taken in the *Groundwork* where Kant offers a positive characterization of freedom as autonomy, but without proving that it is real; and (3) finally, the third is taken in the *Critique of Practical Reason* where Kant shows that it is just a *Faktum* that reason determines the will, that is, pure reason is practical by itself alone.

First of all, I would like to clarify better the internal connections (argumentative links) between the three works where the proof of the reality of freedom is presented or, what is the same, that pure reason is practical. In the preface to the second *Critique*—published in 1788—Kant clarifies that this work presupposes the *Groundwork* published three years before because the latter text establishes the supreme principle of morality and *justifies* a specific formula (*Practical Reason*, 5:8–9). However, in the *Groundwork* Kant makes no effort to prove either that there is something one may call "morality" or that freedom is real. The step forward that the *Critique of Practical Reason* takes is the following: the problematic judgment on the mere assumption of freedom to explain how autonomy as the supreme principle of morality is possible must become apodictic. But the *Groundwork* itself presupposes an argumentative step. Kant writes at the end of the third section of this work that freedom and causality must both be accepted.[12] In this way, freedom can only be considered a necessary assumption for the possibility of autonomy if it is in some way compatible with the law of causality. This observation shows an important link between the *Groundwork* and the first *Critique* published in 1781: practical philosophy depends upon theoretical reason since the later needs to show that freedom and causality can coexist.

Before reconstructing the steps taken to prove the reality of freedom, I wish to recall the fundamental rules of a transcendental proof, which, according to Kant, must control pure reason. Here is one: "The first rule is, therefore, not to attempt any transcendental proofs until we have considered, with a view to obtaining justification for them, from what source we propose to derive the principles on which the proof are to be based, and with what right we may expect success in our inferences" (*Pure Reason*, B814).

This rule makes clear what is specific in a philosophical proof. It appears also when Kant formulates the third rule of the transcendental proofs (*Pure Reason*, B817) (the second is trivial: there is just one proof), saying that they must be ostensive, that is, they must not only establish the truth of the proposition to be proved, but also expose the grounds of its truth. Given that the sciences are composed of a priori synthetic propositions, it is a task of philosophy to clarify *how* such a priori knowledge is possible at all. This is the main problem that transcendental philosophy must resolve also in an a priori manner. Thus, natural sciences and philosophy belongs to distinct domains. Therefore, a transcendental proof is sui generis: it has to present a justification of the sources of what it needs to prove together with the attempt to show the truth of the proposition. In the next section I will return to this point, giving a more detailed discussion of the nature of this kind of proof.

Let me then try to reconstruct how Kant shows the possibility of freedom without contradiction with the assertion of the universal validity of the law of causality. In fact, they are contrasted in the third antinomy. This conflict of the transcendental ideas is presented in the following way:

> *Thesis:* Causality in accordance with laws of nature is not the only causality from which the appearances of the world can one and all be derived. To explain these appearances it is necessary to assume that there is also another causality, that of freedom.

> *Antithesis:* There is no freedom; everything in the world takes place solely in accordance with laws of nature. (*Pure Reason*, B471–72)

Kant presents a proof to each of these propositions showing that both are true. The proof has the form of a reductio ad absurdum. Generally speaking, the proof of the thesis is this: Suppose that there is no freedom. Now, given that everything that happens is connected to a previous condition causally determined, and this event to another previous condition, and so on, this series cannot go on to infinity because otherwise it will be nothing at the present moment. But there are events happening now; therefore, one must admit that the thesis is true, that is, one must accept also a causality of freedom in the world. The antithesis is also proved, as can be seen in B473–75. What Kant has then is a pair of propositions, one denying the other, and both having the same truth value. But this constitutes a clear transgression of the logical principle of the excluded middle. To solve this conflict, Kant shows that in fact both are true, but each of them refers to two different aspects of the same object. Thus, causality is an a priori category that applies to the object as phenomenon. Causality of freedom is also an a priori idea understood as spontaneity, but it is an attribute of the thing-in-itself (noumenon) and not of the phenomenon. In this way, the distinction between phenomenon and thing-in-itself allows Kant to dissolve the antinomy between causality and freedom and to accept both, simultaneously.

If both propositions are true and the condition for this is that they refer to different aspects of the same object—the antagonism is apparent and arises out of the confusion between phenomena and noumena—then what the thesis presupposes is obviously true, that is, that freedom is possible. The question then is: what does the word "freedom" mean here? The answer is this: transcendental freedom or cosmological freedom. This means simply that spontaneity must be admitted, namely, the beginning of a causal chain without a previous natural cause. If this kind of freedom can be attributed to a rational being—or to a rational and sensible being such as humans—then free action would be possible, that is, an act would have a spontaneous cause. Thus, taking Kant's own example, if I decide to get up from this chair right now, this decision will start a new chain of natural events in the world as its consequence, but its cause is not determined as a natural event because freedom is an attribute of the agent taken as a thing-in-itself and not as phenomena. In other words, the action is free. Therefore, the proof of the spontaneity of the world allows us to think in terms of new spontaneous series into the natural world, that is, to admit a free faculty of action. But an important observation needs to be made now: freedom as spontaneity is here admitted without having been postulated by the necessity of the moral duty. In Kant's example, it is an amoral action to decide to get up from this chair. However, it is a free action.

Before discussing the second step in Kant's proof, I would like to call attention to a particular point: the distinction between phenomenon and thing-in-itself is here seen as a purely logical distinction, which in the theoretical domain does not imply any ontological duplication of a Platonic kind, namely, the belief in the existence of two worlds. Kant is not always careful when he is using his terminology, but the preface of the second edition of the *Critique of Pure Reason* leaves no doubt regarding the distinction between phenomenon and thing-in-itself. Kant writes: "But if our Critique is not in error in teaching that the object is to be taken *in a twofold* sense, namely as appearance and as thing in itself" (*Pure Reason*, Bxxvii). As can be seen, it is the same object taken in two different senses and not two different objects. In this way, phenomenon is the object taken in its cognitive relationship to a subject, that is, while it is outside the mind and affecting one's sensibility and thus represented by intuitions, which will be subsumed into categories. The thing-in-itself is the same object taken independently of this relation, that is, just the denial of the object as phenomenon that one can think of, but one cannot know any of its attributes. Therefore, the distinction is not ontological, but rather purely logical, or, in other words, it is the same object taken in a double sense.

What Kant reaches in dissolving the antinomy between causality and freedom by showing that they refer to two different aspects of the same object, is simply to indicate that it is possible to admit freedom without denying the necessity and universality of the laws of nature. Thus, freedom is compatible with causality. To show this point is *the first step* in Kant's proof that pure reason can determine the will to action.

The *second step* is taken by Kant in the *Groundwork* when he shows that freedom is a condition for autonomy. The first question then is: what is autonomy? The third formula of the categorical imperative gives the following expression to autonomy as the supreme principle of morality: "never to perform an action except on a maxim such as can also be a universal law, and consequently such *that the will can regard itself as at the same time making universal law by means of its maxim*" (*Groundwork*, 4:434).

In other words, what Kant holds is that the expression of the supreme principle of morality is the self-imposition of those laws that a rational being is capable of assuming. It may be worth stating the Rousseauian formulation here: freedom is nothing else but obedience to the laws that one gives to oneself. Therefore, autonomy is freedom in his positive sense, namely, as self-determination. Now, if one asks, how is autonomy possible? the answer will be the following: under the necessary assumption of freedom in its transcendental sense presented above as spontaneity. For this reason, Kant holds that the transcendental concept of freedom is the basis of the practical concept of freedom.

I would like to insist upon this point, namely, that autonomy is not the condition of freedom, but, on the contrary, the latter is the condition of the former. It is exactly this that Kant has in mind when he writes: "Now I assert that every being who cannot act except *under the idea of freedom* is by this alone—from a practical point of view—really free; that is to say, for him all the laws inseparably bound up with freedom are valid just as much as if his will could be pronounced free in itself on grounds valid for theoretical philosophy" (*Groundwork*, 4:448). Thus, it is a necessary and sufficient condition for a rational and sensible being to be free that it thinks of itself as free. It is sufficient to act under the assumption that one is free in order to be really free. It is clear, however, that freedom is an attribute of the intelligible character of the agent and not of its empirical self as a phenomenon among phenomena. But it is also worth noting that there are no "two selves" of the same agent, namely, the empirical self and the intelligible one, but rather it is one and the same ego seen from two different points of view, as phenomenon and as a thing-in-itself.

The step taken by Kant in the *Groundwork*, however, has many conditionals, as I pointed out earlier. Kant never tries to demonstrate in this work that morality is real, that there are obligations that are categorical imperatives, that reason can determine the will, etc. The *Groundwork* argues in this manner: if morality exists, then its supreme principle is this . . . ; if there are duties, then their formula is this . . . ; if reason determines the will, then. . . . As can be seen, the whole argument is conditional, that is, constructed under hypothetical premises. The understanding of this point is paramount for an adequate interpretation of the *Faktum* reason, which is a decisive moment in the proof Kant is trying to present.

The *third step* is taken in the *Critique of Practical Reason* where his author simply postulates that pure reason is practical for itself and that this is a *Faktum*. Thus, one has here the right measure to understand better the use of the expression "*Faktum* of reason." Kant has no alternative, given that (1) freedom is an attribute of the thing-in-itself, as the first *Critique* showed; and (2) that rational beings who act under the idea of freedom are *eo ipso* free, but to declare that pure reason is itself practical and that this is a *Faktum*. To say that pure reason is practical, that is, that it can determine itself to action and be the efficient cause of action, has no less degree of evidence or less certainty than the inevitability of an empirical fact.

In this way, the proof of the reality of freedom is completed. The proof can be summarized, taking the risks of an oversimplification, in this way: The freedom of the will is possible and it is not opposed to the natural causality. Now, rational beings who act under the assumption of freedom are for this very reason free. Therefore, freedom is a *Faktum* of reason.

This way of presenting the proof has an important advantage, namely, it avoids the objection that there is a vicious circle in the proof of the reality of freedom if it is done starting from the *Faktum* of the moral law. Kant himself was aware of this circle in the *Groundwork*: in the order of efficient causes, we assume ourselves free to conceive ourselves as subject to moral laws in the order of ends; but afterward we conceive ourselves as subject to the moral laws, because we attributed to ourselves freedom of will. Thus, the appearance of the vicious circle that would undermine the argumentation is avoided when freedom is correctly understood as the raison d'être of the moral law, since without freedom, that is, only under natural laws, it does not make sense to speak of obligations.

The Nature of the Proof

The understanding of the expression "*Faktum* of reason," as we saw earlier, depends upon the recognition that it is a step in a proof. For that reason, it was necessary to reconstruct the steps Kant takes to show the reality of freedom. Thus, what I would like to do, in this last section, is to discuss the nature of Kant's proof and whether it is a good one or otherwise.

First, it is necessary to go back to the discussion on what is a philosophical proof. According to Kant, such proof is not strictly speaking a demonstration. Then, what is a demonstration? In the *Critique of Pure Reason*, a demonstration is an apodictic proof that involves intuition. In this sense, only mathematics and not philosophy contains demonstrations, since it constructs concepts presenting the related intuitions.[13] Philosophical proofs are not demonstrations in this strict sense. In Kant's own words: "I should therefore prefer to call . . . *acroamatic* (discursive) *proofs*, since they may be conducted by the agency of words alone (the object in thought), rather than *demonstrations* which, as the term itself indicates, proceed in and through the intuition of the object" (*Pure Reason*, B762–63).

One can realize in this quotation that Kant is making a distinction between the kind of philosophical proof that can be presented in philosophy and the kind of proof that can be done in a science such as mathematics. Independently of the name the proof, the important point is to understand that a philosophical proof, especially in the practical domain, cannot be intuitive. That is to say, one cannot ask for an intuition of freedom or morality, since that would mean to ask for a representation of an object that would be given in an experience. This is exactly the limit of all practical philosophy: it cannot present an intuition of its concepts. Reason will go beyond all its limits if it demanded an intuition of its objects that are part of the intelligible world (*Groundwork*, 4:458). What the third part of the *Groundwork* does is to stress that it is not possible to present a *demonstration* of the reality of freedom. It is exactly this point that Kant is making at the end of that section: "Reason would overstep all its limits if it took upon itself to *explain how* pure reason can be practical. This would be identical with the task of explaining *how freedom is possible*" (*Groundwork*, 4:458–59).

The limit of pure reason is exactly that of being unable to *explain* how it is possible for pure reason to be practical. Trying to explain that would be the equivalent of asking for an intellectual intuition that is not possible for finite creatures such as human beings. In other words, given that freedom is an attribute of the thing-in-itself, and in the case of humans, as rational beings of their intelligible self, the price to be paid is the inexplicability of freedom itself. One can only understand that it is not possible to explain, that is, to demonstrate the reality of freedom.

If the proof of the reality of freedom, as a philosophical proof, is not a demonstration, then what it is? Is it possible to compare it with the transcendental deduction of the categories? Or better: is the proof of the reality of freedom a transcendental deduction? This is what Beck and H. J. Paton think. The later explains what he understands by a transcendental deduction in this way: It seeks to justify a synthetic *a priori* proposition by tracing its origin to the nature of mind as such and in particular to the activity of reason itself. Such a justification is what Kant calls a 'transcendental deduction.'"[14]

Perhaps this way of seeing the transcendental deduction is oversimplifying. To understand the deduction better it is important to remember that a transcendental argument is composed of two parts. The first is to show that a certain concept is a priori. The second, a transcendental deduction, tries to show the objective reality of this concept. There is a transcendental argument when, for example, one explains the possibility of a priori synthetic judgments in mathematics by showing that humans beings have a pure intuition of space and time (metaphysical deduction) and that this intuition is constitutive of geometry and arithmetic, respectively (transcendental deduction). In the same way, when one deduces a priori categories from the table of judgments, this is a metaphysical deduction. But when one shows that the categories are constitutive of experience referring to objects, or better, explains *how* they refer to objects, this is a transcendental deduction. It is also worth pointing out that a transcendental argument does not have a logical form that is distinct from the other kinds of proof: it follows the same logical principles. What makes it a philosophical proof and not a scientific one is the nature of its problems.

If this is correct, then to explain the sources of a concept is not to make a transcendental deduction yet. If a concept is showed to have its source in the reason alone and therefore it is a priori, then this is a metaphysical deduction. For that reason, the way Paton explains the transcendental deduction may not be accurate. However, Paton himself says, after defining transcendental deduction, that in some cases the purpose of the transcendental deduction is just to explain the possibility of a priori concepts and in other cases is to establish them. This seems really the case. For instance, the existence of a priori judgments in the domain of the natural sciences is just a fact, but in the domain of morality it is necessary first to establish them.

A transcendental deduction is not a demonstrative proof, but it is rather a special kind of justification. According to the *Critique of Pure Reason*, it deals with a question of *iuris* and not a matter of fact. That freedom is not an empirical fact, but an a priori idea, was already well established. Its objective reality was also shown in the second section of this paper. For this reason, the proof that pure reason is practical can be seen as a kind of transcendental deduction. But to deduce does not mean here *to infer* a proposition from another accepted one by valid rules. This is the main mistake that many of Kant's commentators make: they think that when one speaks of deducing freedom, what one has in mind is to infer it from another concept, namely, from morality. This is not the case. What Kant is trying to do is to justify it, that is, to present reasons to show its objective reality. This is the source of many misunderstandings that could be avoided. For instance, Allison holds that the deduction of the third section of the *Groundwork* fails because Kant wants to deduce freedom from amoral premises, and that in the second *Critique* Kant makes an inversion, namely, he is deducing freedom from morality. However, Allison's arguments to show the supposed failure in the third section are weak and I really cannot see any significant inversion.[15] To avoid this confusion, it is important to pay attention to a methodological difference between the two works. It is sufficient to remember that *Groundwork*'s method is analytical, that is, it moves from common moral knowledge to its principle, the categorical imperative. But the *Critique of Practical Reason* uses a synthetic method, that is, it moves from examination of the principle to common knowledge. Therefore, there is a change in the methodology of the two works, but not an inversion or a failure in one of the two deductions.

I will try to clarify this point in another way. The central question of the third section of the *Groundwork* is this: how is the categorical imperative (autonomy) possible as an a priori synthetic proposition? The answer is, roughly speaking, this: under the necessary assumption of freedom. It starts from morality regressing to its condition. The second *Critique* starts from freedom as a condition—and we should remember that it is a *Faktum*—and arrives at morality. Furthermore, the sequence between the *Groundwork* and the second *Critique* is clearly established at the end of the second section of the *Groundwork* (4:445), namely, Kant cannot admit a synthetic use of pure practical reason without making a critique of practical reason.

If this point is sound, namely, that Kant avoids admitting a synthetic use of pure reason without making a critique of practical reason, then the way in this paper that the proof of the reality of freedom was reconstructed must be correct. What I did was to show the argumentative sequence between the main works. Consequently, there are not two transcendental deductions, but taking into consideration the methodological differences, just one transcendental deduction, a justification, of freedom. This was exactly the point I was trying to make: freedom is a distinct *Faktum* of reason, though not completely independent of, the *Faktum* of morality.

A final question remains: is this a good proof? Yes and no!, one may say. Yes, because in the end it manages to convince one of the reality of freedom. No, because it is a proof unable to produce an empirical evidence of what is the object to be proved, that is, in the end it is not possible to make an intuitive representation of freedom. But this apparent problem may indirectly be compensated. That is to say, since it is not possible to demonstrate the reality of freedom, then one can proceed by refutation. In other words, if it convinces us of the reality of freedom and that point is denied, then it is possible to reject that negation. This is the case because the skeptic cannot deny freedom, since it is not possible to have any intuitive representation of it. In other words, the skeptic loses his ground for arguing. That may be what Kant has in mind when he writes, at the very end of the third section of the *Groundwork*: "But where determination by laws of nature comes to an end, all *explanation* comes to an end as well. Nothing is left but *defense*—that is, to repel the objections of those who profess to have seen more deeply into the essence of things and on this ground audaciously declare freedom to be impossible" (*Groundwork*, 4:459). Transcendental argumentation can lead to this defense against the skeptic, like an arbor that provides shelter from the rain. It is not a demonstration, but the proof that it can produce is sufficient to repel the denial of freedom.

Notes

1. David Hume, *A Treatise of Human Nature* (Oxford: Clarendon Press, 1978), 458.

2. Ibid., 415.

3. The term is also used in, for example, the *Critique of the Power of Judgment* (§91, 5:468) and *Doctrine of Right* (6:252).

4. Kant is also very careful at using another word taken from the Latin, namely, *Realität*, to characterize the reality of, for instance, freedom, and not the German word *Wirklichkeit*. The latter word is used to qualify phenomena and in this sense to characterize what fulfills the material conditions of experience. Freedom is an idea of pure reason and its objective reality cannot be proved by experience. That does not

mean, however, as I will shown, that it must be considered an empty idea or simple unreal.

5. Lewis White Beck, *A Commentary on Kant's "Critique of Practical Reason"* (Chicago: University of Chicago Press, 1960), 167.

6. Ibid., 168.

7. Ibid., 169.

8. Henry Allison, *Kant's Theory of Freedom* (New York: Cambridge University Press. 1991), 232.

9. Ibid., 233.

10. Beck, *Commentary*, 169–70.

11. After giving examples that one first recognizes the duty and then one considers oneself to be able of doing what one must do, Kant writes: "He judges, therefore, that he can do something because he knows that he ought, and he recognizes that he is free—a fact which, without the moral law, would have remained unknown to him" (*Practical Reason*, 5:30). However, one could appeal here to particular circumstances, as the examples given above, where there is the consciousness that something must be done, but it may not be possible to do it.

12. "Reason must therefore suppose that no genuine contradiction is to be found between the freedom and the natural necessity ascribed to the very same human actions; for it can abandon the concept of nature as little as it can abandon that of freedom" (*Groundwork*, 4:456).

13. "An apodeictic proof can be called a demonstration, only in so far as it is intuitive. . . . Mathematics alone, therefore, contains demonstrations, since it derives its knowledge not from concepts but from the construction of them, that is, from intuition, which can be given *a priori* in accordance with the concepts" (*Pure Reason*, B762).

14. H. J. Paton, *The Categorical Imperative: A Study in Kant's Moral Philosophy* (London: Hutchinson of London, 1948), 200.

15. Allison, Kant's Theory of *Freedom*, 227–29.

7

Critique, Deduction, and the Fact of Reason

Guido Antônio de Almeida

Kant's *Critique of Practical Reason* differs in a striking way from his other critical works, since it does not include what he calls a "deduction" of the principles of the criticized faculty, that is, a proof of the objective validity of its a priori principles. To be sure, one finds there the chapter "On the Deduction of the Principles of Pure Practical Reason." However, the aim of this chapter is not exactly that of working out a deduction of these principles but, instead, to show that, in a critique of *practical* reason, such a deduction is in fact impossible, and, indeed, not only impossible but also dispensable, since what has to be ensured by a deduction in the other critical works is guaranteed in the present one by recourse to a so-called fact of reason—a mysterious and apparently paradoxical notion that I will discuss in this paper after considering Kant's reasons for discarding a deduction of pure practical principles.

In the earlier *Critique of Pure Reason*, on the contrary, an essential part of his critical project, which was that of ascertaining the possibility of a priori knowledge, was the deduction of the categories, taken to be pure concepts of the understanding through which one thinks the essential predicates of any object of knowledge as such. Indeed, without such a deduction, the philosopher would be incapable not only of justifying the claim to have a priori knowledge, but he would also be incapable of justifying the claim to know *empirical* objects as something distinct from the perceptions in which they are given. Consequently, he would also be incapable of ascertaining the right we have to ascribe to our objective judgments a necessity and universal validity that we deny to judgments about our perceptions.

In the later published *Critique of the Power of Judgment* as well, the deduction of the principle of our judgments of taste was also a decisive part of the critical project. Indeed, without it, the philosopher would not be able, when examining the credentials of our aesthetic judgments, to establish our presumed right to distinguish judgments of the beautiful from judgments of

The original version of this paper appeared as "Crítica, dedução, e facto da razão," in *Analytica* 4 (1999): 57–84. Translated by the author.

the agreeable, ascribing to the former a universal validity we deny the latter, although both are based on a subjective state of our mind, which is the feeling of pleasure.

It is worthy of notice that, in the *Groundwork of the Metaphysics of Morals*, a deduction of the categorical imperative to act on universalizable maxims, taken to be the principle of all our moral judgments, also played a decisive role in the task of establishing this principle. In fact, without this deduction—so it seemed to Kant—the philosopher would not be able to establish the right we have of ascribing to our moral judgments a necessity and universal validity that we deny to our pragmatic judgments about what we think is beneficial for us.

It should not go unnoticed too that in the *Groundwork*, it is the *deduction* of the categorical imperative that gives the work the right to bear the title of a *Groundwork*, insofar as it makes possible the transition from the mere metaphysical exposition[1] of the content of the categorical imperative to the critical *Groundwork* of its possibility. Indeed, the third and last chapter, dealing with the "Transition from the Metaphysics of Morals to a Critique of Pure Practical Reason," contains essentially a *transcendental deduction* of the categorical imperative, based on the proof that every rational agent is endowed with a free will and on the assumption that all agents endowed with a free will necessarily see themselves as bound by moral law.[2]

I do not mean to say that the critique of pure practical reason that Kant contemplates here should be reduced to the deduction of the categorical imperative, and that this critique, therefore, had already been accomplished in the third chapter of the *Groundwork*. But it is quite clear that, without this deduction, it would not be possible to carry out the project described in the Introduction as consisting in the *Aufsuchung und Festsetzung*, that is, in "searching for" and "establishing" the principle of our moral judgments (*Groundwork*, 4:392).[3] Really, this investigation program can only be carried out if we move from the level attained in the second chapter, whose task is that of discovering and formulating the principle of our moral judgments (*Aufsuchung*), to the upper level occupied by a *critique* of pure practical reason, whose purpose is to establish the validity of this principle (*Festsetzung*) and thus to dispel the suspicion raised by the skeptical philosopher that our moral judgments might be based on a chimerical notion.

In the *Critique of Practical Reason*, however, a deduction of the principle of our moral judgments is declared not only impossible but also unnecessary, because the validity of the principle should be taken as an undisputable "fact of reason"—which might come as a surprise to anyone who took seriously Kant's worries about the possibility of skepticism in moral philosophy in his previous work. Consequently, Kant also abandons the project of a "critique of *pure* practical reason" that he had outlined and carried out in the central part of *Groundwork*, and replaces it by the less ambitious project of a "critique of *practical reason*." Such is nothing more than the examination of the principles that make it possible for reason to be practical of itself, that is, to determine our actions by itself, without taking heed of any interest based on needs stemming from our sensuous nature. Instead of a deduction, it involves only: (1) showing "through a fact"[4] that reason can determine the will by a synthetic principle *a priori*; and (2) defending this principle of reason against dialectical arguments that purport to reduce practical reason to empirically conditioned principles.

The abandonment of the attempt to give a deduction by having recourse to a fact of reason did not satisfy the majority of Kant's readers,[5] even those more inclined to look with favor on his philosophical views about morality. Indeed, the two basic points of the new doctrine seem to be quite unconvincing, perhaps because of the extreme concision with which they are formulated.

On the one hand, resignation to the impossibility of a deduction not only appears to entail relapsing into precritical dogmatism in moral philosophy, but also seems to be insufficiently argued for. Indeed, if the relevant passages are read with care, as we shall see, one gets the impression that Kant's explanation is insufficient on two counts: as an explanation of the *possibility* of giving a deduction in the case of the principles of *knowledge*, and as an explanation of the *impossibility* of giving a deduction of the principle of *morality*.

On the other hand, having recourse to a so-called fact of reason not only appears to entail a regression to dogmatism in moral philosophy, but the notion itself also seems to be obscure and even paradoxical. First, the meaning of this expression is ambiguous, since the word "fact" can be taken both in the cognitive sense of an immediately certain *truth* (suggesting a cognitivist account of morality), as well as in the volitional sense of an *act or deed* of reason (suggesting a decisionist account of morality). Besides, Kant gives at least five different characterizations of the expression "fact of reason," and it is not immediately clear how these characterizations relate to each other.[6] However, I will not deal here with these difficulties. I will take for granted that, even if the expression "fact of reason" might have for Kant the etymological sense of an *act* or *deed* of reason, what really matters and has to be considered when we investigate the validity of the principle said to be a fact of reason is the manner in which we become *aware* of it. I will suppose too, without proof, that the expression "fact of reason" characterizes in the first place our consciousness of moral law and that all other formulations may be derived by analysis from this initial formula.[7]

However, even if we were to make these suppositions about the meaning of the expression "fact of reason," the concept remains obscure and appears to involve some paradox. Indeed, if a fact of reason is a state of affairs or a truth established by reason, this cannot be achieved by any reasoning (as one would normally expect of a truth discovered by reason), since that would amount to giving a proof, which is deemed impossible and unnecessary. Consequently, it has to be taken as an immediately certain truth. Its immediate certainty, however, can be based neither on intuitive evidence, since it concerns a concept of reason, nor on mere conceptual clarification, since it concerns a synthetic proposition. What, then, might be its basis, since neither reasoning, nor intuitive evidence, much less conceptual clarification qualifies as such?

I shall therefore concentrate here on two questions that seem to me more important for an evaluation of Kant's critical project, namely: (1) Why is a deduction impossible or, in other words, what is the obstacle that from the start would make the project of giving a deduction an unfeasible one? (2) On what exactly is consciousness of the moral law based, or, to put it otherwise, why does the principle of our moral judgments force itself upon our will and what gives us the right to say that we are conscious of this as a *fact*?

I believe that these are the decisive points for a correct understanding and evaluation of Kant's theory. In fact, the *impossibility of a deduction* appears, on the one hand, to threaten Kant's project insofar as it has a *critical* aim. How can we ascertain the right to distinguish between a *moral* point of view and a merely *pragmatic* point of view for evaluation of our actions, if we must in the end give up all attempts to establish the validity of the principle of moral evaluation and accept it on the faith of a bald assertion? On the other hand, the appeal to a *fact of reason* as an ersatz, a second-best substitute for a desired but impossible deduction, seems only to consecrate the abandonment of the critical project with a barely disguised backsliding into dogmatism. Against these appearances, however, I want to explore the possibility that, correctly understood, none of Kant's points do really endanger his critical project in moral philosophy. Of course, to achieve a correct understanding, it will be necessary to explore and expand Kant's explanations, which one must admit to be, at least, too brief and dense to be quite satisfactory.

The Impossibility of a Deduction

Under what conditions is a deduction possible or, eventually, impossible? The explanation we find in *Critique of Practical Reason* (5:46) can be reduced to three points. The *first* one explains what a deduction is, defining it as a proof of the objective validity of a synthetical principle a priori (whatever it may be) through the demonstration that this principle is a condition of possibility of the *knowledge* of the objective nature of that which may be *given* independently from it. The *second* one explains why a deduction of the synthetic principles *of understanding* is possible, by claiming that it is possible to prove that these principles are conditions of possibility of the knowledge of the objective nature of that which can be given "from elsewhere" (*anderswärts*) *in sense intuition.* The *third* one, finally, explains why a deduction of moral law is impossible by claiming that it is not possible to prove that moral law is a condition of the possibility of knowledge of anything that might exist independently from it.

I submit that, read with attention, this explanation proves to be insufficient both as an explanation of the *possibility* of giving a deduction of the principles of the understanding and as an explanation of the *impossibility* of giving a deduction of moral law. It is easy to see that the first point is based on Kant's official explanation of the deduction of the pure concepts of the understanding, in the first *Critique*, as consisting in the proof that these are conditions of possibility, not of intuitions, but rather of experience.[8] Now, this explanation has an obvious difficulty that his interpreters do not leave unnoticed. Indeed, according to this explanation, a deduction depends on the premise that we do in fact have what Kant calls "experience," that is to say, knowledge of the objective nature of that which is given in sense intuition (or, more simply, of the objects given in sense intuition).[9] For that very reason it cannot be accepted as a proof of the *objective validity* of the principles of understanding by anyone who puts into question the possibility of objective knowledge, and therefore can at best be accepted only as a proof of the a priori nature of the principles of understanding on which experience (supposed possible) is based.

However, the starting point of the argument actually developed in the deduction of the first *Critique* is not the presumption of the possibility of *experience* in the sense of *objective knowledge* (expressed, to use Kant's terminology of the *Prolegomena*, in "judgments of experience"), but rather empirical *consciousness* of what is given in intuition (expressed in "judgments of perception"). Given this premise, the deduction may be broadly divided in two large steps,[10] the first one being the proof of the necessary relation that *empirical consciousness* of what is given in sense intuition has to *self-consciousness*, and the second being the demonstration of the necessary relation between self-consciousness and the power of making *objective judgments* (in conformity with categories and the respective principles of understanding).

This argument derives its plausibility from the fact that it does not seem to be possible to deny the objective validity of the a priori pure concepts and principles of understanding without denying at the same time what they make possible, namely, experience, and, with this, epistemic self-consciousness and empirical consciousness of one's own epistemic states. Thus, supposing all steps of this argument are really correct and it is possible to prove, as purported by Kant, (1) that there is a necessary connection between empirical consciousness of sense intuitions and self-consciousness, and (2) that there is also a necessary connection between the latter and empirical knowledge of objects, one could not accept the possibility of having *consciousness of sense intuitions* without accepting at the same time the possibility of having *knowledge of the objects* of sense intuitions, that is, experience.

The canonical formula of the deduction as a proof of the objective validity of the categories and principles of the understanding by means of the proof that these are conditions of possibility of experience should be understood, therefore, as an abbreviation of a much more complex argument than that immediately suggested by it. In consequence, the derived formulation found in the second *Critique* (as a proof that the principles of the understanding are conditions of the possibility of knowledge of the objective nature of something that is given from elsewhere in sense intuition) should be understood as an attempt to prove that the *validity of these principles* and, with them, *knowledge* of objects *made possible by these principles*, are presupposed by empirical consciousness of the intuitions in which objects are given.

Let us consider now the explanation given in the same passage of the *impossibility* of a deduction of moral law. According to this explanation, it is impossible to give a deduction of the latter because moral law does not concern knowledge of objects that might be given "from elsewhere" to reason, but rather knowledge of something whose existence depends on moral law itself, that is, on the will insofar as it operates in conformity with moral law.

This explanation seems to be based on the sole observation that principles of the understanding are conditions of *knowledge*, but not of the *existence* of the objects that come to be known in conformity with them (since the objects known must be given in sense intuition), whereas moral law is a condition not only of knowledge, but also of the existence of objects known in conformity with it (because these cannot be given in sense intuition). Indeed, moral law is a principle of practical reason, and of practical reason one can say that it makes possible not only knowledge, but also the existence itself of certain objects, namely, the fact of there being morally good or morally evil objects, which cannot be found as such in sense intuition, so to speak given "from elsewhere" to practical reason.

Now, this comparison does not appear to be quite in order. *On the one hand*, it is not true without qualification that the objects of *practical* reason (namely, whatever is liable of being evaluated as *good or evil*) and, in particular, that the objects of *pure* practical reason (namely, whatever may be evaluated as *morally good or evil*) might not be given independently from their principles in sense intuition. Good and evil are predicates that we apply to actions that are possible by means of the causality of our will, that is, in conformity with the representation of our ends, or maxims. Now, insofar as they are determined in conformity with maxims, actions that one evaluates as morally good or evil can exist independently from moral evaluation. Indeed, we might even admit that, in a certain sense, they might also be given in sense intuition, insofar as they are or involve physical actions or motions (known by the external sense) and consciousness of ends, or purposes (known by the internal sense). Thus, for example, the act of maliciously killing a man, which is murder, exists for practical reason only insofar as it is morally evaluated as evil. But the act of killing itself may be said to exist independently of moral evaluation insofar it is a physical action intentionally brought about and that may be described as such (and eventually assessed as instrumentally good or evil for one's purposes) without moral evaluation.

On the other hand, it is not true without qualification that objects known in conformity with principles of the understanding might exist as such independently of the understanding. They certainly can exist as appearances (*Erscheinungen*), that is, as "indeterminate objects of empirical intuition" (*Pure Reason*, A20/B34), but not as determinate objects, that is, things or physical events existing or coming about independently from the intuitions through which we become acquainted with them. Indeed, one can say that things and events, or objects of experience in general, are, in a similar way to objects of practical reason, products of a constitutive activity of the understanding (subsumption of intuitions under concepts). It is true that principles of the understanding are not a condition of the appearances themselves, but they certainly are a condition of the *objects of knowledge* as such. That is precisely the Kantian doctrine condensed in the formula: "The conditions of the *possibility of experience* in general are at same time conditions of the *possibility of the objects of experience*, and on this account have objective validity in a synthetic judgment *a priori*" (*Pure Reason*, A158/B197).[11]

Were this all we had to go by, we might say that our actions, insofar as they can be known as morally good or evil, are not on a very different standing than the data of sense intuition, insofar as these can be recognized as appearances of objects distinct from them. *On the one hand*, the concepts and the principle of pure practical reason are not necessary conditions of the actions to which they apply (since the capacity of making moral evaluations is not a condition of performing actions, even rational ones), just as the concepts and principles of understanding are not conditions of the appearances to which they apply (since the capacity to use concepts is not a condition of intuiting appearances). *On the other hand*, exactly as concepts and the principle of pure practical reason are necessary conditions of knowing actions as morally good or evil, in the same way the concepts and principles of understanding are necessary conditions of knowing what is given in sense intuition as appearances of objects that we take to exist independently from them.

So, should we leave things at this point, without further commentary, we would still lack a satisfactory explanation of the presumed impossibility of giving a deduction of moral law. Indeed, if moral law relative to actions is on a par with the principles of understanding relative to the data of sense intuition, and if this piece of information is all we have to guide us, there is no reason to suppose that a deduction, deemed possible in one case, must be impossible in the other.

What then is lacking in Kant's explanation of the impossibility of a deduction of moral law? I think we can find a clue toward solving our problem, if we pay attention to what was found missing in the explanation of the *possibility* of a deduction of the principles of the understanding. Indeed, we saw that a deduction of the pure concepts and synthetic principles a priori of the understanding cannot be based on the sole claim that the objective validity of these concepts and principles is a condition of experience (understood as the knowledge of the objective nature of what is given in sense intuition). The reason was that it depended too, if we were to avoid skepticism, on the proof that experience has a necessary relation to self-consciousness, which is, in its turn, necessarily related to the empirical consciousness of what is given in intuition and to the subjective judgments ("judgments of perception") in which we express this consciousness. The crucial point in the deduction is, then, the claim that empirical *consciousness* of our sense intuitions has a necessary relation to our self-consciousness as subjects capable of making objective judgments, that is to say, judgments about the objects of our experience.

Now, if the principle and the concepts of pure practical reason were indeed in the same standing as the pure concepts and synthetic principles a priori of understanding (relative to the items to which both apply), then one would have to accept the possibility of giving an *analogous* deduction of the pure concepts and a priori principles of both the understanding and practical reason. Such a deduction, however, would have to be a proof that moral law, or consciousness of its validity for our will, should be seen as a condition of being conscious of our actions insofar they are possible through our will.

Let us consider then, how, according to Kant, we may be said to have consciousness of our actions. According to his explanation, a human being is conscious of its actions as determined by its power of choice (its *Willkür*, or *arbitrium*, that is to say, its *will* in the strict sense), which may be affected but not necesssitated by sensuous impulses, insofar as a reason furnishes its will with "imperatives" (practical propositions stating what is good or evil to do). That is a point that Kant made clear, already in the first *Critique*, in the context of his analysis of practical freedom, that is, considered as the property of a power of choice (*arbitrium*) that is *sensitivum* (in the sense that it may be affected by impulses of the sensibility), but not *brutum* (that is, not determined by these impulses).[12] The human being, says Kant there, knows itself through "pure apperception, and indeed in actions and inner determinations" that "cannot be ascribed do to the receptivity of sensibility" and therefore have to be taken as effected through a "causality of reason" that becomes "clear" to us "from the imperatives" that it proposes to our power of choice.[13]

This allows the conclusion that, in Kant's conception, imperatives are the condition under which a rational agent is aware of its own actions. However, this does not certainly suffice for a deduction of moral law, since it is necessary to distinguish two kinds of imperatives according to their prescriptive force: pragmatic imperatives (which are subjective principles, or maxims, of our will) and moral imperatives (which are objective principles, or laws, for our will). Thus, if we wanted to present moral imperatives as such as a condition of being conscious of our actions in general (as it would be necessary for a deduction), it would be necessary to disqualify pragmatic imperatives as a *sufficient* condition for being conscious of acting consciousness and to make their existence depend on the existence of moral imperatives. Which would boil down to claiming that one could not be conscious of acting in conformity with pragmatic imperatives if one could not also be conscious of acting on a moral imperative (or rather, in such a way that it could be possible to evaluate it according to a moral imperative).

Now, this seems to be not only counterintuitive but also conceptually incorrect. It seems to be counterintuitive because one can easily give examples of individuals capable of responding to sanctions and acting on pragmatic imperatives, but apparently incapable of making moral judgments, such as little children and psychopaths. Moreover, it certainly is conceptually incorrect since pragmatic and moral imperatives are hierarchically related, so that the former serves as a basis for the application of the latter but not vice versa. Indeed, pragmatic imperatives formulate possible maxims, or subjective principles with which we directly evaluate our actions (or the particular end of each action), regarding its compatibility with other ends. The moral imperative, on the contrary, is an objective principle with which we evaluate our own pragmatic imperatives concerning its compatibility with the imperatives of anyone else. In this sense, it can be said to constitute a restrictive condition for the adoption of pragmatic imperatives. Thus, the relation that subsists between them is exactly the reverse of what would be necessary for a deduction, since it is the moral imperative that presupposes the existence of pragmatic imperatives, and not vice versa.

This point is clear enough in itself and it is no wonder that we do not find in Kant any effort to carry out a deduction following this plan, at least in an obvious manner. Kant did follow, all the same, a similar strategy in some of his attempts. These are based on two considerations: (1) on the reciprocity of the concepts of freedom and morality; and (2) on the spontaneity of our judgments (cognitive as well as practical) insofar as they are determined according to reasons and not by causes (provisional argument in *Groundwork* III and several *Reflections*),[14] or at least insofar as the power of judgment is connected in us with practical reason, or the will (conclusive argument in *Groundwork* III).[15]

Kant gave up his first attempts after convincing himself (as recorded in certain *Reflections* to which Dieter Henrich was the first to call attention) of the unfeasibility of deriving "transcendental" from "logical freedom," that is to say, of the impossibility of deriving freedom of the will from the mere spontaneity of judgment.[16] Indeed, it is quite possible to think of a subject as being free in its *judgments*, in the sense of not being causally determined to judge as it does, but not free in its *will*, in the sense of being causally determined to act (as in the case of compulsion) or, at least, in the sense of having do adopt the maxims on which it bases its decisions by force of a superior causality it is not aware of.[17]

Kant's last attempt to give a deduction is set down in *Groundwork* III. It is based in the endeavor to bridge the gap separating logical freedom (spontaneity of judgment) from transcendental freedom (freedom of the will) by means of an additional premise. This premise consisted in the claim that consciousness of the spontaneity of judgment implies consciousness of belonging to an intelligible world, and was meant to support the conclusion that any individual capable of judging and endowed with a will must see itself as a belonging to an intelligible word and therefore as endowed with a free will. The problem with this proof strategy lies, of course, in the appeal to the concept of an "intelligible world," which is an indeterminate concept and, therefore, allows no positive determination of whatever object to which it may be applied. So it is not surprising that Kant abandoned too this last attempt to rescue his deduction, and, even though he did not make explicit his reasons for doing so, we may presume that it concerned the use of the concept of an "intelligible world."

Moral Law and the Fact of Reason

Having considered what might have been Kant's reasons for asserting the impossibility of a deduction of the moral principle, let us tackle now our second difficulty concerning the notion of a moral "fact of reason." In the case of cognitive and aesthetic judgments, one can say that acknowledging the impossibility of giving a deduction of their principle would amount to espousing skepticism about the possibility of making such judgments, that is, skepticism as to the possibility of distinguishing them from subjective judgments about the mental states we find ourselves in when we purport to make cognitive or aesthetic judgments. However, according to Kant's new doctrine, this does not hold for moral judgments. Recognition of the impossibility of giving a deduction of their principle does in no way lead to skepticism about our right to make moral judgments as something different from subjective evaluations, and this precisely because the principle they are based on allegedly forces itself upon our will as a fact against which no philosophical argument can prevail. The difficulty we have to solve now is explaining what Kant actually means when he speaks of a "fact of reason" and why he considers moral law, or consciousness of moral law, a fact of reason.

A first step toward this explanation can be given by considering Kant's idea that moral law is expressed for us in a proposition that we have to take, as in the case of the principles of understanding, as being at the same time synthetic and a priori. Indeed, if moral law is not to be understood as an analytic proposition, it cannot be a merely conceptual matter, hence it must be in some sense a matter of fact, that is to say, something that happens to be so, but could be otherwise, since it is not logically impossible to think the contrary.

Support for this explanation may be found in a passage in *Judgment*.[18] Kant makes extensive use of the German word *Tatsache* (as well of the Latin expression *res facti*, both employed in the eighteenth century for the English expression *matter of fact*) in order to characterize both empirical propositions about things and their properties, and mathematical propositions about magnitudes of things and the idea of freedom.

Of course, this may only be accepted as an initial step, since the explanation given is not sufficiently specific in order to characterize with precision the sense in which consciousness of moral law is called a fact of reason. Indeed, other synthetic a priori propositions are not considered by Kant as facts of reason, since they have to be established by a deduction (as in the case of the principles of the understanding) or exhibited in pure intuition (as in the case of the axioms of mathematics).

A second attempt to find an answer to our question can be based on the supposition that we know moral law (insofar as it determines our will, that is to say, binds and motivates it) as a consequence of the effect that it produces on our sensitivity (*Gefühl*), namely, a feeling of respect, that distinguishes itself from all other feelings because it allegedly is the only one that can, in some way, be known a priori. Such is the essential point of Henrich's explanation in his classic article on Kant's expression "fact of reason," "Der Begriff der sittlichen Einsicht und Kant's Lehre der Vernunft."

Two points can be made in favor of this approach: (1) The passage in the *Critique of Practical Reason* introducing the notion of a "fact of reason" does not exclude, at least in an obvious manner, the possibility that consciousness of moral law might be based on a kind of moral *feeling*. What it excludes is the possibility of thinking the fact of reason as a truth that we come to know thanks to some kind of *intuition*, be it intellectual or sense intuition. (2) The feeling of respect is, in Kant's analysis, one that (actually, the only one) can be known a priori[19] and because of this it would seem to be a sufficient basis for a fact of reason.

Henrich, to be sure, is careful enough not to identify Kant's notion of a *feeling* of respect to moral law with the traditional notion of a *sensus moralis*, although he does see in Kant's doctrine of a moral "fact of reason" a halfway return to Hutcheson's position, that is to say, to a notion of the moral imperative as something that cannot be based on arguments of theoretical reason.[20] However, in Henrich's understanding (as exposed before propounding his interpretation of Kant's doctrine), the moral imperative is nonetheless an object of a moral *insight* (*sittliche Einsicht*) in which an intellectual and an emotional element are closely bound—although in a manner that no philosopher has yet managed to explain. Nevertheless, this intellectual component is later presented by Henrich (in the context of his interpretation of Kant's doctrine) as being independent in an important sense from the emotional component. Indeed, it concerns *knowledge about the content of moral law* (namely, the requirement that maxims on which our actions are based might be universalized as a condition of morality) and it can be established not only independently of the emotional component, but also, according to Henrich, by *theoretical* reason alone.[21] The latter concerns the *basis of obligation and the moral motive*, namely, the feeling of respect: we acknowledge the law as an imperative for our will because we feel bound by it, and we feel bound by it because we feel respect for it.[22] Thus, according to Henrich, the fact of reason, or the fact that we are conscious of moral law as valid for our will, is an object of moral insight only insofar it is necessary to ascribe to theoretical reason our *knowledge about the content* of the law, whereas it is necessary to ascribe to *feeling* the fact that we acknowledge the law as *binding* and motivating our will. To sum it up: for Henrich, it is a *fact of reason* that we are conscious of moral law as requiring that our maxims can be taken as universal laws, but it is a *fact of feeling*, rather than of reason, that we are conscious of moral law as binding and motivating our will. Henrich, to be sure, does not use the expression "fact of feeling," but I think it does not distort in any way his interpretation.

To my mind this explanation is open to two serious objections, since it appears to imply: (1) taking a sensible content (*feeling*) as an adequate means for exhibiting a concept of reason (*moral law*), that is, showing that it applies to our will; and (2) misunderstanding the real nature of the moral motive, as conceived by Kant, and consequently assimilating the moral imperative to a pragmatic imperative.

The basis for these objections is the consideration that, in Kant's conception, all moral feelings, including the feeling of respect, are effects produced on our sensibility by consciousness of moral law. Because of this, they do not differ qua effects on our sensibility from any other feeling, since they are like the others mere affections, that is, affective contents of which we are aware as the mental states of pleasure or displeasure.[23] They certainly may be said to be intellectual as to their origin, but not in themselves, the notion of an "intellectual feeling" being, one could say, a *contradictio in adiecto*. Thus, the characterization of moral feeling as a nonpathological effect in no way means that it is not, as a feeling, sensuous, but only that it is a feeling brought about in our sensibility by our own spontaneity (*selbstgewirkt*), as a result of moral knowledge, different from the feelings that are related to our needs and the satisfaction thereof.[24]

If the feeling of respect, however nonpathological and self-effected (*selbstgewirkt*)[25] it may be, is an affection of our sensibility, it is hard to see how both objections could be answered. Indeed, not only is the *content* of moral law (which Henrich is ready to accept as known by "theoretical reason") an idea, or a concept of reason, but the representation of moral law itself as a *duty* or *obligation*, that is, as a *categorical imperative*, is also a concept of reason. Now, a concept of reason cannot, as a matter of principle, be exhibited by means of any content of *sensibility*, irrespective of whether this content has a representative value (that is, gives us some information about the objects that cause them, as in the case of *sensations*) or not (as in the case of *feelings* and *emotions* that inform us solely about the state of mind in which we happen to be).

Further, one might also object that, in making the feeling of respect a condition for the acknowledgment of moral law (or of its content) as being imperative for our will, Henrich inadvertently assimilates the moral imperative to pragmatic imperatives. Indeed, what characterizes pragmatic imperatives is precisely the fact that they are hypothetical, that is, that they presuppose as their condition a feeling of pleasure or displeasure with the representation of the prescribed action. Therefore, if the condition for acknowledging the principle of universalization of maxims is a feeling, the specific quality of this feeling is of no importance for determining the imperative force of this principle, since its relation with this principle is conceived of in the same manner as the relation of the feeling of pleasure or displeasure with pragmatic principles, namely, as a relation in which a certain feeling is a previous condition for the acknowledgment of the principle as having an imperative force for our will. In this case, the possibility of making a formal distinction between moral and pragmatic imperatives is no more available. Now, for Kant, as we know, this distinction concerns the form of the imperative, since the former must be taken as a *categorical* imperative, that is, prescribing what is good, or what we ought to do, independent of a presupposed object of the will and of any feeling of pleasure taken as a previous condition. To be sure, the feeling of respect has to be thought of as a *necessary consequence* of our acknowledging moral law as an imperative for our will, but precisely this circumstance makes it useless as an independent criterion for our consciousness of moral law and, consequently, as an explanation of how we can become conscious of a moral law.

Indeed, the *first* objection is that moral law is an *idea*, that is, a concept of reason that as such cannot be exhibited by any sense content, whether this content may have a representative value (giving us some information about the objects to which they are causally or intentionally related, as in the case of those we call *sensations*) or not (as in the case of *feelings* and *emotions* that inform us only about the state we find ourselves in). The *second* objection is that moral feeling presupposes consciousness of moral law and, for that very reason, cannot serve as an independent criterion for recognition of moral law. Indeed, in order to know that a determinate feeling involving inclination and aversion is precisely the moral feeling of *respect* (rather than, for example, that kind of feeling involving fear and love that any tyrant wants to instill in their subjects), it is necessary to know that it is caused by moral law, since it is not feeling so inclined toward its object that turns a precept into a moral law, but, on the contrary, it is the awareness that the precept is a moral law for our will that allows taking the feeling inspired by it as moral feeling. This objection is in fact the same made by Kant to Hutcheson's theory of moral sense, so that accepting, as Henrich does, that Kant's notion of a moral "fact of reason" represents in a way a return to Hutcheson's standpoint is making his theory inconsistent.

To be sure, Kant did speak, in *Groundwork*, of the feeling of respect as the incentive for morality, and this might appear to give some plausibility to Henrich's interpretation of moral motivation. However, it should be remembered that respect is analyzed in *Groundwork* as the "mere consciousness of the subordination of my will under a law, without mediation of other influences upon my sense." Consequently, the feeling of respect has to be understood as an "effect of the law upon the subject" (insofar as one is conscious of it), and not as a "cause" of the law, or rather of its being recognized as a law for my will.[26] *Critique of Practical Reason* dispels any doubt we might still entertain by presenting the moral law itself (or rather our consciousness of the moral law) as the sole moral incentive and by analyzing the feeling of respect, not as a motive for morality, but as morality itself, directly motivated by consciousness of the law.[27]

Among ourselves, Zeljko Loparic offered a variant of Henrich's interpretation as part of his "semantic-transcendental" reconstruction of Kant's philosophy as a problem-solving theory in the domain of practical philosophy.[28] According to this reconstruction, the task of "transcendental semantics" is to establish sense and reference of a priori concepts by showing how they can be they exhibited in sensuous contents, which in the case of practical reason are to be found not in sense intuition, but in feeling. Thus, the feeling of respect makes it possible to sensify the a priori concept of moral law and thereby to relate it to certain objects, namely, actions that can be performed by our will. Kant's expression "fact of reason" is accordingly interpreted as the awareness that moral law is in fact valid for our will insofar it affects our sensibility with a feeling of respect.

This interpretation, of course, is exposed to similar objections to those made above against Henrich. Thus, it has, first, to presuppose what Kant formally denies, namely, the possibility of exhibiting concepts of reason, that is, of establishing its objective reality by means of sensuous contents. Second, by appealing to a moral feeling in order to secure objective reality to moral law, it must presuppose what is allegedly explained by it, namely, awareness of moral law, since the feeling of respect is based on it, insofar as it is an effect rather than a cause of it. However, it is also open to an additional objection, since it implies what Kant thought to be made superfluous by his theory of the consciousness of moral law as fact of reason, namely, a deduction of moral law. Indeed, if moral feelings are to give objective reality to the concepts of pure practical reason, it must be possible for them to be given independently of these concepts. In this case, however, one would have to accept as satisfied that condition refused by Kant for a deduction, namely, the existence of items given "from elsewhere" and making possible a deduction of the pure concepts of practical reason.

A third approach to the problem has been proposed by Henry Allison. Besides its ingenuity, his interpretation has the merit of trying to show that Kant's appeal to a "fact of reason" neither rests on "sheer assertion" nor represents a "reversion to a discredited standpoint" (presumably Hutcheson's, as admitted by Henrich), but rather "offers the best available strategy for authenticating the moral law and establishing the reality of transcendental freedom."[29]

Although the allusion to a "reversion to a discredited standpoint" may possibly contain a veiled objection to Henrich, Allison's interpretation resembles Henrich's in one important aspect. Indeed, in a way similar to that of Henrich, Allison distinguishes between two tasks: that of justifying the claim that we are conscious of moral law as a fact of reason and, therefore, as *valid for every rational agent*, and that of showing that moral law is *obligatory for our* human will. Differently from Henrich, though, Allison thinks that the first task can be accomplished by the doctrine of the "fact of reason," if we understand it as a consequence of Kant's exposition of the concept of morality, whereas the second task has to be solved by a deduction of freedom.

Allison sees the Exposition as starting from an indisputable fact, which even the moral skeptic would have to accept. Such is the fact that rational agents, capable of deliberating, submit their deliberation to moral constraints, and understand the principle on which these moral constraints are based according to the "typified" form of the categorical imperative, which Kant formulates as the requirement to act on maxims that can be regarded as laws of nature.

What is open to doubt and has to be proven by the Exposition is that this fact is a fact *of reason*, that is, that the principle underlying moral constraints on the adoption of maxims has its origin in pure, that is, nonempirically conditioned reason. This task is precisely the task of the Exposition, which accomplishes it by proving that the principle of moral constraint can only be a self-legislated principle of reason. Thus, Kant's claim that our consciousness of moral law must be taken as a fact of reason, far from being a sheer assertion, finds a most satisfactory justification in the Exposition.

However, the argument showing that consciousness of moral law is a fact of reason does not suffice, according to Allison, to establish the *obligatory* force of the moral law. That is so because, even though one may argue that anyone conscious of the moral law as a fact of reason must thereby take an interest in moral law, it is not possible to infer from that alone that one has the capacity to be actually motivated by the moral law. The reason is that it is logically possible to think of our will as being overpowered by stronger motives stemming from needs of our sensuous nature, consequently as not being free in the sense that is required for acting morally.

In order to prove that the moral law is obligatory for our will, it is necessary to have recourse to a deduction of the freedom of our will, based on a transcendental-idealistic premise. Such is the premise that a rational agent conscious of the moral law as a fact of reason necessarily sees himself as a member of an intelligible world.

The starting point of this deduction is the fact that we necessarily have, as rational beings, an interest in moral law, which is a point that we may take as established in the Exposition. From this, it is possible to derive by analysis that we can attribute to our will at least the capacity to be motivated by moral law, consequently that we may attribute to our will freedom in the positive sense of autonomy. Now, this implies that we necessarily see ourselves as members of an intelligible word, therefore that we also can legitimately attribute to our will freedom in the negative sense of being independent of sensuous motives and, thus, the capacity of acting morally.

Allison's interpretation finds important textual support. On its behalf speaks in the first place Kant's assertion that the analysis of our moral judgments suffice to prove that moral law is an undeniable fact of reason.[30] Besides, it is also backed by a remark (*R*7201, 19:275), to which Allison attaches great importance and in which we read that the possibility of pure practical reason cannot be "understood a priori," but has to be "inferred" (*geschlossen*) from something that can only spring from it. "Moral laws are of this nature," continues Kant, "and these must be proven in the manner in which we prove that the representations of space and time are a priori, with the difference being that the latter are intuitions and the former mere concepts of reason."[31]

Allison's interpretation runs into trouble when we consider the hypothetical nature of Kant's argument in the Exposition. It becomes apparent then that his interpretation is exposed to two objections that are fatal for his professed intent of giving an effective defense of Kant's doctrine of the "fact of reason." The objections are that he (1) misconstrues the target of moral skepticism, and consequently (2) overlooks the hypothetical nature of Kant's argument in the Exposition (or at least the fact that it is, without additional considerations, irrevocably hypothetical, and therefore problematical).

The hypothetical nature of Kant's argument in the Exposition is a consequence of the fact that its starting point is a "given concept" of morality, and therefore depends on acceptance of this concept. Thus, even if Kant's doctrine on the consciousness of moral law as a fact of reason could be taken as sufficiently established by the Exposition, the assertion of this fact would still be of a hypothetical nature. Thus, we should not say that the Exposition establishes the strong categorical claim: consciousness of the moral law is a fact of reason, but only the weaker hypothetical claim: if we accept Kant's initial concept of morality, then consciousness of the moral law is a fact of reason. This makes a big difference, because in hypothetical inferences both antecedent and consequent are stated only as problematical judgments, so that even the skeptic who doubts both can accept the hypothetical statement as a whole if the consequence holds.[32]

However, the objection is not, so far, fatal for Allison's interpretation, since he holds that Kant's initial premise is not in itself problematic, and therefore can be asserted categorically, so that all its consequences, up to the statement that consciousness of the moral law is a fact of reason, can also be stated categorically. Thus, he may easily concede the objection that Kant's argument is hypothetical, and still maintain that the consequent can be independently asserted in a categorical way, since the antecedent is not (in his opinion) problematic in itself and can also be asserted categorically.

However, is it really so?

As seen above, Allison holds that the real target of the skeptic is not the fact that we make moral judgments and take them to express moral constraints on our practical deliberations. What the skeptic doubts is, in Allison's opinion, only the fact that moral judgments rest on a principle that is self-legislated by pure reason (and must therefore be taken as a fact of reason). I do not quite agree with that. Of course, the fact that we make moral judgments and that these judgments express some kind of constraint upon our choices is not open to debate. However, the nature of these constraints can be the object of discussion, and the target of the skeptic's doubt is precisely the way in which Kant characterizes the nature of these moral constraints.

Kant's starting point in the Exposition is the concept of morality as something that is unconditionally good, or good without restriction (the "good will"). This concept involves (or rather, is based on) the supposition that judgments about what is morally good are specifically distinct and therefore irreducible to pragmatic judgments, that is, judgments about what is good in the sense of being agreeable or useful. Since what is agreeable or useful is good only on a subjective condition, and since the morally good is from the start presumed to be irreducible to the pragmatically good, the morally good has to be conceived of as good independently of any subjective condition and, in this sense, as being unconditionally good. Therefrom two consequences follow: first, that the morally good cannot be restricted by any consideration concerning whatever may be useful or agreeable to us (since it is unconditionally good). Second, that it can be a restrictive condition, that is, a constraint limiting our choices of whatever is useful or agreeable to us (in case of conflict of what is morally good with what is useful or agreeable).

Now, why should we accept this initial decision by Kant? Even if we can take it as the object of common knowledge, why should the skeptic, speaking on behalf of an enlightened reason, not question the idea that the morally good is irreducible to what is useful or agreeable to us? Without an answer to this question and a justification of his initial claim, Kant's argument in the Exposition remains irrevocably hypothetical.

Kant was of course aware of this, since he demanded additional and independent argument from the deduction of freedom in *Groundwork* III. This argument failed according to most interpreters, including Allison. Allison, however, did offer an interpretation of the deduction of freedom in the *Critique of Practical Reason*, purporting to prove the obligatory character of the law of reason (whose reality as a fact of reason he took to be already proven in the Exposition). This deduction of freedom, however, depends on premises taken from the Exposition, either directly (the fact that one necessarily takes an interest in moral law as self-legislated by pure reason) or indirectly (the fact that interest in a self-legislated moral law attests membership in an intelligible world and thereby the independence of our will relative to motives conflicting with the moral law and its capacity to act morally). However, we saw that the argument in the Exposition is a hypothetical one; consequently, we must take all arguments based on it as being equally hypothetical. The inevitable conclusion is, then, that Allison's interpretation of the deduction of freedom does not add enough to revoke the hypothetical nature of argument in the Exposition.

However, even if Allison has failed in his attempt to save Kant's doctrine of the "fact of reason," to the regret of all Kantian philosophers, like myself, he did show where to look for a solution, in case we have not yet lost all hope of finding one. As already conceded, if there is a solution, the exposition of the concept of morality is the only place where we can look for a clue, since the exclusion of a deduction of moral law leaves us with no other alternative.

Kant claims, in a passage already quoted,[33] that mere analysis of our moral judgments suffices to prove that the moral law (the principle they are based on) is an "undeniable fact." Kant's claim is hardly acceptable if this proof depends on previous acceptance of a determinate concept of morality, namely, the concept of our moral judgments as irreducible to pragmatic judgments and consequently as concerning what is unconditionally good. The reason is that, since we can deny this presupposition, we can very well deny its consequences too. However, Kant's claim becomes quite understandable if we take it to mean that mere analysis of our moral judgments suffices to show that they rest on an immediately certain principle, since we cannot deny or demand proof for what is immediately certain. Our problem becomes, then, that of showing why we should accept the principle of our moral judgments to be immediately certain, that is, certain by itself, without need of proof.

There are only two classes of judgments, according to Kant, that can be accepted as immediately certain. On the one hand, analytic judgments, which are true in virtue of the meaning of their terms and therefore do not depend on our acquaintance with any instance of the concepts signified by them in order to be ascertained as true, but only on the *clarity of the concepts* (that is, on a clear grasp of the marks that constitute the content of the concepts). On the other hand, objectively valid synthetic judgments based on *intuitive evidence*, insofar as their objects can be given in empirical intuition (as in the case of empirical objects), or whose concepts can be exhibited a priori in pure intuition (as in the case of mathematical objects).[34] Our problem, now, is that the principle of moral judgments does not seem to fit into any of these classes, since we must think of it, according to Kant, as an objectively valid *synthetic* (though also a priori) proposition, which, however, cannot be based on any sort of intuitive evidence.[35]

This seems to confront Kant's doctrine of the "fact of reason" with an insurmountable difficulty. How is it possible to ascribe to this fact *immediate certainty* if it can have neither the immediate certainty that belongs to analytic judgments (*conceptual clearness*), nor that belonging to (some) synthetic judgments (*intuitive evidence*)?

A way out of this dilemma becomes possible, to my mind, if we take into account two aspects of Kant's theory, brought forward in the Exposition, but which perhaps have not yet received all due importance (at least in discussing Kant's doctrine of the "fact of reason"). These are: (1) the distinction made by Kant between the moral principle considered as a *law* for a perfect will and as an *imperative* for an imperfect will;[36] and (2) the circumstance that the moral imperative alone is characterized as being expressed by a synthetic proposition, moral law being characterized (at least by implication) as an analytic proposition.[37]

It is easy to understand why the *moral imperative* is characterized as a synthetic proposition. Indeed, in Kant's theory, it connects with the concept of an imperfect will the other concept of a line of action required by the moral principle (namely, to act on maxims that can be taken as universal laws). Now, an imperfect will is a will that does not necessarily conform to precepts of reason, either because of ignorance or because of weakness. Thus, a necessary and sufficient condition in order to have an imperfect will is acting on maxims of any sort, moral or nonmoral. That is why it is impossible to extract moral duty analytically, that is, the necessity to act on the kind of maxims required by the moral principle, from the concept of an imperfect will. As seen above, the impossibility of a deduction of the moral law is precisely a consequence of this. Indeed, acting on maxims, whichever they may be, is a necessary and sufficient condition for any rational agent to be aware of what it does, for that very reason it is impossible to prove that, in order to explain the possibility for a rational agent to be conscious of what it does, it would be necessary to accept the moral principle as a presupposition of this.

Despite disagreement of important interpreters,[38] I think that there are good reasons to hold that moral *law* has to be taken as an analytic proposition. Indeed, moral law connects with the concept of a perfect will the idea of acting as required by the moral principle (which is, as we know, acting in accordance with maxims that may be universalized). Now, *will* is in Kant's conception nothing other than *practical reason*, that is, the capacity to determine our actions in accordance with precepts formulated by reason itself.[39] Thus, a *perfect will* is a *perfectly rational will* and a perfectly rational will is a *will that infallibly conforms to precepts of reason* that it necessarily knows (otherwise it would not be a perfect will). But acting on maxims required by the *moral principle* is a *precept of reason*, since only the adoption of such maxims can be justified in a valid manner for all rational agents. For that very reason—one can see now—it is a necessary and sufficient condition for having a perfect will to act on such maxims as are required by the moral principle. As a consequence, if it is conceded that acting on maxims as required by the moral principle is a condition for having a perfectly rational will, then it must be analytically true for a perfect will that it necessarily acts in accordance with maxims such as required by the moral principle.[40]

The distinction between the categorical imperative, taken as expressed by a synthetic proposition, and the moral law, as expressed by an analytic proposition, gives us all the orientation we need in order to find a way out of the dilemma described above. The dilemma was a consequence, as we saw, of Kant's attributing to the principle of our moral judgments an *immediate certainty* that it apparently could not have, since it could neither possess the immediate certainty of synthetic judgments (*intuitive evidence*), nor the immediate certainty of analytic judgments (*conceptual clarity*). Now, the distinction between what Kant calls a *law* and what he calls an *imperative* allows us to think of the imperative as a consequence of being aware of the law. Since the fact of reason, according to its canonical formula, is the consciousness of a moral law, the moral law, however, is expressed as an imperative for rational agents endowed with an imperfect will, we can say that the fact of reason is precisely the consciousness a rational agent endowed with an imperfect will has of the moral law. Now, to be conscious of the *law* is to be conscious of an analytically true proposition. This consciousness is not, however, a necessary condition of having an imperfect will. Thus, if an agent endowed with an imperfect will has consciousness of the moral law, he is conscious of something that in itself is the object of that certainty that belongs to analytic propositions, but in such a way that the relation of the law with his own imperfect will is expressed in a synthetic proposition.

I hope the explanation I gave is faithful both to the letter and to the spirit of Kantian thought. It respects its letter since it has textual support and does not depend on any significant reformulation or reconstruction of Kant's doctrine. More important, it accords too with the critical spirit of Kant's doctrine, since it gives a reasonable justification of Kant's claim that consciousness of the moral law is an undeniable fact. Indeed, being analytically true of agents who infallibly act on maxims that can be taken as universal laws, the principle of our moral judgments qualifies as an immediately certain, therefore undeniable proposition.

I believe further that the proposed interpretation is sufficiently simple to correspond to our moral intuitions, insofar these are based on an irreducible distinction between what is morally good and what is good in the sense of being useful or agreeable. Indeed, if Kant's analysis of the implications of this initial distinction (that it is to say, the Exposition) is correct, it shows that the principle of moral judgments based on this distinction forces itself as a categorical imperative upon our imperfect will, and does so only because we are aware of it as a law for the will of an agent endowed with a perfect will, since it is only in this capacity that it can be taken as an immediately certain proposition. Of course, whether the analysis itself is correct in all its steps is debatable, but that issue must be the subject of another investigation.

Notes

1. A "metaphysical exposition" is, to put it briefly, an analysis of the content of an a priori concept. See its definition in the first *Critique*: "I understand by *exposition (expositio)* the distinct (even if not complete) representation of that which belongs to a concept; but the exposition is *metaphysical* when it contains that which exhibits the concept *as given a priori*" (*Pure Reason*, B38).

2. Kant characterizes his argument in chapter 3 of *Groundwork* as a *deduction of the concept of freedom* (*Groundwork*, 4:447) and as a *deduction of the categorical imperative* (4:457). It is true that Kant does not characterize it explicitly as a *transcendental* deduction, but since it deals with a *quid iuris* question, concerning the justification of a synthetic proposition a priori, which is the kind of question that, according to the

first *Critique*, requires a transcendental deduction, we have the right, as explained by H. Allison in *Kant's Theory of Freedom* (Cambridge: Cambridge University Press, 1991), 279 n. 1, to consider the deduction of the categorical imperative as a transcendental deduction.

3. "The present groundwork is, however, nothing more than the search for and establishment (*Aufsuchung und Festsetzung*) of the *supreme principle of* morality" (*Groundwork*, 4:392).

4. M. J. Gregor translates: "by what it does," and also admits as a possible translation: "by a deed." A "proof through the fact" (*Beweis durch die Tat, argumentum de facto*) consists in the refutation of a thesis by presenting a counterexample, no matter how this may be established. It is in this sense that Kant uses the expression in *Critique of Pure Reason* when referring (in the context of a discussion of the ontological proof of the existence of God) to the attempt to refute the thesis that the notion of an absolutely necessary being is an empty concept (as Kant wants it to be) by the allegation that there is at least an absolutely necessary being, namely, the object of the concept of a most real being, for the existence of this being would necessarily follow from the mere possibility of thinking it without contradiction (*Pure Reason*, A596/B624). "*Argumentum de facto*" is the expression used in the Latin translation of *Critique of Pure Reason*. Immanuelis Kantii, *Critica Rationis Purae*, latine vertit Fredericus Gottlob Born (Lipsiae, 1796; reimpr. Frankfurt: Minerva, 1969), 413. It is in the same sense that Kant uses the expression in *Critique of Practical Reason*, when referring to the moral law as the only fact of reason that escapes censure (*Practical Reason*, 5:46), with implicit reference to the thesis in the first *Critique*, according to which all "facts of reason" (transgressions of which pure theoretical reason is guilty when it extends the use of categories beyond the limits of possible experience) are liable to a justified censure by the sceptical philosopher (*Pure Reason*, A760/B788).

5. Schopenhauer and Hegel are always remembered as the initiators of this negative reception of Kant's doctrine. Thus, Schopenhauer accuses Kant of having opened the doors to all "philosophasters and dreamers" belonging to romantic irrationalism by presenting the categorical imperative "as a hyperphysical fact, as a Delphic temple inside the mind, from whose dark sanctuary infallible oracles proclaim, alas, not what *will*, but what *ought* to happen." Arthur Schopenhauer, *Die beiden Grundprobleme der Ethik*, 3rd ed. (Leipzig: Brockhaus, 1881), 146. Hegel, in turn, referring to the expression "fact of reason," characterizes it as a "revelation given to reason" that remains "in the stomach" as "an indigestible lump." Georg Wilhelm Friedrich Hegel, *Vorlesungen über die Geschichte der Philosophie*, 20 vols., ed. Moldenhaur and Michel (Frankfurt am Main: Suhrkamp, 1979), 20:368–69. Both passages quoted by Dieter Henrich, "Der Begriff der sittlichen Einsicht und Kant's Lehre der Vernunft," *in* G. Prauß, *Kant: Zur Theorie von Erkennen und Handeln* (Köln: Kiepenheuer & Witsch, 1973), 235. Prauß himself esteems that, for the simple reason of having "to equate moral law not only as a fact, but also as an 'apriorical fact,'" Kant is forced to infringe an essential tenet of transcendental philosophy, which is that of having recourse to an a priori only "insofar as this admits of being deduced or derived." G. Prauß, *Kant über Freiheit als Autonomie* (Frankfurt: V. Klostermann, 1983), 68.

6. In *Practical Reason*, the expression "fact of reason" is successively characterized as the "consciousness of moral law" (5:31); as "autonomy in the principle of morality"

(5:42); as "consciousness of freedom" (5:42); as the "moral law" (5:43); and finally as the "inevitable determination of the will by the mere conception of moral law" (5:44).

7. I discussed these issues in two other papers: "Kant e o 'facto da razão': 'Cognitivismo,' ou 'decisionismo' moral?" *in Studia Kantiana* 1, no. 1 (1998): 53–81; and "Kant e o facto da razão," in *Saber filosófico, história, e transcendência*, ed. João A. MacDowell (São Paulo: Edições Loyola, 2002), 87–108.

8. In fact, the idea that giving a deduction consists in proving that categories (and one might add, synthetic a priori principles of the understanding) are conditions of possibility of experience is presented as the *principle (Prinzipium)* of deduction, "toward which the entire investigation must be directed" (*Pure Reason*, A94/B126). If we admit that the proof of this "principle" *has already been given* in the preceding paragraph of §14 (as suggested by the reference to the "objective side of the deduction" in the Preface of the first edition, Axvi–xvii), we must understand this "principle" as the starting point of a deduction yet to be completed (in the "subjective side" of the deduction), namely, as the major premise of an argument that will have as its minor the insight that the empirical consciousness of intuitions in us presupposes a self-consciousness that is only actualized as the consciousness of the power to make judgments about the objects of *experience* (of which categories are precisely, according to the already demonstrated "principle," conditions of possibility). Therefore, we cannot consider it as a formula encompassing the whole argument of the deduction. If, on the contrary, we do not admit that a proof of the "principle" has already been given and consequently that it will be given in the next chapter, with much more reason we will have to refuse it as a formula for the whole deduction, since this, precisely, is yet to be given in its entirety.

9. Taken in its proper sense, the term "experience" means empirical knowledge (of objects given in intuition), which is, in Kant's analysis, a product of the understanding and results from the subsumption of what is given in sense intuition under concepts of objects (see *Pure Reason*, A1). However, insofar as empirical knowledge is itself explained as knowledge *from experience (aus der Erfahrung)* (*Pure Reason*, B1), the term "experience" may be taken as referring to empirical intuition and its sensuous content, which is the source of empirical knowledge, or at least as the subjective synthesis of our perceptions, that is to say, of our intuitions insofar as we are aware of them as subjective states of our mind. (see in this regard, *Prolegomena* 4:275: "Experience itself is nothing but a continual joining together (*synthesis*) of perceptions," and a commentary on this passage in Helmut Holzhey, *Kant's Erfahrungsbegriff* (Basel: Schwabe, 1970), 168–69, 210–11). If we take the term "experience" in the first sense, it is clear that a deduction can only be understood as a refutation of an *empiricist* philosopher who questions, not the possibility of knowing empirical objects as something distinct from the subjective states of whomever knows them, but only the existence of a priori cognitions. If, on the contrary, the term "experience" is taken in the second sense, deduction can be understood as the refutation of a *skeptical* philosopher who accepts the possibility of being aware of the subjective states that we find ourselves to be in when we say, or think, that we know something, but does not admit that we can know any object that might be taken as existing independently from these subjective states. See in this regard P. Guyer, *Kant and the Claims of Knowledge* (Cambridge: Cambridge University Press, 1987), 79–85.

10. Such is the outline of the proof we find in the "Provisional Explanation of the Possibility of the Categories as *a priori* Cognitions" (*Pure Reason*, A111). I have tried to show that the proof given in the deduction actually follows this outline in "Consciência de si e conhecimento objeto na dedução transcendental das categorias," *Analytica* 1, no. 1 (1993): 187–219.

11. Kant presents this claim as the supreme principle of all synthetic judgments a priori, the possibility of which can be said to the object of the transcendental deduction, insofar as the task of this deduction is to show that and how is it possible to subsume sense intuitions under the pure concepts of the understanding.

12. For the concept of practical freedom, see *Pure Reason*, A534/B562.

13. See *Pure Reason* A546–58/B574–86. Why this is so remains largely implicit in Kant's explanation, but it is not hard to bring it out. In fact, we consider our actions to depend on our will insofar as it is up to us to do or to not do them. Now, actions are up for us to do or to not do insofar as they result from a decision-making deliberation, although not infallibly so, as if the action or the decision to act followed from the deliberation as an effect from a natural cause, but in such a way that we are left free to make the decision resulting from the deliberation process. Now, we may say that imperatives, in Kant's theory, are precisely rules for decision-making deliberation. Indeed, they say to us, according to Kant, what is *good* to do (and we might add: rather than to not do). Saying, however, that it is good to do something amounts to saying that we have *reasons* (or *grounds*, *Gründe*) to do it rather than not do it, although we do not necessarily do it for the sole reason that reason represents it as being good (and we might add: but only if we decide to do so). That is the reason why an imperative expresses what is deemed good to do by saying that we *should*, or *ought* to do it, even if we in fact decide not to do so. See *Groundwork* II, parag. 12 for Kant's analysis of the predicate "good."

14. *Groundwork*, 4:448, and *Reflections*. 4220, 4338, 5441, 5442. See also *Metaphysik* L_1*/Pölitz*, 28:268–69.

15. *Groundwork*, 4:450–53. See also the *Review of Schulz* (8:14). Henrich, who has best studied Kant's attempted deductions in the *Reflections*, distinguishes between two kinds: (1) attempts of an "indirect deduction," based on the concept of freedom; and (2) attempts of a "direct deduction," based either on considerations on the requirement of consistency in our actions or on the maximization of our chances to achieve happiness. See passages quoted by Henrich, "Begriff," esp. *Reflections*, 6853, 7196, 6221. See also *Vorlesung über Ethik*, ed. P. Menzer (Berlin: Panverlag, 1925); rev. ed. G. Gerhardt (Frankfurt: Fischer, 1991), 54. However, I do not believe that attempts of a so-called direct deduction may be considered as attempts at a deduction properly speaking, since they are empirical arguments based on considerations on the search of happiness as a motive of human action and intended as giving a foundation to the moral principle taken as a *subjective* principle *of* the term "execution" (that is, as a maxim of our will), and not as an objective principle of evaluation of our maxims. Should we accept them as deductions proper, we would have to accept that a deduction was already present in the first *Critique*'s Canon of Pure Reason, which is certainly unacceptable. To be sure, we could always describe them as attempts at giving an empirical deduction, not a transcendental one, but in this case, we would not be using the word "deduction" in its proper sense.

16. See R5442.

17. Such is the possibility suggested by Kant in the Canon of *Critique of Pure Reason* (A803/B831), when he accepts the possibility of an empirical and nontranscendental concept of practical freedom.

18. See *Judgment*, 5:468. *Tatsache* is a neologism invented in 1756 by J. J. Spalding as a translation of *matter of fact*, which is itself a translation of *res facti*. See Jacob and Wilhelm Grimm, *Deutsches Wörterbuch*, and *Lexikon der deutschen Sprache*, ed. R. Köster (Frankfurt: Ullstein, 1969). The assertion that mathematical propositions are questions of fact (that is, not analytical, but rather synthetical propositions based on intuitive evidence) is clearly opposed to Hume, according to which they are based on "relations of ideas," being therefore expressed, to say it in Kantian terminology, in analytical propositions. Likewise, the characterization of freedom and of moral law as a fact of reason may be understood in two ways. *On the one hand*, as an important but not decisive step toward Hume (the concept of moral law as valid for us and of our will as being free is not based on mere relations of ideas, but rather on knowledge of a *fact*, that is, of a contingent state of affairs). *On the other hand*, it expresses a position taken against Hume's claim that the conception of moral law and of freedom of will as "truths of reason" is nothing but a *chimera* of imagination, since Kant holds that the validity of moral law for us is precisely a fact of *reason*. See David Hume, *Treatise of Human Nature*, ed. I. A. Selby-Bigge (Oxford: Clarendon Press, 1978), 3.1, 455–76.

19. See *Practial Reason*, 5:73, 78–79.

20. "So hat sich die kantische Ethik nach langen Jahren, in denen sie im Prinzip einer deduktiven Ethik den Stein der Weisen zu finden hoffte, wieder der Position angenähert, von der sie ausgegangen war. Es ist der Standpunkt von Hutcheson, die Skepsis in Beziehung auf eine theoretische Grundlegung der Ethik, den sie nun auf einer höheren Stufe wiederholt." (Thus Kantian ethics, after so many years of hoping to find the philosopher's stone in the principle of a deductive ethics, neared again the position that was its starting point. This is Hutcheson's standpoint: skepticism regarding the project of giving a theoretical foundation for ethics, which it now reiterates on a higher level.) Henrich, "Begriff," 248.

21. "Die theoretische Vernunft kann sich zwar a priori eine Idee von Verbindlichkeit machen. Sie kann ihren Inhalt hypothetisch bestimmen. Denn unter der Voraussetzung, daß Freiheit ist, gilt das Gesetz des kategorischen Imperatives. Sie kann jedoch das Bewußtsein der Verbindlichkeit zum sittlichen Handeln nicht hervorbringen." (Theoretical reason can, to be sure, form an idea of obligation a priori. It can determine its content hypothetically. For, on the presupposition that there is freedom, the law of the categorical imperative is valid. It cannot, however, bring about the consciousness of an obligation of acting morally.) Henrich, "Begriff," 247.

22. Thus, referring to the critique of theoretical reason, Henrich says, first: "Sie kann aber die Billigung und die Entscheidung des Selbst nicht mit vernünftigen Gründen erzwingen. Sie kann nicht zeigen, daß das Selbstbewußtsein wesentlich Freiheit ist, und ihm ad oculos demonstrieren, daß es sich einer Forderung unterstellen, die in deduktiver Methode wissenschaftlich begründet worden ist." (It cannot, however, compel the self with rational arguments to give its approval and make a decision. It cannot show that self-consciousness is essentially freedom and demonstrate *ad oculos*

to the latter that it has to submit itself to a requirement that has been scientifically established according to a deductive method.) Henrich, "Begriff," 248. And a few lines ahead: "Kant's neue Lehre des Faktums der Vernunft hat eine wichtige Änderung in seiner Lehre über das emotionale Element in der sittlichen Einsicht zur Folge gehabt: Er hat zur Lehre von der 'Achtung fürs Gesetz' als der einzig legitimen Triebfeder des sittlichen Willens geführt." (Kant's new doctrine on the fact of reason resulted in a very important change in his doctrine about the emotional element in moral insight: it led to the doctrine on 'respect for the law' as the sole legitimate incentive of moral will.) Henrich, "Begriff," 249.

23. See the following passage in Kant's preparatory remarks for *Anthropology*: "Sinnlichkeit heißt das bloß *subjektive* unseres Vorstellungsvermögens. Kann jenes doch auch objektiv gebraucht werden, d.i. ein Erkenntnisstück werden, so gehört es zum Erkenntnis Vermögen (Zusatz: und heißt Empfindung). Is es aber auf solche Art subjektiv, daß es gar nicht objektiv zum Erkenntnis beiträgt, so gehörts für das Gefühl der Lust, welche also immer zur Sittlichkeit gehört, obgleich die Vorstellung, die sie erregt, intellectual ist." (*Sensibility* designates the merely *subjective* ingredient of our faculty of representation. However, if this can also be used objectively, i.e., become a cognitive ingredient, then it belongs to the faculty of knowledge [added later: and it is called *sensation*]. But, if it is subjective in such a way that it does not provide any objective contribution to knowledge, then it belongs to the feeling of pleasure, which [pleasure] therefore belongs always to sensibility, even though the representation arousing it is intellectual.) *R*227, 15:86–87.

24. See *Practical Reason*, 5:75.

25. Or "self-wrought," as translated by M. Gregor.

26. "What I cognize immediately as a law for me I cognize with respect, which signifies merely consciousness of the *subordination* of my will to a law without the mediation of other influences on my sense. Immediate determination of the will by means of the law and consciousness of this is called *respect*, so that this is regarded as the *effect* of the law on the subject, and not as the *cause* of the law" (M. Gregor's translation, *Groundwork*, 4:401).

27. See *Practical Reason*, 5:71, 75.

28. See Z. Loparic, "O facto da reason—Uma interpretação semântica," in *Analytica* 4, no. 1 (1999): 13–55. See too "Das Faktum der Vernunft eine semantische Auslegung," in *Kant und Berliner Aufklärung, Akten des IX. Internationalen Kant-Kongresses*, vol. 3 (Berlin: de Gruyter, 2001), 63–71.

29. H. Allison, *Kant's Theory of Freedom* (Cambridge: Cambridge University Press, 1990), 230.

30. "The fact mentioned above is undeniable. One need only analyse the judgment that people pass on the lawfulness of their actions" (*Practical Reason*, 5:32).

31. *R*7201 (19:275), as translated by Allison, *Kant's Theory of Freedom*, 234.

32. The real issue (not only for the skeptical philosopher, but for Kant too), is how we can move from the *fact* that we make moral judgments to whatever gives us the *right* to take the principle on which they are based as valid for our will (and thereby the right to make this sort of judgment). From the mere fact that one makes, say, astrological predictions, one cannot infer the validity of the principle on which they are based (namely, the belief that the position of the stars in the sky influences

whatever happens men on earth). In the same way, from the mere consideration that we make moral judgments, one cannot infer the claim that their principle (however it may be formulated) is a valid one, and consequently that we do have the right to make moral judgments.

33. See above, note 31.

34. Alternatively: whose objects can be "constructed" in pure intuition, as in the case of mathematical objects.

35. Reference to any kind of intuition, either to sense intuition, pure or empirical, or to a (problematical) intellectual intuition, is explicitly rejected by Kant in the passage in which the notion of a "fact of reason" is introduced. "Consciousness of this fundamental law may be called a fact of reason . . . because it . . . forces itself upon us as a synthetic a priori proposition that is not based on any intuition, either pure or empirical, although it would be analytic, if the freedom of the will were presupposed; but for this, as a positive concept, an intellectual intuition would be required, which certainly cannot be assumed here" (*Practical Reason*, 5:31).

36. About the distinction law/imperative, see *Groundwork*, 4:412–13; and *Practical Reason*, §1, Remark, 5:19–21.

37. "I connect (*verknüpfe*) the deed with the will without a presupposed condition from any inclination, a priori, and hence necessarily (though only objectively, i.e., under the idea of a reason having complete control over all subjective motives). This is, therefore, a practical proposition that does not derive the volition of an action analytically from another volition already presupposed (*for we have no such perfect will* [emphasis mine—GAA]), but *connects it immediately with the concept of the will of a rational being* [emphasis mine—GAA], as something that is not contained in it" (*Groundwork*, 4:420). The implication of the highlighted phrase seems clear: if we had a perfect will it would be possible to derive *analytically* the volition expressed by the practical proposition (which proposition is, in this case, a practical principle) from the concept of the will of a rational being. I dealt in a more detailed way with the interpretation of this passage in "Kant e o 'facto da razão,'" 66–70.

38. Notably H. Allison, "Kant's Preparatory Argument in *Grundlegung* III," in *Grundlegung zur Metaphysik der Sitten—Ein Kooperativer Kommentar*, ed. O. Höffe (Frankfurt: Klostermann, 1993), 314.

39. "Everything in nature works in accordance with laws. Only a rational being has the capacity to act *in accordance with the representation* of laws, that is, in accordance with principles, or has a *will*. Since *reason* is required for the derivation of actions from laws, the will is nothing other than practical reason" (*Groundwork*, 4:412).

40. The arguments above can be expressed in a more terse way, if we begin with the definitions of an imperfect and a perfect will. An *imperfect will* is, for Kant, a will that does not always do what is good to do, either through ignorance, or as the result of a decision. Because of that, the principle of our moral judgments, saying what is unconditionally good, takes the form of an *imperative* for an imperfect will, that is, of a proposition saying what one *ought* to do, even if actually no one would do it. That is why the categorical imperative, which is the principle of our moral judgments, has to be taken as a *synthetic* practical proposition. Indeed, given the definition of an imperfect will, one cannot say that the concept of the unconditionally good is contained in

the concept of an imperfect will as one of its marks, since an imperfect will may not do what is unconditionally good as the result not only of a decision, but also of ignorance. Therefore, since it is not contradictory to think of an imperfect will belonging to a subject that does not even know what is unconditionally good, the relation between the concepts of an imperfect will and of the unconditionally good must be thought as a synthetic one. Notwithstanding, it must be thought at the same time as an a priori relation, since it says what is unconditionally good.

Now, a *perfect will* is, by hypothesis, one that necessarily knows and wills what is unconditionally good, for otherwise it could not be called a perfect will. That is why the principle of our moral judgments assumes for a perfect will the form, not of an imperative, but of a *law*, since it says what it necessarily wills. Therefore, insofar as it is a law for a perfect will, the principle of our moral judgments is an analytical practical proposition, since it is not possible to think the concept of a perfect will without thinking the concept of a will that necessarily wills what is unconditionally good.

8

The Noncircular Deduction of the Categorical Imperative in *Groundwork* III

Julio Esteves

Introduction

Among the most respected interpreters, there is virtual unanimity that in the third section of the *Groundwork* Kant intends to provide a justification or proof of the validity of the supreme principle of morality previously articulated in the other two sections. The problem dealt with in the third section is a result of the fact that the analytical or regressive-hypothetical method hitherto adopted can satisfy only "whoever holds morality to be something and not a chimerical idea without any truth" (*Groundwork*, 4:445). The question of the validity of the supreme principle of morality requires the synthetic use of pure practical reason, since it concerns a *quid juris* analog to the one dealt with in the *Critique of Pure Reason* regarding the pure concepts of the understanding and the a priori synthetic principles.

Nevertheless, among the interpreters, there is also virtual unanimity that Kant's attempt fails. In fact, Kant himself raises the specter of a kind of circle "from which, as *it seems*, there is no way to escape" (*Groundwork*, 4:449; my emphasis). So, in what follows, I will provide a reconstruction of the argument developed by Kant in the third section of the *Groundwork* and defend it against the overall criticism, paying particular attention to the objection of a hidden circle in it. However, since there is an agreement among the interpreters concerning Kant's intentions and the shortcomings of his enterprise, it would then be convenient, first of all, to put forward some arguments and passages of Kant's texts that could grant at least some initial plausibility to my proposal.

This is a revised but not substantially modified translation of an article published as "A dedução do imperativo categórico na *Fundamentação* III," in *Studia Kantiana* 5 (2003): 79–104. Translated by the author.

Kant's Endorsement of the Deduction

The critics of the deduction in *Groundwork* III start usually from Kant's own admission that the proof is flawed, which should beforehand discourage any attempt to defend it. According to critics, Kant's concession of the objection of circularity would have made him abandon the proof strategy once adopted in *Groundwork* III in favor of a different one later, in the *Critique of Practical Reason*. In the latter work, Kant would have realized that it is impossible to prove morality from an independent proof of freedom, renouncing the train of thought that he had adopted in *Groundwork* III. Thus, in the *Critique of Practical Reason*, Kant would have revised his procedure, recognizing that one cannot start from freedom in order to prove morality, since the latter is the *ratio cognoscendi* of the former (*Practical Reason*, 5:4), and reversed the proof structure. Nevertheless, contra these critics, there are passages in Kant's works, including even those they often quote in which one *cannot* find the acknowledgment by Kant of a failure in the deduction of the supreme principle of morality from an independent proof of freedom.

To begin with, as H. J. Paton pointed out, undoubtedly Kant himself interprets his procedure in *Groundwork* III as consisting in a deduction modeled on the transcendental deduction of the categories in the First *Critique* and "talks about the rightness of his deduction."[1] In fact, Kant talks about "the deduction of the concept of freedom from pure practical reason" (*Groundwork*, 4:447). Moreover, notwithstanding the objection of the circle, Kant warns us against "any censure of our deduction of the supreme principle of morality" (463). Finally, he adds that "the correctness of this deduction" is confirmed by the practical usage of the common human reason (454).

It is equally remarkable that in the Introduction to the second *Critique*, that is, in the very work that is supposed to have definitely ruled out the proof strategy adopted in the *Groundwork* and reversed it, Kant claims that if we surmise the possibility of discovering "grounds for proving that this property [namely, freedom—JE] does in fact belong to the human will (and so to the will of all rational beings as well) then it will through this not only be shown that pure reason can be practical, but also that it alone, and not reason empirically limited, is unconditionally practical" (*Practical Reason*, 5:15).[2] Clearly, the grounds in question that would allow us to attribute freedom to our will would have to be valid independently of the validity of the practicability of pure reason, that is, of morality.

Nevertheless, one could reply that such possibility is undoubtedly rejected in the Preface and in the Analytic of the same second *Critique*. Granted, in the second *Critique* Kant still maintains the "reciprocity thesis," that is, the claim that morality and freedom are reciprocal concepts, which had been an important premise to the proof strategy of *Groundwork* III.[3] But now, in the second *Critique*, Kant alleges that "we cannot start from freedom," for it is the moral law "of which we become immediately conscious (as soon as we draw up maxims of the will for ourselves), that **first** offers itself to us and leads directly to the concept of freedom" (*Practical Reason*, 5:29–30).

However, if one carefully considers the passages in which Kant would have once and for all rejected the possibility of proving the validity of morality from freedom, one comes to a somewhat different conclusion. For the arguments presented by Kant in the passages of the second *Critique* leave the proof structure in *Groundwork* III simply untouched. In fact, Kant argues that, although the self-consciousness of the pure practical reason and the positive concept of freedom could perhaps be identical, our knowledge of the unconditioned practical might not begin with freedom "for we can neither be immediately conscious of this, since the first concept of it is negative, nor can we conclude to it from experience" (*Practical Reason*, 5:29). Now, in the first place, in the *Groundwork* Kant does not seek to infer freedom from experience. On the contrary, whether he is successful or not, in *Groundwork* III Kant intends to prove freedom on the basis of the *concept* of the will of a rational being in general, by rejecting the possibility "to demonstrate it from certain supposed experiences of human nature (though this is also absolutely impossible and it can be demonstrated only *a priori*)" (*Groundwork*, 4:447–48). Second, even if our first concept of freedom were a negative one and, therefore, insufficient to prove the validity of morality, this fact would only generate a serious objection to the proof structure adopted in *Groundwork* III, if in the second *Critique* Kant had put forward further arguments denying an important premise of the earlier work, namely, that the positive concept of freedom flows analytically from the negative one (*Groundwork*, 4:446).

Moreover, it is above all important to pay attention to what Kant really wants to rule out when he states that we cannot start from freedom. In fact, in the Preface to the second *Critique*, Kant affirms that the vain attempts undertaken by the traditional metaphysics to provide a theoretical proof of the immortality of the soul and of the existence of God are, as it were, compensated by practical reason that by means of the concept of freedom confers stability and objective reality to the ideas of God and immortality of the soul (*Practical Reason*, 5:4–5). Now, it is quite remarkable that Kant claims that freedom, instead of morality, gives in the first place objective reality to those metaphysical ideas, and this is so for at least two reasons. First, because such a claim comes after the famous passage in which the knowledge of freedom itself and a fortiori of the other metaphysical ideas is said to depend on the consciousness of the moral law.[4] Second, because the Dialectic of the *Critique of Practical Reason* teaches us that it is morality with its imperative to strive for the highest good that actually postulates the objective reality of God and the immortality of the soul.[5] These passages could by themselves cast doubts on the supposed rejection of a prominent role played by freedom in favor of morality in the second *Critique*. Doubtless, though, what Kant definitely rejects in the second *Critique* is that the speculative reason could solve the traditional metaphysical problems whose *Einsicht* should be reserved to the practical use, because "our faculty of speculation is not so well off" (*Practical Reason*, 5:5). Later, in the Analytic, but still in the polemical tune of the Preface, Kant restates "that this is the true subordination of our concepts and that morality first discloses to us the concept of freedom, so that it is **practical reason** which first poses to speculative reason, with this concept, the most insoluble problem" (*Practical Reason*, 5:30). Thus, what Kant claims is simply that the *theoretical-speculative reason* deals with neither the genesis of the problem of freedom nor its solution (and of the other ideas of reason). Thus, what we can conclude from the statements in the Preface and in the Analytic of the second *Critique* is that Kant would reject any attempt to start from a supposed *theoretical-speculative proof* of freedom seeking to prove morality, which does not exclude him from still admitting the possibility of providing a *practical proof* of the former, evidently from morally neutral premises, in order to prove the objective validity of the latter.

Nevertheless, to my mind, we can find in the Preface to the second *Critique* the strongest evidence that Kant did not cast doubts on the rightness of the deduction once undertaken in *Groundwork* III. In fact, Kant writes that the *Critique of Practical Reason* "presupposes, indeed, the *Groundwork*, but only insofar as this constitutes preliminary acquaintance with the principle of duty and provides and *justifies* (*rechtfertigt*) a determinate formula of it" (*Practical Reason*, 5:8; my emphasis). Now, when discussing the justification (*Rechtfertigung*) of an a priori principle or concept, the critical Kant always means by the term "justification" the procedure of providing a deduction, that is, a proof of the objective validity of the a priori principle or concept. Now, on the basis of the passage quoted above could we not conclude that, far from rejecting the argument presented in *Groundwork* III, in the second *Critique* Kant simply started from the assumption that not only a formula of the principle of morality had already been given, but also its deduction and justification?[6] And could it not be the case that, just because he considered the deduction in *Groundwork* III to be successful and complete, Kant eventually came to the infamous doctrine of the "fact of reason" in the second *Critique*, a step that was interpreted by an authoritative interpreter such as Dieter Henrich as being a renouncement by Kant of the deduction of the principle of morality and thereby of a distinctive feature of the critical philosophy?[7]

The Self-Refutation of Universal Determinism

Thus, there are no indications that Kant had been dissatisfied with the deduction in *Groundwork* III. Obviously, though, he could have been wrong in his estimation of the proof. That is why, in the following two sections, I will attempt to reconstruct the argument in *Groundwork* III and to show that Kant was not wrong in his judgment. In the last section, I will discuss the objection of circularity such as it is usually understood by the interpreters and provide an alternative interpretation and solution to this problem.

We must distinguish two steps in the argument in *Groundwork* III. First, Kant seeks to provide a proof of freedom by showing that the thesis of universal determinism is self-defeating, that is, that the very presuppositions of universal determinism entail its falsehood. Second, Kant applies the results of this first argument to the particular case of beings that possess a will.

First of all, it is important to be clear about the character of the thesis of determinism that Kant was trying to refute. It seems strange that Kant wanted to refute determinism, since he had provided a proof of the principle of causality in the Second Analogy of Experience in the first *Critique*. Now, we can take determinism in general as the thesis according to which everything that happens has its necessary and, more important, *sufficient* conditions exclusively in natural causes preceding in time. Having said this, we must keep in mind that Kant's refutation of determinism is directed at a determinate variant of it, according to which the principle of causality would be universally and absolutely valid. In other words, determinism to be refuted by Kant is the metaphysical-dogmatic version of it that claims that the principle of natural causality is valid for things and events as they are in themselves, independent and regardless of the descriptions under which they fall and of the contexts in which they can be considered. By contrast, the proof in the Second Analogy contains the restriction of the universal validity of the principle of causality to things and events insofar as they are objects of empirical knowledge, that is, appearances.

Besides, although I cannot deal adequately with this question here, I maintain that causality by Kant means above all a relation between tokens, not between types, and that in the Second Analogy his target is to prove the necessary validity of only one law or transcendental principle, namely, that everything that happens has any cause (whatsoever). In other words, appealing to the very illuminating formula introduced by Lewis White Beck, in the Second Analogy Kant intends to justify the principle "every-event-some-cause," challenged by Hume in the *Treatise*, and not the principle "same-cause-same-effect," challenged by Hume in the *Enquiry*.[8] In this way, since it represents a dogmatic extension of the principle of causality in the Second Analogy, the version of determinism Kant wants to refute consists of minimal, but extremely strong, requirements. It does not rely on the possibility of foreseeing or foreknowing which events will happen from the given conditions; nor does it rely on the possibility of specifying completely the nature of the causal conditions, namely, whether they are genetic, neurophysiological, social, environmental, and so on. In fact, the version of determinism to be refuted states simply that every single event in the world, even every particular event in one's life, both taken as things in themselves, finds its necessary and sufficient conditions in nothing more than preceding natural causes, even though we are not in a position yet to establish exhaustively the nature of such conditions and foresee for sure what will happen.

Kant's argument can be found condensed in the following passage: "Now, one cannot possibly think of a reason that would consciously receive direction from any other quarter with respect to its judgment, since the subject would then attribute the determination of his judgment not to his reason but to an impulse. Reason must regard itself as the author of its principles independently of alien circumstances" (*Groundwork*, 4:448).

Although Kant himself did not present it so, I think it is convenient to put forward Kant's argument in a polemical style, and this is so for at least two reasons. First, because the argument has the same structure as the polemical and antifatalist argument developed by Kant in his *Rezension* to Schulz's moral theory.[9] Second, and more important, because both arguments rest in an implicit analysis of the act of judging that, as we will see, has a polemical structure.

Now, given that what is impossible to be thought is everything that involves contradiction, and since the supposed contradiction is a self-referring one ("a reason that would *consciously* receive direction from," *Groundwork* 4:448, my emphasis), so we can provide a paraphrase of Kant's argument in the following terms: a reason that in its judgments admits to receive direction from something else than from itself, that is, not from its own patterns of rationality, incurs in a self-contradiction in the very moment that it judges, and that would be the determinist's error. In the very act of judging, better, of asserting the universal and absolute validity of the thesis of determinism, the determinist would be thereby conceding that this judgment receives direction from something else than his reason and incurring in contradiction. Thus, to understand Kant's argument correctly, we must reflect on what is involved in the act of judging or asserting.[10]

To begin with, let us be clear that, since every sentence *p* can be denied, then the act of asserting *p* essentially anticipates the possibility of a denial, a counterassertion, that is, the assertion of *not p*. Thus, to assert, that is, to judge that *p* is true is to deny in anticipation the truth of *not p*. We can see that assertion presents in its essence a *polemical* character, because it can be understood as a *challenge* in which a speaker challenges someone to take up the counterposition. That is why, following an idea that stems from Wittgenstein, Michael Dummett suggests that assertion can be compared with a game, such as a bet, in which two partners play against each other and the rules are such that they lead to a final position that consists in one having won and the other having lost.[11]

Now how should we understand precisely the opening move in the assertoric game? Someone who opens an assertoric game by employing a sentence *p* offers a *guarantee* that it is true that *p*, while the partner's countermove is already fixed, which consists in the utterance of *not p* with the correspondent guarantee that it is true that *not p*. Well, whoever guarantees the truth of an assertion guarantees that, first, she or he *knows* the truth conditions of the assertoric sentence and, second, *knows* that these truth conditions are actually fulfilled. Now, what are these truth conditions? Concerning utterances made in daily life, we can conceive of such truth conditions as semantic rules on the basis of which we can verify if a general term applies to an object identified by a singular term. However, concerning utterances made in scientific or even in philosophical contexts, the relevant truth conditions consist mainly in patterns of justified rational evidence and of formal valid inference.

Applying these considerations to our problem, we can say that, asserting the thesis of universal determinism, the determinist opens an assertoric game thereby offering a guarantee that the patterns of evidence and rational inference are in favor of the truth of her thesis and of the falsehood of the opposite thesis, according to which there can be exceptions to the universal causal determinism, so that the defender of the latter thesis would have lost the game and should agree with the former.

Now, let us consider if the determinist is in fact in a position to maintain the guarantee she offered to her adversary so that the latter would be obliged to acknowledge that he lost the game. Well, this guarantee includes the determinist's admission that she is *conscious* that the patterns of rational evidence and of formal valid inference speak in favor of the thesis of universal determinism. However, according to determinism, every event without exception, and even every particular event in one's mental life, is nothing but a mere result of preceding causal conditions that would sufficiently account for it. Such causal conditions are of strictly physical-material character without any reference to consciousness of patterns of objective rational evidence or consciousness of a nexus between premises and conclusion. Now, given that the assertion of the thesis of universal determinism is itself an event, to wit, a mental event in the determinist's life, then according to her own admission it must also be considered as a mere result of physical conditions. However, if the preceding physical-material conditions account *sufficiently for* the event asserting-the-truth-of-determinism, then the consciousness of the patterns of rational evidence that was supposed to be the guarantee offered by the determinist is not after all a *necessary* condition of the determinist's assertion. But if the consciousness of the relevant patterns of objective rational evidence was not a necessary condition of the determinist's assertion, then that consciousness *does not explain* determinism's assertion and, consequently, it is not grounded in reasons and remains *unjustified*.

Thus, if she were consistent, the determinist would admit that her assertion of the truth of determinism is not grounded in reasons, which would undermine the guarantee supposedly offered. It means that the determinist did not after all win the game against her adversary.

We must pay attention to the centrality of the *effective* role that the consciousness or the act of recognition of patterns of rational evidence must play in judgments claiming to be objectively valid. In fact, we must distinguish between the mere existence of a reason that I even recognize as relevant for a determinate judgment, on the one hand, and, on the other hand, the fact that such reason is really the reason why I judge, that is, the *effective ground* for my judgment. Thus, for example, I can have a reason that would justify my asserting that the neighbor's dog is dangerous, namely, because of the many times I have seen it muzzled and observed that postmen approach the house very carefully in fear, and so on, but, in spite of this, that assertion might have had another motive, namely, the (by now unconscious) fact that the dog looks like the one that bit me when I was a child. On this hypothesis, the consciousness of the rational evidence *was not effectively the cause or reason* of my judgment, which is, consequently, unjustified.[12]

Thus, if the determinist herself admits that her acceptance of the thesis of determinism can be completely and sufficiently explained as conditioned by natural causes, then she must also admit that the recognition of reasons or patterns of rationality plays no role and is not necessary for her asserting the thesis of determinism, which is consequently unjustified. As Kant affirms, the determinist admits consciously that her judgment on the truth of determinism receives direction from another quarter than her reason, even though she still claims to be appealing to reason while making her judgment.

But perhaps the determinist still has a chance to respond. After all, the argument hitherto rests on a principle that expresses an exclusive disjunction: either natural causes are regarded as sufficient for the judgment in favor of determinism, which would impair the cognitive value of such judgment; or such judgment can legitimately claim objective validity, but only insofar as the determinist admits that the consciousness of reasons is a necessary condition for it. Now, suppose that the mental state "recognition of reasons," which I will call state *R*, is identical or supervenient on a given physical state *P1*, which in turn is the condition of another physical state *P2*, on which the mental state taking-position-in-favor-of-determinism, which I will call state *T*, is supervenient or identical.[13] Now, according to such a model, if the physical state *P1* is a necessary condition for the physical state *P2* and if the mental state *R* and the mental state *T* are supervenient on or even identical to each of them, then we could appeal to a principle of transitivity and still claim that the recognition of reasons is also a necessary condition for determinism assertion.

However, if we consider the question very carefully, we come to the conclusion that such "harmonious parallelism" between physical and mental states collapses. To make it clear, consider the following: According to the model just proposed, what does effectively govern the reasoning process that culminated in the acceptance of determinism? Was the reasoning process governed by rational evidence in accordance with principles of formal valid inference? Or is it rather the case that the process was completely determined by physical conditions in accordance with physical principles making rational evidence once more unnecessary for the process? Now, if the determinist holds firmly the absolute validity of the principle of causal closure, then she cannot admit that rational evidence *as such* could govern the reasoning process. In fact, according to the proposed model, the state *R* is supposed to be a necessary condition for *T just because* the former is supervenient on or identical to the physical state *P1*, which in turn is a necessary condition for *P2*. In this way, one can still maintain that the recognition of reasons somehow could explain the judgment in favor of determinism, but not the recognition *qua* recognition or *qua* consciousness of something *as a good evidence*, but *only in sofaras* it is supervenient on a physical state that determines another physical state, on which that judgment in favor of determinism is in turn supervenient.

In sum, according to the model suggested by the determinist, the recognition of reasons as good evidence for a judgment becomes epiphenomenal, without playing any effective role in governing the reasoning process. In fact, since the determinist's assertion is completely explained by necessary and sufficient natural causal conditions, then the reference to reasons for such an assertion can perfectly be put aside, and we can maintain that taking position in favor of determinism would *necessarily* happen in the determinist's mental life quite *independently* of such reasons.

Thus, Kant's argument reconstructed shows that determinism cannot be elevated to a universal and unrestricted valid principle. For, in the very act of stating her thesis, the determinist creates an instance that falsifies it. In fact, this is the determinist's dilemma: either she overtly maintains that her judgment rests on reasons and not on natural causes, but then she must admit that universal determinism is false; or she refrains from defending determinism publicly, that is, from arguing on the basis of reasons for the truth of determinism, though she can maintain her conviction silently for herself. Sure, the determinist could yet reply that the argument has shown at best that the thesis of universal determinism cannot be defended on the basis of reasons, which does not exclude that it can be true in itself. Now, such a reply would hardly surprise us, since we are dealing with a dogmatic determinist that holds that the principle of natural causality is valid for things in themselves, independent of the descriptions under which they can fall. However, if the determinist makes this desperate step, she will thereby give up once more her right to claim a particular distinction for her thesis against the adversary. For, to begin with, this last step consists once more and again in a judgment, to which the argument hitherto developed equally finds application. Besides, the determinist's adversary can also argue that his own thesis can be true from the point of view of the things in themselves. Nevertheless, the latter is in the more advantageous position of defending his thesis because he can appeal to reasons, since his thesis contains nothing that collides with the conditions of possibility of judgment.[14]

Freedom as a Necessary Presupposition of the Will

Nevertheless, we must take into account that the argument reconstructed above can be found in a subsection in *Groundwork* III under the title Freedom Must be Presupposed as a Property of the Will of All Rational Beings (*Groundwork*, 4:447). Thus, the argument, if successful, would have shown not the *objective reality* of freedom properly speaking, but only that it is a necessary *presupposition* and worse, at least thus far, exclusively of the *theoretical* act of judging. So we could cast doubts on the sufficiency and adequacy of such a proof for the justification of the *objective reality* of the supreme *practical* principle.

Now, concerning the first problem, all that we can find in Kant's text as a hint of a possible answer is the seemingly dogmatic remark, according to which the demonstration of the necessity of presupposing freedom in the actions is as good as the theoretical demonstration of its reality. However, the suspicion of dogmatism begins to vanish as soon as we recall that Kant's treatment of the third Antinomy in the first *Critique* has shown that the theoretical-speculative philosophy must leave unsettled the question of the reality of freedom.[15] If this is correct, then it becomes understandable why practical philosophy can be satisfied with the demonstration of the necessity of presupposing freedom. In fact, if practical philosophy does not need to expect a confirmation or fear a refutation from theoretical philosophy, then it can start with the necessary presupposition of freedom and move on to the claim of its reality and then, subsequently, conclude that all laws that are inseparably bound up with freedom are valid for a being that necessarily presupposes freedom in its actions.

However, concerning the second problem above, it is not clear that the argument reconstructed has demonstrated freedom from premises of practical philosophy properly speaking. For, at best, we would have proved that freedom is a necessary condition of the activity of judging in general, and Kant has to show that freedom is a necessary presupposition of the will of rational beings. Perhaps, we could even concede that freedom was proven both in a negative sense, namely, as a capacity of *not* being determined by natural causes in his judgments, and in a positive one, namely, as a capacity to determine his judgments by reasons conceived as something that cannot be reduced or assimilated to physical causes. Nevertheless, as so often objected, it is possible to think of beings free in their judgments of understanding and that possess reason conceived as a theoretical capacity, but who would not be free in their actions and lack reason with practical capacity, in other words, rational beings that would lack a will.[16] In sum, freedom was hitherto demonstrated only in the theoretical sense as a necessary feature of the *epistemic* spontaneity. And it would be useless to try to escape from the objection by arguing that the acts of judging and asserting should be more adequately conceived even in the theoretical context just as a kind of "acts." For, to have a will is not merely to have the capacity to produce free acts of judging, but mainly to have the capacity to make such judgments effective in the actions.

In fact, Kant's critics very often argue that he would have never tried to settle the existence or reality of will.[17] For my part, I think it is after all not clear what the critics expected Kant to have done. For, in a sense, it is not possible to settle the reality of the will, that is, to prove that we really make effective our practical judgments in our actions, because it would require the possibility to prove that the reasons that are supposed to determine our judgments and that, as mentioned, cannot be reduced or assimilated to natural causes actually have causality on the actions in the phenomenal world. Now, this is as impossible as it is to prove that there is really at least one action with authentic moral worth in the same phenomenal world. For, in both cases, from the fact that we cannot find a natural cause determining the action, we cannot conclude that such natural cause does not exist and, instead of the practical judgment or the consciousness of moral duty, that it actually does not even determine the action.

Nevertheless, the impossibility of settling the reality of the will does not constitute a paralyzing objection. Because, although the critics do not realize it, the same objection can be raised against reason in its epistemic and theoretical spontaneity that they do not consider objectionable. In fact, we cannot prove once and for all that our theoretical judgments actually rest on the reasons we bring forward and not, for example, on unconscious hidden causes. However, against a systematic skepticism about freedom concerning our theoretical judgments we can reply that such freedom is a necessary presupposition for the skeptic stating his doubts, because he can only cast his doubts on freedom in our judgments by judging. And, similarly, we could perhaps show that the will with the correspondent capacity to make the practical judgments effective in the actions is a necessary presupposition for the moral skeptic in the very moment when he casts his doubts on the validity of the moral law.[18] But where is such a will to be found, a will that could be characterized independently of the validity of the moral law and would constitute the very starting point for the skeptic stating his doubts on the moral law?

Now, in paragraph 12 of *Groundwork* II Kant analyses a concept of will or practical reason that is weak enough to be accepted even by the skeptic, according to which the will is "the capacity to act **in accordance with the representation** of laws, that is, in accordance with principles" (*Groundwork*, 4:412). Since it is in this passage that Kant begins his analysis of rational agency that will lead to the formula(e) of the categorical imperative, the laws in question cannot include, at least immediately, the moral law, but only "mere maxims." In other words, Kant's starting point for discovering the principle of morality is itself morally neutral and, therefore, must be accepted by the moral skeptic. According to Kant, to have a will in this sense means to have the capacity to act knowing what one is doing, that is, it means to be able to will individual actions as instances of determinate concepts[19] or principles, and *just because* they are instances of these concepts and principles. In sum, Kant's starting point is a concept of will or rational agency conceived as a capacity to act in accordance with judgments, and that consists in a capacity to take a position before given inclinations and desires as possible principles of determination.

Now, in order to state his doubts the moral skeptic must at least admit that he has a will in this sense, that he knows what he is doing, thereby acknowledging that his practical judgment is determined by reasons, and not by causes, and has causality on his actions. For otherwise he could not claim that he knows what he is doing and cast his doubts on the validity of the moral law. In fact, if the moral skeptic does not admit at least that his judgments based on reasons have causality on his actions, then the very question of the validity of the moral law simply would not concern him. In this case, he would better remain silent, like the plant in Aristotle's argument for the validity of the principle of contradiction.

Now, following the argument, whoever admits to have a will in this sense admits also that he has a causality with the property of freedom, that is, "that property of such causality that it can be efficient independently of alien causes **determining** it" (*Groundwork*, 4:446). But such a concept of freedom is not sufficient for Kant's purposes yet. For all we know thus far is that such will has the capacity *not* to be determined by alien causes, but we do not know positively what could determine such will to action. Kant's next step is to show that the positive concept of freedom flows analytically from the negative one. In fact, since every causality has laws, and since the will cannot be governed by the natural law, that expresses "a heteronomy of efficient causes, since every effect was possible only in accordance with the law that something else determines the efficient cause to causality" (4:446–47), then the only alternative available is to think of the will as a cause that has the law to determine itself to act, that is, to determine itself autonomously to causality. But as Kant had shown in *Groundwork* II, the moral law is nothing more than the expression of the autonomy of the will in its legislation. In this way, if the moral skeptic admits that he has a will and knows what he is doing, then he must admit that he is subjected to the moral law.

Suspicion of a Circle

Thus, whatever the shortcomings contained in it, the only objection it seems we cannot raise to Kant's argument is that it is circular. But Kant himself writes:

> It must be freely admitted that a kind of circle comes to light here from which, *as it seems*, there is no way to escape. We take ourselves as free in the order of efficient causes in order to think ourselves under moral laws in the order of ends; and we afterwards think ourselves as subject to these laws because we have ascribed to ourselves freedom of will. (*Groundwork*, 4:450; my emphasis)

This intriguing passage, in which Kant seems to be so unfair to himself, has challenged many of the most authoritative interpreters. Its paradigmatic interpretation was provided by Paton, usually a very sympathetic Kant's interpreter, and it has influenced the discussion on the subject. According to Paton, "In plain fact the objection totally misrepresents his argument. He never argued from the categorical imperative to freedom, but at least professed, however mistakenly, to establish the presupposition of freedom by an insight into the nature of self-conscious reason quite independently of moral considerations."[20]

Thus, according to Paton, the objection of circularity would amount to the acknowledgment by Kant that his proof of freedom was not actually grounded in independent, morally neutral premises, on the basis of which the validity of the morality in turn could be proven. In sum, Paton claims that Kant eventually admitted that he had proven freedom from morality in order to prove morality from freedom, thereby incurring in a circular reasoning. However, if we consider the text carefully, we conclude that Paton's paradigmatic interpretation simply does not correspond to Kant's own diagnosis of the problem. In fact, in the passage quoted above, where Kant mentions the alleged circle for the first time, he claims that "we take ourselves as free in the order of efficient causes in order to think ourselves under moral laws in the order of ends; and we afterwards think ourselves as subject to these laws because we have ascribed to ourselves freedom of will." Now, the two sentences that would constitute the semicircles of the alleged circular argument express in each case that *freedom is the condition of being subjected to the moral law,* and not the opposite. And we can observe the same in the passage where Kant claims to have once and for all removed what amounts to nothing but a suspicion of a circle.

> The *suspicion* that we raised above is now removed, the suspicion that a hidden circle was contained in our inference from freedom to autonomy and from the latter to the moral law—namely that we perhaps took as a ground the idea of freedom only for the sake of the moral law, so that we could afterwards infer the latter in turn from freedom, and that we were thus unable to furnish any ground at all for the moral law but could put it forward only as a *petitio principii* disposed souls would gladly grant us, but never as a demonstrable proposition. (*Groundwork*, 4:453; my emphasis)

I think one of the difficulties of comprehension of the passage above, at least concerning the Portuguese- and English-speaking interpreters, rests on a problem in the translation. For, in contradistinction to the new English translation quoted above that renders the expression "*nur um des sittlichen Gesetzes willen*" correctly as "for the sake of the moral law," Paton translated it inaccurately as "only because of the moral law." In fact, in the entry "*um . . . willen*" of the Langenscheidts Taschenwörterbuch Deutsch-Englisch we find the correspondent expressions "for the sake of" and "in behalf of." Now, if Paton had observed that simple linguistic convention, then he could have avoided a number of misleading interpretations of Kant's text inspired in his translation. For Paton's translation implies that Kant conceives the moral law in his argument as, so to speak, the *efficient cause* of presupposing freedom. If it would be the case, then Kant would actually have entirely misrepresented his argument by claiming that the moral law, and not the activity of judgment, was the cause for presupposing freedom. But, according to the correct translation and correspondent interpretation, Kant conceives the moral law as, so to speak, the *final cause* of presupposing freedom. In fact, what Kant is correctly claiming is that he takes as a ground the idea of freedom only on behalf of or in the interest of morality, and not on behalf of or in the interest of anything else. Sure, this interpretation does not put us in a position to understand Kant's problem yet. But at least it permits us to reject definitely Paton's paradigmatic interpretation as incorrect.

It is also worth remarking that, in both the passages where he mentions the more and more enigmatic circle, in addition to claiming that freedom is the condition to be subjected to the moral law, and not the opposite, Kant casts no doubt on the premise of freedom itself, but only on the moral law, which we could not put forward as "a demonstrable proposition." This is a very important remark because the interpreters often argue that, in a desperate attempt to escape from the circle and to prove freedom from independent and morally neutral premises, Kant would have made an appeal to the transcendental distinction sensible/intelligible world. Thus, according to the transcendental distinction, when we represent ourselves as rational beings we represent ourselves as members of the intelligible world, and, consequently, we represent ourselves as free from the natural law only valid for the sensible world. In this way, freedom would be proven from morally neutral premises and could in turn ground the validity of the moral law. However, Kant's attempt would have failed because the requirements of his own theoretical critical philosophy would forbid any *entrée* into the intelligible world except for that one provided by the consciousness of being under pure practical principles.[21]

Nevertheless, it should be noted that the appeal to the intelligible world is *not* intended by Kant as a means to have an independent access to freedom. On the contrary, Kant invites us to "inquire whether we do not take a different standpoint when *by means of freedom* we think ourselves as causes efficient *a priori* than when we represent ourselves in terms of our actions as effects that we see before our eyes" (*Groundwork*, 4:450; my emphasis). In other words, according to Kant, it is freedom already proven, namely, on the basis of rational agency conceived as a capacity to act in accordance with judgments, which gives us access to the intelligible world, and not the opposite.

In fact, the alleged circle, or rather, in Kant's own words, the *suspicion* of a circle from which there *seems* to be no way to escape consists at bottom in a very simple problem. *Groundwork* III deals with a question inherited from the prior section, which is the following: "How is a categorical imperative possible?" (*Groundwork*, 4:420). However, Kant approaches this question from two different, although interrelated, sides or perspectives. On the one side, he means the problem of explaining "how the *necessitation* of the will, which the imperative expresses in the problem, can be thought" (4:417, my emphasis). Kant considers this to be a very acute problem because, in contradistinction to the hypothetical imperative that commands under some presupposition as its condition, the categorical imperative requires explaining how an unconditional binding imperative is possible for finite rational beings like us. On the other side, Kant means the problem of explaining how the categorical imperative conceived as an a priori synthetic *proposition* is possible (4:444). So conceived, the question requires the above reconstructed justification or deduction of the principle of morality as an a priori synthetic proposition from the necessary practical presupposition of freedom. The puzzle for Kant arises when he realizes that if "freedom of the will is presupposed, morality together with its principle follows from it by mere analysis of its concept" (4:447). In other words, the presupposition of freedom would transform the supreme principle of morality into a proposition analytically contained in our will with the consequence that the categorical imperative would thereby lose its character of an imperative or of a necessitation or obligation for us. This state of affairs finds its (not very happy) expression in the propositions quoted above. "We take ourselves as free in the order of efficient causes in order to think ourselves under moral laws in the order of ends" refers to the deduction of morality from the necessary presupposition of freedom, and "we afterwards think ourselves as subject to these laws because we have ascribed to ourselves freedom of will" refers to the problem of explaining the possibility of being subjected to the unconditional principle of morality. Thus Kant realizes that there seems to be, if not a circle in the classical sense, at least some logical inconsistency here. For if freedom is presupposed, then we are both subjected and not subjected to the moral law. We are subjected because freedom is the condition of possibility of being under the moral law. We are not subjected because freedom makes us members of the intelligible world so that, if we were only this, all our actions would naturally be in conformity to the moral law. In sum, the successful deduction of morality from freedom seems to make it difficult to account for the fact that we are *subjected* to the moral law and "hence **on what grounds** [*woher*] **the moral law is binding**" (4:450). And now we understand how the transcendental distinction is supposed to solve this seemingly inconsistency.

> For we now see that when we think of ourselves as free we transfer ourselves into the world of understanding as members of it and cognize autonomy of the will along with its consequence, morality; but if we think of ourselves as put under obligation [*als verpflichtet*] we regard ourselves as belonging to the world of sense and yet at the same time to the world of understanding. (*Groundwork*, 4:454)

Notes

1. H. J. Paton, *The Categorical Imperative: A Study in Kant's Moral Philosophy*, 3rd ed. (London: Hutchinson, 1958), 202. Astonishingly enough, though, Paton also concludes that the deduction of *Groundwork* III is flawed.

2. I added the words "through this" to the English translation, rendering the German word *dadurch*, contained in the original, in order to point out the character of a deduction in the usual, logical, sense of morality from freedom that is also present in the proof structure in *Groundwork* III.

3. See *Practical Reason*, 5:29, *Groundwork*, 4:450; and Henry Allison, *Kant's Theory of Freedom* (Cambridge: Cambridge University Press, 1990), 201–13.

4. Nevertheless, in 5:3–4, Kant had already claimed, in a similar vein, that freedom is the keystone (*Schlußstein*) of all use of reason, even of the speculative reason.

5. And the objective reality of freedom itself, but only as a condition of possibility of autocracy.

6. It is also worth mentioning that, in a letter written after the publication of the second *Critique*, more precisely, in a letter of April 20, 1790, addressed to Kiesewetter, Kant still states confidently that "Der Begriff der Freiheit, als Kausalität, wird bejahend erkannt, welcher ohne einen Zirkel zu begehen mit dem moralischen Bestimmungsgrunde reciprocabel ist" (11:155).

7. Since I am interested in the deduction in *Groundwork* III, I cannot deal with the doctrine of the "fact of reason" in full. Nevertheless, since I intend to offer a defense of the deduction in the earlier work, I must give at least some hints of what I take to be the *Stellungwert* of the doctrine of the "fact of reason" in the second *Critique*, in which, according to the prevailing interpretation nowadays, we could find the "real" deduction of the principle of morality. To begin with, starting from a suggestion made by Robert Paul Wolff, *The Autonomy of Reason: A Commentary on Kant's Groundwork of the Metaphysic of Morals* (New York: Harper & Row, 1973), 24–8, we should always keep in mind that Kant's works, and even partial sections of his works, are directed at distinct audiences with correspondent layers of argument. Thus, for example, in the *Groundwork*, we have the first section directed to ordinary people not versed in philosophy and the second section directed to the "popular philosophers" of his time, both audiences holding morality to be something real and not a chimerical idea or a phantom of the brain, in contradistinction to the moral skeptic, to whom the third section is directed. Now, the hypothetical interlocutor of Kant in the Analytic of Principles of the second *Critique* is not the moral skeptic, but rather the philosopher who accepts the objective validity of morality as an undeniable fact and finds it only difficult to accept Kant's thesis that its principle or ground is to be found in the pure reason. In other words, as the polemic in the Analytic of Principles shows sufficiently, Kant's interlocutor is the moral philosopher who defends the traditional thesis according to which happiness constitutes the supreme principle of the actions or morality. Now, what Kant must show to such interlocutor is that the validity of morality has a character not of an empirical fact, but rather exactly of a fact of reason.

8. See Lewis White Beck, "A Prussian Hume and a Scottish Kant," in *Essays on Hume and Kant* (New Haven: Yale University Press, 1978), 126.

9. This is also noted by Allison, *Kant's Theory of Freedom*, 217.

10. In what follows, I appeal to Tugendhat's analysis of assertions. E. Tugendhat, *Traditional and Analytical Philosophy: Lectures on the Philosophy of Language*, trans. P. A. Gorner (Cambridge: Cambridge University Press, 1982), esp. 198–200.

11. Michael Dummett, *Frege: Philosophy of Language* (Cambridge: Cambridge University Press, 295–301.

12. Davidson says: "A person can have a reason for an action, and perform the action, and yet this reason not be the reason why he did it. Central to the relation between a reason and the action it explains is the idea that the agent performed the action **because** he had the reason. . . . The justifying role of a reason depends upon the explanatory role." Donald Davidson, *Essays on Actions and Events*, 2nd ed. (Oxford: Clarendon Press, 2001), 9.

13. This possible reply is also examined by Henry Allison, "Kant's Refutation of Materialism," in Allison, *Idealism and Freedom: Essays on Kant's Theoretical and Practical Philosophy* (Cambridge: Cambridge University Press, 1996), 100–101.

14. In his polemical *Review of Schulz*, Kant comes to the same conclusion: "Although he would not himself admit it, he has assumed in the depths of his soul that understanding is able to determine his judgment in accordance with objective grounds that are always valid and is not subject to the mechanism of merely subjectively determining causes . . . hence he always admits freedom to think, without which there is no reason" (8:14).

15. In claiming that we cannot start from freedom to prove morality in the passages of the second *Critique* discussed above, Kant is once again recalling this critical diagnosis of the third Antinomy, because he is denying that we can start from a *theoretical* proof of freedom, as I tried to show, since the theoretical-speculative philosophy cannot take position in favor or against the reality of freedom.

16. A paradigmatic example of this kind of objection can be found in Allison, *Kant's Theory of Freedom*, esp. 217–18.

17. Gerold Prauss, for example, is not alone in claiming "dass Kant seine Praktische Philosophie insgesamt, . . . zuletzt doch nur auf Sand gebaut hat. Denn die Grundlegung für sie, das heißt, ein von Moralität noch unabhängiges Kriterium für Wirklichkeit von Wille, Freiheit und Handlung als solche ist er schuldig geblieben." Gerold Prauss, *Kant über Freiheit als Autonomie* (Frankfurt am Main: Vittorio Klostermann, 1983), 10.

18. As mentioned above, we should always keep in mind that Kant's texts and arguments are directed to determinate audiences.

19. See Paton, *Categorical Imperative*, 81.

20. Ibid., 225.

21. See Allison, *Kant's Theory of Freedom*, 227–28.

9

The Distinction between Right and Ethics in Kant's Philosophy

Ricardo Ribeiro Terra

The analysis of the relation between morality and right requires that one makes precise the meaning of these terms that sometimes carry a narrow, sometimes a wide sense.[1] When distinguishing laws of nature from laws of freedom, the moral term in Kant acquires a wide sense: the latter are called moral laws. Kant affirms that, while they are "directed merely to external actions and their conformity to law they are called *juridical* laws; but if they also require that they (the laws) themselves be the determining grounds of actions, they are *ethical* laws, and then one says that conformity with juridical laws is the *legality* of an action and conformity with ethical laws is its *morality*" (*Doctrine of Right*, 6:214). Morality in its wide sense comprehends the doctrine of morals, encompassing right as well as ethics. Thus, one cannot take as correlatives the pairs moral/right and morality/legality. An interpretation identifying them would lead to a separation between right and ethics without pointing out the common elements.[2] Regarding ethics, Kant designated that it meant the doctrine of morals, and afterwards designated only a part of it the doctrine of virtue (*Doctrine of Virtue*, 6:379).

As division of the doctrine of morals, right opposes itself to ethics (doctrine of virtue) and not to morality, which is wider than this; what may cause some confusion is calling morality the agreement of actions with ethical laws. (It is noteworthy that Kant has not always maintained the meaning of the words as they were stated here, which evidently does not make the reader's task easier.)

For Kant some concepts are common to both parts of the metaphysics of morals, for instance, duty and obligation. Duty is understood as "that action to which someone is bound . . . [which] is therefore the matter of obligation." Obligation is "the necessity of a free action under a categorical imperative of reason" (*Doctrine of Right*, 6:222). Before insisting on the common points

This article was first published as "A distinção entre direito e éthica na filosofia kantiana," in the *Revista de Filosofia Política* 4 (1987): 49–65. Translated by Cauê Cardoso Polla.

between right and ethics, it is necessary to explain their distinctiveness. Laws that relate to external actions, which must conform to them, have been opposed to laws that ought to become the determining principles of actions. The distinction between these two fields lies in the difference of the incentive (*Triebfeder*): "that lawgiving which makes an action a duty and also makes this duty the incentive is *ethical*. But that lawgiving which does not include the incentive of duty in the law and so admits an incentive other than the idea of duty itself is *juridical*" (*Doctrine of Right*, 6:219). In the first case, the incentive, that is, "the subjective ground of desire" (*Groundwork*, 4:427), is duty itself. The action is realized not only according to an objective ground of determination, universally valid, but also by duty, revealing a feeling of respect for the moral law itself. Hence, the incentive is the respect for the moral law and only this incentive is ethical. Juridical law, however, admits another incentive that not the idea of duty, that is, incentives that determine choice (*Willkür*) pathologically, and not practically or spontaneously, that is, through sentiments that cause aversion given that the law must obligate in an effective manner. Returning to the distinction made above: in the juridical sphere there is *legality*, the correspondence of an action with the law, even though the incentive may be pathological; and in the ethical sphere there is morality, where this correspondence turns out to be insufficient because the respect for the law is demanded as the incentive of the action.

In the juridical sphere one does not dwell on the realm of intention, since only the exteriority of actions is considered.

> Duties in accordance with rightful lawgiving can be only external duties, since this lawgiving does not require that the idea of this duty, which is internal, itself be the determining ground of the agent's choice; and since it still needs an incentive suited to the law, it can connect only external incentives with it. On the other hand, ethical lawgiving, while it also makes internal actions duties, does not exclude external actions but applies to everything that is duty in general. (*Doctrine of Right*, 6:219)

According to rightful lawgiving, duties as well as their incentives are external, which makes it possible to judge the fulfilment (or nonfulfilment) of the action and the ways to ensure its realization. Because ethical lawgiving demands that its incentive be the respect for the law, it cannot be an external lawgiving. It is impossible to determine an intention through external laws given that the intention cannot be controlled by a judge that is not the agent itself. However, ethical lawgiving can accept duties from an external law and make it its own—so all duties belong in some way to ethics. Kant points out that the juridical laws concern freedom in its external usage, and ethics in both its external and internal usages; and compares them with theoretical philosophy: "only objects of outer sense are in space, whereas objects of outer as well as of inner sense are in time, since the representations of both are still representations, and as such belong together to inner sense" (*Doctrine of Right*, 6:214). There are duties that are directly ethical, but the juridical ones, while they are duties and also concern internal lawgiving, are indirectly ethical. For instance, to abide by a contract is a juridical duty, and one can be obligated through an external coercion to fulfil it; but if the external incentive cannot casually be exercised, in the ethical sphere the fulfilment of the contract remains a duty, taking into account the difference that in this case the action would be virtuous and not only in accordance with the law. "The *Doctrine of Right* and the doctrine of virtue are therefore distinguished not so much by their different duties as by the difference in their lawgiving, which connects one incentive or the other with the law" (*Doctrine of Right*, 6:220, 384). Although it can have duties in common with right, ethics does not have an external way of obligating as does the former.

There is a certain difficulty in the Kantian system, as Gerhard Dulckeit emphasizes,[3] when all duty is considered duty of virtue (the juridical duties considered as indirectly ethical), which is more complex when all duties are regarded as embraced by the general ethical duty. However, this becomes more comprehensible when one understands the ethical duty as relating only to "the formal aspect of the determination of will which through a virtuous disposition (*tugendhafte Gesinnung*) is the determination principle of the power of choice."[4] The duties of virtue and the juridical duties are subjected to the general ethical ones; what happens is that "the system of the doctrine of duties in general is now divided into the system of the *Doctrine of Right* (*ius*), which deals with duties that can be given by external laws, and the system of the *doctrine of virtue* (*ethica*), which treats of duties that cannot be so given; and this division may stand" (*Doctrine of Virtue*, 6:379). Right and virtue are part of the doctrine of morals and have the same basis, which is a consequence of the unity of practical reason, both types of lawgiving being derived from the autonomy of will. "The autonomy law of the categorical imperative is thought at the same time as law of the will of oneself (ethics) and as of the others' will (right)."[5] The autonomy of will is the basis of both types of lawgiving, the supreme principle of the doctrine of morals is the categorical imperative (*Doctrine of Right*, 6:226).[6]

Both the definition of right and the universal principle of right are composed of the same basic elements. "Right is therefore the sum of the conditions under which the choice of one can be united with the choice of another in accordance with a universal law of freedom" (*Doctrine of Right*, 6:230). The universal law of right is in turn thus formulated: "so act externally that the use of your choice can coexist with the freedom of everyone in accordance with a universal law" (6:231). This regards external relations, actions of people able to influence others' actions; from this perspective the dispositions do not matter and the universal law of right is not necessarily taken as the incentive of the action (given that it is not about virtue, but about right). What does matter is not the content of the choice (the end one has) but rather the form of the relations among the powers of choice of the people involved (6:230); for example, when one negotiates with another over an object, the benefit that one may or may not obtain is not taken into account, and what matters is only the form of the relation among the powers of choice, both bargainers being considered free and equal and the coexistence of their freedom being in accordance with a universal law. The basic elements are two: on the one hand, a reciprocal relation of the powers of choice, on the other, the universality of the law.

The first element affirms the specificity of right while it concerns the external relation between people, but also simultaneously characterizes freedom as coexistence or mutual limitation of freedom, what is highlighted in *Theory and Practice*: "*Right* is the limitation of the freedom of each to the condition of its harmony with the freedom of everyone insofar as this is possible in accordance with a universal law" (8:289–90). This conception of freedom as mutual limitation is suited to the defense of individual freedom, the right of each person extending to the line where the other's right begins. Now, the universality of law points to practical reason, to right as one of the branches of the doctrine of morals—laws being given a priori and founded in freedom understood as autonomy. The tension between freedom understood as mutual limitation and freedom as autonomy will be present in many parts of Kant's work.

If right concerns the numerous external relations and cannot have duty itself as incentive, it needs an external coercion (*Zwang*) that demands the realization of a determined action. In the sphere of virtue there is not an external, but rather a personal coercion (*Selbstzwang*) (*Doctrine of Virtue*, 6:379). When someone who lends money to another person has the right to repayment, it does not mean that the lender can persuade the debtor to pay the debt, instead, it means that a legal coercion may force the latter to pay; in this case, "right and authorization to use coercion therefore mean one and the same thing" (*Doctrine of Right*, 6:232). The problem presented here is the one regarding the reconciliation of coercion with freedom, which is solved this way:

> Whatever is wrong is a hindrance to freedom in accordance with universal laws. But coercion is a hindrance or resistance to freedom. Therefore, if a certain use of freedom is itself a hindrance to freedom in accordance with universal laws (i.e., wrong), coercion that is opposed to this (as a *hindering of a hindrance to freedom*) is consistent with freedom in accordance with universal laws, that is, it is right. (*Doctrine of Right*, 6:231)

Coercion is in accordance with freedom because it is the hindrance of the one that opposes freedom, the faculty to coerce the unjust ones is just in itself. Kant even compares right with the body's movements—limitation of freedom, its coexistence, and the "the law of a reciprocal coercion necessarily in accord with the freedom of everyone under the principle of universal freedom" would be analogous to "the law of the *equality of action and reaction*" (*Doctrine of Right*, 6:232; see also *Theory and Practice*, 8:292).[7] Here one finds the same tension; on the one hand, reciprocal coercion, the law of the equality of action and reaction, on the other, the principle of universal freedom.

This tension in Kant's thought fosters a plurality of interpretations. Besides, positivistic-oriented jurists tend to bring Kant to their side. The same thing happens with the liberals, democrats, or socialists who try to see in Kant an adept of their respective positions (not to mention the polemics about whether Kant's philosophy of right bears a critical character or not).

Diverging interpretations, as they explore one aspect of Kant's thought, excluding others, may teach a lot about the internal difficulties of the analyzed text. This is particularly true regarding the notion of right, its relation with morality and the conception of freedom. In this sense we will see three different interpretations, two referring to the relation of morality and right and one about the notion of freedom.[8]

Giole Solari, for instance, is concerned with the independence of right from morality, and thus centers his interpretation on this question. For him, Kant would hold the merit of affirming the autonomy of right, as Machiavelli would hold the merit of affirming the autonomy of politics from morality. The autonomy of right would have an important historical meaning within a liberal perspective against the absolutist state because it intended to "extend its action to the ethical domain and contribute its ways to the happiness of individuals. In speculation about the distinction between right and morality, the question of the nature and the limits of political activities regarding the individual's respect was implicit."[9] Liberalism would find in Kant its juridical shape, as in Locke it had found its economical.

In another work Solari develops the problem further, posing the problem of the metaphysics of right. Would it be like the metaphysics of nature, a system of principles to comprehend and unify the juridical experience? Or like ethics would it give the practical norms for juridical action? His answer is the former. Solari develops the analogy made by Kant between right and mathematics, "that wouldn't be extrinsic and symbolic, but innermost and perfect."[10] The juridical problem is thought of as the problem of the coexistence of external freedoms, as a plurality of powers that are in equilibrium in terms of the law of the equality of action and reaction.

> Thus, the juridical synthesis comes to be an external-mechanical synthesis . . . we are induced to believe that the *Doctrine of Right* is to Kant more a product of pure reason than of practical reason, and must itself be included more in the theoretical sciences than in the ethical and deontological sciences. If one thinks that the application of the mathematical methods and criteria measures, for Kant, the theoretical validity of knowledge and its level of perfection, the science of right comes to be situated in a favored condition in relation to all the other moral disciplines, allowing itself to build its concepts *a priori* and with mathematical accuracy.[11]

Maybe Solari goes too far in affirming this analogy between right and mathematics and the theory of movement, which is in accord with his reading of the theory of right and the conception of freedom as liberal, and with the exigency of a radical separation between right and morality. The charge one must accept in this reading is a certain "forgetfulness" regarding the notions of autonomy, the unity of practical reason and metaphysics of morals, despite the fact that Solari tries to show the accord between right and morality. However, his analysis does not take into account that metaphysics of morals encompasses the *Doctrine of Right* and the doctrine of virtue, as well as the Kantian emphasis in the rational universality of the practical law.

A much earlier work, from Kurt Lisser, goes in an opposite direction in two fundamental aspects. First, he considers ethics in a narrow sense (doctrine of virtue) together with right as parts of ethics in a wider sense (doctrine of morals). Second, he evaluates the concept of freedom and the analogy to the law of the equality of action and reaction, which will be considered here.

For Lisser, the great difficulty imposed by the concept of Kantian right consists in the fact that it does not properly consider economy, and so starts from the state of nature and its constant struggle. The concept of right does not start from social relations, but rather from "the concept of an individual threatened by all the others. Thus, from the beginning, it turned out to be impossible for Kant to discover a definition of right that could be anything but a mere tautology."[12] The individualistic perspective leads to a conception of freedom as mutual limitation, and one looks for "delimiting the individual's sphere of freedom against the other's,"[13] which is as unfruitful as the definition of right. In this perspective Kant could make an analogy of right with the law of the equality of action and reaction because in the juridical state there would be equality between the action and the reaction of the powers of choice that limit each other reciprocally. The mistake in this analogy consists in that the juridical state is an idea, a task to be realized, and not only a factical situation in which effective forces are in confrontation: the analogy effaces that binding between right and ethics in its wide sense. "This analogy leads to error and one can suppose that Kant's tautological definition of right bases itself upon it."[14] The only definition of freedom that is in accord with the Kantian system is the one of freedom as autonomy, which in the juridical sphere would be: each individual obeys external laws to which he can adhere, resulting in conformity to ethics in its wide sense and its principle of autonomy.

What is interesting in the confrontation between Lisser and Solari is that each one must reject or not dwell upon some aspects of Kant's philosophy. Solari leaves aside the doctrine of morals and Lisser rejects the definition of right and one of the definitions of freedom so as to find the coherence of the system in the notion of autonomy. Against Lisser one could say that Kant does not merely take the threatened person as starting point, because human beings are transformed once the state of nature is an idea, not a fact; it is the correlate of the exigency to enter into the civil state, which is an a priori rational exigency. Thus, the starting point would be this rational exigency, and even more: when he deals with the coexistence of a plurality of powers of choice, Kant insists that it happens under universal laws; again one sees the universal perspective of rationality. Nonetheless, Lisser touches on a problem whose meaning is worth looking into because, even though the perspective of rationality may be found in the whole process, the "why" regarding the question of the social contract, of the state of nature, of the coexistence of the powers of choice, of the mutual limitation of freedom, and the much quoted analogy of right with the law of action and reaction, remains.

Some clues for the development of this question are found in an article by Norberto Bobbio where he tries to characterise the two notions of freedom present in Kant's thought. In order to analyze the question in Kant, Bobbio first establishes a distinction between the two basic meanings of the word "freedom" (a distinction first made by Benjamin Constant): "Freedom means now the faculty to realize or not certain actions, not being impeded by the others who live with me, or by the society as an organic complex or merely by the state power; now, the power to not obey other norm than the one that I impose myself."[15] The first conception is the liberal one, defended by Montesquieu. The second is the democratic one, defended by Rousseau. The peculiarity here is that both would be found in Kant—the democratic would be the explicit definition and the liberal conception would orient his theory. The explicit definition would be found in many passages, for instance, in *Perpetual Peace* (8:350) or in the *Doctrine of Right* (§46). But in the definition of right, in the conception of state and in the philosophy of history, the liberal conception would be predominant, and to Bobbio, "the liberal conception of history—history as the theater of antagonisms—sustains, in Kant's thinking, the liberal conception of right—right as condition of the coexistence of individual freedoms—and the liberal conception of the state—the state having as its purpose not to guide the subjects toward happiness, but rather to guarantee order."[16] Bobbio's major concern is to distinguish both conceptions of freedom in order to classify Kant's thinking as liberal. However, he opens up the way to consider the relations between right and the philosophy of history, and also to think that the maintenance of both conceptions may be bound to the commitment of an individualistic political anthropology and the universalizing exigency of reason. One must admit that for Kant right has its specificity, coercion is one of its fundamental characteristics and the liberal elements are undeniable; but the *Doctrine of Right* belongs to the *Metaphysics of Morals* and the notion of autonomy is essential to its basic principles. An analysis of this notion in morality and right, and the examination of the notion of natural right, may cast some light upon these questions.

In Kant's philosophy the problem of the connection between freedom and law, freedom and obedience, will be solved through the path opened up by Rousseau, who affirms: "the obedience to the law that one prescribes oneself is freedom."[17] Thus, law can be thought of not only as a restriction of freedom, but the obedience to law and freedom's spontaneity can also be thought of together, not as opposing each other. This theme is so fundamental for Kant's philosophy that Beck suggests calling it "by analogy to the 'Copernican revolution,' the 'Rousseauian revolution' in moral," although "while Rousseau established the essential link between law and freedom primarily for the political domain, where his doctrine was adopted almost unchanged by Kant, the doctrine of the autonomous government ruled by the free citizens of a republic is deepened by Kant with a moral, metaphysical and even religious conception."[18] Rousseau brings about a revolution in the sphere of political theory when he binds the justification of the obedience to the authorship of the law by those who must respect it. Kant would "deepen" the theme in the moral sphere, developing the question of autonomy of will, placing it as the principle of morality.[19] In the political sphere Rousseau's theory would be transformed, by Kant, much more than Beck suggested. Nevertheless, the "Rousseauian revolution" is central both to morality and to Kant's political philosophy and philosophy of right.

Kant understands the autonomy of will as that "property of the will by which it is a law to itself (independent of any property of the objects of volition). The principle of autonomy is, therefore: to choose only in such a way that the maxims of your choice are included as universal law in the same volition" (*Groundwork*, 4:440). Autonomy in the strict sense demands not only that the law not be given by the object, but also that the will not be determined by sensible inclinations. If the will searches for the law outside itself, or is determined by inclinations, it ceases to be a lawgiver and becomes heteronomous. If will is autonomous it can only be determined objectively by the moral law, subjectively by the respect for this law (see *Groundwork*, 4:400). The incentive of the will must be the law itself, and thus, "of every action that conforms to the law but is not done for the sake of the law, one can say that it is morally good in accordance with the *letter* but not the *spirit* (the disposition)" (*Practical Reason*, 5:72). In the ethical sphere the action is not only realized in accordance with duty but also from duty, the incentive is included in the law and one must fulfill the letter that also accords with the spirit of the law. In the sphere of right one admits an incentive other than the idea of duty, and what is of interest here is the conformity (or not) of the action to the law, without taking into account the incentive. Even more: in right, incentives "must be drawn from *pathological* determining grounds of choice, inclinations and aversions, and among these, from aversions; for it is a lawgiving, which constrains, not an allurement, which invites" (*Doctrine of Right*, 6:219). Juridical laws must use the possibility of coercion to obligate those who intend to infringe them by creating an unpleasant situation. The power of choice is determined by aversive pathological principles. One can be in accord with the law itself, but what matters is the conformity of the action with the law. Hence, in right, the autonomy of will is not realized as in ethics because the former admits incentives that introduce heteronomy.[20] This does not mean that right is alien to the autonomy of will. Instead, since "*heteronomy* of choice . . . does not ground any obligation at all" (*Practical Reason*, 5:33), the juridical obligation, as well as the exigency of the coexistence of the freedoms according to a universal law, must be based in practical reason. Even though the incentives of right impede the complete realization of autonomy as virtue, the juridical constraint does not impede freedom; instead, it serves as "*a hindering of a hindrance to freedom*" (*Doctrine of Right*, 6:231). There must thus be a common point between freedom as the autonomy of ethics and juridical freedom.

Autonomy in its narrow sense, as it is defined by Kant, has its role in right once the categorical imperative is the supreme principle of the doctrine of morals; but lawgiving and juridical duties, although they share a common ground with ethical laws and duties, are distinct from them:

> The concept of duty stands in immediate relation to a *law* (even if I abstract from all ends, as the matter of the law). The formal principle of duty, in the categorical imperative "so act that the maxim of your action could become a universal *law*," already indicates this. Ethics adds only that this principle is to be thought as the law of *your* own will and not of will in general, which could also be the will of others; in the latter case the law would provide a duty of right, which lies outside the sphere of ethics. (*Doctrine of Virtue*, 6:388–89)

In ethics law is the principle of subjective and objective determination, and is thought as the law of the will itself; in right, law can also be the other's will, which will ground an external juridical duty. The relationship between the wills in right will be thought under a general will, which sends one back to autonomy in right, because all take part in the lawgiving to which they subject themselves. Thus, the juridical relations must occur under the universal law of freedom; hence, external freedom (juridical) is defined as "the warrant to obey no other external laws than those to which I could have given my consent" (*Perpetual Peace*, 8:350).

Autonomy can be thought of in a wide sense as the need for the participation of everybody in lawgiving, without taking into account the incentive; one returns to Rousseau, to a certain extent, conceiving of autonomy both in the juridical and political spheres.[21] The positive conception of freedom will function as a common ground for the juridical-political ideas such as state of nature, original contract, republican constitution, and perpetual peace. In the political sphere the original contract shows the need for autonomy and demands that popular sovereignty and will serve as a parameter to lawgiving, given that it will be a fair law if it is derived from the united will of a whole people. The idea of a contract binds itself to the idea of state as the gathering of men under juridical laws necessary a priori, and demands a republican constitution that guarantees the realization of these laws; this constitution must allow the formulation of a federation of nations that has perpetual peace as its purpose. These juridical-political ideas form a system of patterns that provides the criteria for the adequacy of the laws and political institutions. In virtue of their freedom, human beings demand a government in which the people legislate (*Conflict*, 7:87). In this sense it can be stated that through the legislative, executive, and judicial powers, "a state (*civitas*) has its autonomy, that is, by which it forms and preserves itself in accordance with laws of freedom" (*Doctrine of Right*, §49, 6:318). The autonomy of the state is not mere independence from other states, or its self-sufficiency, because it encapsulates the need for the realization of the universality of the laws of freedom, not of happiness. Autonomy of the state is made possible by the union of distinct powers that come from popular sovereignty. The state's security lies in the maximal agreement of the constitution with the principles of right, which, in turn, are themselves grounded in the autonomy of will. The need for autonomy to include them both gives unity to right and politics and also points to its cohesion with ethics, despite the differences. Both ethics and right affirm the connection of freedom with the law in the form of the obedience to the law that was prescribed by human beings for themselves, providing the cohesion of the unity of practical reason.

Given that the notion of autonomy provided a solution to the question of the connection of freedom with the law, it remains to be explained why the moral law and also the juridical one are formulated as imperatives. If human beings are the lawgivers, why think in terms of the duties of virtue and the juridical duties? The moral law is valid for all rational beings. In limited rational beings such as human beings that have wills and inclinations, and thus are able to follow the incentives that do not coincide with law, will is not always in conformity with reason, so the determination of the will according to laws is a necessitation (*Nöthigung*), and "the representation of an objective principle, insofar as it is necessitating for a will, is called a command (of reason), and the formula of the command is called an **imperative**" (*Groundwork*, 4:413). A holy will would follow the objective law without being obligated, for the law would not be for it an imperative because will would be always in accordance with reason.[22] However, two distinct points of view must be considered: as having sensibility, a human being has its inclinations and appetites that put him in the sphere of the heteronomous natural laws; as having intelligence, he belongs to the intelligible world, and is autonomous. He is a lawgiver while he belongs to this intelligible world, but belongs also to the sensible world and is subject to inclinations that can move him away from the rational law considered an imperative. This double standard is also essential in the sphere of right. Here, as the coercion is external, the problem of the punishments for crimes committed, and also the problem of the criminal as the author of the law, is raised:

> As a colegislator in dictating the *penal law*, I cannot possibly be the same person who, as a subject, is punished in accordance with the law; for as one who is punished, namely as a criminal, I cannot possibly have a voice in legislation (the legislator is holy). Consequently, when I draw up a penal law against myself as a criminal, it is pure reason in me (*homo noumenon*), legislating with regard to rights, which subjects me, as someone capable of crime and so as another person (*homo phaenomenon*), to the penal law, together with all others in a civil union. (*Doctrine of Right*, 6:335)

Each one is the lawgiver from the point of view of the intelligible; lawgiving comes from pure reason, thus all are colawgivers because all are rational. Juridical and ethical laws come from the same practical reason, and in order to understand them one must adopt the same point of view, that is, that of the intelligible world; but as human beings also belong to the sensible world, both the ethical and juridical laws will appear as imperatives, and actions in accordance with laws appear as duties.

Just as Kant maintains certain basic concepts of the political philosophy of the seventeenth and eighteenth centuries, as state of nature, original contract, republican constitution (transforming them into ideas), he also maintains the term natural right to refer to the discipline that bundles those concepts. They serve as a norm, an ideal model bound to the autonomy of man: "the idea of a constitution in harmony with the natural right of human beings, one namely in which the citizens obedient to the law, besides being united, ought also to be legislative, lies at the basis of all political forms" (*Conflict*, 7:90–91). Thus, one has a criterion for the reformations and improvements of the constitution to be promoted by the chief of the state and also a criterion for the elaboration of positive laws: the laws that the people cannot promulgate to themselves, the lawgiver cannot give them.

Natural right is one that is not statutory, it is a "right that can be cognized a priori by everyone's reason" (*Doctrine of Right*, §36, 6:296); it is the system of the rational juridical laws a priori. Natural right constitutes, then, a system of rational juridical laws a priori and thus cannot be identified only with right in the state of nature. In *Reflection* 7084 Kant raises this question: "Since the phrase 'natural right' is used ambiguously, we must make use of a subtlety in order to eliminate this ambiguity. We distinguish 'natural *right*' (*Naturrecht*) from '*natural* right' (*natürlichen Recht*)" (*R*7084, 19:245). In the *Doctrine of Right* this distinction is raised again: "The highest division of natural right (*Naturrecht*) cannot be the division (sometimes made) into *natural* and *social* right (*natürliche und gesellschaftliche*); it must instead be the division into natural and *civil* right (*natürliche und bürgerliche Recht*), the former of which is called *private right* and the latter public right. For a *state of nature* is not opposed to a social but to a civil condition" (*Doctrine of Right*, 6:242). Natural right (*Naturrecht*) encompasses both private right (natural right in narrow sense) and public right. The distinction between natural right and positive right is not confused with the distinction between private natural right and public right (civil right). Public right can be seen both in the sphere of rational laws, and thus in *Naturrecht*'s sphere, and in the sphere of positive laws.[23]

Natural right is necessary and comes a priori from a universal lawgiver, from the idea of the united will of a people, from reason itself; it is already the "positive (statutory) right, which proceeds from the will of a legislator" (*Doctrine of Right*, 6:237), and this is why the positive law is contingent (*zufällig*) and chosen (*willkürlich*) (6:227). As positive laws come from a determined lawgiver who holds the power of the state, they form an effective lawgiving; and the state has the coercive means to make these laws obeyed. But both natural as well as positive laws are external:

> Obligatory laws for which there can be an external lawgiving are called *external* laws (*leges externae*) in general. Those among them that can be recognized as obligatory *a priori* by reason even without external lawgiving are indeed external but *natural* laws, whereas those that do not bind without actual external lawgiving (and so without it would not be laws) are called *positive* laws. One can therefore contain only positive laws; but then a natural law would still have to precede it, which would establish the authority of the lawgiver (i.e., his authorization to bind others by his mere *choice*). (*Doctrine of Right*, 6:224)

In contrast to ethical laws, natural juridical laws are external, but like ethical laws they ground themselves a priori in reason. Natural right, to use

Dulckeit's terms,[24] has an ideal value (regulative) and a real one (obligatory). It serves as ideal parameter to the lawgiver but also obligates him just as it does other individuals. This obligation is a priori rational and indicates its common origin with ethics.[25] Just as the idea of a sovereign, rational being representing the whole people needs a physical person in order to be effectuated (*Doctrine of Right*, 6:338), natural right, despite the fact that it obligates, needs positive laws to be effectuated safely: "Civil legislation has as its essential supreme principle the realization of the natural right of human beings, which is a mere idea in the *statu naturali* (before the civil alliance), that is, to bring all under universal public precepts, accompanied by appropriate coercion, in accordance with which the right of each can be secured or provided" (Letter to Jung-Stilling, March 1789, 11:10).[26] Thus, positive civil lawgiving adds to the obligation of natural right, which is a rational obligation, an obligation bound to external public coercion, ensuring that this law is not violated.

However, as the positive laws come from the will of a lawgiver, they are chosen and contingent, and only obligate when promulgated, that is, when they are effective external laws. In order that this obligation be not a mere act of power it must be grounded in something that goes beyond the lawgiver's power of choice, he himself and the laws he promulgates. The lawgiver's authority is grounded in natural right that "must supply the immutable principles for any giving of positive law" (*Doctrine of Right*, 6:229).[27] Civil legislation must realize natural right, but, on the other hand, natural right gives the rational ground to positive lawgiving. However, a problem arises: the possibility that the positive law might be in disagreement with natural right. Kant states that it must be obeyed and, moreover, that it is an imperative to obey the authority currently in power, and he does not admit the right to resist. Regarding the notion of sovereignty one faces some difficulties and tensions in Kant's thought.[28] This is due to the violent origin of the state and to the imperative of obeying the established authority, on the one hand, confronted with natural right, on the other. But this conflict must be resolved by taking into account political prudence, Kant's peculiar notion of the representation, and the tendency of the transformations of the state in history, which would be a theme for other articles.

Notes

1. This article was written in the 1970s, in France, while the debate between the French and Italian interpreters pointed confusedly to a juridical positivistic interpretation of Kant's doctrine. My intention was to clarify this key aspect, that is, the distinction between right and ethics, trying to cast some light upon the discussion of this problem.

2. "Kant sharply detached his ethics from right. To the former, morality is appropriate, the ethical disposition, to the latter legality, the conformity with the juridical law." G. A. Walz, *Die Staatsidee des Rationalismus und der Romantik und die Staatphilosophie Fichtes* (Berlin: W. Rothschild, 1928), 192; see also G. Luf, *Freiheit und Gleichheit* (Vienna: Springer-Verlag, 1978), 53.

3. G. Dulckeit, *Naturrecht und positives Recht bei Kant* (Leipzig: Berger, 1932; repr. Aalen: Scientia Verlag, 1973), 15.

4. Ibid., 12.

5. Ibid., 16.

6. See K. Lisser, *Der Begriff des Rechts bei Kant* (Berlin: Reuther & Reichard, 1922).

7. "Such is an analogy between the legal relation of human actions and the mechanical relation of moving forces: I can never do anything to another without giving him a right to do the same to me under the same conditions; just as a body cannot act on another body with its motive force without thereby causing the other body to react just as much on it. Right and motive force are here completely dissimilar things, but in their relation there is nonetheless complete similarity" (*Prolegomena*, 4:357).

8. M. A. Cattaneo, in *Dignità umana e pena nella filosofia di Kant* (Milan: Giuffrè Editore, 1981), 120, lists forty-five authors who have studied this relation of morality and right, and groups their interpretation in three main tendencies: "The first is the group of the interpretations that I'll define as 'intermediaries,' which hold that Kant has an oscillating position, or not sharply defined, about the relations between morality and right, or that in his thinking morality and right are not neither strictly bound neither rigidly separated; the second group is the interpretations that sustain the thesis of a rigid separation between morality and right in Kant's thinking, above all based in coercion as a characteristic element of right; the third group is the interpretations that affirm the presence, in the Kantian practical philosophy, of a substantial connection between morality and right, or of a subordination of the latter to the former (based in a devaluation of the element 'coercion' and an emphasis on the element 'duty')."

9. G. Solari, *La formazione storica dello stato moderno* (Torino: G. Giappichelli, 1962), 95. G. Vlachos, in *La pensée politique de Kant* (Paris: Puf, 1962), 264, also dealing with other philosophers besides Kant, wrote: "it is the necessity of tracing strict limits to the state's action that engenders, within the German liberalism of the end of the eighteenth century, the tendency of ensuring right with a doctrinal autonomy as complete as possible in relation to morality."

10. G. Solari, *Studi storici di filosofia del diritto* (Torino: G. Giappichelli, 1949), chapter 8, "Scienza e metafisica del diritto in Kant," 214.

11. Ibid., 215.

12. Lisser, *Begriff*, 14–15.

13. Ibid., 22.

14. Ibid., 23.

15. Norberto Bobbio, "Kant e le due libertà," in Bobbio, *Da Hobbes a Marx* (Naples: Morano Editore, 1965), 147.

16. Ibid., 161.

17. Jean-Jacques Rousseau, *Du contrat social*, vol. 3 of *Oeuvres complètes*, ed. Bernard Gagnebin and Marcel Raymond (Paris: Gallimard, 1964), 365.

18. L. W. Beck, "Les deux concepts Kantiens du vouloir dans leur contexte politique," in *La philosophie pratique de Kant* (Paris: PUF, 1962), 130. Lewis White Beck, "Kant's Two Conceptions of the Will in Their Political Context," in *Selected Essays on Kant*, North American Kant Society Studies in Philosophy, vol. 6, ed. Hoke Robinson (Rochester: University of Rochester Press, 2002), 62–63.

19. The statement that Kant has deepened the Rousseauistic doctrine is frequent. However, it would be more interesting if it was followed by an analysis regarding the meaning of the appropriation of a problematic born from the political theory and that migrated to morality, or, in a wider way, what does this "deepening" of the French and English political questions in German philosophy mean.

20. Regarding this issue, Goyard-Fabre wrote: "To recognize that virtue is to itself its own purpose and to found the strict right on the possibility of an external coercion results in distinguishing them as autonomy and heteronomy. Such is, according to Kant, the essential difference between morality and right: morality is only possible through a reference to the ideas of person and autonomy, to which right does not make use of." Simone Goyard-Fabre, *Kant et le problème du droit* (Paris: Vrin, 1975).

21. A more comprehensive interpretation of the idea of autonomy can be read in B. Rousset, *La doctrine Kantienne de l'objectivité: L'autonomie comme devoir et devenir* (Paris: Librairie Philosophique J. Vrin, 1967). For Rousset, in Kant's metaphysics of right there would be an addition of a minimum of an empirical element, that is: "the mere empirical existence of something that is externally given to reason. One has the laws of autonomy related to the possible relations between the former and an external existence in general" (508). But one cannot take into account the particular empirical data, the facts and the characteristics of the things and persons; metaphysics of right will have to be built from the mere form of freedom, and "treating about property or society, we must content ourselves with making explicit the 'agreement of freedom with itself'; the existence of things and persons is only the occasion to make precise the content of the ideas and principles that we had already given: the autonomy and the respect of the rational being as its own purpose in the moral world; no new purpose is added: the deduction of right is entirely 'analytical.' The only difference is that autonomy is now defined in its relation to exteriority: it takes on a new appearance" (509). From the perspective of the individual subject, right "seems to be a law that realizes freedom, while the latter is purely external to the former, and would represent only a limitation of its power, a coercion due to the presence of things and other subjects; on the one hand, to the extent that it only defines its external relations, it does not concern the intrinsic rationality of the intentions of its will, but only its acts and their external accordance with rationality in general" (509).

22. "It is a very common mistake to say of Kant that for him the moral law is always a command or an imperative. On the contrary, we must take a sharp distinction between the moral law and the moral imperative. The moral law appears to us *under human conditions* as a command or imperative, because in us reason has not full control over the inclinations; but this characteristic does not belong to moral law as such. For the will of a perfect being the moral law is a law of *holiness*; for the will of

every finite rational being it is a law of duty." H. J. Paton, *The Categorical Imperative: A Study in Kant's Moral Philosophy* (Philadelphia: University of Pennsylvania Press, 1971), 70.

23. See Dulckeit, *Naturrecht*, 47.

24. Ibid., 51–52.

25. As A. P. d'Entrèves highlighted: "The notion of natural law partakes at the same time of a legal and of a moral character. Perhaps the best description of natural law is that it provides a name for the point of intersection between law and morals." A. P. d'Entrèves, *Natural Law: An Introduction to Legal Philosophy* (London: Hutchinson, 1979), 111.

26. Quoted and translated from a fragment of the letter at 11:10. A complete version of the letter is at 23: 494–95. See also, *R*7084, 19:245: "Without civil order, the entire right of nature is merely a doctrine of virtue, and bears the name of a right solely as a plan for possible outer coercive laws, hence of civil order."

27. "General division of the *Doctrine of Right* in natural and positive, the latter must not only not contradict the former, but also in what concerns the principle of the lawgiving, must be derived from it *a priori*" (*Opus Postumum* 21:462); see also *Doctrine of Right*, §9, 6:256.

28. See R. R. Terra, "O idealismo politico kantiano" (Kantian political idealism), in *Cadernos de História e Filosofia da Ciência* 53, no. 5 (1983): 39–57.

10

Right and the Duty to Resist, or Progress toward the Better

José Nicolau Heck

Politics, Right, and History in Kant

Kant held the unshakeable conviction that right could only be perfected within a given established order.

Denial of the right of resistance, apostrophized by the German philosopher, derives from a simple argument. The possibility of legal resistance to the monopoly of power implies having authority to define the conditions, analyze the criteria, and choose the means for disobedience itself. Thus, every political opponent assumes the power of decision and acquires the privileges of a ruler. If there is someone in the state holding power, nobody can demand the right of resistance to this ruler, unless he himself is not the supreme ruler of the state, but is the person opposing him in the command of the state. According to Kant, for a people to be authorized to resist, there must be a public law that permits resistance. In other words, the supreme law would have to include a disposition that it is not sovereign, which, by one and the same criterion, would make the people sovereign in terms of subjects in relation to the person to whom they are subjected. "This is self-contradictory," concludes the juridical teacher, "and the contradiction is evident as soon as one asks who is to be the judge in this dispute between people and sovereign" (*Doctrine of Right*, 6:320).

The moment the pacifying activity of the state is considered an unconditional presupposition for the obedience of the citizens, the presumed juridical relevance of the historical origins of the state loses its significance. The binding power of the legal system of the state disguises the violent means that the present holder of power may have used earlier when taking over control. For Kant, the historical source of the civil constitution contains the idea as a principle of practical reason, according to which "the presently

---

This is a revised but not substantially modified translation of an article published as "Direito e dever de resistência ou o progesso para o melhor," in *Veritas* 49 (2004): 803–24. Translated by P. J. O'Sullivan.

existing legislative authority ought to be obeyed, whatever its origin" (*Doctrine of Right*, 6:319).

Even when faced with regicide, the formal execution of the monarch, Kant rigidly maintains his juridical arguments. The German philosopher avoids creating a dialectic between the origin of right and the idea of morality that would legitimize it forever in absolute form. The unconditional submission of the popular will to the will of a ruler is *Tat*, or in other words, it constitutes a political fact as a historical gesture. Such a will can only be installed through force and it establishes, in the first instance, a public right. Granting citizens the right to resist the original heir to power is glaringly contradictory, given that it would annul the jurisdiction that determines what is or is not to be publicly a right. "This principle," wrote Kant in the conclusive phrase of the appendix to the *Doctrine of Right*, "is already present *a priori* in the idea of a civil constitution as such, that is, in a concept of practical reason." And he concludes: "Although no example in experience is adequate to be put under this concept, still none must contradict it as a norm" (*Doctrine of Right*, 6:372).

Whether the holders of sovereign power are founders of the republic or lords of the latest revolution, Kant abstains from branding them with the stigma of a political and philosophical type of original sin. Just as in an anarchical scenario, when reason empowers every human being to force fellow humans to join in a legally communitarian state, that is, establish by force a primordial order of peace, Kant groups all those who have usurped established power throughout the ages either by force, blackmail, or revolution under the title of guardians of the idea of a constitution. The scholar of right is coherent when he welcomes the French Revolution, while vehemently repudiating the beheading of Louis XVI as a sin against the Holy Spirit. As an established order, the victory of the great revolution unveils a new juridical starting point in history, in humanity's ongoing progress toward the better.

According to Kant, the struggle to perfect right is fought with the weapons of argumentation. What is in question is an attempt to emancipate the juridical community from the shackles of the violent dominion of its origins and direct it toward a republican state steeped in freedom. The process leads to the constitution of a state established by the union of a multitude of human beings subjected to rightful laws, in which the people exercise sovereignty through their representatives, and the powers of the republic are committed to implementing right and making it effective.

Right, Humanism, and Violence

For Kant, a right of resistance signifies the collapse of each and every policy of juridical security. The state that officially foresees, guarantees, or tolerates it, brings violence on itself and condemns its citizens to a return to the natural state. To the extent that the right of resistance makes the resolution of conflict at the heart of the state unviable, the existence of a positive norm that legitimizes this right is the equivalent of the dissolution of the state. In this case resistance procedures enjoy the shield of positive law, but even so continues to be totally illegitimate, because, according to Kant, revolutionary behavior "would make every rightful constitution insecure and introduce a condition of complete lawlessness (*status naturalis*), where all rights cease, at least to have effect" (*Theory and Practice*, 8:301).

The Kantian thesis of the prohibition of resistance becomes relevant when faced with the impasse of political contractualism at the dawn of modernity, needing to guarantee, in the one hand, the adherence of citizens to state authority, and, on the other, being obliged to establish parameters of justice for the political control of the state. To the careful observer, the apparent convergence of contractual criteria merely prolongs indefinitely the anarchy of the state of nature, to the extent that observance of contractual duties is a fortiori conditioned to the justice of laws previously submitted to the control of established norms. The state of nature, since Hobbes, had been nothing other than indecision between the legitimization of political power and the validity of norms sustained by justice. In this respect, prohibition of the right of resistance, in Kant, ratifies the state more as a rational figure par excellence than as a contractual configuration.

The rational outline of the Kantian state is quite distinct from the moral rationality of the German philosopher. While morality postulates revolution in people's minds, politics is carried out, occurs, and operates under the law of continuity. In other words, in the moral field, the law prevails prohibiting any commitment between what is true or false, correct or incorrect, good or bad, and so forth, whereas in the world of politics historical continuity constitutes a presupposition for the tiniest and slightest advance of justice.

This is not the case in the humanist tradition that has come down to us from Cicero. According to *De officiis*, a republican "has nothing in common with tyrants, which is also a reason why it cannot be against nature to kill them."[1] In Western political history, marked by the tradition of natural right, humanism invariably honors the supremacy of natural right over positive law, when it is a question of sustaining a suprapositive right of resistance.

In the wake of Hobbes, the German philosopher breaks with this political legacy of the most edifying doctrinal pole of European humanism, that is, the diabolical incarnation of the tyrant. According to this tradition, any ruler subverting the common good should suffer resistance and, if he does not yield to collective happiness, he should be removed from power or killed. Where humanists see flowers sprouting from corpses, Kant perceives the return to "the condition of anarchy . . . with all [its] horrors" (*Theory and*

Practice, 8:302), when a party inflicts injustice on another at the heart of the people and the rebels try to forcefully impose a constitution that is more oppressive than the one they revolted against. The philosopher clarifies: "There is, therefore, no right to sedition (*seditio*), still less to rebellion (*rebellio*), and least of all is there a right against the head of a state as an individual (the monarch), to attack his person or even his life (*monarchomachismus sub specie tyrannicidi*), on the pretext that he has abused his authority (*tyrannis*)" (*Doctrine of Right*, 6:320).

Kant's stance against a right to revolution is so visceral that the philosopher maintains the antirevolutionary principle of right, even where positive law guarantees its citizens the power of resistance, revolt, or revolution as soon as constitutional presuppositions are fulfilled. Such insurrectionist behavior is the only legal action over which Kant sustains the superiority of the right, even if, in this case, it is a question of resistance according to the constitution, or in other words, the respective ruler could not even claim that he is suffering an injustice. By strictly limiting the juridical excellence of the right to safeguarding constituted powers against an uprising based on a revolutionary positive law, the German philosopher honors politics as a human sphere where the law of continuity of the Enlightenment project as freedom from superstition holds sway. To the extent that revolutions are forbidden only in the name of positive law, right is extraordinarily enlightening for endorsing what is simply negative. It is in this that the later Kant discovers the quintessence of the Enlightenment,[2] a negative without a corresponding positive, something like the Mephistophelian premise of modernity.

In *Perpetual Peace*, the German philosopher insists that an initial juridical configuration is better than none, even if it only minimally corresponds to the right (*Perpetual Peace*, 8:373, note). He distinguishes between an embryonic juridical situation and one that has reached the proper juridical term. Although the former does not totally conform, the scholar considers it sufficiently structured to the point of demanding obedience. Kant situates this elementary juridical constellation between the state of nature and the civil state, and as such, embodies the negation of both, to the extent that it is no longer a state of nature and not yet a state under the rule of right. In other words, it treats of the state as a natural event, in which scattered individuals are submitted to the determinations of the will of whoever brings them together as a united people.

No matter how deficient it may be, the empirical foundation of a state transforms the idea of the constitution into political representation and thus enforces the matrix of the normative relations for human living. As soon as there is a political power acting in the name of the law and holding a monopoly of power, it should be accepted as a rational demand of the idea of the constitution. For Kant, not even the duty of obedience of subjects united by force nor the right to rule of successful state founders derives its reason for being from the mere existence of political power. The juridical origin of both resides exclusively in the establishment of a society based on right. A political order that comes about through violent means does not constitute an argument against the established state authority. Be they usurpers, revolutionaries, coup organizers, or dominators, no holders of power need fear that the manner by which they seize the title will incriminate them or justify resistance against their political power. Kant writes: "Moreover, once a revolution has succeeded and a new constitution has been established, the lack of legitimacy with which it began and has been implemented cannot release the subjects from the obligation to comply with the new order of things as good citizens, and they cannot refuse honest obedience to the authority that now has the power" (*Doctrine of Right*, 6:323).

Once people have been pacified, the origin of common living becomes insignificant. "Reason in the rightful state demands that the subject forget," writes Wolfgang Kersting, and he adds: "there is no court on earth which could incriminate the person who wields power."[3] Even though it violates right, Kant recognizes that a revolution is victorious because, as the supreme ordering power, it provides a new opportunity for the ongoing and uninterrupted perfecting of right. It does not matter if any contract had been signed at the origin of the present state or if power had been imposed by force and only later exercised by law. Be that as it may, according to Kant, it is not up to a people already subjected to civil law to investigate "into the origins of the supreme authority to which it is subject, that is, a subject ought not to reason subtly for the sake of action about the origin of this authority" (*Doctrine of Right*, 6:318).

While the connection between moral law and the hope of being happy, or rather, the exact proportion between happiness, justice, and morality claim God and immortality as constituents of a moral kingdom opposed to death, for Kant history is constituent of right directed toward the progressive realization of republican ideas and perpetual peace, that is, political practice in harmony with morality amounts to a "doctrine of right put into practice" (*Perpetual Peace*, 8:370).

For the philosopher of right, nothing can revert or arrest the continuity of the historical progress of right. No education is capable of corrupting a human being to such an extent that he or she becomes unspeakably evil, lacking all sensitivity, heteronomous by rational definition, and for whom all other people would become superfluous. Even the so-called innate evildoers (*geborene Bösewichter*), who are "quite incapable of improvement as far as their cast of mind is concerned" (*Practical Reason*, 5:99), do not break the continuity of history that successively reconciles the state of nature with a juridical state that progressively harmonizes with right.

It is only when addressing the trials of Charles I and Louis XVI that the German philosopher dwells on the profile of extreme evil, which "strikes horror in a soul filled with the idea of human rights" (*Doctrine of Right*, 6:321). Kant asks himself how one can explain this sentiment of horror, which is not a sentiment of affinity, "but [rather] moral feeling resulting from the complete overturning of all concepts of right" (6:321). Kant compares the formal execution of the two monarchs with "(*crimen immortale, inexpiabile*) . . . what theologians call the sin that cannot be forgiven either in this world or the next" (6:321), an explicit evil, high treason, without any justification, which, even though it is wrong for humans to commit it, "is not to be ignored in a system of morals (although it is only the idea of the most extreme evil)" (6:322). For the German scholar the principle that leads to putting a state authority on trial is contrary to the law not just because it is an act of omission. With the formal execution of the monarch, the people do not only act against the law but also end up diametrically opposed to the law. In other words, the principle of their conduct appears contradictory in relation to the law, "for it is as if the state commits suicide" (6:322), Kant says.

Nevertheless, the German philosopher does not admit to historical gaps in the sphere of right. He refutes the idea of malice in the origins of the judicial order and faithfully upholds humanity's constant tendency toward the better. In addition, in the worst situations of injustice, humanity continues to keep the idea of right alive. For Kant, every juridical order in force, even that born of violence, but that does not have violence as the norm, is healthier than the absence of a form of justice and is thereby in harmony with the highest principle of autonomous thinking, invariably directed toward the self-preservation of reason, struggling against the workings of evil, the sectarian, the prophet, the fanatic, and all types of superstition and illusion.

The principle of noncontradiction is configured in Kant's political and juridical cosmopolitanism in the profile of the unjust enemy. For Kant the unjust enemy is the state whose will, publicly expressed, "reveals a maxim by which, if it were made a universal rule, any condition of peace among nations would be impossible and, instead, a state of nature would be perpetuated" (*Doctrine of Right*, 6:349). Modern right comes to terms with the supposed contradiction between right and injustice, but does not tolerate the negation that violence imposes on right. While the Kantian ban on the right of resistance occurs on the plane of opposition between right and injustice at the heart of established states, the duty to fight the unjust enemy is located at the core of the noncontradiction between right and violence. Even if the figure of the unjust enemy is still part of the doctrine of people's rights, the constitutions of certain countries prescribes citizens' rights to passive and/or active resistance to the holders of power, whenever the constitutional law is being ostensively slandered by the holders of state power.

Practical Reason and Political Philosophy

In the light of the principles of pure practical reason it is necessary to accept, as the real object of our will, the progress that constantly moves in the direction of total conformity between morality and happiness.

Such a perfect union constitutes the highest good, according to Kant. For him this becomes possible "only on the presupposition of the existence and personality of the same rational being continuing endlessly (which is called the immortality of the soul)" (*Practical Reason*, 5:122). As well as this progress ad infinitum, unprovable as a theoretical proposition, the principles of practical reason equally ensure that happiness ends up exclusively destined for those who deserve it. Thanks to a simple impartial reason, whose presupposition is found in the existence of a cause appropriate to this effect, pure practical reason postulates and rational faith (*Vernunftglaube*) recognizes "the existence of God as belonging necessarily to the possibility of the highest good" (*Practical Reason*, 5:124). The existence of God, as the supreme cause of nature, ratifies the second element of the highest good. For Kant, it is the equivalent of the wise government that justly distributes the happiness that people need, that is, exactly proportional to the morality of the human being.

The postulates of pure practical reason with respect to the immortality of the soul and the existence of God fully respond to the demands of finite rational beings whose morality does not in itself analytically contain happiness, but whose reason demands that they be happy to the exact same extent that they are worthy of happiness. The German philosopher is insightful about this. On the one hand, he states that "happiness and morality are two specifically quite different elements of the highest good and that, accordingly, their combination cannot by cognized analytically" (*Practical Reason*, 5:112–13). On the other hand, he makes it clear that a person lacking happiness yet worthy of it, and who does not experience it "cannot be consistent with the perfect volition of a rational being that would at the same time have all power, even if we think of such a being only for the sake of the experiment" (5:110).

Just as moral perfection, corresponding to perfect happiness, requires endless time, so too the progress of which Kant speaks in mastering the principle of pure practical reason refers to the world and beyond, since infinite progress starts here and goes on for all eternity.

To the extent that they fulfill their function, the two postulates do not, however, respond adequately to the demand of the categorical imperative that imposes on a person in this world the unconditional duty of obeying the moral law. The lack of harmony and fit of pure rational faith in moral perfection (immortality of the soul) and the harmony between happiness and morality (existence of God) with the moral law as the legislating element of pure practical reason, as the freedom of finite beings, takes the form of inducing an apparent contradiction between the constant frustrations of human happiness in carrying out the duties of this world and the full proportionality of morality to happiness in the world of the future. After all, why would human beings do good when zealously pursuing the highest good on earth, when, according to Kant, in this world there is no possibility of achieving the moral perfection that corresponds to the happiness of which they are worthy? Besides, nature is not normally an extravagant mother when distributing happiness among her children.

Throughout the work of Kant, both before and after the second *Critique*, there are several indications that the philosopher had perceived the risk that human progress could be an illusion, perhaps nothing more than a daydream wrapped in the fictitious webs of future whims; in short, progress might be nothing more than an extrarational reference full of trivialities.

In the final proposition of his 1784 essay on the idea of universal history, the author asks himself, why exalt the majesty and wisdom of creation if we despair of the history of humanity to the point of thinking that its full rational development can only be expected in another world? (*Idea*, 8:30). In his 1786 study on the meaning of self-orientation through thought, the philosopher insists that it is necessary to prevent the concept of the highest good, along with all morality, from being considered a pure ideal (*Orient*, 8:139). In the third part (against M. Mendelssohn) of the essay "Theory and Practice" (1793) and in *The Conflict of the Faculties* (1798), Kant observes that not admitting humanity's ongoing progress means that humanity's mere fluctuation between good and evil of human beings on the globe must be seen as a simple farcical comedy (*Possenspiel*) (*Conflict*, 7:82; *Theory and Practice*, 8:308).

Just like humanity, human nature and history are not per se equal to individuals, nor can individuals be receivers of the categorical imperative, nor in need of happiness. Moral progress and just government, while components of the postulates of the immortality of the soul and of the existence of God, are simply inconsequential in relation to the historical subjects of progress unless they are people of flesh and blood.

The type of progress that involves the highest moral good is not the same as that which, according to Kant, "can lead to continual approximation to the highest political good, perpetual peace" (*Doctrine of Right*, 6:355). Not only are the objects of progress different but, above all, the alternatives to be discarded are not the same. The highest moral good dispenses with the monsters of Theosophists and mystics and dreams of every type. It also frees man from anthropomorphism as a source of superstition, fanaticism, prejudice, and suprasensitive intuitions (*Practical Reason*, 5:120–21; 5:135–36), whereas the highest political good protects humanity from the illusions of just war, the lack of distinction between violence and injustice, as well as moralistic Manichaeism, in such a way that humanity's analogical use of the postulates of the immortality of the soul and the existence of God in mastering progress for the better is not suitable.[4]

While both the first and second *Critique* place the highest good in the future life, the third *Critique* locates it, as the world's highest good (*das Weltbeste*), in the universe of sublunary coordinates. After guaranteeing that "we are determined a priori by reason to promote with all of our powers what is best in the world," the philosopher explains that this good consists in linking the highest good of rational beings in the world "with the highest condition of the good for them, i.e., the combination of universal happiness with the most lawful morality" (*Judgment*, 5:453), and he adds:

> For the objective theoretical reality of the concept of the final end of rational beings in the world it is thus requisite not merely that we have a final end that is set before us a priori, but also that the existence of creation, i.e., the world itself, has a final end. . . . For if creation has a final end at all, we cannot conceive of it except as having to correspond to the final end of morality (which alone makes possible the concept of an end). . . . Thus we have a moral ground for also conceiving of a final end of creation for a world. (*Judgment*, 5:454–55)

At the end of the first part of his *Critique of the Power of Judgment* Kant formulates the criteria according to which taste declares a certain pleasure valid for humanity in general and not just for the private feeling of each human being in particular. He writes, "taste is at bottom a faculty for judging of the sensible rendering of moral ideas (by means of a certain analogy of the reflection on both)" (*Judgment*, 5:356). Such a derivation of the aesthetic pleasure from moral sentiment is preceded by a short compact digression on a handful of allusive political references to humanity, sociability, lasting collectivity, and legal coercion.

On the question of the humanities as preliminary knowledge for the highest degree of all the fine arts, the German philosopher makes a double reference to the humanistic studies of ancient Greece and Rome. First, he says that these works of art do not refer to concepts, but rather are impregnated with the faculties of the soul, "presumably because humanity means on the one hand the universal feeling of participation and on the other hand the capacity for being able to communicate one's inmost self universally" (*Judgment*, 5:355); they are properties that together constitute sociability, characteristics proper to man, and that, according to Kant, distinguish us from the animals. Later, the philosopher evaluates the artistic collections of the Greeks and Romans as a product of a certain human way of living, and for that very reason, as producers of political traits that remind one more of the great revolution than of the ancient political greatness of Athens and Rome.

Referring to the time and peoples whose impulse for legal sociability led them to set up a lasting collectivity, bringing together freedom and coercion more out of duty than out of fear, Kant writes that such a time and such people "had first of all to discover the art of the reciprocal communication of the ideas of the most educated part with the cruder," and thus invent the middle term between culture and nature, "and in this way to discover that mean between higher culture and contented nature which constitutes the correct standard, not to be given by any universal rule, for taste as a universal human sense" (*Judgment*, 5:355–56).

The philosopher neither names the invention to which he refers nor identifies the people who brought it into the world. Since for Kant invention is not deduced from a general rule, but rather comes from the harmony between the expansion and refining of the more cultured with the natural simplicity and originality of the less cultured (*Judgment*, 5:356), it could be supposed that the philosopher is envisaging the General Declaration on Human Rights, approved by members of the Estates General during their first meeting as the National Assembly, six months before the appearance of the third *Critique*.[5]

This hypothesis finds support in a passage from *Anthropology from a Pragmatic Point of View*, where people are seen as inventive beings. To the extent that the evil that one inflicts on others increases, they see no other way out than by putting the private feeling of some under the unified common feeling of all and thus decide, even against their own wishes, to submit themselves to civil coercion, to which they only subject themselves in accordance with the laws passed by themselves. And, in the light of the awareness that they have of all of this, they "feel themselves ennobled by this consciousness; namely, of belonging to a species that is suited to the destiny of the human being, as reason represents it to him in the ideal" (*Anthropology*, 7:329–30).

From the Third Critique to History

Political readings of the third *Critique* and other Kantian texts, made by Hannah Arendt during a seminar on Kant's political philosophy in 1970 at the New School for Social Research, adopt an aesthetic judgment, from a reflexive teleological perspective as a model for political judgment.[6] In contrast to the Benjaminian proposal of the politicization of art, Arendt's aestheticization of politics neutralizes the definitive role of *Perpetual Peace* and the *Doctrine of Right* in favor of the aesthetic reflexive judgments that start from the exception in search of the rule. Arendt's analyses of the spectator of the French Revolution are paradigmatic. According to Kant, the spectator is caught up in "a wishful participation that borders closely on enthusiasm" (*Conflict*, 7:85).[7]

From a list of Kantian texts, written over a ten-year period, Arendt extracts what she calls Kant's political philosophy, without registering the context or differentiated theme of the works involved. The plank that confers identity to her studies on Kantian political thought is the connection between moral judgments and common sense in an aesthetic-communicative sense, the normalization of the political judgment that pervades the so-called human affairs (*anthropon pragmata*) of healthy understanding (*der gemeine Menschenverstand*), a favorite theme in the tradition of Aristotelian *bios politikos* and one to which Kant returns, in paragraph 40 of the third *Critique*, the text *An Answer to the Question: What Is Enlightenment?* (1784).[8]

The nature of Arendt's revolutionary spectator is exemplarily moral. The marks of publicity, generality, impartiality, and finally enthusiasm, attributed by Arendt to the spectator of the French Revolution in Kant's *The Conflict of the Faculties* really illustrate the conclusive phrase of the critique of the faculty of aesthetic judgment (*Critique of the Power of Judgment*, part 1), where Kant says: "It is evident that the true proaedeutic for the grounding of taste is the development of moral ideas and the cultivation of the moral feeling, for only when sensibility is brought into accord with this can genuine taste assume a determinate, unalterable form" (*Judgment*, 5:356). Even if Arendt's analyses of Kant's political thought had faced the concept of legal sociabilility (*gesetzliche Geselligkeit*),[9] interpreting the figure of the Kantian revolutionary spectator in *The Conflict of the Faculties*, a prisoner of reflexive judgments of the third *Critique*, would continue to be an anachronism. Different from the aesthetic communitarian direction given by Arendt to the spectator of the great revolution, Michel Foucault sees in the second section of *The Conflict of the Faculties* the continuity of *What Is Enlightenment?* While Arendt's reflections on art and politics place all human history in the care of aesthetical discernment as *sensus communis*, Foucault identifies in the Kantian continuity of the Enlightenment the question about "our topic, the current field of possible experience," in short, "an ontology of the present, an ontology of ourselves."[10]

By letting human history penetrate aesthetical discernment, as an idea of communitarian meaning (*gemeinschaftlichen Sinnes*), the interpreter does not hold the same position as the philosopher when facing an event of our times, and so she does not perceive, like Kant, that "the revolution of a people full of spirit" (*Die Revolution eines geistreichen Volks*) is the equivalent of a historical sign (*Geschichtszeichen*) for the spectators, not signifying for them the mere sharing of sentiments connected to a given representation, lacking the mediation of a concept.

What Is Enlightenment? introduces a moral and not a juridical discourse. Thinking for oneself is accepting will as a principle. Daring to make use of one's own understanding is the equivalent of using will as a duty, refusing to have recourse to criteria alien to the motives that inspire the action. Kant observes the action of two types of actors: on the one hand, the great masses (*ein grosser Haufen*), Rousseau's blind multitude, and on the other, enlightened man, *der Selbstdenkende, l'homme eclaré et indépendante* (the enlightenened and independent man) of the Genevan philosopher. Both types are rational agents and act within the regime of Kantian morality. The former are lazy, cowardly, and to be blamed for the insignificance in which they willingly live. As rational beings, they have nobody to blame for the situation because they are as free as the others. They are a living testimony that their freedom is in the origin of the protected state in which they find themselves. Reason shows its autonomy in the possibility of reverting it, in other words, heteronomy is not something unusual for it, the reason why it can only be suspended each time, based on the first. The latter, the enlightened man himself, is responsible for not becoming apathetic, as he is free, living under the protection of others. He uses his understanding, accepts rational challenge, is decisive and courageous, and only submits to the autonomy of his reason. Because of his daring, the future is his. Reason considers him the subject of historical progress, according to Kant.

Criticism is a weapon of Enlightenment morality because thinking or acting without consequences is neither critical nor moral. Those who are happy obeying orders do not think and act in an irrational manner, but their actions and reasoning do not change the mechanism of obedience. Whoever uses his understanding to lord it over others, keeping alive precepts and formulas of a lasting minority, is not enlightened. Criticism is the only enlightened weapon because it does good to those who use it but without needing to do so at the cost of those who do not use it. As a privilege of reason, criticism damages just as little as reason harms. Consequently, enlightened criticism neither uses force nor exerts pressure.

"A revolution," writes Kant, "may well bring about a falling off of personal despotism and of avaricious or tyrannical oppression, but never a true reform in one's way of thinking" (*Enlightenment*, 8:36). The Kantian objection to revolution is of a moral nature, since "new prejudices will serve just as well as old ones to harness the great unthinking masses" (8:36). As it is imposed by force, a revolution simply substitutes old preconceptions with new ones, because it holds on to the cycle of cycles begun by the guardian who oppressed a certain group of people. For the simple people, nothing changes, except the person of the guardian. Because it is an event on the tactical plane, the philosopher compares revolution with a normative-rational principle, called *Reform der Denkungsart* (reform of the way of thinking).

The great masses, Kant insists, are burdened by revolutions. They produce guardians, without whom it would be difficult to survive, and the masses are comforted by the fact that the new guardians themselves are now bound by the same yoke that the former had imposed on them. The Enlightenment, therefore, remains in the hands of the *Selbstdenkenden*. They alone support it. It is only in them that enlightened reason finds historical support, and is not deceived by them, that is, guaranteeing that the primary bountiful nature does not become an oppressive nature. For Kant, enlightened men are right not to lead revolutions. They must be committed to reform in the way of thinking.

In the second section of *The Conflict of the Faculties*, the German philosopher takes a stand on "an event of our time" and reaches conclusions that alter previously recognized thinking. Although maintaining the primacy of the moral point of view, the text presents arguments until then unknown within the perspective of Kantian morality. Kant writes:

> This occurrence consists neither in momentous deeds nor crimes committed by human beings. . . . No, nothing of the sort. It is simply the mode of thinking of the spectators which reveals itself publicly in this game of great revolutions . . . [and] thus demonstrates a characteristic of the human race at large and all at once, owing to its disinterestedness, a moral character . . . which not only permits people to hope for progress toward the better, but is already itself progress insofar as its capacity is sufficient for the present. (*Conflict*, 7:85)

The primacy of morality holds, despite the interplay of interests inherent to the revolutionary process. Through its universality, the event shows a moral character, in the predisposition it denotes. The moral viewfinder, however, is no longer fixed on actors, or actions, or crimes of individual people. That it seems like this is because of the way the spectators understand what is happening. The *Denkungsart*, no longer the privilege of a handful of wise men, becomes the way of being of the multitudes. Objectively speaking, the event does not just indicate greater or lesser security for the future—rather, in itself it is already progress. Kant reflects: "The revolution . . . may succeed or midcarry, it may be filled with misery and atrocities to the point that a right-thinking human being, were he boldly to hope to execute it successfully the second time, would never resolve to make the experiment at such cost" (*Conflict*, 7:85). The philosopher continues emphatically: "This revolution, I say, finds in the hearts of all spectators . . . a wishful *participation* that borders closely on enthusiasm . . . this sympathy, therefore, can have no other cause than a moral predisposition in the human race," the juridical and not the biological subject of history.

The public spectators are the real interpreters of the French Revolution as a historical sign (*signum rememorativum*, *demonstrativum*, *prognostikon*). Their generalized and disinterested solidarity with humanity, in the realm of practical reason, culturally determines what only respect for the moral law is capable of developing, and inspires men of goodwill. As a clue to the future, the great revolution marks the starting point of a new theoretical order, that is, the right of a people not to be thwarted by other powers, when they set up a civil constitution. The categorical imperative persists. The principle of right does not substitute or limit it, but becomes its ally. While the former refers to the self-consciousness of existence—the lifespan of every person as a living being—the latter includes the future, inconceivable without otherness and unthinkable without humanity. Kant reasons:

> Not an ever-growing quantity of morality with regard to intention, but an increase of the products of legality in dutiful actions whatever their motives. That is, the profit (result) of the human being's striving toward the better can be assumed to reside alone in the good deeds of human beings, which will become better and better and more and more numerous; it resides alone in phenomena constituting the moral state of the human race. (*Conflict*, 7:91)

The ethical destiny of the species is, for Kant, due to internal principles of right (*innere Rechtsprinzipien*), according to which the phenomenon of the French Revolution, in the course of time a causal event, unites nature and freedom, an event that according to Kant, "no politician, affecting wisdom, might have conjured out of the course of things hitherto," but having happened, it constitutes "a phenomenon in human history [that] will not be forgotten" (*Conflict*, 7:88).

Concluding Observations

It is only by means of the rational juridical order that humanity perceives progress. The fact that practical reason morally determines will is no longer seen by Kant as the only rational power for universal control. The idea of uniting the multiplicity of human desires through the legalization of the external actions of people, which does not demand self-coercion, but rather coactive coexistence under the self-dominion of law (*Selbstherrschaft des Gesetzes*), does not amount to "an empty figment of the brain, but rather the eternal norm for all civil organization in general, and averts all war" (*Conflict*, 7:91), which is for Kant the obstacle par excellence of morality.

The normative regime of right, which touches human culture, leads the German philosopher to invert the course of things, claiming that moral progress does not happen "from bottom to top but from top to bottom." Kant, an enthusiastic reader of Rousseau's *Emile, ou de l'éducation*, is skeptical about the formation of youth that is limited to home and school instruction and reinforced by religious teaching; yet he believes that this formation could reach, on an increasing intellectual and moral scale, the point of not just forming good citizens, but also of educating for the good what could still progress and be preserved. According to Kant, the success of such a plan "is hardly to be hoped for" (*Conflict*, 7:92). With the French Revolution, the Kantian *Doctrine of Right* is elevated to the realm of reason, that is, it is possible to know a priori the conditions under which beings of impulse and inclinations act rationally. Kant formulates such conditions when he writes: "If we were able to attribute to the human being an inherent and unalterably good, albeit limited, will, he would be able to predict with certainty the progress of his species toward the better, because it would concern an occurrence that he himself could produce" (*Conflict*, 7:84).

In the Supplement to *Perpetual Peace* there are repeated indications that juridical political principles are historically feasible, since the moral principle in the human being is never extinguished and reason is in constant progress through culture (*fortschreitende Kultur*); in addition, Kant guarantees that "pure principles of right have objective reality, that is, that they can be carried out" (*Perpetual Peace*, 8:380). In *The Conflict of the Faculties*, in turn, after referring to the historical narrative, anticipatory to that which awaits us in the future, the German philosopher explains that it is a question of "a possible representation a priori of events which are supposed to happen," and he asks: "But how is a history a priori possible? Answer: if the diviner himself makes and contrives the events which he announces in advance" (*Conflict*, 7:79–80). The synthetic practical a priori judgment of Kantian history does not consist of a reflexive subsistence but rather of an exemplarily narrative, one that "the human race has always been in progress toward the better and will continue to be so henceforth" (7:88).

Having moved to the plane of experience and affirmed that there must be an event that refers to the constitution and faculty of humanity being both cause and author of progress, the German philosopher states that starting from a given cause an event can be predicted as its effect when there are circumstances that contribute to it. Nevertheless, in general terms, just as in the calculation of probability in a game, it can be seen that, at a given moment, events will occur, so it is impossible to determine if such an event will occur in my lifetime or if I will experience this, thereby confirming the fortuitous prediction. Therefore it is necessary to seek an event pointing to the existence of such a cause and equally to the act of its causality in humanity, even if the time is not determined. On identifying the existence of such, it would be possible to infer progression as an indisputable consequence, and thus, Kant writes, it would be possible to judge "the tendency of the human race viewed in its entirety, that is, seen not as individuals . . . , but rather as divided into nations and states (as it is encountered on earth)" (*Conflict*, 7:84).

Zeljko Loparic argues in chapter 11 of this volume that such a demonstration reflects an original concept of "a mixed nature" in Kantian practical philosophy, "since it designates on the one hand the noumenal cause that authors political-juridical progress . . . and, on the other hand, the concrete ways in which this cause manifests itself in factual history."[11] The novelty in the semantic sphere of a priori political and historical judgments does not lie in the abstract idea of a general unified will, but rather, according to Loparic, "because he elaborated the idea of a general sensitized will, more precisely of the concept of a collective subject for history," with a moral and juridical tendency toward the better, which "has not only purposes and capacities for action but also other faculties that were up until then commonly reserved for individuals, such as memory."[12] For Kant, the French Revolution and the conquest of a legitimate republican constitution legitimize the moral claim of reason that mankind is journeying, as it has always been, toward a better future. It is worth mentioning that the most typical element of the supreme law of right is the legalizing publicity of the French Revolution.

The specific development of the text *The Conflict of the Faculties* in relation to *The Doctrine of Right* is that the interpretation of pure practical concepts as pure theoretical concepts of understanding no longer refers to individuals, but rather to humanity and the practical application of pure practical concepts to pure theoretical concepts of understanding by means of pure projects and empirical examples. According to Loparic, "this semantic turn . . . allows the later Kant" to reconcile nature and freedom with a solution "at once rational and sensitized, in terms of the theory of the physical performability of a priori principles of moral politics."[13]

Kant achieves the height of Enlightenment, that is, freedom from superstition. For the German philosopher this consists in the great preconception of "representing nature as not subject to the rules that understanding, through its own essential law, presents as a basis" (*Judgment*, 5:294).[14]

Notes

1. Cicero, *De officiis*, book 3, *The Conflict between the Right and the Expedient*, vol. 4 of *Oeuvres complètes*, trans. M. Nisard [bilingual ed.] (Paris: Dislot, 1859), 494.

2. See *Judgment*, where Kant says, "Liberation from superstition is called enlightenment," and continues in a footnote, "it must be very difficult to maintain or establish the merely negative element (which constitutes genuine enlightenment) in the manner of thinking (especially in that of the public)" (5:294).

3. Wolfgang Kersting, *Wohlgeordnete Freiheit: Immanuel Kants Rechts- und Staatsphilosophie* (Frankfurt am Main: Suhrkamp, 1993), 475.

4. For a different position on this topic, see David Lindstedt, "Kant: Progress in Universal History as a Postulate of Practical Reason," *Kant-Studien* 90 (1999): 143: "Two postulates, then, are needed, which are analogous to the postulates of immortality and God. The first, nature as working providentially, functions analogously to the postulate of the existence of God in the second *Critique*. . . . But a second postulate, similar to the immortality of the individual, is needed so that one may hope for the achievement of perfect morality."

5. Markus Arnold, "Die harmonische Stimmung aufgeklärter Bürger: Zum Verhältnis von Politik und Ästhetik in Immanuel Kants, Kritik der Urteilskraft," *Kant-Studien* 94 (2003): 24–25.

6. Hannah Arendt, *Lectures on Kant's Political Philosophy*, ed. R. Biener (Chicago: University of Chicago Press, 1982); and Hannah Arendt, *The Life of the Mind*, 2 vols. (New York: H. B. Jovanovich, 1978).

7. See Ricardo Terra, "É possível defender a legalidade e ter entusiasmo pela revolução?: Notas sobre Kant e a Revolução Francesa," in Ricardo Terra, *Passagens: Estudos sobre a filosofia de Kant* (Rio de Janeiro: Editora UFRJ, 2003), 101–29; and Ricardo Terra, "Juízo político e prudência em *À paz perpétua*," in *Kant no Brasil*, ed. Daniel Omar Perez (São Paulo: Escuta, 2005), 121–33.

8. Kyriaki Goudeli, "Kant's Reflective Judgement: The Normalisation of Political Judgement," *Kant-Studien* 94 (2003): 31: "Kant's *Critique of Judgement* has been proved to be a resourceful text of major significance for contemporary debates on aesthetics, politics and epistemology. Its implicit political implications have been mainly broached by H. Arendt's innovative reading."

9. See Valério Rohden, "Sociabilidade legal: Uma ligação entre direito e humanidade na 3 *Crítica* de Kant," *Analytica* 1 (1994): 97–106.

10. Michel Foucault, "Qu'est-ce que les Lumières?" *Dits et écrits (1980–1988)*, vol. 4 (Paris: Gallimard, 1994), 687.

11. Zeljko Loparic, "The Fundamental Problem of Kant's Juridical Semantics," chapter 11, this volume, 227.

12. Ibid., 227–28.

13. Ibid., 229.

14. This passage is taken from the first edition of the *Critique of the Power of Judgment*. The second edition altered the passage; the Cambridge edition follows the second edition.

11

The Fundamental Problem of Kant's Juridical Semantics

Zeljko Loparic

The Concept of Practical Philosophy in Later Kant

Kant defines a philosopher as "the legislator of human reason" (*Pure Reason*, B867). The philosopher's legislation has two objects, nature and freedom, and therefore contains both the laws of nature (natural laws) and the laws of freedom (moral laws). The former determine a priori *what is* and comprise the system of nature; the latter determine a priori *what should be* and make up the system of freedom.[1] Theoretical or speculative philosophy takes care of the former; practical philosophy takes care of the latter.

In Kant's later writings, practical philosophy is split into a "metaphysics of morals" and a "moral anthropology" (*Doctrine of Right*, 6:217). The former contains a priori the principles that dispose of "freedom in both the external and the internal use of choice" (*Doctrine of Right*, 6:214),[2] and for that reason is also called "anthroponomy" (*Doctrine of Virtue*, 6:406).[3] The latter, moral anthropology, comprises the study of subjective conditions, pertaining to human nature, that are either favorable or contrary to the *execution* of the laws of practical reason (*Doctrine of Right*, 6:217).

This distinction is a novelty relative to the first *Critique*. In the first *Critique*, Kant contrasts practical philosophy, especially pure morals, which deals with the principles that "determine **action** and **omission** a *priori* and make them necessary," with anthropology, conceived as an empirical, scientific theory. He says, for example, that "the metaphysics of morals is really the pure morality, which is not grounded on any anthropology (no empirical condition)" (*Pure Reason*, B869–70). This thesis is maintained in the *Metaphysics of Morals* (1797), but then the problem of the basis and validity of the a priori laws of the doctrines of right and of virtue is formulated according

First published as "O problema fundamental da semântica jurídica de Kant," in *O filosofo e a sua história: Uma homenagem a Oswaldo Porchat*, ed. Michael Wrigley and Plínio Smith (Campinas: CLE, 2003), 477–520. Translated by Rogério Passos Severo; revised by A. Blom.

to the results of the *Critique of Practical Reason* (1788). Hence, it demands a demonstration of the *immanent* applicability of practical laws, that is, that they can be valid in the domain of actions that can be effectively carried out by free human agents.[4] This shift in focus is reflected in Kant's remark that "a metaphysics of morals cannot be based upon anthropology but can still be applied to it" (*Doctrine of Right*, 6:217). One of the main innovations of the *Metaphysics of Morals* that was inspired by the second *Critique* is precisely the addition of the *realm of acts that can be freely performed* to the *realm of possible objects* specified in the first *Critique*. This paved the way for the development of an *a priori theory of the application* of the concepts and laws of the metaphysics of morals to the former realm, that is, for an *a priori semantics* as part of Kant's practical philosophy. This is an indispensable task, according to Kant:

> But just as there must be principles in a metaphysics of nature for applying [*Prinzipien der Anwendung*] those highest universal principles of a nature in general to objects of experience, a metaphysics of morals cannot dispense with principles of application, and we shall often have to take as our object the particular *nature* of human beings, which is cognized only by experience, in order to *show* in it what can be inferred from universal moral principles. (*Doctrine of Right*, 6:217–18)

In other words, the constitution of a metaphysics of morals put forth in the *Doctrine of Right* implies, as a necessary subtask, the elaboration of the principles for applying the fundamental propositions of the *metaphysics of morals* to the realm of human acts. This incumbency is conceived by Kant in exact parallel to the task carried out in his 1786 *Metaphysical Foundations of Natural Science*, which provided rules for determining the "objective reality, that is, meaning and truth" of the fundamental concepts and propositions of the *metaphysics of nature* (*Natural Science*, 4:478). Thus, an "excellent and indispensable" service was rendered to general metaphysics, insofar as "examples (instances *in concreto*) in which to realize the concepts and propositions of the latter," that is, "to give a mere form of thought sense and meaning [*Sinn und Bedeutung*]" were provided (4:478).

Rather than eliminating it, this parallel highlights a significant difference between Kant's theories of the "sense and meaning" of natural and moral a priori concepts: whereas the former are interpreted onto the objects of experience, the latter refer to freely performable acts, which is the subject matter of moral or pragmatic anthropology. As opposed to "physiological" anthropology, that is, the anthropology that is part of natural science and "concerns the investigation of what *nature* makes of the human being," pragmatic anthropology is concerned with "the investigation of what *he* as a free-acting being makes of himself, or can and should make of himself" (*Anthropology*, 7:119).

The Order of the Problems in the Doctrine of Right

The final—not merely the initial or partial—total goal of the *Doctrine of Right*, which is to be carried out within the bounds of mere reason, is the establishment of a universal and permanent peace. But why perpetual peace? Because the rational regulation of social life demands that what is mine and what is yours should be safely *secured*, and in a multitude of human beings living as neighbors to one another, only a state of peace enforced by laws offers that assurance. To be sure, these are a priori juridical laws assembled in a civil constitution according to the ideal of "association of human beings under public laws as such" (*Doctrine of Right*, 6:355).

Formulated in terms of a *Doctrine of Right*, the solution to the problem of perpetual peace therefore presupposes the solution to problems concerning private ownership, in particular, the problem of finding out *if* and *how* reason can say whether something can be rightfully mine. It seems unproblematic to say a priori that something that is in my physical possession—something that I hold—can also be rightfully and even legally mine, since everything leads us to think that the suppression of this possibility is equivalent to the pure and simple suppression of all external use of free choice. It is much harder to justify, based on pure practical reason alone, that something is mine even when it is not in my physical possession. Kant refers to this way of having something be mine as "merely rightfully" (*bloss-rechtlich*) mine, or as "intelligible possession," which are phrases that designate a basic concept of practical reason. The practical objective meaning of this concept must be warranted, since it is used in judgments or propositions[5] of the type "this external object is mine," which state the *first* lawgiving *acts* of Kant's natural right. When I make such a statement, I understand "externally mine" as something that "I would be wronged by being disturbed in my use of it *even if I am not in possession of it* (not holding the object)" (*Doctrine of Right*, 6:249; see also 6:245). Here we have a lawgiving act, Kant says, by means of which "an obligation is laid upon all others, which they would not otherwise have, to refrain from using the object" (6:253). Kant reaffirms the same point by saying that "when I declare (by word or deed) that I will that something external is to be mine, I thereby declare that everyone else is under obligation to refrain from using that object of my choice, an obligation no one would have were it not for this act of mine to establish a right" (*Doctrine of Right*, 6:255).

Such declaration includes a presumption that the possession is *rightful*, a prerogative of right (*Doctrine of Right*, 6:257) that lays upon all others a duty of right prior to the existence of positive laws warranting its *legality*. Because it cannot be derived from the concept of the external use of freedom (free choice), the statement of the presumption is *synthetic*; and because it purports to be universally valid and necessary, it is *a priori*. Hence, "reason has then the task of showing how such a proposition, which goes beyond the concept of empirical possession, is possible *a priori*" (6:250). Kant formulates this task as follows: "how is a *synthetic a priori* proposition about right possible?" (6:249), namely, a proposition such as "this external object is mine," where the term "mine" means "mine in terms of natural right."

The deduction of the possibility of propositions of this type is a prior condition for dealing with the problem of the possibility of all other propositions about natural right, both private and public, or civil. Propositions of this type are constitutive of Kant's *Doctrine of Right*. The latter is conceived within the bounds of mere reason and based solely on the a priori principles of practical reason, and has as its final goal that of securing perpetual peace.[6] Furthermore, the task of warranting the possibility of these propositions precedes that of deciding whether the juridical claims that they convey are valid. Propositions of the type "this external object is mine" are therefore *basic* in Kant's *Doctrine of Right*, and the task of showing that they are possible is its *fundamental problem*.

According to Kant, showing that a synthetic a priori judgment is possible (that it *can be* objectively valid or invalid) means making explicit the conditions under which it can be applied in a realm of *sensible* data.[7] Likewise, an a priori concept is said to be possible if its referent and its meaning can be sensitized in this way. Judgments and concepts possible a priori are said to be *objectively real* theoretically if they are theoretical, and *objectively real* practically if they are practical. The objective possibility or reality[8] of the former is warranted by the *givenness* of objects;[9] and that of the latter by the *performability* of actions.[10] Givenness is a topic of Kant's theory of possible experience; performability, a topic of moral anthropology, or pragmatics.

According to the interpretation I presented elsewhere,[11] the task of making explicit the possibility of synthetic a priori theoretical judgments is part of the a priori semantics of those judgments. Therefore, the problem of the possibility of basic a priori juridical propositions is the fundamental problem of Kant's *juridical semantics*.[12]

According to the first *Critique*, the "general problem" of transcendental philosophy is that of the possibility of synthetic a priori theoretical judgments (*Pure Reason*, B73). The remarks I have just made allow us to conclude that, in working out the project of a transcendental philosophy, the later Kant extended that problem in order to encompass not only a priori theoretical judgments, but also any other synthetic a priori judgment. Thus, the generalized problem of transcendental philosophy became the following: how are synthetic a priori judgments in general possible? The answer to this question also aims at another goal: justifying the *decision procedures* for these judgments, that is, the procedures by which it is possible to determine whether they are valid. In some cases (theoretical and moral judgments, for example) these procedures provide *proofs*; in other cases (aesthetic judgments, for example) they provide decisions based exclusively on certain reflexive argumentative strategies.[13]

The Definition of the Concept of Rightful, Restrictive External Action

Since the synthetic a priori proposition whereby I state that an external object is mine "in terms of natural right" is something that I do unilaterally, thus laying upon all others an obligation or duty and restricting their external freedom, it becomes necessary to determine also a priori the conditions under which lawgiving acts of this kind can be justified. In other words, the study of the semantics of basic juridical propositions requires a clarification of the concept of *rightful, restrictive external action.* Kant takes on this task right away in the Introduction to the *Doctrine of Right* (Part 1 of the *Metaphysics of Morals*), and says clearly that it is an analysis preliminary to the study of the central problem, which, as we have just seen, is that of the possibility of propositions stating acts whereby one gains intelligible possession over something.

Kant defines the concept of rightful restrictive external action in terms of the conditions laid by pure practical reason upon practical external interpersonal relations among human beings. These conditions are part of the external lawgiving of practical reason, which is the subject matter of juridical science. In this context, human beings are thought to be agents who have free choice. To choose is to be able to act or refrain from acting according to one's wishes, which is connected with the consciousness of the capacity to perform actions that produce objects or modify them. A choice is free if it can be determined by the laws of pure reason, in particular, by the moral law (*Doctrine of Right*, 6:213). The concept of right presupposed by the external lawgiving of Kant's *Doctrine of Right* is therefore a moral concept, but that does not imply that juridical laws are themselves moral laws.

The relations among people endowed with free choice can be studied from three distinct points of view. First, insofar as their actions are affected by other human beings. These actions, as "*Facta*" (i.e., free human *deeds*), "can have (direct of indirect) influence on each other" (*Doctrine of Right*, 6:230). For example, the act whereby I declare an object to be mine influences the actions of others in the sense that it lays upon them an obligation to refrain from using that object.[14] Second, insofar as they have to do exclusively with the relation between one's choice to the choice of others (one's capacity to act freely on what is outside oneself), but not the relation of one's choice to the mere wishes or needs of others. Third, disregarding the matter, that is, the ends sought by free choices, but taking into account only the forms of their reciprocal relations, that is, the condition whereby "the action of one can be united with the freedom of the other in accordance with a universal law" (6:230).[15]

That said, Kant defines right (*das Recht*) as "the sum of conditions under which the choice of one can be united with the choice of another in accordance with a universal law of freedom" (*Doctrine of Right*, 6:230).[16] Juridical science is the "*systematic* knowledge" of those conditions (6:229). Thus conceived, the subject matter of right is the fundamental principle of the external lawgiving of practical reason, which assures rights and duties in the external use of freedom and lays restrictions upon its use.

Juridical doctrine is based on the universal criterion by which it is possible to recognize whether an act that imposes restrictions on the free will of others is right (*recht*) or wrong (*unrecht*). This criterion is made explicit by Kant in the form of a "universal principle of right": "An action is **right** if *it* can coexist with everyone's freedom in accordance with a universal law, or if on *its maxim* the freedom of choice of each can coexist with everyone's freedom in accordance with a universal law" (*Doctrine of Right*, 6:230; my emphasis in italics). This principle, also known as the "axiom of right," in fact offers the *definition* of rightful restrictive external action in terms of a formal property of its maxim, namely, the compatibility of one's maxim with the maxims of external actions of all other free agents, in accordance with an unspecified universal law.[17] This is merely a *nominal* definition, obtained through an analysis of the idea of free external action that allows for a conceptual distinction between right and wrong actions but does not specify the conditions under which rightful actions are to be performed. As usual, here too the analysis of concepts given a priori precedes the solution of the problem of its a priori synthesis; in the case at hand, the problem of warranting the possibility of an act of synthesis whereby I declare something as rightfully mine.[18]

From this analytic definition of rightful action, and taking into account that external actions are *facta* (deeds), that is, that they influence one another, one can draw a consequence containing the elements for the *real* definition of rightful action. Kant begins by introducing the concept of hindrance to a rightful action: "If then my action or my condition generally can coexist with the freedom of everyone in accordance with a universal law, whoever hinders me in it does me *wrong*; for this hindrance (resistance) cannot coexist with freedom in accordance with a universal law of freedom" (*Doctrine of Right*, 6:230–31).

After adding that "whatever is wrong is a hindrance to freedom in accordance with universal laws," Kant goes on to say: "Therefore, if a certain use of freedom is itself a hindrance to freedom in accordance with universal laws (i.e., wrong), coercion that is opposed to this (as a *hindering of a hindrance to freedom*) is consistent with freedom in accordance with universal laws, that is, it is right" (*Doctrine of Right*, 6:231).

From this one concludes that performing of a rightful action is always accompanied by an authorization for offering *effective* resistance to the hindrance of its actualization. In Kant's own words, "there is connected with right by the principle of contradiction an authorization to coerce someone who infringes upon it" (*Doctrine of Right*, 6:231). Therefore, a *principle of external coercion* follows analytically from the universal principle of right (more precisely, from the maxims of right). As an analytic consequence of the definition, that is, of what is "in the idea" of external freedom, this principle should be considered an *analytic* proposition. Kant says so explicitly in the *Doctrine of Virtue*. The "supreme principle of right," according to which "in accordance with the principle of contradiction . . . if external constraint checks the hindering of outer freedom in accordance with universal laws (and is thus a hindering to the hindrances to freedom), it can coexist with ends as such," and does not need to go "beyond the concept of freedom to see this," whatever the end sought. Therefore, Kant continues, "the supreme *principle of right* is therefore an analytic proposition" (*Doctrine of Virtue*, 6:396). According to this analysis, the right to perform a rightful action can also be represented as the possibility of a universal "reciprocal use of coercion that is consistent with everyone's freedom in accordance with universal laws" (*Doctrine of Right*, 6:232). Kant concludes his analysis by stating: "Right and authorization to use coercion therefore *mean* one and the same thing" (6:232; my italics).

The Semantics of the Concept of a Universal Reciprocal External Coercion

Due to the synonymy between the natural right to perform a rightful act justified on the basis of reason alone and the authorization to exert coercion (as long as it is backed by a universal law) on the free choice of others who oppose its execution, it follows that the objective reality of the a priori concept of *rightfulness* is warranted. This assures the objective reality of the a priori concept of *coerciveness* backed by law. As it happens, both are concepts of practical reason, but according to the transcendental semantics presented in the first *Critique*, of no concept of reason, theoretical or practical, can an adequate example be exhibited. None can be presented in a realm of sensible data provided by intuition. Hence the suspicion that these concepts might be empty, with the consequence that, if this is the case, they ought not to be used in juridical propositions that have doctrinal purposes.

However, some of these concepts can be made sensible *indirectly*. In particular, the concept of universal reciprocal external coercion can be given an example in "intuition *a priori*," only not directly, but also "by analogy," namely, by "presenting the possibility of bodies moving freely under the law of the *equality of action and reaction*" (*Doctrine of Right*, 6:232). The law at hand is obviously the "third analogy" of the theoretical understanding.[19] This principle, says Kant, is "as it were, the *construction*" (6:232) of both the concept of universal reciprocal coercion and—due to the above-mentioned synonymy—the concept of right, which renders possible the factual (sensible) "presentation" of these two concepts of practical reason, and hence their application to the realm of performable actions.

A short digression is in place here. In this context, "construction" designates the way theoretical concepts are given reference and meaning, that is, how they are schematized.[20] A schematized concept of the theoretical understanding—for example, a category—is said to be "realized" (*Pure Reason*, B185), that is, referred directly to the realm of possible experience, thus receiving a theoretical objective reality (see *Pure Reason*, B185–86, 221, 268). This procedure for giving reference and meaning to the concepts of the theoretical understanding should be distinguished from *schematism by analogy* or *symbolization*, used in sensitizing ideas of reason in general.[21] "The symbol of an idea (or a concept of reason)," Kant says, "is a representation of the object by analogy" (*Progress in Metaphysics*, 20:280). A concept schematized by analogy, or symbolized, is not "realized," since the content or objective reality that is assigned to it has a rather fictional character. Thus, such a concept *cannot* be used to convey knowledge. Nonetheless, the symbolization of concepts of reason is of great *operational* significance, since it allows the ideas of reason to be used in the construction of the system of nature—as is the case of theoretical ideas that can give *order* to the collection of natural laws produced by the understanding[22]—as well as in establishing the system of freedom, that is, the rational regulation of human courses of action, which is the goal aimed at by sensitized practical ideas.

Once the analogy between universal reciprocal practical coercion and physical coercion is accepted, what is *subsumed* under the concept of right and belongs to pure practical reason is not directly this or that act of free choice, but rather the pure concept of action and reaction of the *theoretical* understanding: the category of community, employed in the formulation of the third analogy (*Doctrine of Right*, 6:252–53, 268). The advantage of this subsuming is that, although it is not an empirical representation, the category in question can be schematized (sensitized, made intuitive) in two ways: (a) by its schema, and (b) by mathematical models.[23] Kant takes the schema of the category of community for granted and makes explicit only a mathematical analogy that represents the rightfulness of an act. In mathematics, there is only one straight line between two given points; likewise, within right there is only one way of assuring the rightfulness and correctness of the reciprocal influence between two free agents. In mathematics, only one perpendicular line can be constructed on a given point of a straight line; likewise, within right there is only one way of deciding: impartially.[24]

Establishing the analogy between the practical concept of universal reciprocal external coercion—which agrees with everyone's freedom in accordance with a universally valid law—and the category of community of physical objects—which corresponds to the a priori principle of action and reaction of the understanding—is the key to Kant's semantics of the a priori concepts of the doctrines of right and virtue. Kant stresses the significance of this symbolization when he says, at the beginning of the *Doctrine of Virtue*, that in the theory of the duty of right, "*what is mine* and *what is yours* must be determined on scales of justice exactly, in accordance with the principle that action and reaction are equal, and so with a precision analogous to that of mathematics" (*Doctrine of Virtue*, 6:376 note). This mathematical analogy finds support, in part, on the fact that we experience that others "are to be considered fellow human beings, that is, rational beings with needs, united by nature in one dwelling place so that they can help one another" (6:453).

Kant extends this point of view to all his theory of rights, that is, to all his metaphysics of morals, saying: "In speaking of laws of duty (not laws of nature) and, among these, of laws for human beings' external relations with one another, we consider ourselves in a moral (intelligible) world where, by analogy with the physical world, *attraction* and *repulsion* bind together rational beings (on earth)" (*Doctrine of Virtue*, 6:449). Schematization by analogy—this is a very important point for the understanding of Kant's juridical semantics—does not render the concept of right a theoretical concept and does not determine it precisely. It remains a practical concept, not directly applicable to the realm of performable actions.

The Exposition of the Concept of "Externally Mine"

Following this semantic analysis of the concept of rightful external action, Kant shifts his focus, already in the body of the first part of the *Doctrine of Right*, which is dedicated to public right, to the problem of the rightfulness of acts that declare something as mine "merely in terms of natural law." He then asks, first, what it *means* to say that an external object is mine or yours. That is, he begins to deal with the semantics of the predicate "mine" as it is used in natural right.

Kant begins by noting that, so as to be able to call something rightfully mine, I must rightfully possess it. Thus a new problem emerges: what does it mean to possess something in general and, in particular, rightfully possess it? The answer to this question entails the specification of what the possible objects of possession are. Objects of possession can be external or internal. An object of external *possession* is something *outside me*. This last phrase has two senses: on the one hand, it designates something distinct from me as a human being; on the other, something that is to be found elsewhere in space and time (*Doctrine of Right*, 6:245). Objects taken in the first sense are merely intelligible; the others are necessarily sensible.

The object of *internal* possession is one only: my innate freedom, that is, "independence from being constrained by another's choice, insofar as it can coexist with the freedom of every other in accordance with a universal law" (*Doctrine of Right*, 6:237). Here freedom is neither defined in terms of the moral law, nor as the possibility of behaving as one wishes, nor simply as free choice (appetitive capacity connected to the consciousness of the capacity to perform object-producing actions, determined by pure practical reason), but by the axiom of right made explicit above. This is freedom of choice, or freedom insofar as it is an object of the external lawgiving of practical reason, and the origin of external actions that affect other people and objects of external use.[25]

The internal freedom to act externally, represented by the natural-right concept of freedom, is something that is rightfully mine, that is, my possession of it is directly assured by practical reason. This possession is based on a *natural right* "which belongs to everyone by nature, independently of any act that would establish a right" (*Doctrine of Right*, 6:237), that is, a right that follows from the axiom of right. Thus, it is an *innate* right to freedom, which is also innate and concerns actions that affect external objects and others who are likewise free to perform external actions. The innate right to freedom includes an innate equality and various other authorizations, entailing, according to the axiom of right, the right to resist all obstacles to the external use of internal juridical freedom (that is, of what is internally mine) and the right to resist all violations of the innate right to freedom.[26]

Kant distinguishes two concepts of possession of an external object, which is something that deserves special attention. An external object is said to be in my physical possession (empirical, or sensible, possession: *possessio phaenomenon*) if it is physically mine, for example, if it is on my hands or at the reach of my guns. Physical possession of something is synonymous with having a *physical power* over that thing, which is a kind of "physical connection" to the object. This entails that the object of my possession is also empirical and that there are spatio-temporal relations between me and the object.

On the other hand, I cannot disregard the fact that an object remains mine if I was the first to possess it and declared it to be mine, either by words or by some other means, but from which I *later* moved physically away. This is a case of *intelligible possession* (or *noumenon possessio*) of an external object, which is itself also intelligible. This possession is understood in the sense of a "connection of the subject's will with that object . . . *independently of any relation to it in space and time*" (*Doctrine of Right*, 6:254; my italics). Here the predicate "intelligibly mine" is applied to an external object "with which I am so connected that another's use of it without my consent would wrong me," it would hurt my (natural) right (6:245).

In both cases, the external object that is possessed can be numerically the same. However, when we speak of empirical possession, both the relation of possession and the objects possessed are subject to the conditions of intuition, in particular, the objects possessed must be cognizable empirically and thus be objects for the senses, or appearances (see *Doctrine of Right*, 6:268). On the other hand, the object of a rightful possession must be thought of as a thing in itself (*Sache an sich selbst*), not "as it was in the Transcendental Analytic as an appearance" (6:249).[27] In the *Doctrine of Right*, the object of right, even when it can be cognized empirically, is always regarded as an object of choice, that is, of freedom in its external use, determined by practical reason. Objects of this type are not appearances, but rather "things" to which I am connected by merely juridical relations. Since these relations are noumenal, those "things" must also be thought to be noumenal, or "things in themselves." This analysis indicates yet another feature of Kant's juridical semantics: the objects of possession referred to by basic juridical judgments do not have—to borrow a phrase from Heidegger—the same sense of being as those objects accessible to our cognitive apparatus in possible experience.

The Fundamental Problem of the Semantics of Synthetic A Priori Propositions about Natural Right

Typical examples of *basic propositions* about right are, "this external object is mine," "this external object is not mine," and "this external object is yours (not mine)." Hence, from a qualitative point of view, these propositions are affirmative, negative, or limitative. From the point of view of quantity, relation, and modality, they seem to be singular, predicative, and assertoric. I say "seem" because a finer analysis reveals that they contain a hidden universal quantifier (by saying "this external object is mine," I lay upon *anyone else* that may come to interact with me an obligation to refrain from using that object); they do not express a monadic predicate but rather a relation (being mine is a relation), and state an obligation that is not merely affirmed but also cogent.[28]

Here I cannot articulate Kant's semantics of all the syntactic components of the basic juridical propositions. I will focus exclusively on the difference between the ones in which the *predicate* "mine" (that is, the *relation of possession*) is understood in the empirical sense and those in which that relation has a merely intelligible sense. This point is crucial for the remainder of the semantic analysis of propositions about right offered by Kant in the *Doctrine of Right*.

If "mine" means physically mine, in the sense made explicit above, then the proposition "this external object is mine" is *analytic*. In fact, in this case, what the basic proposition about right *says* is that "If I am holding a thing [*Sache*] (and so physically connected with it), someone who affects it without my consent (e.g., snatches an apple from my hand) affects and diminishes what is internally mine (my freedom)" (*Doctrine of Right*, 6:250). A proposition with that content is analytic because it "does not go beyond the right of a person with regard to himself" (6:250). Which right is that? The one relative to what is "internally mine," my freedom, which I have by virtue of an innate right. The external use of my body—in Kant's example, my hand—"concerns only my outer *freedom*, hence only possession of myself, not a thing external to me, so that it is only an internal right" (6:254). The axiom of right applies both to the innate internal right and to external rights acquired by an act. Thus, the action or maxim of action that consists in snatching an apple from someone's hand cannot coexist with the freedom of my choice in accordance with a universal law. It contradicts the axiom of right. From this it follows analytically that I have a natural right to resist physically the above-mentioned action, that is, to defend physically what is physically mine.

Let us consider now the second case, where the predicate "mine" means "intelligibly mine." In this case, the proposition "this external object is mine" is synthetic a priori. It is a priori because it employs a term from pure practical reason, "intelligibly mine," which does not have any immediate meaning in sensation. It is *synthetic*, because it cannot be derived from the axiom of right, that is, from the definition of the concept of rightfulness (*Doctrine of Right*, 6:250). The axiom of right does not allow us "to put all others under an obligation, which they would not otherwise have, to refrain from using certain objects of our choice because we have been the *first* to take them into our possession" (6:247; my italics). The possibility of stating that an external object is mine in the merely intelligible sense raises a presumption of right, which, because it is a priori, intends to be understood as universally valid and necessary, but because it is *synthetic* still needs to be *justified*. So the *fundamental task* of Kant's *juridical semantics* comes to be determined more precisely as follows: "how is a [basic] synthetic *a priori* proposition about right possible?" (6:249).[29] As we shall see, this task essentially boils down to that of establishing the possibility of a single a priori concept used in propositions of this type: that of intelligible possession.

The Nature of the Problem and the Solution Procedure

It helps to recall here some crucial distinctions of Kant's theory of the proof of a priori synthetic propositions in general. First, the problem of proving the possibility of propositions of this type is different from that of assuring its validity. In the former case, one asks for "conditions of possibility," that is, conditions under which it may or may not be valid. In the latter, one decides based on those conditions that of these two exclusive possibilities is realized: for theoretical propositions, whether they are true or false; for practical propositions, whether or not they hold. In that context, Kant's goal is merely to prove the possibility of propositions of the type "this external object is mine"—that is, to establish that they *can* hold a priori and that lawgiving is therefore possible on the basis of them—and not to decide whether they actually hold. Second, the conditions of possibility and decidability considered by Kant are always defined for a realm of sensible data and are thus objective: those of the synthetic a priori theoretical judgments for the realm of objects of experience, and those of the synthetic a priori practical judgments for the realm of actions performable by free human agents. Hence, the *possibility* or *validity* sought (and sometimes proved) are also said to be "objective."

The method used by Kant for solving the problem of the objective possibility of synthetic a priori propositions about right—the only ones that interest us here—is analogous to the one employed in the first *Critique* for proving the objective possibility of the principles of the understanding. In both cases, at the core of the procedure is the proof that the a priori concepts employed in these propositions—the categories, in the principles of the understanding; the concept of intelligibly mine, in the basic propositions of the *Doctrine of Right*—are objectively possible. According to the general thesis of Kant's semantics of pure concepts, restated in the *Doctrine of Virtue*, logical consistency is not enough to assure the objective reality of a concept (see *Doctrine of Virtue*, 6:382). This requires showing the real possibility of the thing designated by the concept, that is, its referent, by giving a real definition of the concept. In the first *Critique*, Kant does so with respect to the categories in two steps: first, their transcendental deduction, and then their transcendental schematism. In the *Doctrine of Right*, Kant again proceeds in two steps: he first deduces the a priori objective possibility of intelligible possession and then offers a procedure for its application to the domain of actually performable actions.[30] This two-step procedure is analogous, but not at all identical—as will become clear in what follows—to the two-step procedure used in the first *Critique* (transcendental deduction and schematism of the categories).

The Postulate of Right

Kant deduces the concept of intelligible possession by showing that its objective possibility (practical-juridical objective reality) is an "immediate consequence" of the postulate of right of practical reason: "The possibility of this kind of possession, and so the deduction of the nonempirical concept of possession, is based on the postulate of practical reason with regard to rights" (*Doctrine of Right*, 6:252). In one of its formulations, this postulate says: "It is possible for me to have any external object of my choice as mine" (6:250). Here the term "possible [*möglich*]" has the practical meaning of "allowing," since the postulate of right conveys a moral capacity or faculty for unilaterally *laying* obligations upon anyone else with whom I might freely interact. Kant calls the postulate of right a permissive law (6:247, 276). The same point is detailed in the observation: "This prerogative arises . . . from the capacity anyone has, by the postulate of practical reason, to have an external object of his choice as his own. Consequently, any holding of an external object is a condition whose conformity with right is based on that postulate by a previous act of will" (*Doctrine of Right*, 6:257).

The postulate that allows for unilateral coercion is neither a command (*lex praeceptiva*) nor a prohibition (*lex prohibitiva, lex vetiti*), but rather an authorization or permission (*lex permissiva*).[31] As a permissive law, the postulate renders private possession rightful for practical reason, imposing the duty to respect the rightful acts by means of which we secure the private possession of the external objects of free choice (*Doctrine of Right*, 6:250).[32] This component of the meaning of the postulate is explicit in another formulation, which says that "it is a duty of right to act towards others so that what is external (usable) could also become someone's" (6:252).[33] Reason "wills that this hold as a principle, and it does this as *practical* reason, which extends itself *a priori* by this postulate of reason" (6:247).[34]

If the concept of "having as mine" is interpreted in an empirical sense, in which "mine" means "physically mine"—mine in certain spatio-temporal conditions—the postulate of right is an *analytic* proposition, not to mention what the postulate of right already says, which, as we have seen, is also an analytic proposition. In fact, if what is in my physical power to use could not also be in my rightful power, then freedom "would be depriving itself of the use of its choice with regard to an object of choice, by putting *usable* objects beyond any possibility of being *used*; in other words, it would annihilate them in a practical respect and make them into *res nullius*" (*Doctrine of Right*, 6:246). But, Kant goes on, practical reason lays down only formal laws as the basis for using choice and with respect to an object of choice "it can contain no absolute prohibition against using such an object, since this would be a contradiction of our outer freedom with itself" (6:246).

However, if the predicate "mine" is understood in the sense of intelligible possession, the postulate of right "could not be got from mere concepts of right as such" (*Doctrine of Right*, 6:247). It says something new that *extends* the use of practical reason, and must therefore be considered as a synthetic a priori proposition.[35]

Deduction of the Possibility of the Concept of Intelligible Possession

The objective reality of the concept of intelligible possession is an immediate consequence of the postulate of right in its synthetic a priori sense. Kant's argument consists of a single sentence, set up as a hypothetical: "For if it is necessary to act in accordance with that principle of right, its intelligible condition (a merely rightful possession) must then also be possible" (*Doctrine of Right*, 6:252).

In this context, the phrase "principle of right" designates the postulate of right, so that the antecedent of the hypothetical sentence above speaks of the need to act in accordance with the postulate of right. Likewise, the phrase "intelligible condition," which occurs in the consequent of the deduction, is not saying that something might condition intelligible possession, but rather that the possession is implied by the need to act in accordance with the postulate.

This deduction procedure differs in several important points from the one employed by Kant in the transcendental deduction of the categories. The proof of the objective validity of the a priori concepts of the understanding in the realm of sensible objects, offered in the first *Critique*, consists of showing by conceptual analysis that these concepts are a necessary condition of the objective validity of synthetic judgments in general.[36] Kant found this solution by asking for the possibility of synthetic a priori judgments in pure mathematics (Euclidean geometry) and natural science (Newton's physics), considered as *facta* or products of pure theoretical reason (*Prolegomena*, 4:275). Although their validity is undeniable, these judgments are themselves still contingent.[37] The concept of intelligible possession, on the other hand, is deduced by showing that its objective validity in the realm of acts performable by human beings is implied by the objective validity of an a priori practical judgment—namely, the postulate of right, recognized not as a contingent deed of the likewise contingent pure speculative reason, but rather as an *imposition* of the lawgiving will of pure reason on free human agents. The difference between the two deductions can be presented as follows: theoretical reason does not want anything, but merely renders possible the intelligibility of Euclidean geometry, and also its a priori truth for our cognitive apparatus; on the other hand, practical reason does want something, namely, for "merely rightful" possession to be practicable, but it does not warrant the intelligibility of such a practice. It merely warrants the claim that by not allowing for the possibility of intelligible possession we would be contradicting what reason wants and, in *this practical sense*, we would be irrational. "We cannot see how intelligible possession is possible and so how it is possible for something external to be mine or yours, but must infer it from the postulate of practical reason" (*Doctrine of Right*, 6:255).

On the other hand, the deduction procedure for the objective practical reality of intelligible possession is strongly reminiscent of the one by which Kant established the same result for the concept of freedom in the second *Critique*: the objective practical reality of freedom is there also established as an immediate consequence of a law, namely, the moral law, considered as an a priori imperative.[38] In both cases, the deduction does not show the intelligibility of the concept deduced, but merely its practical possibility.[39] Kant himself emphasizes this parallel by saying that no one needs to be surprised by the fact that the remarks about objects that are "mine or yours get lost in the intelligible . . . since no theoretical deduction can be given for the possibility of the concept of freedom, on which they are based. It can only be inferred from the practical law of reason (the categorical imperative) as a fact of reason" (*Doctrine of Right*, 6:252). This observation is particularly instructive, since it highlights the reach of a deduction technique that is essentially different from the one used in the first *Critique* and was applied for the first time in the *Critique of Practical Reason* for the idea of freedom. Later it was employed in various works, including the *Critique of the Power of Judgment* and the *Metaphysics of Morals*.

Despite the parallel indicated, there is an important difference between the deduction of the objective reality of freedom, based on the moral law, and the deduction of intelligible possession, in the context of the postulate of right. The moral law is a categorical imperative or postulate. It says that "one ought absolutely to proceed in a certain way" (*Practical Reason*, 5:31), commanding that our actions be ruled by universal maxims. The postulate of right is also a problematic imperative (not a categorical imperative) in the sense of being compatible with a merely possible practical reason (see *Practical Reason*, 5:11 note). As a permissive law only, it does not command us, but merely opens up an a priori space for a certain way of life.[40] Thus, the imperative of right does not generate a fact (*factum*) of reason, as the moral law does, but allows for these facts to be generated by rightful external actions, that is, actions whose maxims can be made compatible with each other in accordance with a universal law.[41]

This difference can only be properly appreciated in the context of a more detailed reconstruction of Kant's concept of *facticity of reason*. I emphasize here two points of that reconstruction, which are particularly illuminating. First, one should consider Kant's distinction between the *facta* of theoretical reason, which I have just mentioned, and the "sole fact of pure reason," defined in the second *Critique* as the consciousness of being internally coerced to act in accordance with universal maxims, consciousness that is identical to being obligated by the moral law (*Practical Reason*, 5:31). This distinction, in its turn, needs to be analyzed in light of the later Kant's thesis that the theoretical faculty of the human being, though not the *faculty of moral self-obligation*, can very well be a "quality of a living corporeal being," and that we cannot decide either by experience or by pure reason alone whether life is a "property of matter." In moral relationships, however, "the incomprehensible property of *freedom* is revealed by the influence of reason on the inner lawgiving will" (*Doctrine of Virtue*, 6:418). The subjects of these relationships are not bodies and souls, that is, men as sensitive beings characterized by natural properties and belonging to an animal species, but rather men as beings of reason.

Second, one ought to distinguish between the fact of reason, as defined in the second *Critique*, and the facts of reason that comprise valid a priori juridical lawgiving acts or the external actions that follow from them (that which man as a free being—that is, influenced by practical reason—*makes of himself*). The set of *these* facts make up the object of the a priori history of the human race, which is essentially a history of moralizing rationalization and not one of technical-practical rationalization.

Rules for Applying the Concept of Intelligible Possession

The deduction of the concept of intelligible possession showed *that*, given the postulate of right, that concept is objectively possible, but it did not specify *how* the concept can be *applied* to the realm of human praxis.[42] So as to assure the possibility of lawgiving about what is mine or yours using propositions of the type "this external object is mine," one needs to identify the procedures by which it is possible to render *practically real* the relation or link between my will and the external object in question, which is thought a priori by means of the concept of intelligible possession. Only thus can the *Doctrine of Right* go beyond the presuppositions of practical reason and show itself fruitful as a guide for human action (see *Doctrine of Right*, 6:242).

Given that the concept of rightful possession is an a priori concept of *reason*, it "cannot be applied *directly* to objects of experience and to the concept of empirical *possession*" (*Doctrine of Right*, 6:252). In other words, it cannot be schematized in the same way as the categories of the theoretical understanding. Since it is impossible to find a *direct* and *adequate* sensible reference for the concept of noumenal possession, one ought to conclude that this concept is *empty* of any content and has no objective practical reality. Following Kant, one ought not to try to find a less direct or only partially adequate procedure for assuring its applicability to human acts.

Overall, Kant's solution comprises a new *schematization by analogy*. The concept of intelligible possession needs first to be referred, also a priori, to an intermediate concept—the concept of having—which belongs to the *theoretical* understanding, whose object is something external to myself and under my coercive control (*Gewalt*). If I *subsume* the concept of intelligible theoretical possession under the concept of intelligible practical possession, or inversely, if I *interpret* the latter in terms the former, then my statement that an external object is merely rightfully mine—for example, that this land is merely rightfully mine, whereby I presume that it is effectively mine, even when I do not physically occupy it—means that I find myself in "an intellectual relation to an object insofar as I have it *under my control* (the understanding's concept of possession independent of spatial determinations)" (*Doctrine of Right*, 6:253). Thus, the practical objective reality of the concept of intelligible possession is warranted by its applicability to the *realm of physical causal actions* theoretically thought. Kant writes:

> It is precisely in this—in the fact that, *abstracting* from possession in the appearance (of detention) of an object of my choice, reason wants possession to be thought in accordance with the concepts of the understanding, not empirical ones, but rather those that contain *a priori* its conditions—where the ground of the validity of such a concept of possession (*possessio noumenon*) as a universal *legislation*; since that legislation is contained in the judgment "This external object is *mine*." (*Doctrine of Right*, 6:253)

Now, like any other a priori concept of the understanding, the concept of coercive control (or coercive cause) also admits, at least in principle, of being applied to empirical concepts, for example, to the concepts that designate *my physical-empirical causal power* over an external object, such as the power of my weapons. Hence, the a priori juridical concept of rightful possession becomes applicable to the realm of actions (effectively) performable, thus assuring, albeit indirectly and only by means of an analogy, the practical objective reality of the synthetic a priori basic proposition of the metaphysics of morals in the realm of sensible human acts. The problem of the effective applicability of practical reason's concept of intelligible possession—which must not be confused with the problem of the deduction of that same concept, analyzed above—essentially boils down to that of the effective applicability of the theoretical understanding's concept of coercive control. Juridical a priori lawgiving over what is mine or yours can be interpreted and applied in terms of laws for the use of our coercive control, thought in practical-technical empirical terms.

In part 2 of the "Doctrine of Private Right"—from the first half of the *Doctrine of Right* (§§10–31, 6:258–86)—Kant devotes himself precisely to the task of identifying the empirical procedures (effectively taking possession, use of individual force or armed forces, contract, positive laws prior to a public constitution, etc.) whereby we acquire and exert rightful possession over various types of external objects. These same procedures are also used as *instruments of proof*, that is, for deciding what is rightfully mine or yours. As an illustration, I mention Kant's thesis that in the state of nature—therefore prior to the establishment of a civil constitution based on reason and on coercive control by the state—I cannot rightfully claim that an object is mine if I cannot physically defend it. The high seas, for example, cannot be said to be mine given that they are beyond the reach of my guns (*Doctrine of Right*, 6:265).

The schematization of the concept of intelligible possession is similar, but not identical, to the one offered for the concept of universal reciprocal external coercion (see section 4 above). The similarity lies in the fact that in both cases the juridical concepts of practical reason are interpreted by causal concepts (causal relations) of the theoretical understanding. The difference is in the choice of the latter: the concept of reciprocal coercion is symbolically schematized by the category of community (reciprocal, circular causality) and that of intelligible possession by the category of causality (unilateral, linear). This difference brings about a new problem: how can I be *sure* that everyone else will recognize the rightfulness of my unilateral act and behave accordingly?

Kant's answer begins with the observation that the judgment whereby I state that something external is merely rightfully mine contains a reciprocal obligation that "arises from a universal rule" (*Doctrine of Right*, 6:256). However, since a unilateral act of the will about an external possession—an accidental act therefore—cannot on its own serve as coercive law for all, we have to understand that "it is only a will putting everyone under obligation, hence only a collectively general (common) and powerful will, that can provide everyone this assurance" (*Doctrine of Right*, 6:256).[43]

Now, the only mode of social organization in which there is lawgiving accompanied by a universal external (i.e., public) power is the civil state. Therefore, only in a civil state can there safely be a mine and a yours, without both entailing war. Before the establishment of a social organization based on a public legislation, that is, a civil constitution, my intelligible possession of an external object remains legally *provisional*, and only becomes *permanent* after the effective realization of a state of right. When that happens, my unilateral act begins to be thought of as "included in a will that is united *a priori*" (*Doctrine of Right*, 6:263), or yet as proceeding "from practical reason" (6:259). So the permission, given by the postulate of right to human subjects, allowing each to have as one's own any and all objects of external use implies an additional permission to "constrain everyone else with whom he comes into conflict about whether an external object is his or another's to enter along with him into a civil constitution" (*Doctrine of Right*, 6:256).

Toward an A Priori Politics and History

This same a priori permission had been formulated by Kant already in 1795, in a note to the first definite article of peace in *Toward Perpetual Peace*. Given that the state of nature is a state of war, whoever remains in a state of nature "wrongs me just by being near me in this condition," for the lack of legislation is a permanent threat to me. For this reason, "I can coerce him either to enter with me into a condition of being under civil laws or to leave my neighborhood" (*Perpetual Peace*, 8:349 note). This permission is formulated by Kant in the following "postulate": "all men who can mutually affect one another must belong to some civil constitution" (8:349 note).

As with the postulate of right that establishes duties of right or legal duties, this new postulate, which we might call Kant's *fundamental political postulate*, not only states a permission, but also a duty, namely, the basic *political duty* to all people, expressed in the formula: "a people is to unite itself into a state in accordance with freedom and equality as the sole concepts of right" (*Perpetual Peace*, 8:378). A politics developed on this "communitarian" basis according to a social contract, will be necessarily linked to the concept of right, and will essentially be "the *Doctrine of Right* put into practice" (8:370). Thus conceived, politics will always be a *moral politics*, where morality is understood according to the *Doctrine of Right* (*Perpetual Peace*, 8:384). It is clear that the maxims of this politics cannot be extracted from empirical expectations about the well being or happiness of the citizens, but must be issued from "the pure concept of duty of right (from 'I ought,' the principle which is given *a priori* by pure reason" (8:379). This case is precisely that of the three definite articles for perpetual peace. They all state duties, namely, *political-juridical duties*. They are justified by considerations that refer to Kant's 1797 *Doctrine of Right*, and to follow them is to promote the establishment of perpetual peace internationally.

Thus one opens the door to "a politics cognizable *a priori*" (*Perpetual Peace*, 8:378). What does it mean here to be able to cognize a politics a priori? According to the interpretive line of Kant's critical project adopted here, it means to establish a priori the possibility and validity of the fundamental principles of politics, and to warrant the possibility of carrying them out by means of pragmatic-anthropological considerations. The first task unfolds into two: (1) showing that the principles of the *Doctrine of Right* required by political theory are not "empty thought" (8:372); and (2) showing the same for the maxims of politics itself, and especially making evident that the definite articles for perpetual peace are possible and therefore that the idea of perpetual peace is not "ineffectual," but rather a *humanly performable* task.[44]

In both cases, the problem is the same: showing that the principles in question "can be carried out" (*Perpetual Peace*, 8:380). Kant moves toward his solution, indicating the fact that "the moral principle in the human being never dies out, and reason, which is capable of pragmatically carrying out rightful ideas in accordance with that principle, grows steadily with advancing culture" (8:380).[45] Thus, there is a "well-founded hope" that the successive attempts at creating a state of perpetual peace "comes steadily closer to its goal (since the times during which equal progress takes place will, we hope, become always shorter)" (8:386).[46]

These theses about the possibility of accomplishing the task of establishing perpetual peace, defined in terms of the *Doctrine of Right*, anticipate an answer to another necessary question of practical reason: how is an a priori history possible? This inquiry, which was explicitly raised by Kant for the first time in *The Conflict of the Faculties* (1798a, 7:172), can be reformulated as follows: does the human *race* (as a whole) constantly advance toward the better? "Better" here is thought in terms of right, that is, as a quality of a civil constitution comparatively more agreeable to the interests of practical reason. The answer to this question is not only possible, but can be phrased as a "divinatory historical narrative of things imminent in future times," therefore, Kant adds, "as a possible representation [*Darstellung*] of events which are supposed to happen then" (*Conflict*, 7:72). To the narratives that anticipate the future, one can add the ones about the past and the present (7:84). The a priori history sought by Kant consists therefore of *narrative judgments that anticipate*, *recall*, and *observe*, all of which are grounded on the following *fundamental judgment* of Kant's theory of history: "the human race has always been in progress toward the better and will continue to be so henceforth" (7:88–89).

Here one must necessarily face the central question of Kant's critical philosophy of history: how are synthetic a priori judgments about history possible?—a semantic question that becomes ipso facto, the *fundamental problem* of Kant's theory of history. The point here is to find out, first of all, whether the fundamental a priori judgment about history just mentioned is possible—and, if it is possible, how it can be proved. That fundamental judgment, as one can easily see, is not theoretical, moral, juridical, or reflecting. According to the basic rule of transcendental semantics, the proof of the possibility of that judgment requires that it be referred to a sensible experience. It is precisely this demand that Kant reaffirms in the title of section 5 of the *Conflict of the Faculties*: "Yet the Prophetic History of the Human Race Must be Connected to Some Experience." At the very beginning of this section, Kant clarifies what he means by this type of experience: "There must be some experience in the human race which, as an event, points to the disposition and capacity of the human race to be the cause of its own advance toward the better, and (since this would be the act of a human being endowed with freedom), to the human race as being the author of this advance" (*Conflict*, 7:84). The author of such an advance is conceived by Kant as having an *a priori tendency*—in particular, a tendency to establish republican constitutions—which can be seen not in individuals, but in the human race *as a whole*. Here we have a new concept within Kant's practical philosophy. It is a concept that has a mixed nature, since it designates on the one hand the noumenal cause that authors political-juridical progress (namely, the collective rational will, which has universal coercive power) and, on the other hand, the concrete ways in which this cause manifests itself in factual history. The former component of this mixed concept is an important addition to the metaphysics of morals; the second, to pragmatic anthropology. The concept is developed in the last part of Kant's *Anthropology*—published in the same year as *The Conflict of the Faculties*—where Kant deals with the fundamental character traits of the *human species*. There we read that humanity, as a species, due to its rational nature has a tendency "some day to bring about, *by its own activity*, the development of good out of evil" (*Anthropology*, 7:329; my italics).[47] This is why Kant can say, in *The Conflict of the Faculties*, that an a priori history is possible "if the diviner himself makes and contrives the events which he announces in advance" (*Conflict*, 7:80), which is a thesis that makes of this kind of development a *self-fulfilling prophecy*.

Hence, "an occurrence must be thought which points to the existence of such a cause and to its effectiveness in the human race, undetermined with regard to time" (*Conflict*, 7:84). Could there be an event that satisfies these conditions? Yes, there is, says Kant: it is the way in which world public opinion experienced the achievements of the French Revolution. That experience consisted in the "wishful participation that borders closely on enthusiasm" (7:85).[48] The jubilation with which the human race received the development of the republican constitution, revealed by the events in France that marked the end of the eighteenth century, is the sought "*demonstrative sign*" of the "tendency of the human race viewed in its entirety" (Kant no longer says "of the human being") to advance toward what is morally and juridically better. This *experience* is at the same time an "*of remembrance sign*"—which allows us to say, based on other *political-juridical deeds*, that humanity has forever advanced in that way—and a "*prognostic sign*," since it authorizes us to predict a priori that it will continue advancing likewise (7:84).

Kant manages here a decisive step forward for his semantics of a priori judgments about politics and history: not because he introduced the abstract idea of unified general will—that step had already been taken in the *Doctrine of Right*—but because he elaborated the idea of a *sensitized general will*, more precisely of the concept of a *collective subject for history*, characterized by a *tendency* toward what is morally and juridically better. This collective subject has not only purposes and capacities for action but also other faculties that were up until then commonly reserved exclusively to individuals, such as memory: the achievement of a republican constitution by the French people is a phenomenon in human history that "*will no longer be forgotten*" (*Conflict*, 7:88). The possibility of a priori politics and history can then be warranted by the application of concepts and judgments of these two disciplines to the realm of sensible data comprising what the human race can do and cease doing.[49] When not only individuals but also organized groups and even humanity as a whole, living on the terrestrial globe as an actual collective subject, begins to *do* for a priori reasons what public opinion considers *should* happen, when a *universal movement* demands that our legal and political duties be obeyed, then not only the fundamental judgment about history becomes possible, and even demonstrable, but also all narrative synthetic a priori judgments that anticipate a priori real events as outcomes of the progress toward the better (for example, the lessening of violence between individuals and peoples, the raising of social welfare, etc.).

These indications suffice, I believe, to make evident that the judgments about history, whose semantics were sketched by Kant in 1798, comprise a class of its own of a priori judgments, because they differ substantially from foretelling and prophetic judgments—unacceptable in any doctrine that intends overcome Kant's criticism—as well as all other classes of a priori judgments, either theoretical-predictive, moral-determining, juridical-lawgiving, or even reflecting, whose semantics had been laid out by Kant in prior works.[50] Assuring the "sense and meaning" of this new type of a priori judgment not only allows for setting up history as an a priori doctrine, but also opens up new perspectives for a rereading of Kant's political philosophy from the perspective of his philosophy of history.

Practical Philosophy within the Bounds of the Critical Project

The analysis that I have just presented allows for an interesting retrospective on the path followed by Kant in search of a formulation and resolution of the problems of the metaphysics of morals within the framework of his critical project, that is, from the question: how are synthetic a priori judgments in general possible? In both the 1781 and 1787 editions of the *Critique of Pure Reason*, practical philosophy is left completely out of the project of transcendental philosophy and the problem of the possibility of synthetic a priori practical judgments is not even formulated (*Pure Reason*, B833). In the 1784 essay *Idea for a Universal History with a Cosmopolitan Aim*, the history of the human race is conceived as a natural history, therefore without any connection to a theory of a priori practical judgments. The *Groundwork for a Metaphysics of Morals* is the first work in which Kant explicitly formulates the problem of the possibility of synthetic-practical a priori judgments (*Groundwork*, 4:420), but it is generally recognized that he fails to solve it, in part because he sought the answer by having recourse to metaphysical considerations in studying the "practical rational faculty" in human beings. The solution only comes up in the *Critique of Practical Reason* (1788), and consists of the thesis that the consciousness of the need that our will has for the moral law—a need that binds us to act in accordance with universal maxims—is sufficient factual or sensible evidence for the effectiveness of that law, and therefore also of its possibility. In the 1795 essay *Toward Perpetual Peace*, this kind of approach, which replaces ontological-material considerations with questions about the performability of actions governed by practical concepts, comes progressively to the forefront in the treatment of topics of political philosophy. In the *Doctrine of Right*, published a couple of years later, the general line of investigation is directed precisely at questions about whether pure practical concepts of right can be interpreted by pure theoretical concepts of the understanding (concerning the use of physical force). It is also directed toward the practical *application* of the pure practical concepts of right by means of pure schemata, and to providing empirical examples of the latter. The same shift in Kant's focus from the field of ontology to that of semantics can be observed in Kant's theory of history, tightly connected to the theories of natural right and politics, with the difference that in this case the domain of interpretation is not the set of acts of individuals but rather the human race.[51]

This *semantic turn* in approaching the questions of the metaphysics of morals also allows the later Kant to solve, in a novel manner, questions relative to the unity of the *system* of critical philosophy. The problem of the compatibility between nature and freedom, for example, does not remain open, as it had in the first *Critique*, nor does it remain confined to merely reflecting judgments, as in the third *Critique*, but instead receives a solution that is at once rational and sensitized, in terms of the theory of the *physical* performability of a priori principles of *moral* politics. This is a theory that was first presented, as I have shown, in *Toward Perpetual Peace*, and completed in *The Conflict of the Faculties*.

Notes

1. See *Critique of Pure Reason*, B869; and *Doctrine of Right*, 6:218.

2. See also *Doctrine of Right*, 6:219 note. From the standpoint of the source of the obligation, moral lawgiving can be either juridical or ethical. The source of the obligation is external coercion in the former, and internal coercion in the latter. Hence, juridical lawgiving concerns merely the external use of choice, whereas ethical lawgiving applies both to the internal and the external use (internal and external actions) of choice. See *Doctrine of Right*, 6:218.

3. Acts of free choice can be regarded from a formal standpoint and from the standpoint of their goals. Accordingly, the metaphysics of morals is divided into a

Doctrine of Right and a doctrine of virtue or ethics. The former has to do merely with "the *formal condition* of choice that is to be limited in external relations in accordance with laws of freedom" (*Doctrine of Virtue*, 6:375). Ethics, on the other hand, "provides a matter (an object of free choice), an **end** of pure reason" (6:380).

4. In Kant's practical philosophy, the concept of an act of choice plays the same role as the concept of object in "ontology," or theoretical philosophy: just as in the latter, objects are sorted out as "something" or "nothing" (*Etwas und Nichts*), so too practical philosophy begins by distinguishing the acts of free choice that conform to the laws of freedom from those that do not (*Doctrine of Right*, 6:219 note).

5. According to the *Jäsche Logic*, in a judgment (*Urteil*) "the relation of various representations to the unity of consciousness is thought merely as problematic," whereas in a proposition (*Satz*) it is "assertoric" (§30, 9:109). In most contexts, however, Kant does not seem to stick to this distinction between judgments and propositions, but rather uses the two terms interchangeably. In this paper, I merely follow the established translations of the passages I am commenting, and employ either the term "judgment" or "proposition" accordingly.

6. In Kant's later practical philosophy (see *Perpetual Peace* and especially *Conflict*), that which is thought to secure perpetual peace is not nature or providence, as it had been in previous texts (see *Idea for a Universal History*), but rather the human race's acceptance of the moral-juridical duty of living in peace—an acceptance that is *sensitized* by the enthusiasm for the progress toward a republican constitution that was achieved during Kant's time.

7. All empirical judgments are by definition possible.

8. The term "reality" here means "content," so that the phrase "objective reality" is synonymous with "objective content," that is, sensible content. Objective reality can be theoretical (contents accessible in the realm of objects of possible experience) or practical (actions performable by a free human agent). Objective reality is not always actual, so we may distinguish between the objective reality and the actuality of a concept or judgment. Within proof contexts, this distinction plays an essential role.

9. For a concept or some other theoretical knowledge to be possible, logical consistency is not enough. It must also have objective reality, that is, "be related to an object, and . . . have significance and sense in that object." Thus, "the object must be able to be given in some way," that is, it must be givable (*dabile*) in the realm of possible experience (*Pure Reason*, B194).

10. On the synonymy of practical possibility, practical objective reality, and performability, see, for example, *Judgement* (5:457, 472, and 474), *Perpetual Peace* (8:356, 371, and 380), *Doctrine of Right* (6:246), and *Doctrine of Virtue* (6:405).

11. See Zeljko Loparic, "Sobre a interpretação de Rawls do fato da razão," in *Justiça como Equidade*, ed. Sónia Felipe (Florianópolis: Insular, 1998), 73–85; "O fato da razão: Uma interpretação semântica," *Analytica* 4 (1999): 13–55; "Acerca da sintaxe e da semântica dos juízos estéticos," *Studia Kantiana* 5 (2001): 49–90; and *A semântica transcendental de Kant*, 2nd ed. (Campinas: CLE, 2002).

12. In Kant, the solution to the problem of semantic possibility is a condition for the solution of the problem of decidability or demonstrability (see Loparic, *Semântica transcendental*, chapter 1).

13. These theses are presented and argued for in greater detail in Loparic, "O fato da razão" and *Semântica transcendental.*

14. Kant is here, in the context of the theory of right, returning to his doctrine of the natural antagonism between free human agents, which was worked out prior to the *Metaphysics of Morals*. See, for example, *Idea*, Proposition 4 (8:20–22).

15. The concept of a "rightful action," sought by Kant, is thus not a wholly abstract a priori concept, since it refers to actions as anthropological *facta* of the type mentioned above. But is it not merely a posteriori either, since it refers to *free* actions, and the concept of freedom is the one that is proved to be practically real by the moral law. It is a mixed concept, which has both a priori and a posteriori marks, much like some theoretical concepts, such as the concept of change (or movement). In the second edition of the first *Critique*, Kant writes: "Among *a priori* cognitions, however, those are called **pure** with which nothing empirical is intermixed. Thus, e.g., the proposition 'Every alteration has its cause' is an *a priori* proposition, only not pure, since alteration is a concept that can be drawn only from experience" (*Pure Reason*, B3).

16. A similar definition of right can be found in Kant's *Theory and Practice* (8:289–90). However, in this passage both the principle of universal reciprocal coercion and the postulate of right (see below) are yet to be stated.

17. For this reason, the universal principle of right is also called the "principle of all maxims" of law (*Doctrine of Right*, 6:231; see also *Doctrine of Virtue*, 6:283).

18. The "principle of all maxims" of right can also be formulated as a *command*: "so act externally that the free use of your choice can coexist with the freedom of everyone in accordance with a universal law" (*Doctrine of Right*, 6:231). This command, also called the "universal law of right" or "postulate of right," differs from the categorical imperative of ethics in at least two points. First, whereas the moral law asks me to act according to duty, the principle of all maxims of right does not demand that I *should* restrict my freedom by the maxims of right, but says merely that "freedom *is* limited to those conditions in conformity with the idea of it may also be actively limited by others" (*Doctrine of Right*, 6:231). Second, the maxims of rightful action do not have to be, as ethical maxims themselves do, principles of universal lawgiving, but merely compatible with a universal law of practical reason.

19. In the first edition of the *Critique of Pure Reason*, this principle is called the "principle of community" and formulated as follows: "All substances, insofar as they are **simultaneous**, stand in thoroughgoing community (i.e., interaction with one another)." This is also the Kantian version of Newton's third law, of action and reaction (cf. *Pure Reason*, B256–62).

20. In Kant's semantics of theoretical concepts, the model for schematizing is the construction of concepts in pure intuition, as practiced by mathematicians since antiquity (see *Pure Reason*, B299; *Doctrine of Right*, 6:208 note).

21. On this point, see, for example, *Judgment* (§59, 5:351–54).

22. Kant's theory of the systemic use of theoretical ideas is presented in Loparic, *Semântica transcendental*, chapters 8–9.

23. One could add, as Kant occasionally does in the *Doctrine of Right*, another way of sensitizing this same concept, which considers the fact that human beings cannot but "interact" with other human beings (see *Doctrine of Right*, 6:312).

24. It is interesting to note that, according to Kant, there are cases in which we assume a right without explicit coercion and coercion without a right, so that no judge can decide on them (see *Doctrine of Right*, 6:234).

25. See *Doctrine of Right*, 6:249 and 252. Hence, for Kant there are various definitions of the concept of freedom, and we have to determine clearly in each context which of them is being used.

26. According to Kant, it is not correct to say that I *possess* an innate right to freedom, since the fundamental right "is already an intellectual possession," and to speak of possessing a possession "would make no sense" (*Doctrine of Right*, 6:249).

27. Kant calls the object of a rightful possession a "*Sache an sich selbst*" and not a "*Ding an sich selbst*." The latter is more characteristic of his critique of theoretical reason.

28. This same difference between surface syntax and deep syntax can be seen in other cases as well, for example, in theoretical judgments (see Loparic, *Semântica transcendental*, chapter 6) and in judgments of taste (see Loparic, "Acerca da sintaxe").

29. Obviously, the same question needs to be raised and answered with regard to all other synthetic a priori propositions about right before they can be included in the *Doctrine of Right*.

30. Because we are dealing here with an a priori concept of *practical* reason, we must "apply mine and yours to objects not in accordance with sensible conditions but in abstraction from them" (*Doctrine of Right*, 6:253). Thus, in the realm of *theoretical* possible experience, the objective reality of the concept of merely intelligible or rightful possession cannot be proved, or even understood (*Doctrine of Right*, 6:252; see also 6:255).

31. The same distinction is made by Kant in an important note to *Toward Perpetual Peace* (1795, 8:348), in which he calls the attention of juridical scientists to the systematic significance of the concept of permissive law. Kant returns to this point in the Introduction to the *Doctrine of Right* (6:223).

32. If the external object possessed is a corporeal substance, the possession is called property (*Doctrine of Right*, 6:270). However, the possession of services of other people and the actual possession of other people are not property.

33. From this postulate it follows analytically that it is contrary to right any maxim "by which, if it were to become a law, an object of choice would *in itself* (objectively) have to *belong to no one* (*res nullius*)" (*Doctrine of Right*, 6:246).

34. For now I will leave open the question whether this rational will is the one each of us has, or is to be thought as a general will, or as a natural human disposition. These alternatives are laid out explicitly by Kant.

35. Here the question whether and how the postulate of right can be justified remains open, when it is understood in the sense of a synthetic a priori proposition.

36. "The explanation of the possibility of synthetic judgments" is "in a transcendental logic . . . the most important business of all," says Kant in the first *Critique* (B193).

37. The circumstance that the *facta* of theoretical reason are contingent (*Pure Reason* B795), or due to chance, leaves open the way for skeptical doubts about

them. These doubts are only raised by the critique of reason, that is, by the study of the bounds of our cognitive capacities as such (B789).

38. Recalling the thesis presented for the first time in the *Critique of Practical Reason*, Kant says: "that such beings (we human beings) are still free the categorical imperative proves for morally practical purposes, as through an authoritative decision of reason" (*Doctrine of Right*, 6:281 note).

39. Even after it has been demonstrated to be practicably possible, and even practically actual, the concept of freedom could not "realize this thought, that is, could not convert it into *cognition* of a being acting in this way" (*Practical Reason*, 5:49).

40. Kant's use of the term "postulate" is inspired in Greek geometry (Euclid), where it designates an order or imperative to execute an action thought to be easily performable by everyone (see, for example *Pure Reason*, B285–87; and *Practical Reason*, 5:31). During the development of his critical program, Kant extended the concept of postulate so as to encompass propositions that postulate the possibility of *objects* or their properties, such as God and the immortality of the soul (*Practical Reason*, 5:11 note).

41. Kant's distinction between problematic and categorical (apodictic) imperatives is related to his considerations about the modality of practical propositions, which, on its turn, refer to the table of categories of practical reason, that is, to the "categories of freedom" (*Practical Reason*, 5:66).

42. Likewise, the transcendental deduction of the (theoretical) categories establishes only *that* they contain the "grounds of the possibility of all experience," and not *how* they render experience possible (*Pure Reason*, B167).

43. This point is of crucial importance, since it marks the passage from the theory of individual free choice to the theory of the general will. For another formulation of the same thesis, see *Doctrine of Right* (6:263).

44. The "realistic" aspect of Kant's political thought has been appropriately highlighted by other authors, although not in the context of the problem of the sense and meaning of political judgments. See, for example, Lewis White Beck, "Introduction" to Immanuel Kant, *Perpetual Peace* (Indianapolis: Bobbs-Merrill, 1957); Wolfgang Kersting, *Wohlgeordnete Freiheit: Immanuel Kants Rechts- und Staatsphilosophie* (Frankfurt am Main: Suhrkamp, 1993); and José Heck, *Direito e moral: Duas lições sobre Kant* (Goiânia: Editora UFG, 2000).

45. The idea of a capacity or aptitude (*Tüchtigkeit*) of reason to influence human beings on the idea of the authority of the law, as if reason had a physically coercive power, which was made explicit in several other passages from *Toward Perpetual Peace* (see, for example, *Perpetual Peace*, 8:372 and 386), resumes, on the one hand, Kant's doctrine of the fact of reason presented in the *Critique of Practical Reason* and, on the other, paves the way for the *Metaphysical First Principles of the Doctrine of Virtue*, where virtue is defined as "the strength of a human being's maxims in fulfilling his duties" (*Doctrine of Virtue*, 6:394). I cannot therefore agree with Ricardo Terra when he says that in *Toward Perpetual Peace* Kant intends to assure peace from a reflecting-teleological perspective, or that "the admixture, in political judgments, of determining judgments with reflecting-teleological and aesthetic judgments marks that which is specific to the realm of politics" Ricardo Terra, "Juízo político e prudência em *À paz perpétua*," in *Kant e a Instituição da Paz*, ed. Valerio Rohden (Porto Alegre:

Goethe-Institut, 1997), 231. From the point of view of the theory of judgment, it is hard to understand what this type of "admixture" could mean.

46. In the light of this interpretation of Kant's practical philosophy, focused on its semantics of a priori practical judgments, Kant's political philosophy, as presented in *Toward Perpetual Peace*, acquires a consistency to which it had been denied by certain authors guided by different interpretative hypotheses. I have particularly in mind Hannah Arendt, *Das Urteilen: Texte zu Kants politischen Philosophie* (Munich: Piper, 1985), who underestimates the significance of Kant's philosophy of right for the understanding of political matters. She takes *Toward Perpetual Peace* to be a minor text, and refers to the aesthetic-teleological judgments of the third *Critique* for a reconstruction of Kant's political theory. On my interpretation, political life is conceived by Kant as "communitarian-juridical" or, alternatively, "juridically communitarian" (*gemeinschaftlich-gesetzlich*), in the sense that civil society ought to be grounded on maxims dictated by the collective rational will, which become *sensitized* as the human race constantly advances toward the better, as defined by the *Doctrine of Right*. On Arendt's interpretation, the communitarian nature of a politics such as Kant's would be based on a communitarian sense analogous to the aesthetic communitarian sense. My results are akin, however, to some more recent readings of Kant, such as Volker Gerhardt, *Immanuel Kants Entwurf "Zum ewigen Frieden": Eine Theorie der Politik* (Darmstadt: Wissenschaftliche Buchgesellschaft, 1995).

47. This remark suggests the need for a history of Kant's pragmatic anthropology, which would take into account the advances of his remarks about the fundamental concepts of the metaphysics of morals and their applicability to human nature.

48. According to the *Doctrine of Virtue*, the affective participation in the promotion of good is an individual virtue that stems from practical reason (see *Doctrine of Virtue*, §34, 6:456). The "passionate participation on the good" that Kant speaks of in *The Conflict of the Faculties* (7:86) can only be considered to be a collective virtue, and attributed to a collective subject—this is a point that would therefore demand an extension of the metaphysics of morals of 1797.

49. The consequences of this shift in the domain of interpretation of judgments about history have escaped various commentators. Weil, for example, failed to retrace Kant's step that acknowledges humanity as a moral-juridical subject, and for that reason reserves the condition of a "moral subject" to individuals only. Eric Weil, *Problèmes kantiens* (Paris: Vrin, 1982), 140. Philonenko—to mention another well-known commentator—objects that Kant remains in the field of historical utopias, alleging that even in Kant's later writings practical reason remained the *ratio cognoscendi* of divine Providence. A. Philonenko, *Études kantiennes* (Paris: Vrin, 1982), 72. Besides the incompatibility with the analyses presented here, Philonenko's thesis is irreconcilable with paragraph 4 of *The Conflict of the Faculties* and with everything else Kant said about the unavoidable failure of any philosophical attempts at producing a theodicy (see *Theodicy*).

50. The present reconstruction, which is merely programmatic, of the path Kant took in the elaboration of his practical philosophy uses essentially the same material analyzed by Ricardo Terra in *A política tensa: Idéia e realidade na filosofia da história da Kant* (São Paulo: Iluminuras, 1995). The latter is a work that offers a more doxographic approach, and contains a vast array of recent discussions on the topic. The

reader should note that certain divergencies both in the presuppositions—one of them pertaining to the nature of Kant's program for a critical philosophy—and in the results—one of them being the relevance of the problem of a priori synthetic-practical *judgments* for the development of Kant's practical philosophy and in particular of his theory of politics and history.

51. Here would be the place for asking also what Kant has to say about the possibility of an a priori pedagogy.

12

Right, History, and Practical Schematism

Daniel Tourinho Peres

Few philosophers reproduce so faithfully, in the degree of their thinking, the tensions inherent in the object under consideration. Such is certainly the case of Immanuel Kant, for whom this reproduction has a very specific sense, to the extent that the object, through its universal and necessary properties, responds to the determinations of thought. Kant, however, did not consider only the tensions; he also considered equally, as Ricardo Terra has demonstrated,[1] the way of resolving them. It is known that for Kant, history is the history of right, or rather of juridical institutions that place themselves in the path of the realization of the rights of man. On the other hand, we know that politics, as Kant states in *Perpetual Peace*, is the doctrine for implementation of right, or rather it is the ever precarious realization of the idea of law, which must be reviewed or reformed as soon as the necessity for reform becomes clear to the faculty of judgment and conditions are favorable to change. Since "in the carrying out of that idea (in practice) the only beginning of the rightful condition to be counted upon is that by *power* . . . it can be anticipated that in actual experience there will be great deviations from that idea (of theory)" (*Perpetual Peace*, 8:371).

Thus the history of freedom, which is the work of the human being, begins with evil (*Conjectural*, 8:115). The paradox appears to be that freedom, having its origin in reason, places itself on the correct path only with the development of reason itself: "Through progress in enlightenment, a beginning is made toward the foundation of a mode of thought that can with time transform the rude natural predisposition to make moral distinctions into determinate practical principles and hence transform a *pathologically* compelled agreement to form a society finally into a *moral* whole" (*Idea*, 8:21). Enlightenment and politics go hand in hand in delineating the public sphere, where the determinations—and destinies—of life in society are decided upon.

This article was originally published as "Direito, história, e esquematismo prático," in *Discurso* 34 (2004): 109–24. Translated by the author and Simon George Johnson.

Politics presents itself in the public sphere and has in its "foundation" the public use of reason. When approached by means of transcendental reflection and from the perspective instituted by the philosophy of history, it comes to be seen as the gradual institutionalization of the determining activity of judgment and its principles, through which juridical pretensions find their means of legitimization and correction with regard to the agreements that are being empirically woven and at the level of opinion. What is intended here is a brief analysis of the sense of such precarious, historically conditioned agreements as schemata of a basic agreement that is made at the level of judgment and its principles—a basic agreement, the foundation of which is found in *common sense* as a transcendental and regulative principle of human action. If politics is then the "realization" of the idea of a perfect republic, which in truth, being the thing in itself, is never represented as a phenomenon (*Doctrine of Right*, 8:371), it cannot renounce the philosophy of history as a discursive form capable of serving as schema, as a rendering at the level of understanding of that which may only be represented by pure reason. To borrow the words of Gerhard Lehmann, Kant "only excludes the possibility of an intuitive realization (*intuitive*) of intellectual intuition (*Anschaung*); we may 'realize it' discursively."[2]

When analyzed beginning with the elements that are organized by the syntheses of the faculty of judgment in practice, the philosophy of history, as Georg Cavallar states, constitutes the empirical part of Kant's practical philosophy,[3] which has in right its normative instance and in politics its mode of execution. But the philosophy of history is not *only* the empirical, material part of Kant's practical philosophy, since in mediating the tension between the ideal and the real[4] it also serves as guarantee, at the level of judgment, against any possible skepticism or abandonment of all practical perspective linked to freedom. Thus it is necessary to read with a certain reserve Kant's often repeated statement that pure practical concepts, with regard to their objectivity, may dispense with any positivity linked to them. Thus, if it is certain that the idea of a perfect civil constitution, for example, does not cease to be a norm for all juridical ordinance, even if there has never been a constitution close to it, it is also certain that *subjectively* it is necessary to be convinced of the possibility of—and moreover the sense of—realizing such an ideal in the world. Therefore, this second moment of practical judgment is, in its widest sense, the action itself of schematizing, that is, to render a concept comprehensible through analogy with something sensible (*Religion*, 6:65 note). However, in the case of a practical concept, of an idea of reason, time, as a form of intuition, does not serve as an adequate direct schema, so the activity of symbolizing then operates as an analogy of schematism. But schematism or symbolism is not the point of interest, what is of interest is that a pure practical concept, in this case the concept of a perfect civil constitution, is made "comprehensible" when history, in the totality of its course, is considered as "schema," in other words, when the concept is *considered at the time of its realization*—progressive and constant—in sensibility, that is, empirically. "Considered" because such a schema of an idea of reason only supplies the "rule or principle of the systematic unity of all use of the understanding" (*Pure Reason*, A665/B693), here in the case of all use of practical reason.

The philosophy of history contains certain elements as guarantees against possible practical skepticism. As early as 1784 Kant states that all human talents and capabilities can only be fully developed in the species (*Idea*, 8:23). Of course, the individual may have, on the premises of practical reason, as presented in the second *Critique*, grounds on which to base one's hope of seeing the realization of the highest good, a union of virtue and happiness, in which the former is a condition of the latter. With the philosophy of history, with the construction of history from pure principles, it is, in its turn, the species that "in reflecting upon its material and natural conditions becomes conscious of itself as infinite"[5] and sees one—subjective—condition satisfied for the realization of the highest political good.

But the perspective of the species, and that is what is important to my argument, responds to the adoption of a point of view, the cosmopolitan point of view, which in the end determines the capacity to judge [*Vermögen zu Urteilen*], or put better, the understanding and its object. The guiding thread of construction—perhaps it would be better to say (philosophical) reconstruction—of a systematic history of human actions, according to Reflection 1420 and beyond the purposiveness of nature in its legislation upon contingency, which remains nature, is the idea of right (*R*1420, 15:618; and *Idea*, 8:17). It follows that formal elements are present in history, since in it are presented the ways in which free wills, in their external relations, should relate to each other. As Reflection 1404 further states, "In history there is nothing permanent that could readily provide an idea of the changeable except the idea of the development of humanity, and indeed in accord with that which constitutes the greatest unity of its powers, namely civil and national unity" (*R*1404, 15:612).

This philosophical and systematic history, as it is put in Reflection 1471a, is also a task in four moments, each of which corresponds to one of the moments present in the table of categories. Thus, when it is a question of judging history as to its progress toward a greater good and of tracing for it an a priori plan, the human species as a whole (quantity) is taken; the greater good, to which it directs itself, is found in what there is of morality (quality); the internal improvement of each human being is not sought, what is sought are his external relations in society (relation); to connect a priori progress toward the greater good with the causes currently acting in society, in such a way as to consider the necessity of existing progress toward the greater good (modality) (*R*1471a, 15:650). Therefore, it is this table of categories applied to the course of history that presides over the discursive "construction" presented in *Idea for a Universal History*.

The facts that compose history are then objects of reflection; they are not, however, raw facts, but rather works of the imagination. In *Anthropology*, the imagination is presented (§34 A) as the faculty of making the past present (memory) (*Anthropology*, 7:182), of making the future present (the faculty of foresight and divination, §35 and 36) (7:18–90), and of linking both, past and future, to the present (the faculty of using signs, §38) (7:191). It is the faculty of making the future present that, without doubt, is most associated with a philosophy of history, since "recalling the past (remembering) occurs only with the intention of making foresight of the future possible by means of it" (7:186). It is, then, this perspective that Kant assumes in turning, in 1786, toward a possible beginning of human history. Such an account, we well know, is merely conjectural, a simple exercise of the imagination accompanied by reason (*Conjectural*, 8:109); but it is an account, the central point of which is constructed from the juridical categories, or rather from the association between forms of life and ways determining property. The conflict between land owners, a form of life linked to agriculture, and nomadism, linked to hunting and pasturing, will be resolved by the institution of a civil constitution that, if perfect, is the highest purpose of civilization (*Conjectural*, 8:117). But what is important to see is that such a conflict reproduces, at the level of image, a conflict that the *Doctrine of Right* presents in a more abstract way: the conflict between the limitation of possession to purely physical possession and a concept of property that goes beyond physical possession confirm the necessity of considering possession to be intelligible. Thus, in the *Doctrine of Right*, such a conflict generates antinomy, the result of which consists in affirming that only the second conception shows itself to be compatible with the idea of right itself (*Doctrine of Right*, 6:255). At the level of theory, criticism, which for that matter occupies the position of the court, may well resolve these questions. At the level of history, that is, in practice, the solution is political and requires the authority of what is sovereign, through the power capable of administering the law, in other words, of instituting distributive justice, a task that in 1784, in *Idea for a Universal History*, Kant stated to be the most difficult (*Idea*, 8:15). One passage of the *Doctrine of Right* demonstrates the real dimension of the problem, adding new elements:

> The indeterminacy, with respect to quantity as well as quality, of the external object that can be acquired makes this problem (of the sole, original external acquisition) the hardest of all to solve. Still, there must be some original acquisition or other of what is external, since not all acquisition can be derived. So this problem cannot be abandoned as insoluble and intrinsically

> impossible. But even if it is solved through the original contract, such acquisition will always remain only provisional unless this contract extends to the entire human race. (*Doctrine of Right*, 6:266)

The end of this long passage takes us back to the perspective of the 1784 text and its cosmopolitan intent. We are as far from the beginning, when original acquisition of the land by means of first occupation was affirmed as we are from the moment at which the original contract will find itself extended to all of mankind. Clearly, past and future are linked on a plane that, "in a certain way has a guiding thread *a priori*" (*Idea*, 8:30). Thus, empirical elements are linked in a determined form and are constituted, precisely, as cases that *present* this form. It is certain that reflective judgments formulated from the perspective of the philosophy of history, even without producing certainty, may subjectively claim for themselves a sufficient degree of assent to guide determining judgment, and this guidance not only refers to the past or the future but also principally to the present. But in affirming the necessity for the original contract to extend to the whole human species, Kant widens, to the global scale, another point of the *Doctrine of Right*, at once within the ambit of private right and of permissive law: "the way to have something external as one's own *in a state of nature* is physical possession which as in its favor the rightful *presumption* that it will be made into rightful possession through being united with the will of all in a public lawgiving, and *in anticipation of this* holds *comparatively* as rightful possession" (*Doctrine of Right*, 6:257; my emphasis).

Thus, he who first appropriates an external object, he who first states that "this is mine," affirms, at the same time, the institution of legislation, the validity of which is universal and imposes an obligation on everyone (*Doctrine of Right*, 6:253). Conflicts are no longer resolved by private free wills, each judging his right with nothing in common to unify them. Once the right is instituted, it is public judgment that resolves conflicts. But, let us not forget, that since right has its beginning in force, which is authorized by permissive law, it can easily be foreseen how many mistakes will be made before the idea of the original contract extends itself to all mankind. The provisional nature of possession and judicial precariousness appear to imply the necessity for correction, without threatening juridical certainty.

At least three other passages in Kant's texts point in the same direction: one is also found in *Perpetual Peace*, where Kant, discussing permissive law and the right of possession by means of conquest states the following: "The prohibition here concerns only the *way of acquiring, which from now on shall not hold*, but not the *status of possession*, which, though it does not have what is required in order to be called a right, was nevertheless *in its time* (that of putative acquisition) taken to be legitimate according to the public opinion of every state at the time" (*Perpetual Peace*, 8:347; my emphasis). Another passage is found in the *Doctrine of Right*: whomsoever is touched, in his property, by reform enforced by political power, can complain of nothing, since "the reason for their possession *hitherto* lay only in the *people's opinion* and also had to hold *as long as that lasted*" (*Doctrine of Right*, 6:325; my emphasis). But it is in *Perpetual Peace* that we find the formulation that puts the question most eloquently: "political wisdom, *in the condition in which things are at present, will make reforms* in keeping with the ideal of public right its duty" (*Perpetual Peace*, 8:373; my emphasis). That passage can only be disconcerting, for what is the sense of conversion into duty that, from the point of view of reason, always was a duty? Is pure practical reason, which is what would be stated here, in its prescriptions empirically measurable? Does pure practical reason recognize any type of temporal—or even spatial—determination that would limit the validity of its principles? In other words, does the determination of the norm depend, in its own determination, on the circumstances and context of application? On this point history is, then, the result of the imagination as the faculty of using signs (or "designation"): "the faculty of cognizing the present as the means for connecting the representation of the foreseen with that of the past" (*Anthropology*, 7:191)—the faculty of designation, of finding the *signs* that link the past and the future.

Things, however, are not at all simple, and an exhaustive analysis of the question is beyond these notes. An approximation, however, may shed some light on them: in the same way that the categories of understanding are acquired derivatively, that is, a priori, yet are also acquired from reflection and analysis of the syntheses that understanding works on a multiplicity given in intuition so that the sensible synthesis, itself a result of the action of understanding according to its own legislation, operates as an occasional cause for the acquisition of the category,[6] something *analogous* may be said of practical concepts, that is, juridical pure concepts in their link with history. The only difference is that reason is no longer simply a legislative faculty, as is the case of understanding and pure will, which both have their tables of categories, but is also a faculty that, by its nature, determines ends and, beyond that, judges the course of the world according to them: in the case that occupies us here, highest political good, perpetual peace by means of the unification of the freewill of all people, that is, a cosmopolitan society.

It is not, thus, a question of giving primacy to the historical to the detriment of the rational, reducing the latter to the former. Kant warns on more than one occasion of the illegitimacy of such a procedure (*Orient*, 8:140–41; *Doctrine of Right*, 6:229). Far less is it intended to state that practical reason is measured by history, or that time limits pure practical reason. Of course it is a question of affirming history as a condition for the recognition of practical concepts, but in the following sense: practical concepts do not have their genesis in history and continue to be considered as originally acquired a priori concepts; but only in history, by means of history, do such concepts gain clarity and distinctness, because they are recognized in the context of their application. In other words, history provides material for reflection, which will then seek the form that organizes it, a form that has its origin in the superior faculties of the mind, that is, in pure reason. In other words: history—coherent, systematic discourse regarding human actions, which allow themselves to be subsumed under universal practical principles, principles that are merely regulatory and not determining—posits itself as *the fact*, the possible conditions of which are then investigated, *fact* that is demanded by reason itself. This avoids attributing to Kant a historicism that is not his. It merely affirms the necessity, for that matter subjective, for a determined state of things—in which a juridical conflict is present—as an opportunity to achieve clarity as to the pure principles that preside over juridical syntheses and the direction of reform, whenever it is the case. And it is always the case, as soon as the discrepancy between the ideal and its realization is seen and it is possible to discern the possibility of overcoming it.

Kant thinks of political action, in its conformity to the principles of right, as an action of reform of existing institutions and positive legislation. Political action therefore has the task of realizing the republican constitution, the only one fully in conformity with the principles of right in submitting itself to such a principle; it finds its means of expression in republicanism, in the spirit of the idea of the original (rational) contract (*Doctrine of Right*, 6:340). One more important dimension of political action is its solidarity with its discourse, since the latter, to the extent that it mediates between the normative instance and historical effectiveness, positions itself as a condition of possibility of politics. It is a condition of possibility because it is the discourse, which as collectively formed judgment, informed by conjuncture but determined by the form of pure practical reason in its juridical use, in practice, places the moment of recognition of a duty that until then was imposed in theory. It realizes, thus, the function of a schema.

The above passages to which we have referred and that share a temporal determination, not only indicate that the faculty of judgment mediates between pure principles and empirical reality, but they also indicate that at another point in his work Kant reveals his preoccupation with his own time, in which history fulfills its role as guarantee in the most complete way. It is the famous passage from the *Conflict of the Faculties* where Kant makes reference to the French Revolution, which was the historical-political act *par excellence* that marked not only the end of the eighteenth century but also the whole of the subsequent politico-philosophical imagination. In fact, that passage from *Perpetual Peace* in which Kant stated a propitious moment, capable of "generating" a duty, already referred to the revolution:

> Thus political wisdom, in the condition in which things are at present, will make reforms in keeping with the ideal of public right its duty; but it will use revolutions, where nature of itself has brought them about, not to gloss over an even greater oppression, but as a call of nature to bring about by fundamental reforms a lawful constitution based on principles of freedom, the only kind that endures. (*Perpetual Peace*, 8:373)

Without wishing to add anything new here to the many interpretations of these passages from the work of Kant, it is hoped only to emphasize certain points, and as such Renaut's interpretation will be taken as a paradigm. To him, the advent of the French Revolution must be taken as one of those cases in which "nature and freedom are joined in the subjective experience of a philosopher reflecting his feeling of pleasure in the face of the historical progress of right."[7] Thus, it would not be at all unjust to state that such a reading rests on an aesthetic and not a political solution for right. Two questions, however, must be retained: the judgment of aesthetic reflection, with its problematic universality, presents important elements, without doubt, for the analysis by analogy of political judgment in Kant. But it is the second point that is more important here. For what sense—if indeed there is—can an aesthetic solution have for the right? The sense is that by means of the French Revolution, the idea of a republican constitution became clearer, to the extent that, once it had become an object of reflection for the faculty of judgment, it produced an effect on our sense of justice (*Judgment*, 5:293). By going beyond the established legal limits, revolutionary action reveals the limits of *sensus communis*, of the faculty of judgment and shows just how far such limits are from one another. The feeling of pleasure then flows from the recognition of a social order that is more just, because it is closer to the ideal of reason. The French Revolution—and the effect that it provokes in the spectators, the enthusiasm for the affirmation of the rights of humanity—is then a *sign* of the realization of the ideal of right, since it allows one to see more clearly that "the idea of a constitution in harmony with the natural right of human beings . . . lies at the basis of all political forms . . . [and is] the eternal norm for all civil organization in general" (*Conflict*, 7:90).

To make a concept conceivable by means of its presentation is, as has already been seen, the act of schematizing. The shared, communicated sense of approval, serves then as an element for "construction" of the schema of right, the focus of which is the idea of a republican constitution as the only one that fully conforms to reason, the only one that is permanent. In the first *Critique*, it was the imagination that, urged on by understanding, produced the schemata for the concepts. In the *Critique of Practical Reason* it is not the imagination, but rather understanding itself that schematizes a law the origin of which is found in pure reason. Now, it is the *sensus communis* that schematizes, that finds sensible translation that may be located in experience, for the pure concepts. It is this, as the faculty of designation (*facultas signatrix*), that serves as imagination and marks the French Revolution as a sign of progress, linking then, just as a schema, the ideal of reason and the reality of the course of the world. And because it is a product of *sensus communis*, of this sense of community, the schema must be produced publicly, that is, discursively and by means of the public use of reason. But in truth the *sensus communis* is first an idea that possesses transcendental status, to the extent that it, as an operation of reflection, places itself as a condition of the possibility of searching for a judgment that has universal validity (*Judgment*, 5:293–94).

Also in the *Conflict of the Faculties*, Kant states that the enlightenment of the people is public instruction regarding the duties and rights in relation to the state. Furthermore, that it is a question of natural rights, which are derived from the *common human understanding* (*Conflict*, 7:89), from the *sensus communis* in operation, the maxims of which are exposed by Kant in the third *Critique*: (1) think for yourself, (2) think in the place of all others, and (3) think always in agreement with yourself (*Judgment*, 5:294). It is at this moment that critical philosophy shows itself to be supportive of politics and to complement it. Certainly not when imbued with scholastic discourse, but rather when it presents itself as public discourse; in other words, a discourse something like opinion, it is taken to its conclusion by reason in its public use and according to its own method, namely, the public method, the bearer of a universal and cosmopolitan pretension (*R*1439, 15:629), and that operates precisely with the maxims of common human understanding. With these elements it is held that the first task of philosophy, stripped of any scholastic prerogative, consists precisely in affirming as possible a form of politics that does not lose sight of the limits of simple reason, a possibility that is assured, at least subjectively by the critical philosophy of history.

In this task, the philosopher, as with any citizen who makes use of his understanding, starting from a context of pluralism, should take precise care, comparing his judgment with the judgment of others, to construct publicly and discursively the "schemata" that mediate between the normative (theory of political law) and reality (historic-positive law); schemata that, like opinion and collectively formed common will, which bring together the ideal state of practical principles and socially shared expectations regarding the realization of ends (*Perpetual Peace*, 8:386), contribute, at least subjectively, to a certain assent relative to the concept—or rather, to judgment—which they transmit if they are not integrated, thanks to their degree of certainty, to a *Wissenschaft*. In the end, they barely go beyond the registration of an opinion, albeit a well founded one; not for this are they outside the system of reason, since they move precisely in the direction of its unification.[8]

By way of conclusion to these brief notes, it is fitting to state that it is Kant, and not Hegel, who places the bases for the consideration of a reconstructive analysis of history in the history of philosophy, in such a way as to find in it the forms that, even without containing its origin, being rational find their moment of realization there. Once again it is Kant, and not Hegel, who sees in such a reconstruction the way of making our representations, that is, our concepts clearer. The often maligned Kantian apriorism, ready to adhere to any determination, is an image that began to crystallize precisely starting with Hegel. If the philosophy of history, in Kant, takes care to trace an a priori plan for humanity, it is also true that in its course, humanity has known reverses even if they have not shaken its belief in progress. History shows us the right moment; the discourse about history, as a schema of pure concepts, may really favor such a moment. It does not impose itself, however, like something inexorable; and its discourse, closer to opinion than it is usual to accept, offers no certainty at all.

Thus, the political idealism of Kant is far from being an ultrarationalism. The philosopher who imposes limits on his theoretical use of reason is that philosopher who recognizes the fallibility of reason, of the use of reason, it is better to say. In the constellation of practical philosophy perhaps politics is the area that is most subject to error, where the certainties are the slimmest. To recognize such questions is really the first step toward the institutionalization of politics within the limits of simple reason, a politics that does not relinquish a theoretical dimension but that, it can never be sufficiently stated, is far from the dominion of *Wissenschaft*.

Notes

1. Ricardo Terra, *Passagens: Estudos sobre a filosofia de Kant* (Rio de Janeiro: Editoria UFRJ, 2003); and *A política tensa—Idéia e realidade na filosofia da história de Kant* (São Paulo: Iluminuras, 1995).

2. Gerhard Lehmann, *Beiträge zur Geschichte und Interpretation der Philosohie Kants* (Berlin: Walter de Gruyter, 1969), 166.

3. Georg Cavallar, *Pax Kantiana—Systematisch-historische Untersuchung des Entwurfs 'Zum ewigen Frieden von Immanuel Kant* (Vienna: Böhlau, 1992), 292.

4. See Terra, *Passagens*.

5. Hans-Georg Deggau, *Die Aporien der Rechstlehre Kants* (Stuttgart: Frommann-Holzboog, 1983), 306.

6. Michael Oberhausen, *Das neue Apriori—Kants Lehre von einer "ursprünglichen Erwerbung" apriorischer Vorstellungen* (Stuttgart: Frommann-Holzboog, 1997).

7. Alain Renaut, *Kant aujourd'hui* (Paris: Flammarion, 1997), 411.

8. Marco Zingano, *Razão e história em Kant* (São Paulo: Brasiliense, 1989).

13

Cosmopolitanism

Kant and Kantian Themes in International Relations

Soraya Nour

Introduction

On April 5, 1795, Prussia celebrated the *Peace of Basel* with France, abandoning the coalition with Austria and England against France, to whom it yielded its territories on the left bank of the Rhine. In August, Kant finished his work *Toward Perpetual Peace: A Philosophical Sketch*, in which he ironically imitates the form of the peace treaties of his time. Two hundred years later, commemorations for the bicentennial of Kant's *Perpetual Peace* in Germany and elsewhere[1] were not content with the usual philological work: they evaluated the relation of the work to the present, comparing the contemporary world with Kant's rational criteria.[2]

The first part of this work analyzes the conception of peace presented by Kant in his work, addressing the following subjects: political right, international right, and cosmopolitan right. The second part analyzes Kant's reception in the philosophy of international law and international relations, focusing on specific discussions around the so-called Kantian themes. This will allow the evaluation of its positive aspects as well as its limitations.

Kant

For Kant, war and peace have a *structural* character and are bound to the institutional rightful structure. The concept of *structural violence*[3] means that in a *state of lawlessness*, individuals and peoples are not safe either against the violence of another or to do "*what seems right and good*" to them (*Doctrine of*

This text was published as "Os cosmopolitas: Kant e os temas kantianos em relações internacionais," in *Contexto Internacional* 25 (2003): 7–46. Translated by the author.

Right, 6:312). The state of nature (*status naturalis*—a hypothesis, not a historical fact) between human beings is not of peace, but rather of war (due to the permanent threat of hostilities even when there is no effective war). The mere abstention from hostilities does not represent any security for peace, as it does not hinder individuals or peoples from treating one another as enemies. Security is only possible in a rightful state, where I can only treat as an enemy whoever has injured me in fact, whereas in the state of nature, the other "injures me" because I am threatened by the lawlessness of his state (even without injuring me in fact) (*Perpetual Peace*, 8:348–49). The state of nature, therefore, is the state of the absence of right (*status justitia vacuus*). When there is a dispute (*jus controversum*), no competent judge can pronounce a rightfully valid decision that impels others to enter a state of right. Any acquisition is provisory "as long as it does not yet have the sanction of public law, since it is not determined by public (distributive) justice and secured by an authority putting this right into effect" (*Doctrine of Right*, 6:312). If the rules on what belongs to each one prescribe the same in the state as in society, it is only in a state that these rules can be carried through.

Peace must therefore be assured by *institutional rightful structures*: the state of peace must be *instituted* through public right (*Perpetual Peace*, 8:349), that is, we have to leave the state of nature and enter the civil state (*bürgerlichen Zustand*), in which what belongs to each one is defined *by right* (*Doctrine of Right*, 6:312). Public right is defined in *Doctrine of Right* as "the sum of the laws which need to be promulgated generally in order to bring about a rightful condition" (6:311), such as a system of laws for a people or an aggregate of peoples in reciprocal influence, which need a *constitution* (*constitutio*) to enjoin their rights. In the *civil state* (*status civilis*), individuals of a people are in reciprocal relationship; the *state* (*civitas*) is the whole of these individuals and is called *commonwealth* (*res publica latius sic dicta*—republic in the broad sense) because of the "common interest in being in a rightful condition" (6:311); in relation to other peoples, it is called *power* (*potentia*) and because of its supposedly hereditary union, it is called a *nation* (*gens*) (6:311).

The state of nature must be overcome at all levels, not only between individuals, but also between states, as well as between states and individuals. Public right therefore encompasses not only political right, but also international right and cosmopolitan right. Each level depends on the other: "So if the principle of outer freedom limited by law is lacking in any one of these three possible forms of rightful condition, the framework of all the others is unavoidably undermined and must finally collapse" (*Doctrine of Right*, 6:311). This means first that one form of state does not have to overcome the others, but that the three are necessary and must coexist; and second, that no form of state is merely an addition to the previous one: "any form of rightful-political organization below the global level is provisory."[4] Kant radically rationalizes the contractualistic argument, leading to what Kersting calls the "dilemma of the plurality of contractualism." Up until then, contractualism did not give account of the factual plurality of states. This is a basic difference between Kant and his predecessors, for whom the contractual theory refers only to the state and not to relationships between states: "there is only one philosopher who extends the egalitarianism of the social contract and the form of political organization founded on it from a republic of universal law to the cosmopolitan dimension."[5]

The postulate that founds the definitive articles thus has a rightful-constitutional character: "all men who can mutually affect one another must belong to some civil constitution." Therefore, all legal constitution must conform: (1) to *civil right* between persons in a people (*ius civitatis*); (2) to *international right* between states (*ius gentium*); and (3) to *cosmopolitan right* between persons and states considered as world citizens (*jus cosmopoliticum*) (*Perpetual Peace*, 8:349).

Political Right

The first definitive article of *Perpetual Peace* considers republicanism as the first condition for establishing peace: "The Civil Constitution in Every State Shall be Republican" (*Perpetual Peace*, 8:349). If rightful freedom, in the sense of autonomy, is my prerogative to obey only an external law to which I can give my assent, then the only constitution originated from this idea is the republican one, according to which the state is administrated by the laws that a people would give itself (*Conflict*, 7:88). Autonomy is the basis: "To test whether any particular measure can be agreed upon as a law for a people, we need only ask whether a people could well impose such a law upon itself" (*Enlightenment*, 8:39). Therefore, the will of the people has the legislative power. Since right depends on laws, and public law is an act of public will from which all right proceeds, and which cannot be unjust to anybody, only the will of the entire people is possible (*Theory and Practice*, 8:294). In fact, Kant says, it is possible that I am unjust when I decide for another person, but not for myself (*Doctrine of Right*, 6:313). In the political right, the *moral personality* thus becomes *civil personality*. In this way, Kant opposes the notion of *citizen* to that of subject, an essential change in the relation between governors and governed in the theory of the traditional state. The capacity of giving oneself one's own law becomes the capacity to *vote* (*Doctrine of Right*, 6:314).

Kant therefore develops a contractualist theory, distinguished from those of his predecessors in that it does not presuppose that freedom should merely be limited in the state of nature, but left completely in order to achieve freedom as autonomy: individuals in a state abandon "wild, lawless freedom in order to find his freedom as such undiminished, in a dependence upon laws, that is, in a rightful condition" (*Doctrine of Right*, 6:316). Thus, the *original contract* (*contractus originarius, pactum sociale*) is defined as the idea of the act (and not a fact) by which a people constitutes a state, a union of all particular wills forming a common and public will (*Theory and Practice*, 8:297). It is in such a contractualist theory that the idea of a republican constitution is conceived as "the sole constitution that issues from the idea of the original contract, on which all rightful legislation of a people must be based" (*Perpetual Peace*, 8:350).[6]

However, the requirement of a republican constitution may seem to concern only the internal order of a state and not the international order. In tradition, the right of a state seems not to have any role to fulfill in a theory of international peace; and a theory of peace, in turn, seems not to have to address political right. Kant, however, establishes an intrinsic relation between a state's rightful-political structure and its behavior in relation to other states, showing that this requirement of internal order has consequences in foreign matters. Constitutions can be peaceful or not. The republican constitution is presented as functionally peaceful, as it is the only one that expresses the will of those who assume the incumbencies of war and who, therefore, probably will not be in favor of it. Therefore, besides being the only constitution in agreement with freedom, it is the only one that favors an international peaceful order.[7] Peace depends on the will of the people.[8] Kant's argument in this case does not define itself by the criteria of justice, morality, or pacifism, but rather by self-interest:[9]

> When the consent of the citizens of a state is required in order to decide whether there shall be war or not (and it cannot be otherwise in this constitution), nothing is more natural than that they will be very hesitant to begin such a bad game, since they would have to decide to take upon themselves all the hardships of war (such as themselves doing the fighting and paying the costs of the war from their own belongings, painfully making good the devastation it leaves behind, and finally—to make the cup of troubles overflow—a burden of debt that embitters peace itself, and that can never be paid off because of new wars always impending); on the other hand, under a constitution in which subjects are not citizens of the state, which is therefore not republican, [deciding upon war] is the easiest thing in the world; because the head of state is not a member of the state but its proprietor and gives up nothing at all of his feasts, hunts, pleasure palaces, court festivals, and so forth, he can decide upon war, as upon a kind of pleasure party, for insignificant cause, and can with indifference leave the justification of the war, for the sake of propriety, to the diplomatic corps, which is always ready to provide it. (*Perpetual Peace*, 8:351)

This is the basis for Kant's criticism of the British government: although the British people intend for their constitution to limit the will of the monarch through the two houses of parliament that represent the people, Kant observes that these houses decide only what the monarch proposes through his minister. Moreover, the latter also recommends decisions that he expects to be contradicted in order to prove the parliamentary freedom. For Kant, this is a "false publicity" that passes off an *absolute monarchy* for a *limited one* (*Conflict*, 7:90). In an *absolute* monarchy, when the monarch says that there shall be war, there is war immediately; in a *limited* monarchy, people must be asked beforehand if there is to be war, and if the people say no, there is no war. In fact, Kant observes, "the monarch of Great Britain has waged numerous wars without asking the people's consent" (7:90).

Kant thus presents a constitutional theory[10] that distinguishes form of sovereignty (*forma imperii*) from form of government (*forma regiminis*). The form of sovereignty refers to *who* has the power; the form of government refers to *how* power is exercised. The form of sovereignty therefore has as criterion "the different persons who have supreme authority" (*Perpetual Peace*, 8:352) and can be autocratic, aristocratic, or democratic according to the power to be exercised respectively by one, some, or everyone. The form of government, in turn, has as its criterion the fulfillment, or lack thereof, of the rightful principles and can be republican or despotic. At first, the form of sovereignty is indifferent to the rightful quality of the exercise of power, defined only by the two forms of government. The legitimate form of government—republicanism—is based on the principle that legislation belongs to the will of the people. This principle implies three criteria: participation in legislation, power divisions, and representation (8:352–53).

The term "republic" is different from republicanism.[11] This means that the constitution is republican in spirit, but not in letter. States appear in history through violence, which is the opposite of the idea of social contract. However, Kant denies not only the traditional forms of power legitimation, but also the contradiction between rational republic and historical power. Republic is the norm by which to judge any civil constitution, any state that appeared through violence. However, only the historical republic is the adequate form for the idea of republic, in which the accomplishment of right is complete. Republicanism has a provisory character. Only when the constitution becomes a republic "literally" is an "absolutely rightful condition of civil society" constituted (*Doctrine of Right*, 6:340–41). Traditional forms of state must therefore be surpassed, giving place to the republic, in which "the *law* itself rules and depends on no particular person" (6:341).

International Right

Kant's international right addresses the relationship of one state with another state, as well as the relationship between individuals from one state and those from another. However, the right "of peoples" or "of nations"—later termed "international"—since the fifteenth and sixteenth centuries has ruled over relationships between collectives that are no longer termed "peoples" or "nations." Since then, international right is interstate right. Peoples or nations are citizens of international right only when they constitute states. Kant thus affirms in *Doctrine of Right* that what in German is called "right of nations" (*Völkerrecht*) should be called "right of states" (*Staatenrecht*) (*ius publicum civitatum*) (*Doctrine of Right*, 6:343).[12]

Kant's international right supposes basically four elements: (1) reciprocal relationships between states are not rightful; (2) they constitute a warlike condition (the right of the strongest), even when there is no effective war; (3) an alliance between peoples is necessary, according to the idea of an original social contract; and (4) this alliance must not contain a sovereign power, but must only be an *association* (federacy) that can be renewed from time to time. If Kant's problem in the state of natural freedom—of continuous war—is the right *to* war, the right *in* war and the right to abandon this warlike condition, this imposes the task of a constitution that founds a durable peace, that is, of right *after* war (*Doctrine of Right*, 6:343)—Kant's surprising innovation.

Kant establishes an analogy between the state of nature for individuals and states, as well as the necessity for both to leave this situation. This analogy between international right and political right seems at first to be complete, since as much one as the other must submit to coercive laws: "Nations, as states, can be appraised as individuals, who in their natural condition (that is, in their independence from external laws) already wrong one another by being near one another; and each of them, for the sake of its security, can and ought to require the others to enter with it into a constitution similar to a civil constitution, in which each can be assured of its right" (*Perpetual Peace*, 8:354).[13] According to reason, continues Kant, states must then constitute a *state of peoples* (*civitas gentium*) (*Perpetual Peace*, 8:357)—or, as he said in 1793, a *universal state* (*Theory and Practice*, 8:313–14).

However, peace in a *world state* is a despotic one, a "soulless despotism" in a "graveyard of freedom" (*Perpetual Peace*, 8:367). Peace must originate in freedom and not in despotism.[14] Kant thus reflects on differentiations between political right and international right that make the analogy inadequate. The first argument is that sovereign states do not admit any subordination. Since international right is reciprocal, such federacy could be an *alliance of peoples*, but not a state of peoples, for in a state there is the relationship between a *superior* (legislator) and an *inferior* (who obeys). In fact, Kant says, each *state* considers as its majesty not to submit to any rightful exterior coercion (*Perpetual Peace*, 8:354). A second argument is that since states already have a lawful internal constitution, they would be free from the other's coercion to submit them to a wider one (8:355–56). Kant's third argument consists of states' will: "since this is not the will of the nations, according to their present conception of international right (so that they reject *in hypothesi* what is true *in thesi*), the positive idea of a *world republic* cannot be realized" (8:357). In *Doctrine of Right*, the idea of a state of peoples is rejected because of a practical difficulty: due to its great extension, it would be impossible to govern it (*Doctrine of Right*, 6:350).

If the idea that states join to form something analogous to a universal state, as an institutional basis for cosmopolitan right, is taken apart by these several reasons, Kant demands, however, that cosmopolitan right has some institutional basis. Therefore, Kant proposes a negative substitute: a federation.[15] It is thus a *federation of nations* and not of a state of nations (*Perpetual Peace*, 8:354): "in place of the positive idea of a *world republic*" there can be "only the *negative* surrogate of a league" (8:357.)[16] Kant also calls it an *association* of some *states* and, finally, of one *permanent congress of states*, to which all neighboring states can associate. Moreover, such a congress would be subject to possible dissolution in such a way that it can be defined as "a voluntary coalition of different states which can be dissolved at any time, not a federation (like that of the American states) which is based on a constitution and can therefore not be dissolved.—Only by such a congress can the idea of a public right of nations be realized, one to be established for deciding their disputes in a civil way, as if by a lawsuit, rather than in a barbaric way (the way of savages), namely by war" (*Doctrine of Right*, 6:351).

Kant has in view a historical model:

> Something of this kind took place (at least as regard the formalities of the right of nations for the sake of keeping the peace) in the first half of the present century, in the assembly of the States General at the Hague. The ministers of most of the courts of Europe and even of the smallest republics lodged with it their complaints about attacks being made on one of them by another. In this way they thought of the whole of Europe as a single confederated state which they accepted as arbiter, so to speak, in their public disputes. But later, instead of this, the right of nations survived only in books; it disappeared from cabinets or else, after force had already been used, was relegated in the form of a deduction to the obscurity of archives (*Doctrine of Right*, 6:350–51).[17]

Furthermore, Kant believes that this idea can be carried through due to its positive interpretation of the French Revolution, which makes him consider that a state that becomes a republic can begin this federation: "For if good fortune should ordain that a powerful and enlightened people can form itself into a republic (which by its nature must be inclined to perpetual peace), this would provide a focal point of federative union for other states, to attach themselves to it and so to secure a condition of freedom of states conformably with the idea of the right of nations; and by further alliances of this kind, it would gradually extend further and further" (*Perpetual Peace*, 8:356).

With such a federation, Kant accepts rightful and political pluralism in the international order.[18] Kant's peace, therefore, does not demand an "ultimate convergence of political ends."[19] As Vlachos observes, "Kant recognizes, through his biological, anthropo-geographic and historical studies, the originality of each people and grants to it a certain positive mean in his conception of International Law."[20] However, some authors find this conception problematic because it invokes an empirical element: the fact that states of his time do not want to constitute a single world state. At this point, political philosophy pondering on experience would thus seem to condition rightful philosophy, as Cavallar concludes on Kant: "in its evident concern not to fall into the utopian, he excessively accommodates . . . his *Doctrine of Right* to reality in the second definitive article."[21] Sidney Axinn, defending the thesis that the world community should be under the rightful and military force of a single world government, considers that although Kant gave two answers to the structure of the rightful world system (the federation of states and world government), the technical barriers that had made him abandon this second argument (it would be too big a state to govern and would fail in protecting its citizens) have been surpassed.[22] However, this is not the case of an "accommodation to reality," and even less of a mere technical consideration. It is, rather, recognition of the positive sense that reality has, even in opposition to reason, for the very accomplishment of rational ideals. For Kant, a world state is not only impossible from a political point of view, but also unacceptable from a moral one: the diversity of cultures, something morally desirable, must be preserved. In his precritical studies on natural sciences, Kant considers the material world not atomically, but dynamically, as a force field of attraction and repulsion. The spiritual world follows the model of the material world: a system of forces in conflict. Society, science, and culture, in analogy to the material world, develop from antagonisms (*Idea*, 8:20).[23]

Cosmopolitan Right

Until Kant, right had two dimensions: political right, that is, the internal right of each state, and international right, that is, the right of the relationships between states, and between the individuals from one state and those from another. In a footnote in *Perpetual Peace*, Kant adds a third dimension: cosmopolitan right, the right of the world citizens, which considers each individual not as a member of his or her state, but as a member, alongside each state, of a universal state of mankind (*Perpetual Peace*, 8:350). The relation of this cosmopolitan right to the two previous types of right follows the table of categories of *Critique of Pure Reason*: a single state (political right) corresponds to the category of unity; some states (international right) correspond to the category of plurality; all human beings and states (cosmopolitan right) correspond to the category of totality, which unites the two previous states (*Pure Reason* A80/B107).[24] The premise is the same for all three rights: the reciprocal "physical influence." Since the surface of the earth is not infinite but limited (*Doctrine of Right*, 6:311), the spatial proximity to other natural or rightful people cannot be prevented. However, it is only in the modern era that this reciprocal influence refers to all of humanity in such a way that, as Brandt observes, historical time is a constitutive element of this right.[25] The inhabitants of the whole earth begin to constitute a system in which "a violation of right in *one* place of the world is felt in *all*" (*Perpetual Peace*, 8:360).

Cosmopolitan right is presented in the third definitive article of *Perpetual Peace* as the third positive condition for peace. Kant affirms its rightful character: "Here, as in the previous articles, it is not a question of philanthropy but of *right*" (*Perpetual Peace*, 8:357). Similarly, in the *Doctrine of Right*, Kant opens the third section of public right on cosmopolitan right, pointing out: "This rational idea of a peaceful, even if not friendly, thoroughgoing community of all nations on the earth that can come into relations affecting one another is not a philanthropic (ethical) principle but a principle *having to do with rights*" (*Doctrine of Right*, 6:352). The third definitive article is thus formulated: "Cosmopolitan right shall be limited to the conditions of universal *hospitality*" (*Perpetual Peace*, 8:357). It is established from the principle that all originally have the same right to land (*Doctrine of Right*, 6:352) and, therefore, "no-one originally has any greater right than anyone else to occupy any particular portion of the earth" (*Perpetual Peace*, 8:358). The right to land is not an "acquired right" (*Doctrine of Right*, 6:238), such as the right that we can have to things (as in Kant's "Private right"), but is a right that comes from the right to freedom, an "original right." From this right stems the right to one's own body and, since body needs a place, the original "community of land" (*Doctrine of Right*, 6:352).

This conception is the basis for the "right to visit" (*Perpetual Peace*, 8:358), that is, the right of every citizen on earth to enter into community with everybody and, in view of this end, *to visit* all regions of the earth (*Doctrine of Right*, 6:352); as well as the "right to hospitality" (*Perpetual Peace*, 8:358), that is, in this attempt at entering into community with others, the right to not be treated as an enemy by foreigners (*Doctrine of Right*, 6:352). Right is injured, in this case, when one who arrives at a place is not accepted by those who are already there.

In contrast to the two previous articles, the third is formulated with a restrictive character: cosmopolitan right *is limited* to the right of hospitality and cannot be more than this. In this case, right is injured when—and this was the main problem for Kant in unjust "inhospitality"—one who arrives in a territory extends his own empire upon it. Cosmopolitan right is thus opposed to the right to *settle* on foreign territory (*accolatus*) (*Doctrine of Right*, 6:353). These rightful principles allow Kant to base his severe criticism of European attitudes toward peoples on other continents on a rigorous theory of right,[26] denouncing colonization procedures that, while alleging to bring to savages the benefit of civilization, appropriate lands by force or fictitious purchase. A people can install themselves in lands recently discovered only while keeping distance from the residence of the first people who installed themselves there, and not causing it any harm. But when the first people are shepherds or hunters (like most of the American nations) whose subsistence depends on great extensions of unpopulated lands, this process of installation can take place only through contract, which should not exploit the lack of knowledge of the inhabitants—which, of course, was not the case. Kant thus contests any justification that such violence leads to a better world, condemning the maxim according to which the aims justify the means: "all these supposedly good intentions cannot wash away the stain of injustice in the means used for them" (*Doctrine of Right*, 6:353).[27]

Kant criticizes thus the discourse of civilized nations that euphemistically describe the conquest of other peoples as a visit: "If one compares with this the *inhospitable* behavior of civilized, especially commercial, states in our part of the world, the injustice they show in *visiting* foreign lands and peoples (which with them is tantamount to *conquering* them) goes to horrifying lengths" (*Perpetual Peace*, 8:358). Europeans' behavior toward natives is seen by Kant as a reduction of the other to nullity—which makes relationships between *people* impossible: "When America, the negro countries, the Spice Islands, the Cape, and so forth were discovered, they were, to them, countries belonging to no one, since they counted the inhabitants as nothing" (8:358). Kant argues not only on the *illegitimacy* of the conquest, but also on its devastating *effect* on the complete destructuring that directly or indirectly stems from it: "In the East Indies (Hindustan), they brought in foreign soldiers under the pretext of merely proposing to set up trading posts, but with them oppression of the inhabitants, incitement of the various Indian states to widespread wars, famine, rebellions, treachery, and the whole litany of troubles that oppress the human race. . . . China and Japan (*Nipon*), which had given such guests a try, have therefore wisely [placed restrictions on them]" (8:358–59). Finally, Kant shows the bond between commercial expansion and wars between European powers: "The worst of this (or, considered from the standpoint of a moral judge, the best) is that the commercial states do not even profit from this violence; that all these trading companies are on the verge of collapse"; they serve only to provoke more wars in Europe (8:359).

The next section will analyze the result of Kant's reception in the contemporary discussion of following subjects: (1) the peaceful character of the republic; (2) the rightful international institutions; and (3) the rightful statute of human rights.

Kantian Themes

The Peaceful Character of the Republic

In *Perpetual Peace*, the first requirement for peace is that states should be republics—that is, a people should give itself its own laws, which in the reception of Kant's political philosophy is identified with the conception of contemporary democracy. The republican—or democratic—constitution in the internal order can have peace as a consequence in the external order, since it is determined by the will of those who will assume the onus of war and who will therefore probably not want it.

Such an idea invigorated internationalists in the interwar period such as Georges Del Vecchio, Christian Lange, and Boris Mirkine-Guetzévitch. Del Vecchio recognized as a great merit of some thinkers in preceding centuries that they saw what would become relatively easy to understand only in his own time: the close ties between a state's internal organization and the possibility of international coordination. This conception inspired Rousseau's criticism on Abbé de Saint-Pierre's project and it would not be by chance that Kant established it as the first definitive article of *Perpetual Peace*.[28] This also explains Lange's commentary: "without any doubt, Kant's work marks the most important stage in history of pacifist doctrine. He disclosed the error of Saint-Pierre and almost all his predecessors who believed that dynasties could create the international federacy. Thus, he established the close link between internationalism and democracy."[29] In pointing out that article 1 of the Pact of the League of Nations considers the existence of a constitutional regime an essential condition for its members, Mirkine-Guetzévitch reminds us that for Kant international peace is possible only between peoples who have a constitutional regime: "parliamentary control of foreign policy is only one aspect of this great problem, formulated and resolved by Kant. The parliamentary control of foreign policy even allows us to infer that Kant's idea is just not only on the abstract level, but also and above all in historical reality. Studying the historical evolution of representative institutions and their role in foreign policy, we prove that parliamentary control is guarantee of peace."[30]

However, the idea of democracy was to have a strong ideological function in international relations. The Cold War was presented by the West as a fight between democracies and dictatorships. The Truman Doctrine, such as it was presented in March 1947, evoked a dualist conception of world:

one side would be led by the majority will represented in free institutions and legitimately elected governments, assuring individual freedoms, freedom of expression, and freedom of religion; the other would be oppressed by a minority power, using terror, control of the press, and the suppression of individual freedoms. The American President Eisenhower interpreted this conception as a confrontation between forces of good and evil. The Soviet bloc, in turn, presented itself as an opponent of American imperialism and the destruction of democracy. Western democratic countries, however, supported Latin American dictatorships and signed alliances with countries that failed to respect human rights in Africa, Asia, and Latin America, tolerating Franco's Spain and Salazar's Portugal. The United States, which presented itself as the democracy *par excellence*, took the initiative in innumerable conflicts. The idea of the peaceful character of democracies lost its force.[31] Thus, in the postwar period, the notion predominated that violence in the international system has its cause in the very structure of the system, and not in the countries—therefore, not in systems of domination: the systemic structure, contrary to Kant's thought, is not influenced by the systems of domination of each country, which cannot explain a state's behavior in foreign affairs. It is also the anarchical system structure that explains what it is called the *dilemma of security*: preventative security measures are no longer distinguished from offensive preparations, which results in the arms race.[32]

This conception was first contested by liberalism in the 1970s. In 1976, Melvin Small and David Singer published the article "The War-Proneness of Democratic Regimes 1816–1965," and in 1983, Michael Doyle published "Kant, Liberal Legacy and Foreign Affairs."[33] These two articles, criticizing the realist conception that the nature of political regimes does not influence international relations, which are much more determined by relationships of power, interests, and security needs, defended the idea that democracies do not make war between themselves. Through the fall of the Soviet bloc, which, presented as the potential aggressor, strengthened the idea of the bellicose character of nondemocratic states, as well as through the expansion of democratic politics in the 1980s, the idea of democratic peace came back in vogue, resulting in innumerable publications in the 1990s.[34]

Contemporary analyses seek to recover the Kantian bond between republic and peace—which would consist of the basis of modern democracy: political decisions must address social requirements, reflecting, therefore, the citizen's aversion to violence. For Ernst-Otto Czempiel, "if this political interest is transferred without restrictions through decision processes in the political system, and if it is implemented by this system in accordance with this aim, then the use of violence will no longer be possible for a civil democracy. The thesis of the peaceful character of democracies finds endorsement in this social-political nexus."[35]

Research in the postwar period, according to Czempiel, consisted basically of analyses of empirical data. Without going deeply into theory, they did not dispose of refined hypotheses of inquiry. This resulted in divergences in data analyses and the weak explanatory force of these works. This research showed that democracies began wars as much as authoritarian states. The difference is that democracies, in contrast to authoritarian states, never fight among themselves. The international debate, however, does not explain this contradiction. According to Czempiel, such research suffers a double deficiency: they use a nonselective concept of democracy and do not insert their analysis into broader theoretical reflections. The problem of these analyses is that they do not rigorously distinguish between democracies and nondemocracies. Kant, however, offers the most important criterion: the comanagement of citizens. According to Czempiel, no country in the nineteenth century satisfied this Kantian requirement, which means that all statistical analyses of this period, initiated in 1815, "say nothing about their subject." There was comanagement not by those who were affected by war, but by the particular groups of interested parties. Czempiel reminded us that Kant criticized the court that surrounded and "advised" the monarch.[36]

This situation did not changed significantly in the twentieth century: "it cannot be affirmed that Kant's requirement has been fulfilled in the western democracies. Those who have to support the burden of war do not participate in the decision, and those who make the decision do not suffer the consequences of war."[37] In fact, the author continues, recalling Kant, only those who are directly affected by war are against war, that is, those who are obliged to fight personally, to defray the costs of the war with their own possessions or at least to assume the onus of the war debt: "here, in this case described by Kant in very concrete terms and in an empirical-sociological way, lies the true means to stop recourse to violence. For this to function, the decision-making, war and the onus that it provokes cannot be dissociated."[38]

Kant's republicanism is also recouped by Klaus-Gerd Giesen as an argument against the technification of massive and prompt use of nuclear armaments, the effectiveness of which depends upon decisions not subjected to democratic process. Kant, in §55 of *Doctrine of Right*, says: "Citizens . . . must always be regarded as a colegislating members of a state . . . and must therefore give their free assent, through their representatives, not only to waging war in general but also to each particular declaration of war" (*Doctrine of Right*, 6:345). According to Klaus-Gerd Giesen,

> Kant is concerned with assuring the primacy of political control above any consideration of a purely military or technical order. . . . The republican configuration Kant imagines is basically anti-decisionist by its very nature and desires above all to be an endorsement against de-politicization of crucial decisions for the nation. The automation of today's nuclear armament systems,

> indispensable to the "good" functioning within the time constraints *imposed* by the very technique, leads to the technification of decisions and removes the autonomy of politics. On behalf of human beings' freedom of action, Kant, in his time, *decisively* opposed this principle.[39]

On the other hand, however, the *soft power* of the idea of Western democracy has been strengthened, accompanied by the conception that democracy can be imposed from outside, justifying conditionalities in international forums and interventionism, with the implied contradictions of promoting the market economy in detriment to democracy. Moreover, the dissociation between formal democracy (the right to vote, freedom of thought, of expression, etc.) and real democracy (habitation, education, health, etc.) increases. To confer the title of citizen does not correct domination relations that hinder the recognition of ignored rights as well as the real exercising of rights already declared.[40] Proclamation of republican principle therefore requires inquiry into the social relations that destroy it and condition the struggle for its accomplishment.

For Kant, republican constitution is, however, only the first condition for peace—necessary, but not sufficient. The second condition is that the republics should constitute a federation of states—or what is today called an international organization.

International Rightful Institutions

The second definitive article in *Perpetual Peace* prescribes that "the right of nations shall be based on a *federation* of free states" (*Perpetual Peace*, 8:354). The Kantian idea that states must constitute international rightful institutions in order to have peace became fundamental in the pacifist movement and internationalist theories of the interwar periods. This can be apprehended in Alfred Zimmer's view of the League of Nations: "It will create . . . a good entente between all peoples who have the same thirst for peace. It will be for us the solution to the problem of our security. . . . Thus, the word of order in the post-war period is to place all our hopes in the League of Nations, which will at the same time replace the balance of powers and ancient vanished supremacies. In short, it is the *deus ex machina*, it is Providence."[41] In the same sense, Alfred Fried considered that not the absence of war, but rather "*the world organization is the foundation of the modern idea of peace*."[42] The new spirit of international right is identified with the spirit of the League of Nations: "isolated agreements, according to the spirit of the old regime and its methods, can only bring superficial results. There is true and strong peace only in the solidarity of peoples, as expressed by the League of Nations, acting directly and publicly."[43]

During the Cold War, however, security was taken to be a military issue, attributed to the competence of military alliances such as NATO and the Warsaw Pact—an anti-Kantian conception. In the 1990s, however, there was a strengthening of Kant's requirement that an international organization such as the UN, considered illusory by some theoreticians in the postwar period, be active, supported, and respected. Although everyone criticized its functioning and its possibilities,[44] "the fact that we are conscientious today of the limitations and imperfections of an institution such as the United Nations should not make us forget something that Kant's pamphlet shows with clarity: *there is no other way*."[45] Institutions for resolving controversies, which promote measures of adjustment and arbitration, are required—"which involves the requirement that right, as international law, becomes the foundation for all political action."[46]

The discussion turned toward security systems, which in the 1990s took on different roles in relation to those they had played until then. The Charter of the United Nations of 1945 distinguishes three security systems: "a universal system of collective security,"[47] "the inherent right of individual or collective self-defense,"[48] and "regional agreements or agencies" designed to address issues of regional security.[49] During the East-West conflict (1946–89), the collective self-defense system prevailed, in which NATO and the Warsaw Pact were inserted as military alliances. In the 1990s, however, there was a strengthening of the idea that "the bipolar system of collective self-defense through alliances is being replaced by a new multipolarity and renaissance of universal and regional strategies of collective security."[50]

In the Cold War world based on a bipolar system of alliances, security politics was a military issue; in the post–Cold War world, the liberal idea prevails that security is based on regional agreements in which cooperative interaction and rightful mechanisms for resolving controversies must dominate, such as arbitration, bound to the common efforts of assuring the survival of humanity and the environment. Problems such as water scarcity, population growth, migrations, and climatic changes, as well as economic issues and nationalistic conflicts, can no longer be decided by old strategies of competition.[51] The liberal confidence in cooperation strategies and rightful institutions destined to collective security[52] opposes the theoretical perspective of classic realism, for which only collective self-defense systems—that is, military alliances, such as NATO and the Warsaw Pact—can handle the problem of security. This idea was also affirmed by Boutros Boutros-Ghali when he was general secretary of the UN. He stated in his report of June 17, 1992, "An Agenda for Peace": "Regional arrangements and agencies have not in recent decades been considered in this light, even when originally designed in part for a role in maintaining or restoring peace within their regions of the world. Today a new sense exists that they have contributions to make."[53]

For Czempiel, then, the second definitive article would offer, together with the first, a strategic orientation: "the fact that peace is already assured in the European Union thanks to democratization and with the aid of international organization, is not only a considerable confirmation of Kant's two basic opinions. This evidence also contains an important reference to the strategy that external politics concerned with guarantee of peace must develop. Those who wish to pacify an international subsystem must democratize the systems of domination within countries and create between them an international organization."[54]

However, this is not being done with countries in Eastern Europe and in the Commonwealth of Independent States (CIS). The political task of integrating Russia as a nuclear power and permanent member of the Security Council in a new regional collective security system has been neglected. Since 1990, political leaders have failed in the project and construction of the new global and European architecture of security.[55] Kant's theorems would allow us, according to Czempiel, to identify the problematic aspect of this situation and to indicate an action criterion: "in Kant's sense, but also in the sense of political science theory, the most correct action would be to extend the European Union and activate the Organization for Security and Cooperation in Europe (OSCE) as the organization that encompasses all countries in the Atlantic Union." This, according to Czempiel, shows Kant's contemporary importance:

> Kant's theorem is significant not only in the history of philosophy and political theory; it also has strategic importance for the present time. It synthesizes, in an innovative and cautious way, two discoveries made and diffused before, bringing them under the correct heading. Democratization and International Organization are the two strategies that allow stanching the two principal sources of violence in international relations, that is, anarchy in international system and the non-democratic quality of national domination systems. This must be said to all supporters of *Realpolitik* in our days.[56]

Czempiel concluded that Kant's theorem is confirmed by empirical evidence that democracies have an aversion to violence. Deviances occur, however, when a still insufficient degree of democratization hinders society's requirements from being duly transmitted in decisions of external politics and when democracies are not integrated with their partners in an international organization, and therefore must confront the security dilemma. Kant's two articles, according to the author, can still guide the discussion on changes in Europe:

> The importance of Immanuel Kant's theorem is that it showed the existing nexus between the republican constitution of a country (democracy) and its

> external politics, founding this importance in terms of political science. With reference to *foedus pacificum*, to international organization, he mentions the second necessary condition for accomplishing peace: the permanent absence of war and continuous non-violent administration of all conflicts through corresponding procedures. From the results of scientific discussion, it is also possible to distill an orientation for the discussion on the rearrangement of Europe, which has been on course since the mid-1990s: Europe's systems of domination must be organized in a democratic fashion and all countries must be integrated to international organizations. Democracy and *foedus pacificum*—here is the direction toward which Kant's theorem points.[57]

The main difficulty today is that neoliberal orientation, which has been shaping diverse processes of regional integration, contradicts social and political priorities. Moreover, the global South still attempts with great difficulty to impose itself on international forums, in which it is clearly not in a privileged situation, submitting itself further to the neoliberal orientation of international organizations destined to regulate commerce and international finances (FMI, World Bank, and WCO), which in no way resemble the federation of states that Kant considered. Integration into an international organization does not eliminate relations of domination that condition how international right is accomplished, and only the analysis of these relations makes the reaction against them possible.

Cosmopolitanism

Kant added a third dimension to right, which was until then limited to political right and international right: cosmopolitan right, which considers the individual as a member of a society in a world dimension (*Perpetual Peace*, 8:357; *Doctrine of Right*, 6:352). Kant's cosmopolitan idea was taken up again in the 1990s as a guideline for cosmopolitan human rights policies. However, its manipulation by some states degenerates into an autodestructive moralization of politics. The risk is that when a state combats its political enemy on behalf of humanity, it identifies itself with a universal concept against the adversary: it demands peace, justice, progress, and civilization for itself, which are denied to the enemy. Human rights policies would serve as a negative moral appreciation of an opponent, which would frustrate the rightful institutionalized limitation of a political confrontation or military combat.

Addressing this problem, Jürgen Habermas sought to differentiate the rightful nature of the human rights concept from the deviated use of this concept. What confers an appearance of moral rights to human rights is that its validity exceeds the jurisprudence of state-nations. The texts of historical constitutions evoke "innate rights" and take on the form of a declaration, stating that the legislator in power cannot make use of them as he wishes.

That is: it is not only a question of their being valid and carried through by state sanction; they are intended to have a rational justification, which confers on them a universal validity. However, Habermas continued, this type of justification does not transform fundamental rights into ethical norms:

> Rightful rules—understood in the modern sense of positive right—conserve their rightful form regardless of the reasons that allow the founding of their intention toward legitimacy. They receive this character from their structure and not from their content. According to their structure, fundamental rights are demandable subjective rights, and have precisely the function of liberating the citizens from ethical demands, granting to the actors the rightful margins of an action founded on the preferences of each one. Moral rights are founded on obligations that bind the free will of autonomous persons. Rightful obligations, on the contrary, result only from authorizations to act freely in virtue of the rightful restriction to these subjective freedoms." For this reason, Kant defines right as "the sum of the conditions under which the choice of one can be united with the choice of another in accordance with a universal law of freedom."[58]

For Kant, stated Habermas, human rights have their place in the frameworks of the *Doctrine of Right*: "the establishment of a cosmopolitan state means that human rights infractions are not *directly* judged and fought according to ethical criteria, but pursued, in the framework of a state juridical order, according to institutionalized judiciary procedures, as criminal actions."[59] The jurisdictionalization of the state of nature guarantees against confounding ethics and right, assuring to the defendant a protection against ethical discrimination. The difference between right and ethics means that a part of the behavior (disposition of spirit and motives) is excluded from any rightful regulation. In order for politics not to suffer a direct moralization, which transforms divergences into an issue of good or evil, it is not necessary to abandon the concept of human rights, but rather to give it a rightful framework. This can be done, according to Habermas, with the Kantian concept of cosmopolitan right—hence, its importance to the present day.

The debate reached the newspapers with NATO attacks in Kosovo. Habermas observed in the periodical *Die Zeit*, referring to the recent disappearance of the state's reasoning rhetoric evoked during the Gulf War, that "obscure tones are fortunately absent from the German public realm. . . . Supporters and opponents of the NATO attack make use of a crystalline normative language."[60] Reinhardt Brandt, in an article published in the periodical *Frankfurter Allgemeine Zeitung* entitled "The Unjust Enemy: What Kant Would Have Said on the War in Kosovo," asked, "How well founded are the NATO attacks against Serbia? Which philosopher can be carried in a pilot's knapsack? We must go back two hundred years to enter again in the conceptual world that is today demanded by NATO political leaders."[61] Hegel, the author reminded us, concentrated on the singular Germanic state. Marx and Nietzsche distanced themselves from ideas of right. Therefore Kant remained the most modern classic author to consider a rightful peaceful world order. Brandt warned his readers that "Kant's writing of *Perpetual Peace* is still a key text to appreciating a universal human rights policy. The current question on how the rightful principle of non-interventionism is compatible with the principle of humane intervention was already addressed, in its basic elements, in 1795."

Habermas, however, allowed an exception to the demand he made four years earlier that infractions against human rights should be pursued rightfully. Faced with a blocked Security Council, the NATO intervention in Kosovo could be based on an "aid in need" principle of international right even without a UN mandate, since human rights have a moral content, sharing with moral norms an intention of universal validity.[62] This argument was contested by several authors. Among them, the Brazilian jurist Marcelo Neves argued that "according to this conception of the moral character of humanitarian interventions unilaterally conducted by great western powers, Habermas' suggestion does not result exactly in a *world internal* politics to achieve human rights, but in a *westerner external* politics of supervision of the human rights policy. And in this case, decisions about the attack and its selective, arbitrary application are not submitted to control of procedures according to the state model of rights and democracy."[63]

Among the critical reactions to Habermas's argument formulated from a Kantian perspective was an argument by Reinhard Merkel two weeks afterwards, also in the *Die Zeit*, that all international acts need the mandate of a rightful authoritative body recognized by the international community. A war without mandate destroys the conditions for the jurisdictionalization of international relations, and is a threat to the future of the international order as a rightful one, Merkel stressed, stating that he does not argue in realist terms for the precarious scale of autolegitimized powers.[64] In the same sense, Reinhardt Brandt, considering the absence of an UNO mandate for the NATO action, said that "Kant . . . would have seen an extremely grave offence to right in the weakening of an international forum."[65]

Four years later, Habermas opposed the Iraq war of 2003 and American external policy, requiring that Europe redefine its "foreign policies." He identified external European policy with "a Kantian hope for an internal world politics," in which, however, he recognized absolutely no role for the nations of the global South—except that of following the "European model."[66] This exclusion of the South does not correspond to Kant's cosmopolitan idea.

The achievement of the Kantian cosmopolitan right is hindered by relations of domination and violence that provoke the dizzying increase in the portion of humanity that is, lawfully or not, excluded from the right of being represented as political subject: the elimination of resistances incompatible with system reproduction (functional violence), the elimination of "human excess" in the expansion of capital (nonfunctional violence, with an objective character), and the elimination of "alterity" in conflicts of "identity" (nonfunctional violence, with a subjective character).[67] Social movements have been resisting these relations in global and local dimension, but their aims are far from being achieved.[68] If Kant presented the *conditions of possibility* for peace, its achievement today depends on the explicitation of *conditions of struggle* against the hegemonic relations that destroy them.

Appendix: Commemorations of the Two-Hundredth Anniversary of Perpetual Peace.

In March 1995, the Department of Philosophy at the Johann Wolfgang Goethe University in Frankfurt/Main organized the international conference "Kant's Idea of Peace and the Problem of a Rightful and Peaceful International Order Today," in honor of two hundred years of Kant's *Perpetual Peace* and fifty years of the Charter of the United Nations. The following year, Matthias Lutz-Bachmann and James Bohman published the proceedings of the conference in a volume the title of which takes up the motto of the pacifist movement inspired by Kant in the beginning of the twentieth century: *Frieden durch Recht*, or "Peace through Right."[69] In 1997, these same authors published *Perpetual Peace: Essays on Kant's Cosmopolitan Ideal*, stressing in the introduction that these essays show the contemporary relevance of Kant's text, the central issue of which is the peaceful effect of right and the idea that a peaceful order can be created only through a cosmopolitan right establishing the rights of the world citizens in substitution to classic international law. The new historical context—with a massively unequal distribution of resources, nuclear weapons, nationalism, ethnic separatism, and religious fundamentalism—seem to have made Kant "more interesting." All essays in the volume are Kantian, the authors affirmed, because they all agree that peace must be "positive and cosmopolitan."[70]

Also in March 1995, the Friedrich Naumann Foundation and the Association for German Writers Schleswig-Holstein organized the congress "Honoring Kant: Kant's Work *Perpetual Peace*." Its organizers justified the event by stressing that "Kant's writing is two hundred years old. Nonetheless, it develops an impressively important idea of peace for the present time," since "according to Kant, perpetual peace should not remain a mere Idea, if we see it as our duty and legitimate hope to carry through international law step by step and continuously."[71] In October 1995, the Institute for Cultural Research on Peace and Conflict in Hannover organized the symposium "200 Years of Kant's Project *Perpetual Peace*" (the proceedings of which were published the following year), with the aim of discussing what its main organizer, Volker Bialas, called "a classic text with highly important content for the present time," a serious attempt to bind peace to right and to ground the idea of a "just world order as a rightful world order."[72] Reinhard Merkel and Roland Wittmann also organized a volume dedicated to Kantian reformulations of international issues, pointing out that Kant's writing contains a series of principles that not only affected the development of modern international law, but also still have "surprising importance for the present time." For these authors, "Kant develops the essential characteristics of the state of peace to be founded with such precise content that it leads to reflections on a completely new direction in the current meaning of Kantian ethics, and particularly, review the habitual accusations raised against this ethics of formalism and rigorism."[73] Jane Kneller and Sidney Axinn also organized a Kantian volume, observing that the renewed interest in Kant's political and social philosophy in the last decade has resulted in important works of political theory written by authors such as John Rawls, Onora O'Neill, Ronald Beiner, Howard Williams, and Susan Shell, among others. Some of these authors use Kant as a starting point for their own theories, whereas historians of philosophy began to look more attentively at Kant's own works in these areas. The volume they organized was intended to show some of the recent results of these Kantian readings in social and political issues. If in some places the vision still persists that Kant would have too abstract and arid an ethics to be used in contemporary issues, Kneller and Axinn call their volume a Kantian collection in a broad sense: its authors define their social theory as Kantian, although it is not similar in many points to Kant's own thinking. Each one shows in his or her own way that Kantian philosophy supplies conceptual resources in the analysis of contemporary social issues, far from the barren formalism that is generally attributed to it.[74]

The discussion also took place in Brazil. In 1995, a symposium was organized at the Goethe Institute of Porto Alegre on "Kant and the Establishment of Peace." In his presentation to the symposium proceedings, its executive director, Hartmut Becher, affirmed that

> Kant's pamphlet *Perpetual Peace* contributed more than any another philosophical text toward the configuration of political institutions. Its conditions for peace, such as the assurance of fundamental rights and freedom of opinion, the observance of rules in international diplomacy, the federative league of states or the nonviolent regulation of conflicts, have lost none of their validity. . . . In the preparation for this symposium, many voices accused the subject to be devoid of practical reference: the Goethe-Institute of Porto Alegre would be incurring the risk of abandoning its guideline of recent years of dealing mainly with social issues, and the dialogue would take place in an ivory tower. The continuation of the colloquium proved the opposite: Kant's pamphlet

is no barren academic treatise that would only be interesting in courses for PhD candidates. It is today—in a historical context different from that of his time—more relevant to the present time as ever before.[75]

Notes

1. In the French world, see Pierre Laberge, Guy LaFrance, and Denis Dumas, *L'année 1795: Kant, Essai sur la paix* (Paris: Vrin 1977). In Italy, see Società italiana di studi kantiani, *Kant politico: A duecento anni dalla pace perpetua* (Pisa-Roma: Instituti editoriali e poligrafici internazionali, 1996). See appendix to this article for a description of these commemorations in Germany and Brazil.

2. Christine Chwaszca and Wolfgang Kersting, "Vorwort," in *Politische Philosophie der internationalen Beziehungen* (Frankfurt am Main: Suhrkamp, 1988), 7–8.

3. Wolfgang Kersting, "Die bürgerliche Verfassung in jedem Staate soll republikanisch sein," in Otfried Höffe, *Immanuel Kant: Zum ewigen Friede* (Berlin: Akademie Verlag, 1995), 87–108.

4. Wolfgang Kersting, *Die politische Philosophie des Gesellschaftsvertrags*, 2nd ed. (Darmstadt: Primus, 1996), 213.

5. Kersting, *Gesellschaftsvertrags*, 212–13.

6. "This basic law, which can arise only from the general (united) will of the people, is called the *original contract* (*ursprünglichen Vertrag*)" (*Theory and Practice*, 8:295).

7. Kersting, *Gesellschaftsvertrags*, 351.

8. Peter Burg, *Kant und die französische Revolution* (Berlin: Duncker & Humblot, 1974), 247.

9. Kersting, *Gesellschaftsvertrags*, 351.

10. Kersting, "Bürgerliche Verfassung," 99–104.

11. Ibid., 104–7.

12. See Antonio Truyol y Serra, "Théorie du droit international public," *Recueil des Cours* 173 (1981): 29–30. Here is stressed the distinction between the German concepts *Staastrecht* and *Staatenrecht: Staatsrecht* is the right of the state, or political right ("First Definitive Article of a Perpetual Peace"); *Staatenrecht* is the right of the states, or international right ("Second Definitive Article of a Perpetual Peace").

13. Georg Cavallar, "Die Systematik des Rechtsphilosophische Teils von Kants Entwurf *Zum ewigen Frieden*," in *Kant e a instituição da paz*, ed. Valerio Rohden, trans. Peter Naumann (Porto Alegre: Ed. Universidade/UFRGS, Goethe-Institut/ICBA, 1997), 58–77.

14. Reinhard Brandt, "Vom Weltbürgerrecht," in *Immanuel Kant: Zum ewigen Frieden*, ed. Otfried Höffe (Berlin: Akademie Verlag, 1995), 69–86, 139.

15. James Bohman, "The Public Spheres of the World Citizen," in *Perpetual Peace: Essays on Kant's Cosmopolitan Ideal*, ed. James Bohman and Matthias Lutz-Bachmann (Cambridge: MIT Press, 1997), 179–200.

16. Many authors such as Lachs mistakenly interpret Kant's international right to be founded on the idea of a world state. See Manfred Lachs, "Teachings and Teaching of International Law," *Recueil des Cours* 151 (1976): 161–252.

17. The Abbe de Saint-Pierre, writing early in the eighteenth century, said: "I investigated whether Sovereigns could find some degree or *enough security* in the fulfillment of mutual promises, establishing between them a perpetual Arbitration. In my opinion, if the eighteen main Sovereigns of Europe, in order to remain in the government to prevent war between them and to seek all the advantages of a perpetual commerce from Nation to Nation wanted to establish a Treaty of Union and a Perpetual Congress . . . , I think that the weakest would have *enough security*, that the great power of the strongest could not harm them, that each would accurately keep reciprocal promises, that commerce would never be interrupted, and that all future controversies would be resolved *without war* through an arbitrator." Abbe de Saint-Pierre, *Projet pour rendre la paix perpétuelle en Europe* (Paris: Garnier Frères, 1981; orig. ed. 1713), 130–31.

18. In this way, Ténékidès observes, "if Kant's internationalism supposes a minimum legal orientation and convergent politics of the interested States . . . , he understands this homogeneity in a very broad sense that includes in the "federacy of free states" states with political regimes very different one from another, but which tend to common ends of freedom and justice." See Georges Ténékidès, "Régimes internes et organisation internationale," *Recueil des Cours* 110 (1963): 335–36.

19. Bohman, "Public Spheres," 180.

20. Georges Vlachos, *La pensée politique de Kant* (Paris: PUF, 1962), 571–74.

21. Cavallar, "Systematik," 77; see also Matthias Lutz-Bachmann, "Kant's Idea of Peace and the Philosophical Conception of a World Republic," trans. David W. Loy, in Bohman and Lutz-Bachmann, *Perpetual Peace*, 74.

22. Sidney Axinn, "World Community and its Government," in *Autonomy and Community: Readings in Contemporary Kantian Social Philosophy*, ed. Jane Kneller and Sidney Axinn (Albany: State University of New York Press, 1998), 119–29.

23. Brandt, "Vom Weltbürgerrecht," 141.

24. Ibid., 142.

25. Ibid., 143.

26. Ernest Hamburger, "Droits de l'homme et relations internationales," *Recueil des Cours* 97 (1959): 293–429, 316.

27. See Victor Delbos, *La philosophie pratique de Kant*, 3rd ed. (Paris: PUF, 1969), 564–65.

28. Georges Del Vecchio, "La société des nations au point de vue de la philosophie du droit international," *Recueil des Cours* 38 (1931): 541–649.

29. Christian L. Lange, "Histoire de la doctrine pacifique et de son influence sur le développement du droit international," *Recueil des Cours* 13 (1926): 349.

30. Boris Mirkine-Guetzévitch, "La technique parlamentaire des relations internationales," *Recueil des Cours* 56 (1936): 294–95.

31. Pascal Boniface, *Le monde contemporain: Grandes lignes de partage* (Paris: PUF, 2001), 203–13.

32. Ernst-Otto Czempiel, "Kants Theorem und die aktuelle Diskussion über die Beziehung zwischen Demokratie und Frieden," in Rohden, *Kant e a instituição da Paz*, 99–120.

33. See Melvin Small and David Singer, "The War-Proneness of Democratic Regimes 1816–1965," *Jerusalem Journal of International Relations* 1 (1976): 50–69; and

Michael Doyle, "Kant, Liberal Legacy, and Foreign Affairs," in two parts, *Philosophy and Public Affairs* 12 (1983): 205–35 and 323–53.

34. Jean-Jacques Roche, *Théories des relations internationales* (Paris: Montchrestien, 2001), 88–91.

35. Czempiel, "Kants Theorem," 100.

36. Ibid., 101–5.

37. Ibid.

38. Ibid., 111.

39. Klaus-Gerd Giesen, "Kant et la guerre de masse," in *Actes du IIIe Congrès de la société internationale d'études kantiennes de la langue française* (Athens: Union scientifique franco-hellénique, 1997), 338–39.

40. Étienne Balibar, *La crainte des masses* (Paris: Galilée, 1997), 23.

41. Alfred Eckhard Zimmern, "La puissance britannique dans le monde," in *Les empires coloniaux* (Paris: Alcan—PUF, 1940), 94.

42. Alfred H. Fried, "Die Friedensidee in moderner Auffassung," in *Der deutsche Friedens-Kongress in Stuttgart* (Stuttgart: Verlag der Deutschen Friedensgesellschaft, 1909), 15–16.

43. A. Aulard, "La propagande pour la Société des nations." *La Paix par le Droit* 37 (1927): 235–38.

44. Eduardo Rabossi, "Kant y las condiciones de posibilidad de la sociedad cosmopolita," in Rohden, *Kant e a instituição da Paz*, 189.

45. Daniel Brauer, "Utopia e historia em el proyecto de Kant de una 'Paz perpetua,'" in Rohden, *Kant e a instituição da Paz*, 212.

46. Wolfgang Thierse, "Frieden als politische Kategorie und Herausforderung," in Rohden, *Kant e a instituição da Paz*, 143–60, 159.

47. Chapter 6, on "pacific settlement of disputes," articles 33 to 38; and chapter 7, on "action with respect to threats to the peace, breaches of the peace and acts of aggression," articles 39 to 50.

48. Chapter 7, article 51.

49. Chapter 8, on "regional arrangements," articles 52 to 54.

50. Hans Günter Brauch, "As Nações Unidas e as organizações regionais. Uma contribuição ao sistema de segurança coletiva: O caso europeu," *Contexto internacional* (Rio de Janeiro) 16 (1994): 209–11.

51. Ibid., 221.

52. Ibid., 213.

53. Boutros Boutros-Ghali, *An Agenda for Peace: Preventive Diplomacy, Peacemaking, and Peace-keeping*, document A/47/277–S/24111, June 17, 1992, New York, Department of Public Information, United Nations, par. 65. See Brauch, "As Nações unidas," 217–18.

54. Czempiel, "Kants Theorem," 116.

55. Brauch, "As Nações unidas," 236.

56. Czempiel, "Kants Theorem," 116–17.

57. Ibid., 118–19.

58. Jürgen Habermas, "Kants Idee des ewigen Friedens: Aus dem historischen Abstand von 200 Jahren," in Jürgen Habermas, *Die Einbeziehung des Anderen: Studien*

zur politischen Theorie (Frankfurt am Main: Suhrkamp, 1996), 224–25, quoting from Kant, *Doctrine of Right*, 6:230.

59. Ibid., 226.

60. Jürgen Habermas, "Bestialität und Humanität: Ein Krieg zwischen Recht und Moral," *Die Zeit* 54, no. 18 (1999): 1.

61. Reinhard Brandt, "Der ungerechte Feind: Was Kant zum Krieg im Kosovo zu sagen hätte," in *Frankfurter Allgemeine Zeitung*, May 7, 1999, 11.

62. Habermas, "Bestialität"; and Sharon Anderson-Gold, "Crimes against Humanity: A Kantian Perspective on International Law," in Kneller and Axinn, *Autonomy and Community*, 103–11.

63. Marcelo Neves, *Zwischen Themis und Leviathan: Eine schwierige Beziehung; Eine Rekonstruktion des demokratischen Rechtsstaats in Auseinandersetzung mit Luhmann und Habermas* (Baden-Baden: Nomos, 2000), 207.

64. Reinhard Merkel, "Das Elend der Beschützen," *Die Zeit* 54, no. 20 (1999): 10.

65. Brandt, "Der ungerechte Feind," 11.

66. Jürgen Habermas and Jacques Derrida, "Nach dem Krieg: Die Wiedergeburt Europas," *Frankfurter Allgemeiner Zeitung*, May 31, 2003, 33.

67. Balibar, *La crainte*, 42.

68. Étienne Balibar, "Préface," in Étienne Balibar and Immanuel Maurice Wallerstein, *Race, nation, classe: Les identités ambiues* (Paris: La découverte, 1988), 14.

69. Matthias Lutz-Bachmann and James Bohman, *Frieden durch Recht: Kants Friedensidee und das Problem einer neuen Weltordnung* (Frankfurt am Main: Suhrkamp, 1996).

70. Bohman and Lutz-Bachmann, *Perpetual Peace*, 3–6.

71. Machael Hauberg and Wolfgang Beutin, "Vorwort," in Hauberg and Beutin, *Hommage à Kant: Kants Schrift "Zum ewigen Frieden"* (Hamburg: von Bockel, 1996), 7.

72. Volker Bialas, "Einleitung," in *200 Jahre Kants Entwurf "Zum ewigen Frieden" Idee einer globalen Friedensordnung*, ed. Volker Bialas and Hans-Jürgen Hässler (Würzburg: Königshausen & Neumann, 1996), 9–10.

73. Reinhard Merkel and Roland Wittmann, "Einleitung," in *"Zum ewigen Frieden": Grundlagen, Aktualität, und Aussichten einer Idee von Immanuel Kant*, ed. Reinhard Merkel and Roland Wittmann (Frankfurt am Main: Suhrkamp, 1996), 7–11.

74. Kneller and Axinn, *Autonomy and Community*, vii–viii.

75. Harmut Becher, "Apresentação," in Rohden, *Kant e a instituição da Paz*, 9–10.

14

A Typology of Love in Kant's Philosophy

Maria de Lourdes Borges

In this paper I shall analyze what Kant says about the different kinds of love, trying to reconstruct what I call a typology of love. I begin with the feeling of sympathy in the *Groundwork*. Then, I examine the love of benevolence in the *Doctrine of Virtue* as a duty to love other human beings, which is a duty of virtue toward other people. The introduction of a feeling like love seems, at first sight, strange to the Kantian system, since the moral action should be practiced from duty and not because of sensible inclinations.

I shall show that the duty to love, one that implies the derived duties of beneficence (*Wohltätigkeit*), gratitude (*Dankbarkeit*), and sympathy (*Teilnehmung*), does not reject the purity of moral law. Although the a priori origin of the moral law remains valid, the *Metaphysics of Morals* deals with the moral applied to rational sensible beings, for which some feelings can be useful in the accomplishment of moral actions, when the respect for the law is not enough. Finally, using the *Anthropology*, I compare the virtue of love and three other kinds of inclinations: desire, the love-affect, and the love-passion.

Sympathy in the *Groundwork*

Sympathy[1] for other people's fortune, as a feeling that leads to beneficence, is analyzed in the well-known example of the *Groundwork*. When explaining the difference between acting from duty and according to duty, Kant presents the interesting example of two philanthropists, distinguishing the one that possesses a close pleasure in spreading joy to his fellow human beings from the one who helps other people out of a sense of duty:

> Suppose, then, that the mind of this philanthropist were overclouded by his own grief, which extinguished all sympathy with the fate of the others, and that while he still had the means to benefit others in distress their troubles did

---

This article was first published as "Uma tipologia do amor na filosofia kantiana," in *Studia Kantiana* 2 (2000): 19–34. Translated by the author.

> not move him because he had enough to do with his own; and suppose that now, when no longer incited to it by any inclination, he nevertheless tears himself out of this deadly insensibility and does the action without any inclination, simply from duty. (*Groundwork*, 4:398)

Kant also asks if we would consider that his action would have a higher worth if nature had put very little sympathy in his heart, and the answer is: "By all means! It is just then that the worth of character comes out, which is moral and incomparably the highest, namely, that he is beneficent not from inclination but from duty" (*Groundwork*, 4:398–99).

We can clearly distinguish in the example of the two philanthropists an action done in accordance with duty from an action done from duty: the first one is carried out of compassion and the second one is performed even if the philanthropist does not care about other peoples' misery. The difference between one and the other is that the incentive of the first philanthropist is sympathy, which is a sensible inclination, while the action of second philanthropist is performed out of respect for the moral law. Kant considers that, if compassion for the other person's fate is the incentive of an action, then this action does not have a true moral value. If we consider this example in light of the history of philosophy, we see that it is clearly provocative. To affirm that the benevolent action of a man who is not touched by the other person's misery does not have any moral value obviously emphasizes the difference between Kant and the empiricists, such as Hume and Hutcheson, who attribute to the natural feelings of sympathy the role of a virtuous incentive of moral actions.[2]

Despite the example of the philanthropist in the *Groundwork*, which clearly indicates that the mere presence of moral feelings prevents an action from having moral worth, the analysis of some commentators, such as Barbara Herman and Christine Korsgaard, grant that the mere presence of some feelings, such as sympathy, does not make an action morally unworthy, had the respect for moral law been a sufficient incentive for the accomplishment of the action. Herman considers that the vision, according to which the absence of inclinations is a necessary condition for the morality of an action, would not be satisfactory: "The apparent consequence of this view . . . is at least troubling in that it judges a grudging or resentfully performed act morally preferable to a similar act done from affection or with pleasure."[3] Korsgaard also maintains that when sympathy is present, but the person is sufficiently motivated by duty, the action has moral value and "yet her native sympathy will contribute to her enjoyment of the action."[4]

The thesis supported by Herman as well as Korsgaard—for example, that the mere presence of a feeling does not diminish the moral value of an action, if this feeling is not the incentive of a moral action—is corroborated by the difference that Kant establishes between utility and moral feeling. In the *Groundwork*, when analyzing the role played by moral feeling in Hutcheson's philosophy, Kant argues that this feeling is closer to morality than the principle of utility, which only teaches us how to calculate better. Despite the fact that they are both empirical principles and do not give us the necessary purity and formality of a moral principle, at least the moral feeling remains closer to morality:

> On the other hand, moral feeling, this supposed special sense, . . . nevertheless remains closer to morality and its dignity inasmuch as it shows virtue the honor of ascribing to her immediately the delight and esteem we have for her and does not, as it were, tell her to her face that it is not her beauty but only our advantage that attaches us to her. (*Groundwork*, 4:442–43)

In the *Critique of Practical Reason*, the necessity to support morality in a nonmaterial practical principle leads, obviously, to the refusal to ascribe the role of moral incentives to feelings such as love, benevolence, and sympathy. The aim of this work is to prove at least the possibility of practical reason, that is, that reason can be capable of compelling us to act morally, in spite of the good or bad feelings we have. To prove that pure reason can be practical is to prove that it can, alone, determine the will. We would fail to prove it, if the will was always dependant on empirical conditions. If the will was always based on feelings or passions, this would mean that pure reason cannot be practical and that the causality of freedom is impossible. The *Groundwork* as well as the *Critique of Practical Reason* have as their goal an arrival at the categorical imperative and the moral law, respectively, in an attempt to prove that reason can determine the will without the help of empirical incentives. The critique of sympathy and benevolent feelings in general can be understood in this context, since these would be empirical and contingent, unable to be taken as the basis of the determination of will, either objective (motive) or subjective (cause), being, however, inappropriate for morality based on reason.

However, the same sympathy that does not have any intrinsic moral value in the *Groundwork* comes out in the *Doctrine of Virtue* as a feeling of pleasure and displeasure that should be used to promote benevolence, being itself an incentive for moral actions:

> Sympathetic joy and sadness (*sympathia moralis*) are sensible feelings of pleasure and displeasure (which are therefore to be called "aesthetic" at another's state of joy or pain (shared feelings, sympathetic feeling). Nature has already implanted in human beings receptivity to these feelings. But to use this as a means to promoting active and rational benevolence is still a particular, though only a conditional, duty. (*Doctrine of Virtue*, 6:456)

In this quotation, Kant explicitly admits the possibility of using the feeling of sympathy as an incentive, a way to activate benevolent actions. What is more, the use of sensible feelings is called a duty of humanity. It seems that here we are confronted with a modification in the understanding of the role of feelings as incentives. Does Kant change his mind about the role of feelings in the later texts, such as the *Doctrine of Virtue* (1797)? A provisory answer can be found on the remark he makes about the duty of humanity: "It is called the duty of humanity (*humanitas*) because a human being is regarded here not merely as a rational being but also as an animal endowed with reason" (*Doctrine of Virtue*, 6:456). In the *Metaphysics of Morals*, Kant seems to have abandoned the pure a priori domain of practical reason. It is not anymore a matter of incentives that work for pure rational beings, but rather incentives that work for animals endowed by reason. If one is no longer in the pure practical domain, why call this work the *Metaphysics of Morals*?

Love in the Doctrine of Virtue

Kant admits that a *Doctrine of Virtue*, as part of a metaphysics of morals, should be built upon a system of concepts, which are independent of empirical intuitions: "A philosophy of any subject (a system of rational cognition from concepts) requires a system of pure rational concepts independent of any conditions of intuition, that is, a metaphysics" (*Doctrine of Virtue*, 6:375). The philosopher who wants to construct a metaphysics of morals looks for rational pure concepts, unconstrained by empirical conditions. To be faithful to the spirit of the *Metaphysics of Morals*, it should be possible that the *Doctrine of Virtue* gives us a system of rational pure concepts:

> If one departs from this principle and begins with pathological or pure aesthetic or even moral feeling (with what is subjective rather than objectively practical); if, that is, one brings to the matter of the will, the end, instead of with the form of the will, the law, in order to determine duties on this basis, then there will indeed be no metaphysical first principles of the doctrine of virtue, since feeling, whatever may arouse it, always belong to the order of nature. (*Doctrine of Virtue*, 6:376–77)

A doctrine of virtue, being a part of a metaphysics of morals, cannot be based on feelings, since feelings are always physical, related to pain and pleasure. Although in the Preface to the *Metaphysics of Morals* Kant clearly states that morality cannot be based on empirical feelings, here we come across the duty to love as a first section (Of the Duty of Love to Other Human Beings) of the first chapter of the second part (Duties of Virtue to Others) of the *Doctrine of Virtue*.

A metaphysics of morals seeks to build a system of duties, which are free from pathological feelings. In this context, how can we have a duty to love? Another problem that occurs here is the possibility of a priori construction that leads to a theory of virtue, since virtue is usually defined as habits that belong to the empirical domain. Aristotle defines virtue as a *héxis proairetiké*, that is, a habit to act deliberately. If we accept this definition, a theory of the virtues would belong to the technical-practical domain. But Kant seems to look for a way to establish a metaphysics of morals in the pure practical domain. Is this really the case?

To answer this question, it will be necessary to correctly understand the conception of a metaphysics of morals as that doctrine that contains in itself principles of application of the universal law to the "particular nature of human beings, which is cognized only by experience" (*Doctrine of Virtue*, 6:217). The other side of a metaphysics of morals is a practical anthropology, which gives the conditions for the acceptance or rejection of the moral law by human beings. This means, Kant claims, "that a metaphysics of morals cannot be based upon anthropology," but "that it can still be applied to it" (6:217). In the *Groundwork*, Kant clearly distinguishes between a metaphysics of morals that presents "the laws in accordance to which everything must happen" and a practical anthropology that exhibits "the laws in accordance to which everything happens" (*Groundwork*, 4:388). Twelve years later, however, the idea of a metaphysics of morals includes in itself empirical knowledge of the nature of human beings, without which it would not be possible to determine a concrete system of duties for human beings. Allen Wood correctly analyzes this displacement in the conception of a metaphysics of morals that occurs between 1785 and 1797, regarding the separation between the empirical and pure part of ethics.

> In shifting the content of a "metaphysics of morals" toward the empirical, Kant is in no way abandoning or modifying his fundamental thesis that the supreme principle of morality is wholly a priori and borrows nothing from the empirical nature of human beings. He is withdrawing only his earlier claim that a "metaphysics of morals" can concern only "the idea and the principles of a possible pure will and not the actions and conditions of human volition generally" (*Groundwork*, 4:390–91). In other words, Kant now no longer regards a metaphysics of morals as constituted solely by a set of pure moral principles (with the pure moral law as its only foundation). It is instead the system of duties that results when the pure moral principle is applied to the empirical nature of human beings in general.[5]

The application of the pure moral principle to the empirical nature of human beings gives us a system of virtues, defined as ends that are, at the same time, duties. Kant enumerates two ends that should be considered as duties: self-perfection and the happiness of others. These two ends lead to two different types of duties: the duties of a human being to himself, and duties to others, among which we find the duty to love, that consists in promoting the happiness of others. However, this virtuous love is not a love related to the pleasure experienced in the presence of other person, but it is a principle to do benevolent actions:

> In this context, however, love is not to be understood as feeling, that is, as a pleasure in the perfection of others, love is not to be understood as delight in them (since others cannot put one under obligation to have feelings). It must rather be thought as the maxim of benevolence (practical love), which results in beneficence. (*Doctrine of Virtue*, 6:449)

By the duty to love, Kant means not the love of delight (*amor complacentiae*) but rather the love of benevolence (Wohlwollen, *amor benevolentiae*), since the latter could be demanded from someone, but not the former, given that it would be a contradiction that somebody should have the obligation to feel pleasure. The love of benevolence, since it is not a feeling of pleasure, admits something near an Aristotelian cultivation, a disposition that can be awakened by habit. Kant writes:

> So the saying "you ought to love your neighbor as yourself" does not mean that you ought immediately (first) to love him and (afterwards) by means of this love to do good to him. It means, rather, to do good to your fellow human beings, and your beneficence will produce love of them in you (as an aptitude of the inclination to beneficence in general. (*Doctrine of Virtue*, 6:402)

For this reason, Kant distinguishes the virtue of love from the love in which one feels pleasure or satisfaction. Moreover, we cannot have a duty to love if love were to be understood as a feeling or pleasure, because a duty cannot constrain someone to have pathological feelings, nor can moral law induce someone to love somebody.

The duty to love must be understood as a principle of benevolence that consists, not in wanting the good of others without contributing practically to it, but rather in a practical benevolence, or beneficence, that consists in considering the good of others an as end in itself. *The benevolence principle* will produce, in turn, the *duties of beneficence* (to help the needy to find their happiness) and of *gratitude* (to honor a person for a favor that was received) and of sympathy (*Teilnehmung*). Kant accepts that to participate in the pain or joy of others is, without a doubt, a feeling, which cannot serve as a material determination for morality. The introduction of this feeling of sympathy must be interpreted, however, not as a ground of determination for the action, but as a natural feeling that we must use in order to accomplish benevolent actions. It will be our duty, therefore, to cultivate in us that sympathetic feeling, although the moral law should not be based on that, but on pure reason.

In the *Doctrine of Virtue*, Kant presents a more complex moral theory on the role of the feelings in relation to moral actions. Even though sympathy can be an incentive for the accomplishment of a moral action (or an incitement to practical love), this does not mean that all sharing of feelings is positive. We can see it in the division of the humanity in *humanitas practica*, "the capacity and the will to share in others' feelings," and *humanitas aesthetica*, "the receptivity, given by nature itself, to the feeling of joy and sadness in common with others" (*Doctrine of Virtue*, 6:456). The first one is desirable, but not the second, because the first one is free and depends on the will, while the second is spread among people, "since it is like receptivity to warmth or contagious diseases" (6:457).

The reason for praising the *humanitas practica* and disapproving the *humanitas aesthetica* is that compassion, when not followed by a practical action, is a way to increase the evil in the world. If a friend is suffering and I cannot do anything to diminish his pain, I have no duty of being sympathetic to his feelings, because this would only make me increase the suffering and troubles of the world.

Kant without a doubt recognizes that feelings of sympathy may play the role of moral incentive when the representation of the duty by itself will not be enough, "for this is still one of the impulses that nature has implanted in us to do what the representation of duty alone might not accomplish" (*Doctrine of Virtue*, 6:458). The feeling of sympathy is added to a moral incentive (respect) to accomplish the moral action. If the representation of the law will not be enough to bring about the action, it is a duty to promote our natural good feelings to add a natural incentive to a rational moral one. Going, therefore, beyond the spirit of the *Groundwork*, Kant admits that sympathy, duly cultivated to answer to the correct situations, can be the incentive of a moral action that is carried through by the motive of duty. In this case, this duty must be understood on two levels: first, one to carry out moral actions; second, a derived duty to use natural feelings when the consideration about the moral correction of the action is not enough to start the action.

The role that Kant attributes to sympathy is, therefore, of a provisional moral feeling, which can assist in the accomplishment of good actions, when the feeling of respect for the moral law is not yet sufficiently developed. As Nancy Sherman argues, this is a morality *faute de mieux*, that is, a type of provisional morality: it is a morality of an inferior type, an immature morality that finally will be substituted in the progress of the individual. Sherman, however, admits that feelings such as sympathy, compassion, and love possess a perceptive moral role in Kant, that is, that "we still require the pathological emotions to know when and where these ends [of the moral law and its spheres of justice and virtue] are appropriate."[6]

Sherman seems to be correct and faithful to the texts when she examines the provisional role of feelings such as compassion, love, sympathy, since Kant really admits a function for these in the accomplishment of moral actions, when the mere respect for the law will not be strong enough to trigger the action. The perceptive role, however, is more doubtful, since the idea that emotions are blind seems to remain a constant in the Kantian corpus, without variations from the *Groundwork* to the *Doctrine of Virtue*. The critique of sympathy as a possible incentive for a moral action was based, in the case of the philanthropist, not in the absence of contempt for sympathy in itself, but in the idea that sympathy, for itself, could not show us which course of action is the moral one. A good example given in the contemporary literature is supplied by Barbara Herman: we hear somebody crying out for aid to load something heavy, we help this person, later we come to know that a sculpture from an art museum was stolen by a thief. In this example, one ended helping a thief to carry out his misdemeanor. And this was done out of sympathy.

In the *Doctrine of Virtue*, sympathy can play the role of a moral incentive, if it is trained and controlled by the will, which will also tell when this feeling must be activated. This is the reason why humanity is divided into free and nonfree humanity. The free humanity (*humanitas practica*) is the capacity and the will to use the feeling of sympathy to promote the happiness of others, which includes a procedure to decide in which cases I must set in motion these feelings. A stoic that decides that he will not set in motion his feelings of sympathy, acts in such a way because he knows he cannot do anything to help his friend; however, if he had something practical that he could do, he would activate his feelings of compassion, since these would have as consequence a real beneficent action. Consequently, in this new vision of sympathy presented in the *Doctrine of Virtue*, this feeling is capable of being controlled by reason, which contradicts the negative approach of sympathy presented in the *Groundwork* and is confirmed by the *Mrongovius Anthropology* lecture transcripts (1784/85). According to these notes, one of the reasons that sympathy is inappropriate as an incentive is its sensible register: "If [sympathy with joy and pain] becomes an affect, then the human being becomes unhappy. The human being becomes, through sympathy, only sensible and he does not help others" (*Anthropology Mrongovius*, 25:1348).

So, in order to make sympathy effective and turn it into beneficence, one should go to hospitals and other places in order to see other people's suffering; it is a duty, says Kant, "not to avoid the places where the poor who lack the most basic necessities are to be found but rather to seek them out, and not to shun sickrooms or debtors' prisons and so forth in order to avoid sharing painful feelings one may not be able to resist" (*Doctrine of Virtue*, 6:457). This *habitus* does not aim at developing compassionate personalities, but rather at training our feelings of compassion and sympathy so that they can be used as a means to accomplish good actions. However, the feelings of love, sympathy, and compassion are, in themselves, morally blind, depending on moral principles to be set in motion in the correct situation.

Desire, Affect, and Passion: The Anthropologic Modalities of Love

In the book *Anthropology from a Pragmatic Point of View* (1798), Kant presents his division of faculties: the faculty of knowledge, the faculty of pleasure, and the faculty of desire. In his division, affects, appetites, or inclinations in general belong either to the feeling of pleasure and displeasure, or to the faculty of desire. To the faculty of desire belong the instincts, propensities, inclinations, and passions (*Anthropology*, 7:265); affects belong to the faculty of the feeling of pleasure and displeasure.

A first and primitive level of love could be attributed to instinct, according to the division of the faculty of desire. The mating instinct is common to human beings and animals, and sexual desire in itself does not possess anything related to morality or to the promotion of dignity. In the *Doctrine of Right*, Kant defines the sexual union as a use that a human being makes of the sexual capacities of the other; "in this act," he claims, "a human being makes himself into a thing, which conflicts with the right of humanity" (*Doctrine of Right*, 6:278). The only way to restitute his personality is to possess the other equally as a thing. The difference between prostitution and marriage consists in the fact that marriage preserves the right of humanity only by adding the contractual aspect that gives the right to use the other in turn. "In marriage, the other has the right to use your sexual organs, but you have the right to use theirs, and moreover you have the exclusive possession of that use (a right never enjoyed by either prostitutes or their customers).[7]

After this first instinctive and natural level of love there follows a second one, which belongs to the category of affects, stormy and temporary feelings, which make reflection and deliberation on action difficult. The love-affect must be distinguished from the love-passion, since passion, even if it is violent, may coexist with reason and "takes its time and reflects, no matter how fierce it may be, in order to reach its end" (*Anthropology*, 7:252). Kant metaphorically explains the differences between affect and passion: "Affect works on our health like an apoplectic fit; passion, like consumption or emaciation. Affect is like drunkenness that one sleeps off, although a headache follows afterward; but passion is regarded as a sickness that comes from swallowing poison" (*Anthropology*, 7:252). It can be seen here that love-affect differs from the love-passion with regard to the intensity, duration, and degree of danger of each emotion. The first one is more intense; however, it does not last as long as, and is less dangerous than passion. For this reason, Kant affirms that where there is much affect, there is little passion, since stormy emotions are depleted quickly, and do not allow the cold evaluation of the lived situation and the deliberation on reaching an end: "Affects are honest and open, passions on the other hand are deceitful and hidden" (*Anthropology*, 7:252). While affects are genuine explosions of emotions, passions can, in turn, coexist with dissimulation. The innocence of the love-affect compared with the dissimulation of the love-passion can be evidenced in the following situation: "In the presence of his beloved, a serious lover is embarrassed, awkward, and not very captivating. But a man who merely *pretends* to be in love and has talent can play his role so naturally that he gets the poor, deceived girl completely into his trap, just because his heart is unaffected and his head is clear" (*Anthropology*, 7:264). The love-affect resembles the feeling of falling in love with someone, denoting a romantic, uncontrollable love, whose manifestation can make the person blind to the defects of the objects of desire: "The person who *loves* to be sure can still remain quite clear-sighted; but the person who *falls in love* is inevitably blind to the faults of the beloved object, though the latter person will usually regain his sight a week after the wedding" (*Anthropology*, 7:253). The emotion of this passionate person is an affect, in Kantian terms. The term passion is reserved for more deliberative attitudes, being able to coexist with a cunning dissimulation, since this, as shown in the example above, can contribute to possession of the object of desire. Therefore, Kant affirms that passions are not like affects; affects, at least, may coexist with a good intention, while passions reject any attempt of improvement. Such is the case when a person acts moved by a strong affect, what Kant characterizes as a weakness of the will. Passion, on the contrary, chooses a principle in accordance with inclination. The passion of love, however, possesses an advantage regarding other passions, such as ambition, vanity, or greed, which are illnesses of reason because they possess a permanent character, since, according to Kant, "they are never completely satisfied" (*Anthropology*, 7:266). The passion of love, in contrast, ceases when the desire, or the physical love, is satisfied. If it is possible to go crazy because of obsession caused by other passions, such as ambition, vanity, and greed, the saying that one "went crazy because of love" contains some implausibility; therefore the one who went crazy because of a refusal by the one loved was already disturbed enough to have chosen the wrong person as the object of his affect and desires. Such was the case, very common at the time of Kant, of people who fall in love with others of a superior social level: "Falling in love with a person from a class of whom to expect marriage is the greatest folly was not the cause but rather the effect of madness" (*Anthropology*,

7:217). This seems to have happened to Kant himself, when, in the years 1762–63 he fell in love with a student who would later marry someone richer and of a better social level than his own.

Love, in the form of affect or passion, even in its most violent manifestation, is not so harmful as the passions of ambition, vanity, and greed. However, it is not as helpful to morality as the feeling of sympathy, since love implies a feeling between dissimilar people. Or, as Kant writes in one of the *Reflections* grouped in the *Nachlass* on Anthropology: "We need to be honored more than to be loved, but we also need something that we can love with whom we are not in rivalry. So we love a bird, a dog, or a young, fickle and darling person" (*R*1471, 15:649).

Although, apparently, this claim reveals a prejudice of the time regarding feminine inferiority, in another *Reflexion*, Kant affirms that "men and women possess a reciprocal superiority over one another" (*R*1100, 15:490). Despite the fact that this superiority of each one is relative to different aspects, the reciprocal inequality is what stimulates and promotes love as affect or passion. The fact that these feelings need a reciprocal moral inequality indicates that their *locus* is strange to morality, which consists of considering the other as equal and promoting its happiness.

Conclusion

The figures of love assume different positions in the Kantian philosophy, some have moral value, others do not. Love as benevolence can be considered a practical principle—to do good and to help people, from which the love for the others can also be awakened. This was clear in the analysis of the Kantian text, where it is said that it is not necessary to love and, therefore, to do good to human beings, but only to act morally, and through this habit, to awaken feelings of sympathy for human beings. The feeling of sympathy can also be used by the agent to stimulate moral actions in which the respect for the moral law was not strong enough as an incentive. This is not in opposition to what is explained in the *Groundwork*, in which the moral value of an action resides in the fact that respect for the law is the incentive for the action. To use the feeling of sympathy is only a provisional morality that, empirically, can and must use these feelings of pleasure and displeasure for other people's fate to encourage good actions, until our respect for the law is sufficiently strong to be a possible incentive.

Relative to affects and passions, even if both were criticized as illnesses of reason, the negative effect of the love-affect is less dangerous than the persistence and inversion of principles in the love-passion. However, since the passion of love ceases when its physical desire is satisfied, it does not have the persistence of other cultural passions. However, such feelings of love are not useful to morality, since the love-affect or love-passion are awakened from an idea of inequality alien to morality.

Finally, it is important to emphasize that the analysis of feelings, inclinations, and passions in the *Doctrine of Virtue* and *Anthropology* does not contradict the spirit of the *Groundwork*, since the action with true moral value is still the one whose incentive is respect for the law, and that does not hinder us in using our sensible feelings, such as sympathy, for the purposes of reason.

Notes

1. I take the word "sympathy" as translation for *Teilnehmung*, instead of the word "compassion." *Affekt* will be translated by the word "affect," and *Leidenschaft* by the word "passion." I will reserve the word "emotions" for a generic term that denotes moral feelings, affection, and passions.

2. Hume also doubts the existence of a creature in which sympathy was completely absent, which he calls a "monster of fancy." "It can be said that it does not have such a human creature, for whom the happiness of the others did not provoke pleasure (where it did not have place for envy or revenge), and the appearance of suffering, pain." David Hume, *An Essay Concerning the Principles of Morals*, ed. J. B. Schneewind (Indianapolis: Hacket, 1983), 52.

3. Barbara Herman, *The Practice of Moral Judgment* (Cambridge: Cambridge University Press, 1993), 1.

4. Christine Korsgaard, *Creating the Kingdom of Ends* (Cambridge: Cambridge University Press, 1996), 59.

5. Allen Wood, *Kant's Ethical Thought* (Cambridge: Cambridge University Press, 1999), 196.

6. Nancy Sherman, "The Place of Emotions in Kantian Morality," in Owen Flanagan and Amélie Oksenberg Rorty, *Identity, Character, and Morality: Essays in Moral Psychology* (Cambridge: MIT Press, 1990), 159.

7. Wood, *Kant's Ethical Thought*, 258.

15

The Meaning of the Term *Gemüt* in Kant

Valerio Rohden

Problems of Translation

This essay was born out of difficulties with the translation of the term *Gemüt* that I ran into while working on a Portuguese translation of Immanuel Kant's *Critique of the Power of Judgment*.[1]

By *Gemüt* Kant means the principle that unifies the various faculties that are in reciprocal relations to one another; it has a cognitive transcendental sense and also an animating aesthetic sense for the cognitive faculties. In addition to that, Kant takes the term *Geist* (spirit) as the faculty that creates genius, which he in part differentiates from *Geist* as the spirit of taste. In the latter sense, *Geist* means the same as *esprit* for the French, who, according to Kant, have good taste, but not *Geist* in its proper sense (*R*931, 15:413). *Geist* is the animating principle of our *Gemütskrafte* (powers of the *Gemüt*). Apprehending the *Gemüt* prior to any particular, its "genius consists in this capacity to create the universal and the ideal" (*R*932, 15:413.) Last, Kant takes the term *Seele* (soul) in general to be a metaphysical substance.

Kant provides for the term *Gemüt* the Latin counterparts *animus* and *mens* in the *Opus Postumum*: "Es ist im menschlichen Gemüt (mens, animus) als reinem, nichts als Seele des Menschen einwohnendes empirisch/praktisches . . . Prinzip" [It is in the human *Gemüt* (mens, animus) as a pure principle, not as an empirical/practical principle living in men's soul]. "Erfahrung wovon haben ist ein Akt des Gemüts (animus ohne anima zu heissen)" [To have an experience of something is an act of the *Gemüt* (animus, but not anima)] (*Opus Postumum*, 22:112, 484).

Unlike other languages, Spanish, Portuguese, and Italian have terms that correspond to the Latin *animus* and *mens*. English has only the term *mind* to translate both *mens* and *animus*. French does not have an equivalent for

This is a revised, but not substantially modified translation of an article first published as "O sentido do termo *Gemüt* em Kant," in *Analytica* 1, no. 1 (1993): 61–76. Translated by Rogério Passos Severo; revised by A. Blom.

either, and for that reason *Gemüt* is translated into *esprit* (spirit), and *Geist* (which should be "spirit") into *âme* (soul). Hence, French translations end up without a term for translating *Seele* (which should be *âme*). I personally think that the French would do well to introduce the Latin term *animus* as a translation for German *Gemüt*; then they would have for the term *Geist* its equivalent *esprit*, and for the term *Seele* its equivalent *âme*.[2]

On the term *Gemüt*, I differ from Hermann Friedmann, who states with some exaggeration that the lack of a term in a language may mean also the lack of the thing it designates.[3] I also think that it is wrong to think that we have here a concept obscure by nature and therefore scientifically useless. Rather, in regard to this term in Kant, the problem is that the concept has been misunderstood.[4]

As an introduction, I would like to note schematically:

1. Latin itself and some Romance languages can quite adequately translate the term *Gemüt* as *animus* and *mens*. Portuguese, for example, can translate it as *ânimo* and *mente*.
2. The term *animus* is more readily related than *mens* to the German word *Mut* (courage, disposition)—and to the English word *mood*—and also to *Gemüt* in its aesthetic sense (life), but less so to *Ge-Mut* (joining of faculties) in its transcendental sense.
3. Specialized dictionaries, however, unanimously give for the terms *animus* and *mens* a common sense as the *locus* of the faculties of cognition, feeling, and desire. Even the Grimm dictionary acknowledges that *Gemüt* was for a long time identified with *mens* and *animus*. It contains an interesting quote, according to which *Gemüt* is the king of the soul who decides between the heart and reason, and adds: "In Kant *Gemüt* is still the same as *animus*, quite differently from today."[5]
4. The translation of *Gemüt* into the Portuguese *ânimo* [*animus*] or *mente* [*mens*=mind], however, has some inconveniences:

   (a) The term *ânimo* carries with it an ambiguity, as it points predominantly in the direction of *Gemüt* as a feeling.
   (b) The term *mente* [*mind*] is predominantly associated with the cognitive faculties (as is the case in Robert Paul Wolff's *Kant's Theory of* Mental *Activity*).[6]
   (c) The term *mente* is also confused, in contemporary philosophies of mind, with the metaphysical sense of "spirit," as Peter Bieri has shown in *Analytische Philosophie des Geistes*. According to Bieri, "mental is opposed to physical as a *terminus technicus* that applies to all phenomena which count as non-physical in an ontological dualism. . . . And mental correctly evokes the Cartesian *mens*, and

not the Aristotelian psyche."[7] He concludes that "philosophy of the spirit" is the best title for the analysis of our familiar mentalistic theory of persons: "Using Strawson's phrase, philosophy of the spirit can be said the 'descriptive metaphysics' of the mental."[8]

However, adopting a Kantian sense of *Gemüt*, Hannah Arendt published in English *The Life of the Mind*.[9] The first volume was about thinking, the second was on the will, and the third, unwritten, would have been about judgment.

5. To avoid, at least on my part, the above-mentioned ambiguities,[10] but also with an eye on the construction of a more philosophical language, which would consider not only usage but also reasons for or against a given terminology, I think that one should opt for the translation of *Gemüt* into [the Portuguese] *ânimo*, favored also by Kant as *animus*.

Source of Ambiguities: The Degeneration of the Meaning of *Gemüt*

In his reflections on anthropology, Kant borrowed some phrases on *Gemüt* from Baumgarten's *Psychologia Empirica*. In *Reflection* 165, for example, Kant uses *Sammlung des Gemüts* (gathering of the *animus*) for Baumgarten's phrase *animi collection* (*R*165, 15:61). Baumgarten introduces the term *animus*, in the section on *intellectus*, abruptly and without any prior justification. When referring to the faculty of desire, he uses the phrase *elateres animi*, which Kant takes on as *Triebfeder des Gemüts* (impulsive causes of the *animus*), calling the faculty of desire, insofar as it follows the higher cognitive faculty, *animus*.[11] But both in Baumgarten and in Kant, *Gemüt* comprehends higher and lower faculties, which can be in conflict with each other (*dissensus*) or in harmony with regard to stimuli (*Triebfedern*) that may or may not be opposed to the determination of the motives (*Beweggründe*).

Since there is no theory of the *Gemüt* in Kant, I will limit myself in this paper to a description of how he used the term in several passages, which I will quote. In the few existing investigations on *Gemüt* by other authors, I have not found any that addresses Kant's use of that concept, which according to Hans Vaihinger was Kant's *Lieblingsausdruck*. Stephen Strassner, who was one of the few contemporary philosophers to have taken up the topic, spoke of it from a phenomenological perspective and assigned to it the role of integrating the spirit. In *Das Gemüt* (1956), Strassner dedicated less than a line to Kant, in which he mistakenly asserts that "in Kant *Gemüt* is almost a synonym of *Seele* (soul)."[12] Likewise mistaken is Friedman's *Das Gemüt*.[13] He identified *Gemüt* with the Greek *thymós*, which means affection and passion. In each of these authors we find a different mistake: the former identifies the *Gemüt* with a metaphysical substance, and the latter reduces it to the senses. Whereas in Kant the term meant the totality of the transcendental faculties, today its meaning has been reduced to the faculty of feelings, thus open to values. Already in his *Aesthetic*, Hegel identified it with the heart, as opposed to the abstract universality of the will. According to Lersch, *Gemüt* is an experience that happens whenever there is something that we care about (*am Herzen liegt*), or whenever we have to step outside of the environment that had become familiar to us. The concept that would best explain that experience is that of *binding* (*religare*, in Latin), according to which *Gemüt* is an emotional participation of values in man, essences, or things, and a connection with them in an experience of mutual belonging.[14] In this reductionistic conception of *Gemüt*, I think it is a positive fact that an aspect of Kant's concept has been retained, namely, that *Gemüt* constitutes a link that takes someone beyond himself: to others and to the world. Moreover, Goethe's claim commenting on the reduction of *Gemüt* to the sentimental realm seems to me still applicable: "The Germans should refrain from pronouncing the word *Gemüt* for next thirty years; then the *Gemüt* would regenerate itself. Nowadays it means tolerance for one's own and other people's weaknesses."[15]

Confirming this *Empfindelei* criticized by Goethe, Friedman goes as far as asserting that in the meaning of *Gemüt* "the feminine has a substantive primacy."[16] He also says that for Kant the term means a unification of all the sensory representations in the *Gemüt*. So it is not surprising that he found in the Greek term *thymós* the most perfect equivalent for the German term *Gemüt*. Nevertheless, he contributes to the clarification of the meaning of *Gemüt* on two fronts:

1. He calls attention to the fact that the prefix *Ge* is a sign of integration and reunification, which is something we also find in the *Deustches Wörterbuch* by the brothers Grimm. Thus *Gebirge* means mountain range, *Gewissen* means all knowledge about good and evil, *Gestirn* means constellation. Furthermore, *ge* in a verb characterizes the perfect tense, and signals the perfect conclusion of an action; and in nouns the predominantly neutral gender indicates a universal function, and therefore an integrating function. Thus we may ask what does the *Gemüt* bring together? According to the logic of Friedman's thought, it brings together a great number of *Muten* (dispositions): *Hochmut* (haughtiness, pride), *Übermut* (wantonness, joy), *Kleinmut* (faint-heartedness), *Grossmut* (generosity), etc. This is part of the meaning of the term. Another part is better indicated by the Wahrig dictionary when it refers *Mut* to (*obsolete*) *muot*, which means powers or faculties: therefore *Ge-Mut* means the totality of the faculties of thought, feeling, and willing.[17]

2. Friedman called attention to the sense of *Gemüt* as an objective and intersubjective formative principle: "Wherever a form (*Gestalt*) manifests itself in a given object, i.e., whenever an object comes to the presence of man, who then experiences it, the *Gemüt* also bursts forth inside him."[18] "At the moment man breaks off from a *Ge-meinschaft* (community) that he needs, life loses its meaning (*Gemütskrankheit*=dementia), because *Gemüt* is a quality not only of individual but also of collective life."[19] Some aspects of the Kantian conception are already implicit in what I have said so far: it is a faculty that integrates not only faculties but also people insofar as they participate in a common life. Below we shall see in more detail the two meanings of *Gemüt* in Kant: the transcendental and the aesthetic.

A General Transcendental Faculty

In the *Critique of Pure Reason*, *Gemüt* appears as the totality of all transcendental faculties. Near the end of the introduction, Kant refers without naming to a common and unknown root of the various stems of cognition: "All that seems necessary for an introduction or preliminary is that there are two stems of human cognition, which may perhaps arise from a common but to us unknown root, namely sensibility and understanding" (*Pure Reason*, A15/B29). Already in the introduction to the Transcendental Logic, Kant begins by saying that cognition is grounded on two sources of the *Gemüt*: "Our cognition arises from two fundamental sources in the *Gemüt*, the first of which is the reception of representations (the receptivity of impressions), the second the faculty of cognizing an object by means of these representations (spontaneity of concepts)" (*Pure Reason*, A50/B74). Knowledge is thus part of the outcome of the integration of two faculties. In this sense we may say that the transcendental doctrine of elements of the first *Critique* can be considered as a development of a transcendental theory of the *Gemüt*. But for that to be the case, Vaihinger writes, Kant would have to have been more explicit about his *Lieblingsausdruck* "on whose use he is silent for the rest of the *Critique of Pure Reason*."[20] In two other texts we find the above-mentioned definition. In "Aus Sömmering: Über das Organ der Seele" (1796), Kant writes: "By *Gemüt* we mean only the faculty of combining the given representations and effectuating the unity of empirical apperception (*animus*), not yet the substance (*anima*) according to its nature, which is entirely distinct from that matter, and from which it is abstracted here" (*Soemmerring*, 12:32). In the *Anthropology*, Kant says that the *Gemüt* is "represented as a mere faculty of feeling and thinking" (*Anthropology*, 7:161). Therefore, while using the term *Gemüt* in its transcendental sense Kant abstains from using the metaphysically loaded term *Seele* (soul): "Kant thus favors the word *Gemüt* because of its neutrality and noncommittal character; he wants to avoid the word *Seele*."[21] On the other hand, the Kantian concept cannot be reduced to a faculty of feeling, because then it cannot account for the theoretical, practical, and aesthetic functions that it also has.

At the end of the introduction to the *Critique of the Power of Judgment*, Kant presents the general faculties of the *Gemüt* in a table: the faculty of cognition, of the feeling of pleasure and displeasure, and of desire (See *Judgment*, 5:198). According to the *Anthropology*, each of these faculties is subdivided into a sensitive and an intellectual faculty. These faculties, insofar as they have autonomy, are called higher. Their autonomy comes from their apriority. The autonomy of the cognitive faculty is based on the constitutive principles of the understanding—namely, conformity to laws; that of the faculty of the feeling of pleasure and displeasure is based on the principle of the power of judgment—namely, conformity to ends independent of concepts or sensations; and that of the faculty of desire on the principle of reason—namely, the final end (*Endzweck*). Within the *Gemüt* this concept of the conformity to ends of the power of judgment plays a fundamental role in mediating between the concepts of nature and freedom. These realms are connected by the spontaneity of the faculties of cognition, whereby the feeling of pleasure finds the foundation of the agreement of these faculties. According to that table, we have here an application of the *Gemüt* to these concepts through art. That is, they would not act directly on each other but would be separated by a bridgeless abyss, although freedom may, insofar as it is intelligible, act without contradiction on human nature by means of a use of the concept of final end. The power of judgment facilitates this mediation through the concept of purposiveness. Hence, if it is the power of judgment that provides the rule for this mediation, then we may say that the whole articulation between the faculties of the *Gemüt* is based on the power of judgment.

According to the third section of the introduction to the *Critique of the Power of Judgment*, the faculties of higher cognition (understanding, judgment, and reason) make up a family, which is connected by the power of judgment. The power of judgment connects them without having a legislation of its own. It does have a principle and a certain territory of its own, but no domain of objects. Nonetheless, Kant claims that in explaining the passage from the faculty of cognition to the faculty of desire by means of the power of judgment, the relationship that the faculties of representation (of cognition, feeling of pleasure and displeasure, and desire) have among themselves is more important than the cognitive relationship. The notions of "family" and "relationship" have to do with the nature of the *Gemüt*: it constitutes a series of faculties insofar as they can be derived from a common foundation (*aus einem gemeinschaftlichen Grunde*) (*Judgment*, 5:177), whose autonomy can be called "activity of connecting and separating representations."

From both theoretical and practical perspectives, Kant established an imbalance among the faculties by giving primacy now to understanding, now to reason. From the aesthetic perspective, in its turn, there is a primacy of the faculty of imagination, or perhaps an equilibrium among the faculties, so much so that the presence of laws cannot be noticed in them. It was this way that Friedrich Schiller aesthetically understood the *Gemüt*:

> The *Gemüt* goes from sensations to thought through an intermediary disposition, in which sensibility and reason are *simultaneously* active; precisely because of that they suppress their determining power, and by a contraposition produce a negation. This intermediary disposition, in which the *Gemüt* is neither physically nor morally coerced, and is nonetheless active in both ways, deserves primarily to be called a free disposition.[22]

In the aesthetic state, the *Gemüt* is free to the highest degree. Kant criticized the application of this conception to ethics, but would not have done so if he were approaching it from its properly aesthetic perspective.

The Aesthetic Sense of Gemüt

I now turn to a more thorough explanation of the aesthetic conception of the *Gemüt*. In the *Critique of the Power of Judgment* this concept is elucidated in close connection to the concept of life, and is articulated by means of a relation among the faculties. The judgment of taste only has as its goal a relation of the faculties of representation, which comes about as a promotion of life.

In the "General Remark on the Exposition of Aesthetic Reflective Judgments," Kant writes: "the *Gemüt* for itself is entirely life (the principle of life itself)" (*das Gemüt ist für sich allein ganz Leben [das Lebensprinzip selbst]*) (*Judgment*, 5:278). What does it mean to say that the *Gemüt* is entirely life? The concept of life is defined as "the faculty of a being to act in accordance with its representations" (*Metaphysics of Morals*, 6:211). Representations are ends that the agent sets for itself. Life is a capacity to act according to its own ends. A state of *Gemüt* can be represented as in agreement with an end without it needing to represent that end; it suffices that we represent it according to a certain form, which can be attained by abstracting from the end or from the matter through reflection. Agreement with the subjective conditions of life is called pleasure. Whenever there is such an agreement, life is promoted. Consciousness of that pleasure is consciousness that life is being promoted. Thus, the pleasure we experience in aesthetic judgment is that of a feeling that a certain form of life is being promoted. The feeling of pleasure and the feeling of life are identical: "Here the representation is related entirely to the subject, indeed to its feeling of life, under the name of the feeling of pleasure and displeasure" (*Judgment*, 5:204). More forcefully, Kant wrote in a Reflection: "Consensus with life: pleasure" (*Der consensus mit dem Leben: die Lust*) (*R*1021, 15:457).

The terms *Gemüt* and "life" are related to one another in four different ways: (1) in the interplay of the faculties themselves; (2) in the relation between the faculties of genius and taste; (3) in the relation between *Gemüt* and body; and (4) in the idea of a communal sense.

First, the promotion of life happens through the free play of the faculties of the *Gemüt*, whereby it is animated. According to Kant, poetry is the best example of a complete animation of the *Gemüt*. In poetry the *Gemüt* is completely active in a concert of its faculties. It is through this complete involvement of the faculties of the *Gemüt* that poetry attains maximum beauty: "Poetry is the most beautiful of all play, for it involves all of our powers of *Gemüt*" (*Poesi ist das schönste aller Spiele, indem wir alle Gemütskräfte darin versetzen*) (*R*618, 15:266).

In order for us to appreciate the meaning of this conception in our own time, I quote from the poet Carlos Drummond de Andrade's "The Magic Word":

> A word slumbers within the shadows
> of a rare book.
> Can we disenchant it?
> It is the key to life
> the key to the world
> I'll go look for it.[23]

The animation of the *Gemüt* by means of the free play of the faculties is not distinct from the very notion of beauty, so much so that beauty is defined as awareness that life is being promoted: "Beautiful is that phenomenon which awakens in intuition the awareness that life is being promoted" (*R*789, 15:345). That is why we dwell on its contemplation and renew ourselves through it.

Second, genius is made up by a certain unification of the faculties of imagination and understanding, in which the concept of understanding takes material from the free play of the imagination, not objectively so as to know it, but subjectively so as to animate the cognitive faculties. The principle of this animation is the spirit (*Geist*): "**Spirit**, in an aesthetic significance, means the animating principle in the *Gemüt*" (*Judgment*, 5:313). The Latin term *genius* is made up of *gigno*, which means precisely "the generator of life." The animating principle of the genius is the faculty of presenting aesthetic ideas, that is, unlimited representations of the faculty of imagination, which provide plenty of material for thought but for which no concept can account, and which are formed on the basis of attributes (a large quantity of representations that are akin to one another, linked by their free use). Kant gives an example of these attributes by quoting a poem comparing the radiance of a sunset with the end of a virtuous man's life: the poet "animates his idea of reason of a cosmopolitan disposition even at the end of life by means of an attribute" (*Judgment*, 5:316) (a series of parallel sensations and representations for which one finds no expression). Genius consists in finding ideas for a given concept and expressing them in such a way that the subjective disposition of the *Gemüt* can be communicated. By apprehending the flow of the faculty of imagination—beauty is the expression of the ephemeral—and unifying it in a concept, the genius communicates something previously inexpressible without coercing taste. To achieve that communicability the genius or artist must discipline his lawless freedom and laboriously adapt himself to taste. "The genius is subject to the tribunal (*Richterstuhl*) of taste" (*R*876, 15:384). In other words, taste becomes the main faculty, because it is in it and for it as a public sphere that communication can materialize. Therefore, spirit is an animation of taste.

Third, spirit (*Geist*) is animation by means of ideas. Thus we can understand that that action happens in relation to the body. Beauty awakens in us a sensation of our adaptation to the world (but, I should add, more than just that, also an adaptation to the human universe). We have already seen that man can be a rational-animal unity only through beauty; through it he feels connected to a body, and it is in that connection that life finds its promotion and its obstacles. The sentence I quoted above—the *Gemüt* for itself is entirely life—occurs in the context of an agreement with Epicurus that delight and pain (*Vergnügen* and *Schmerz*) are ultimately corporeal and that awareness of one's well or ill being depends on that relation:

> Because life without the feeling of the corporeal organ is merely consciousness of one's existence, but not a feeling of well- or ill-being, i.e., of promotion or inhibition of the powers of life; because the *Gemüt* for itself is entirely life (the principle of life itself), and hindrances or promotions must be sought outside it, though in the human being himself, hence in combination with his body. (*Judgment*, 5:278)

This connection of the *Gemüt* with the body is not exterior, insofar as it happens through sensibility, in whose domain aesthetic reflection takes place. Kant thinks that life is animated by a principle that unifies man: "The principle of life seems to be a principle of unification of soul and body that acts by itself and over which the will has no sway" (*R*1033, 15:463).

I have tried to illustrate, with these forms of exercising taste and spiritual action, what an animation of the *Gemüt* is. In these examples, animation happens by an interplay of the faculties of imagination and understanding that includes sensibility and reflection, and therefore not only reason but also sensations and the animal side of man.

Fourth, what I mean is that, on the one hand, this animation happens through a relation of the faculties, but on the other hand—and this is what I want to highlight—it is based on an idea of human community: animation is verified on the basis of an idea of *sensus communis* (a communitarian sense for Kant), in which pleasure comes from a universal point of view taken up in the act of judging, virtually including in it the judgments of all others. Kant said in the *Anthropology* that taste is a social faculty: "a faculty of making social judgments of external objects within the power of imagination" (*Anthropology*, 7:241). Taste, as judgment itself, is a *sensus communis*, a common sense. "Sense" here means the outcome of reflection on the *Gemüt*. That is, reflection makes the *Gemüt* common by elevating and extending it to a universal point of view, from which it judges while including everyone else's points of view in the act of judging. Thus, the *Gemüt* does not animate itself only through an internal play of the faculties, but also through an intersubjective communicability of people with one another.

I highlighted the communitarian sense of *Gemüt*. Concluding this paper I would like to make explicit its freedom, and show that the pleasure by which it is animated is a pleasure in its freedom. The *Gemüt*, as a principle of life, is a principle of activity. The more active or spontaneous it is, the more aware of life it will be. "Life is self-activity" (*R*574, 15:248). Life has an essential dynamic of shifts between pleasure and displeasure, hope and fear, work and rest, alertness and dream. Because of its restlessness, the *Gemüt* is always driving toward change. It finds rest in a harmonious play of representations and in free beauty itself. But while beauty satisfies it, it is the spirit (*Geist*) that puts it in motion. *Geist* is the very freedom of the *Gemüt*. Freedom, which is the principle of the *Gemüt*, manifests itself mainly through judgment as an election of a life in common, a free and communicative life as the maximum form of life in man.

We know that judgment, when disinterested, is free and universal. We have seen that it grounds its condition of possibility on the idea of a communitarian sense, and that (according to the *Anthropology*) it is a faculty of social judgment. In this social judgment, the *Gemüt* feels free: "Here the *Gemüt* feels its freedom in the play of images (therefore of sensibility); for sociability with other human beings presupposes freedom—and this feeling is pleasure" (*Anthropology*, 7:241). This form of originary life that is the life of the *Gemüt* is accomplished by reflection insofar as it is free and universal. This is something I find expressed more explicitly in the following Reflection, from the critical period (1780–90):

> Freedom is the original life and, in its coherence, the condition of the correspondence of all life; hence that which [*crossed out*: increases] promotes the feeling of universal life, or the feeling of promotion of universal life, produces a

pleasure. Do we, however, ourselves feel good in the universal life? Universality makes all our feelings agree, although there is no special type of sensation of this universality. It is a form of *consensus*. (*R*6862, 19:183)

I hope to have contributed a little to the understanding of *Gemüt*, which is above all the perspective of faculties in reciprocal relations as a whole. The interpretation of the *Gemüt* in relation to the concept of life is no more than the elucidation of what Kant said in the first paragraph of his third *Critique*. The relation between *Gemüt* and a universal form of life seems to me to present a renewed way of thinking about Kant's aesthetic.

Notes

1. The translation was made by António Marques and myself, and published in Brazil by Editora Forense Universitária, Rio de Janeiro, 1993, and in Portugal by Imprensa Nacional/Casa da Moeda, 1992. English editions of Kant's works usually translate the term *Gemüt* as "mind."

2. On the confusions brought about by the various translations of the terms *Gemüt*, *Geist*, and *Seele*, see the comparative chart on §49 of the third *Critique* in my paper "El término *Gemüt* en la *Crítica de la facultad de juzgar*," in *Filosofia, política, y estética en la Crítica del juício de Kant: Actas del Colóquio de Lima comemorativo de bicentenário de la tercera Crítica*, ed. David Sobrevilla (Lima: Goethe-Institut, 1991), 50–51.

3. Hermann Friedmann, *Das Gemüt: Gedanken zu einer Thymologie* (Munich: C. H. Beck, 1956), 1.

4. Miguel Giusti, "Nota sobre el origen del significado del concepto de 'espíritu' en Hegel," *Revista de Filosofia* (Chile) 29–30 (1987): 27–33. Writing on *Geist* in Hegel, Giusti attempts an approach similar to my own with respect to *Gemüt* in Kant. Giusti's work suggests, to me at least, that the loss of the meaning of the term *Gemüt*, its identification with spirit, and the reduction of its meaning to an aesthetic (if not to a psychological, empirical, or subjective) sense may be due to a romantic or Hegelian influence.

5. Jacob Grimm and Wilhelm Grimm, *Deutsches Wörterbuch* (Leipzig: Verlag von Hirzel, 1885). See especially the third sense of *Gemüt*, on page 3296.

6. Robert Paul Wolff, *Kant's Theory of Mental Activity* (Gloucester: Peter Smith, 1973). An identification of *facultas cognoscitiva superior* with *mens* can also be found in §624 of Baumgarten's *Psychologia Empirica*, reproduced in volume 20 of *Kants gesammelte Schriften*.

7. Peter Bieri, "Generelle Einführung," in *Analytische Philosophie des Geistes*, ed. Peter Bieri (Meisenhem: Beltz, 1981), 4. See also Karl Ameriks, *Kant's Theory of Mind* (Oxford: Clarendon, 1982).

8. Bieri, "Generelle Einführung," 25.

9. Hannah Arendt, *The Life of the Mind*, 2 vols. (London: Secker & Warburg, 1978).

10. A large number of these difficulties and equivocations could be remedied if scholars of German were to concern themselves with the consistency of translations of German philosophers into other languages.

11. See §§669 and 689 of Baumgarten's *Psychologia Empirica*, reproduced in volume 15 of *Kants gesammelte Schriften*.

12. Stephan Strassner, *Das Gemüt: Grundgedanken zu einer Theorie des Gefühlslebens* (Freiburg: Herder, 1956), 122.

13. Friedmann, *Das Gemüt*, 4.

14. Philipp Lersch, *Aufbau der Person* (Munich: Barth, 1951), 234.

15. Quote from the *Deutsches Wörterbuch* by the Grimm brothers. See page 3296.

16. Friedmann, *Das Gemüt*, 91.

17. Gerhard Wahrig, *Deutsches Wörterbuch* (Gütersloh: Bertelsmann, 1968), 2500.

18. Friedmann, *Das Gemüt*, 7–8.

19. Ibid., 15.

20. Hans Vaihinger, *Kommentar zu Kants Kritik der reinen Vernunft* (Stuttgart: von W. Spemann, 1881), 9.

21. Vaihinger, *Kommentar*, 9.

22. Friedrich Schiller, *Über die ästhetische Erziehung des Menschen*, Letter 20, in *Werke in drei Bänden*, ed. Herbert Georg Göpfert, vol. 2 (Munich: Hanser, 1966), 493.

23. "Certa palavra dorme na sombra / de um livro raro. / Como desencantá-la? / É a senha da vida / a senha do mundo / vou procurá-la." Carlos Drummond de Andrade, "Discurso de primavera e algumas sombras," in Carlos Drummond de Andrade, *Nova reunião*, vol. 2 (Rio de Janeiro: Record, 1983), 949.

16

Between Prescriptive Poetics and Philosophical Aesthetics

Ricardo Ribeiro Terra

Peter Szondi began his course Ancients and Moderns in the Poetics of the Age of Goethe[1] by considering the meaning of the word "poetics." Poetics bears a double meaning as the doctrine of both *Dichtung* (poetry) and *Dichtkunst* (ars poetica). On the one hand *Dichtung* is taken as a philosophical problem, as the theory that concerns what poetry is. On the other hand *Dichtkunst* is taken as a technical issue, as the theory of the poetic technique regarding the issue of how to make poetry. Nonetheless, both are interwoven—the reflection on poetry making must lead back to its technique:

> The poetics of Aristotle is both in one: an answer to the question "what is poetry" and an instruction on how to best make an Epic, a Drama. Nothing else but this occurs with the works *de arte poetica*, from Horace to the *Versuch einer Critischen Dichtkunst* that Johann Cristoph Gottsched presented in 1730.[2]

The question "how to make poetry" turns into a normative system, into poetics that prescribe rules. The many "poetic arts" have become greatly relevant, a fact that can be seen in France with Boileau, for instance. In Germany this type of poetics that deals exclusively with the composition of poems weakens from 1770 onward. At the end of the eighteenth century a new species of poetics emerges, the philosophical poetics, "which does not seek for rules that apply in praxis, nor for differences that would be taken into account in writing, but for a knowledge that suffices by itself. Poetics so understood constitutes a branch of general aesthetics as the philosophy of art."[3]

This article was originally published as "Entre as poéticas prescritivas e as estéticas filosóficas," in Ricardo Terra, *Passagens: Estudos sobre a filosofia de Kant* [Transitions: Studies on Kant's philosophy] (Rio de Janeiro, Editora UFRJ, 2003), 131–44; a previous longer version entitled "Kant: Juízo estético e reflexão" [Kant: Aesthetical judgment and reflection] was published earlier in a collection of essays organized by Adauto Novaes, *Artepensamento* [Art-thinking] (Sâo Paulo, Cia. das Letras, 1994; 2nd ed. 2006), 113–26. Translated by Cauê Cardoso Polla.

In the age of Goethe these poetics were elaborated mainly by philosophers that used to give courses on aesthetics, as did Schelling (*Philosophy of Art*, from 1802 to 1803) and Hegel (*Lectures on Aesthetics*, from 1820 to 1829), or by philosophers who had also elaborated aesthetic considerations, as did Schopenhauer (*The World as Will and Representation*, 1818).

Kant's reflections on taste hold a suis generis theoretical place, given that they can be aligned neither with the prescriptive poetics of the Enlightenment nor with the philosophical poetics; however, they set in motion the aesthetics problems pondered by the former, and open up the way to the philosophy of art. Kant's *Critique of the Power of Judgment* is not a prescriptive manual for how to make a work of art, nor does it even teach one how to judge it, nor does it institute a so-called philosophy of art. These qualities enabled *Judgment* to overcome the aesthetics of the Enlightenment and to prepare for the coming of the aesthetics of German Idealism, although it has kept a considerable distance from German Idealism. Szondi states that the element that would impede Kant from going a step further toward the aesthetics of the age of Goethe was historical thinking.

> For Schiller and for the brothers Schlegel, for Schelling and Hölderlin, for Solger, Hegel and Jean Paul around the turn of the century, this constitutes the common ground of all the attempts to answer in a new way the main questions of poetics in a counter-movement against the Enlightenment. From historical thinking stems the power with which the war against the Aesthetics of the Enlightenment is conducted in the *Sturm und Drang*; the commander is named Johann Gottfried Herder.[4]

Two fundamental questions that arise from Szondi's analysis should be emphasized here. The first relates to the status held by the *Critique of the Power of Judgment* and its relation to the aesthetics of the Enlightenment and the later philosophy of art. Would it be the case that the critical perspective has been simply overcome by the philosophy of art, by aesthetics? Would the third *Critique* be initiated by the aesthetic questions of the Enlightenment or would it be claimed by an intrinsic necessity of completion of the Kantian system? An analysis of the genesis of the third *Critique* may furnish a proper understanding of the position of the aesthetic judgment in this work, its meaning for the whole of the critical-transcendental, and also to make explicit why the third *Critique* is not a work on aesthetics even though it has relevant consequences to it.[5]

The second question, in turn, relates to historical thinking. It is true that Kant did not build up a conception of history as Schiller and Hegel did, but we should not identify his conception with the one held by the Enlightenment thinkers. Wouldn't a sort of historicity be present in the *Critique of the Power of Judgment*?

Kant readers focus on the polemic about the status and the necessity of the third *Critique*. The issue is multifarious, as this project was not indicated in the previous works. Furthermore, how does one handle an apparently heterogeneous work that gathers considerations on the beautiful and the organism, on judgments both aesthetic and teleological?

The *Critique of the Power of Judgment* has its weight because it realizes and resolves, to a certain extent, the aesthetic questions that were in the air during the eighteenth century, simultaneously opening up the way to both the "philosophical aesthetics" and the aesthetics of romanticism. Ernst Cassirer, in "The Fundamental Problems of Aesthetics," the last chapter of *The Philosophy of the Enlightenment*, shows how the efforts for thinking about art in the seventeenth and eighteenth centuries converge somewhat on the critical solution. Even if one censures this historical teleological perspective of thinking—that is, censures the thinkers prior to Kant's preparation of the critical solution—one must recognize that the fruitfulness of Cassirer's approach is possible because of the actual role of the *Critique of the Power of Judgment* as a turning point of an era.

Changing slightly Szondi's angle that only contrasts the prescriptive perspective with philosophical aesthetics, one can regard schematically how the critical philosophy bears relation to the erstwhile aesthetics. The conflicts between reason and imagination, genius and rules, or the foundation of the beautiful on sentiment or on a determined type of knowledge, are the bulk of the problematic, which asks for a synthesis. Nonetheless, writes Cassirer,

> Before this synthesis could be achieved, before it took on definite shape in the work of Kant, the philosophical idea had, so to speak, to go through a series of preliminary stages and exercises by means of which it strove to characterize the problematic unity of opposites from different angles and viewpoints.[6]

During the seventeenth and eighteenth centuries a dissension between two different attitudes toward the beautiful developed: an objectivistic one with rational rules of classicism, and a subjectivist-empirical one that applies a psychological method to analyzing human nature and seeks to characterize common sense.[7]

Classical aesthetics deals basically with the work of art, and attempts to define it in circumscribing its genre. Hence the doctrine of the invariability of the genres and their objective rules—a way of proceeding that is analogous to the knowledge of nature. Empirical aesthetics, in turn, does not deal directly with the works themselves but rather with the subject and its artistic fruition, basing itself on theories of the feeling of the beautiful and the sublime. Participating in this tendency, Kant, in his precritical work *Observations on the Feeling of the Beautiful and Sublime* (1764), written prior to the change represented by the *Critique of Pure Reason*, continues the reflection of the English thinkers with a text strongly marked by an empirical and anthropological approach concerning the differences between the peoples, between man and woman, and so on.

This attempt of synthesis leads to the foundations of an aesthetics and to the effort to think up the possible autonomy of the beautiful and its distinctiveness in comparison with the perfect and the good. The question concerning taste leads to the discussion about feeling and the faculties, the search for the characterization of a third faculty besides those of knowledge and of desire.[8] With the statement of the autonomy of feeling and the analysis of all these elements, one can affirm Luigi Pareyson's assertion that "the materials of Kantian aesthetics are, for this reason, fundamentally, the materials of seventeenth century and Enlightenment aesthetics. His originality consists in centralizing everything around the discovery of the autonomy of feeling, and above all in founding the possibility of criticizing it."[9] Proceeding to a critique of feeling as an autonomous faculty, Kant rethinks aesthetics prior to him as whole and in so doing radically transforms the question.

However, it is necessary to remember that this was not always Kant's position. In the *Critique of Pure Reason* he himself was unable to see the possibility of a critique of taste not founded only on empirical principles, as he had attempted in his *Observations*. One can read in a large excerpt from the *Critique of Pure Reason*:

> The Germans are the only ones who now employ the word "aesthetics" to designate that which others call the critique of taste. The ground for this is a failed hope, held by the excellent analyst Baumgarten, of bringing the critical estimation of the beautiful under principles of reason, and elevating its rules to a science. But this effort is futile. For the putative rules or criteria are merely empirical as far as their <most prominent> sources are concerned, and can therefore never serve as <determinate> *a priori* rules according to which our judgment of taste must be directed; rather the latter constitutes the genuine touchstone of the correctness of the former. (*Pure Reason*, A21/B35; words in brackets B only)

What led Kant to change his position and seek for an a priori principle to feeling? Even more: could we say that this change is the origin of the *Critique of the Power of Judgment*? If true, how do we explain the second part of this work on teleological judgment? Why not write a critique of taste instead of one on judgment?

At least three different hypotheses can be raised to explain the genesis of the third *Critique*: (1) the discovery of the autonomy of the critique of taste; (2) the discovery of purposiveness; and (3) the third *Critique* would be the place for what remains, that is, what could not be placed in the other two *Critiques*: aesthetics and teleology.

Against the onesidedness of these hypotheses one is able to seek for a synthesis. One can think there is in the Kantian thinking a radicalization of the critical project and a turning to the question of judgment. Schematically it is possible to say that already in the *Prolegomena* there is a movement toward this when one observes the distinction between judgment of perception and judgment of experience; in the Deduction of the Categories in the second edition of the *Critique of Pure Reason* one faces, in comparison with the 1781 text, a different organization that displaces the argumentation axis to an emphasis in judgment.

One can say that the *Critique of the Power of Judgment* is a demand of Kant's system and this is why his starting point was not art. Nevertheless, the first half of the third *Critique* was possible only because Kant took into account the aesthetic questions both from the Enlightenment and from the English tradition, maneuvering them to a critical dimension. Kant elaborates a new approach that will open up the way to the later philosophical aesthetics.

Given the origin of the *Critique of the Power of Judgment*, its results with regard to aesthetics seem surprising. As Cassirer observes:

> For a strange thing came to pass, that with this work, which seems to have grown out of the special demands of his system and to be designed only to fill a gap in it, Kant touched the nerve of the entire spiritual and intellectual culture of this time more than with any other of his works. Both Goethe and Schiller—each by his own route—discovered and confirmed his own essential relation to Kant through the *Critique of the Power of Judgment*; and it, more than any other work of Kant's, launched a whole new movement of thought, which determined the direction of the entire post-Kantian philosophy. That "happy dispensation," by which what was only a consequence of the elaboration of the transcendental schematism could grow into the expression of what were in fact the deepest intellectual and cultural problems in the eighteenth and the early nineteenth centuries, is often a source of wonder, but it has hardly been explained with complete satisfaction. It remains a most noteworthy paradox that upon simply completing the scholastic framework of his theory and working it out in detail, Kant was led to a point that can be called the crucial one of all living intellectual interests in his epoch.[10]

Through the third *Critique* Goethe, and also to some extent Schiller, entered into Kant's philosophy. The junction between aesthetics and teleology in the same work does not provoke strange reactions in his contemporaries; instead, it is what charms Goethe. When Johann Eckermann asks Goethe who among the new philosophers is the best, Goethe answers, "doubtless, Kant. His doctrine is the one that has most spread and taken hold in German culture, in yourself, who have not read it, since it is not even necessary to read more—this doctrine is disseminated everywhere." Nonetheless Goethe tells Eckermann, "so I recommend to you his *Critique of the Power of Judgment*, wherein he handles rhetoric excellently, poetry passably, but the plastic arts insufficiently."[11]

Now to the second question. To clarify the relationship of taste and historical thinking we need to remember briefly some elements of the analytics of the beautiful. In the *Critique of the Power of Judgment* Kant states the autonomy of the third faculty of the mind, the feeling of pleasure and displeasure, along with the faculties of knowledge and desire; he makes his critiques and finds his a priori principle—purposiveness. In doing so he gives a precise status to feeling and opens new horizons to aesthetics. The faculty of knowledge mobilizes in a privileged manner the superior faculty of knowledge, understanding, and faculty-of-desire—reason; the feeling of pleasure and displeasure, by its turn, will mobilize a third superior faculty of knowledge—judgment. In parallel with the laws of nature as the object of the determining judgments of the understanding, and laws of morality as the object of reason, art in its purposiveness is the object for reflective judgment. Now, purposiveness in the *Critique of the Power of Judgment* is regarded not only in art but also in nature's teleology (nature thought as art), which leads to a double standard: aesthetic reflective judgment and teleological reflective judgment.

What interests us here is aesthetic reflective judgment. Beauty and aesthetic judgment are affirmed in their complete autonomy both in relation to knowledge and in relation to practice, that is, to morality. While the beautiful satisfies without any interest, it is distinct, on one side, from pleasure; on the other side, it is distinct from the good, which is bound to interests and refers to the faculty of desire. Moreover, the beautiful satisfies without concept and delights universally.

In a third moment the beautiful is referred to purposiveness without an end, and thus is differentiated from the perfect and the useful that involve an objective purposiveness, be it internal or external. A last characteristic of the beautiful is that it satisfies in a necessary way.

In order to clarify aesthetic judgment it is fundamental to understand what purposiveness without end is to Kant. It is distinct from the objective purposiveness that "can be cognized only by means of the relation of the manifold to a determinate end, thus only through a concept." Now, the beautiful satisfies without concept; the judging of beautiful "has as its ground a merely formal purposiveness, that is, purposiveness without an end" (*Judgment*, 5:226).

In nature one finds objects that seem to have been made in such a way that they envisage an agreement with our faculties. However, this agreement is not seen as being based in a real constitution of the natural object, but rather as bearing relation to the reflective judgment and thus called formal purposiveness.

> In other words, the *formal purposiveness* of nature is not an objective constitution of it but a law of our manner of considering it . . . it is not a real structure but a ruling principle . . . *purposiveness* while nature is seen in its character of accordance with the laws of our cognizance, *formal* while such purposiveness is not a real and objective structure of nature, but laws of our reflection upon it.[12]

The judgment of taste is neither theoretical nor practical, given that there is neither a conceptual nor rational determination; it is a reflective judgment where a free play between understanding and imagination occurs when it is a judgment about the beautiful. Now, regarding the sublime there is a kind of tense disagreement between imagination and reason.

Therefore it is difficult to think any kind of historicity in the judgment of taste when one analyzes the forms of the objects and the relations of the faculties. In the *Critique of Pure Reason* there is no self-constituting historicity of reason; instead, there is a rupture (known as "Copernican revolution") through which metaphysics is led to the safe way of science. And this means that, from this point on, there will be only an amplification of the already known and not the possibility of change in fundamental discoveries. One could agree with Vuillemin's statement that the theoretical part of the critical philosophy "appears as the science of intellectual acts through which man thinks rational mechanics."[13] In this sense the *Critique of Pure Reason* would be bound to Newtonian physics, and even more, would establish the critical foundations of this science as inimical to any future modification.[14]

The situation of the critique of aesthetic judgment is usually viewed in this same way. Since it would not concern history, it would make it possible to make judgments about works of art from all times, without relating them to their times and, besides this, not relating the judgment itself to history. The critical-transcendental perspective asks for an aprioristic and ahistorical attitude.

The Kantian approach is opposed to that of Marx, for whom "the difficulty does not lie in understanding that Greek art and epic are tied up with a certain social form of development. The difficulty is that they still give us artistic enjoyment and serve in a certain relationship as the norm and unreachable standard."[15]

For Kant there is no difficulty in understanding the aesthetic pleasure provided by the ancient works of art because pleasure is bound to a species of agreement between the form of these works and our faculties. The connection with historical social forms is left aside.

Kant himself clearly states:

> Since the investigation of the faculty of taste, as the aesthetic faculty of judgment, is here undertaken not for the formation and culture of taste (for this will go its way in the future, as in the past, even without any such researches),

> but only from a transcendental point of view, it will, I flatter myself, be judged leniently with regard its deficiencies for the former end. But in what concerns the latter aim it must be made firm against the most rigorous examination. (*Judgment*, 5:170)

The aim of the *Critique of the Power of Judgment* is transcendental analysis, although it does not deny the study of the formation and culture of taste and even apologizes for treating it inadequately. Now, when searching for its references to culture, one can show that the preoccupation with history arises in many places of the Kantian text; even more, how it is important in fully understanding art.

In aesthetic judgment there is no determination from the understanding, rather a free play of understanding and imagination. Hence, it is possible to cognize the autonomy of aesthetics as well as the possibility of the formation and transformation of taste. The judgment of taste and the ingenious creation of the aesthetic works are not reducible to the determination of a faculty and are not the expression of a historical period. Nevertheless, they are not ahistorical. This is a theme that is not well considered by the commentaries on Kant's work. Salim Kemal, some time ago, complained about the small bibliography related to this theme and stated that the aesthetic judgment would presuppose culture.[16]

Let's regard briefly the relations between taste, which is "the faculty for judging of the beautiful" (*Judgment*, §1, 5:203), and culture. It is noteworthy that nature is thought of as a teleological system in the second part of this *Critique*. The final end is the human as a cultural being. "The production of the aptitude of a rational being for any ends in general (thus those of his freedom) is *culture*" (5:431).

In other Kantian texts the links between taste, culture, and history are indicated. For instance, one can read in the essay "Idea for a Universal History with a Cosmopolitan Aim": "Thus happen the first true steps from crudity toward culture, which really consists in the social worth of the human being; thus all talents come bit by bit to be developed, taste is formed" (*Idea*, 8:21). Another relevant excerpt is found in the third *Critique*: "the true propaedeutic for the grounding of taste is the development of moral ideas and the cultivation of the moral feeling" (*Judgment*, 5:356).

One must agree with Gerhard Krämling when he states: "Certainly at this point it can be considered that Kant's critical theory of culture (and with this, art) culminates in the program of an association of art and philosophy of history, without abandoning the autonomy of the aesthetic."[17] Something alike happens with practice. The grounding and criterion of morality of action are established independently of the historical and empirical results and conditions; in a series of mediations and passages,

Kant thinks the effectuation of practical reason in politics and history through right—hence, philosophy of history. Now, this transitional system does not imply abandoning moral autonomy. In this relation between the transcendental grounding of action and the meaning of history (whose character is, to a certain extent, aporetical) resides one of the most fruitful aspects of Kantianism: the maintenance of the suprahistorical criteria alongside a philosophy of history. To compare the relations of art and philosophy of history with the connections between morals and history could cast light upon the whole question—but this is a theme for another essay.

Reconsidering the questions posed by Szondi, although we cannot develop them: Is it possible to say that in Kant there is no historical reflection connected with the beautiful or, more precisely, with aesthetic judgment? How ought we to think about their relation with culture? Kant does not have a historical conception as Hegel does—an aesthetics that presupposes a movement that, to a certain extent, deduces the works of art, or at least deduces the great moments in the history of art. There is also no determination process of the ideal until one reaches the artist, or the particularization of the ideal in great cultural periods such as symbolism, classicism, and romanticism, and the singular arts that have privileged relations with a determined period. One cannot find a species of moral and political "program" related to art, nor a "program" of aesthetic knowledge.

However, aesthetic judgment does not ignore speculative knowledge—one can check the discussion of adherent beauty and the conception of the play of the faculties of knowledge. It also does not ignore practice—one can check this easily in examining the sublime and the beautiful as symbols of morality. Finally, although aesthetic judgment doubtless privileges beauty in nature, it does not ignore history completely, given its relation to culture.[18]

For Pareyson, Kant does not err because of a contradiction, but rather because of a lack of completeness, since he does not develop the other aspects of the judgment of taste, their apracticality and atheoreticalness, although he gives many indications of them. Now, many efforts have been attempted to complete Kant's theory. Do they not, in the end, destroy the critical project? Would tension between opposed perspectives not be constitutive of this project?

Notes

1. Peter Szondi, "Antike und Moderne in der Poetik der Goethezeit," in Peter Szondi, *Poetik und Geschichtsphilosophie I* (Frankfurt am Main: Suhrkamp, 1974).
2. Ibid., 13.
3. Ibid., 14.
4. Ibid., 15–16.

5. Regarding the *First Introduction* and the genesis of the *Critique of the Power of Judgment* see Ricardo Terra, "Reflexão e sistema: A propósito da *Primeira introdução* e da gênese da *Crítica do juízo*" [Reflection and system: Apropos of the *First Introduction* and the genesis of the *Critique of the Power of Judgment*], in Ricardo Terra, *Passagens: Estudos sobre a filosofia de Kant* [Transitions: Studies on Kant's philosophy] (Rio de Janeiro: Editora UFRJ, 2003), 27–50.

6. Ernst Cassirer, *The Philosophy of Enlightenment* (Princeton: Princeton University Press, 1979), 276.

7. Regarding the development of aesthetics in the seventeenth and eighteenth centuries, see chapter seven in Cassirer, *Philosophy of Enlightenment*; and also Alfred Baeumler, *Das Irrationalitätsproblem in der Ästhetik und Logik des 18: Jahrhunderts bis zur Kritik der Urteilskraft* (Halle: Niemeyer, 1923; repr. Darmstadt: WBG, 1981).

8. Regarding this topic, see Luigi Pareyson, *L'estetica di Kant* (Milan: Mursia, 1984), 10–11.

9. Ibid., 11.

10. Ernst Cassirer, *Kant's Life and Thought* (New Haven: Yale University Press, 1981), 273.

11. Johann Peter Eckermann, *Gespräche mit Goethe* (Wiesbaden: F. A. Brockhaus, 1975), 188.

12. Pareyson, *L'estetica*, 17.

13. Jules Vuillemin, *Physique et métaphysique kantiennes* (Paris: Presses Universitaires de France, 1955), 3.

14. This way of regarding the question is obviously partial—even in its relation to the *Critique of Pure Reason*—as it does not take into account the metaphysical dimension involved in both the analytics and transcendental dialectics.

15. Karl Marx, "Introduction to the Grundrisse," in Karl Marx, *Later Political Writings*, ed. and trans. Terrel Carver (New York: Cambridge University Press, 1996), 157.

16. Salim Kemal, *Kant and Fine Art* (Oxford: Clarendon Press, 1986), 66. Another interesting book is Gerhard Krämling, *Die systembildende Rolle von Ästhetik und Kulturphilosophie bei Kant* (Munich: Verlag Karl Alber, 1985). About the ideas of culture and history, a noteworthy contribution is Leonardo Amoroso, *Senso e consenso: Un studio kantiano* (Naples: Guido Editore, 1984).

17. Krämling, *Die systembildende Rolle*, 167.

18. See Pareyson, *L'estetica*, 17, and passim.

17

The Purposiveness of Taste

An Essay on the Role of *Zweckmässigkeit* in Kant's *Critique of Aesthetic Judgment*

Pedro Costa Rego

The main concern of Kant's aesthetics in the third *Critique* can be summed up in the following question: Is it in any sense possible that an aesthetic judgment, that is, one that is grounded upon a feeling of pleasure and does not involve any conceptual objectivity, be universally valid? In other words: Do we have the right to claim for a nonobjective and nonconceptual judgment the status of an a priori valid judgment for every judging subject? Given that only the judgment of taste puts forward claims to this sort of nonobjective universality, the problem of the possibility of such an unlikely universality—characterized by Kant elsewhere as a "non-demonstrable" one[1]—is the problem of beauty.

This problem is briefly presented in the Dialectic of Aesthetic Judgment in terms of an antinomy. The thesis of the Antinomy of Taste affirms that "the judgment of taste is not based on concepts; for otherwise it would be possible to dispute about it (decide by means of proofs)." And the antithesis affirms: "The judgment of taste is based on concepts, for otherwise, despite its variety, it would not even be possible to argue about it (to lay claim to the necessary consent of others to this judgment)" (*Judgment*, 5:338–39).

The cryptic solution furnished by the Dialectic cannot be grasped without an examination of the solution proposed both in the Analytic and in the Deduction of Judgments of Taste. In barest outline, the solution is this: no, the judgment of taste is not based upon concepts, at least until we can render intelligible what can be meant by a "transcendental concept of reason of the

This article was published as "A finalidade do gosto: Um estudo sobre o papel da *Zweckmässigkeit* na 'Crítica da faculdade do juízo estética,'" in *Studia Kantiana* 5 (2004): 165–84. Translated by the author.

supersensible," or an "indeterminate concept (namely, of the supersensible substrate of appearances)," referred to in the Dialectic (*Judgment*, 5:339–41). So far as concepts must be considered as determinate discursive representations of the unity of a manifold, judgments of taste are not grounded upon them. And this is the only reason for the Analytic's assertion, in its last moment, that there can be no disputing about their necessity; that they possess a non-apodeictic necessity, that is, literally, a nondemonstrable necessity. But here the antithesis is decisive: we can rightfully lay claim to the assent of all men for our particular judgment because, despite its nonconceptuality, it is based upon an a priori principle, a determining ground belonging to transcendental subjectivity, something that distinguishes the subject-structure and is therefore valid for all subjects. We are in contention about beautiful things because we consider them able to set in motion, to put forward or to stimulate something in us that is not exclusively ours, that belongs to subjectivity, and our contention upon it functions as an attempt to convey such a community, as well as to elucidate the sense of this subjective element that is unexpectedly put into motion whenever we are brought into contact with a beautiful object of nature or of art.

This "something in common" underlying a general approval that cannot be enforced by proofs but that licenses, even stimulates, contention is termed by Kant the *principle* of a judgment, the *ground* of a subsumption. Meant as a condition of the possibility of a proposition of the kind "this is beautiful," the principle of the universal communicability of beauty is the principle of a judgment because it is the "universal" representation to which we refer—and under which we think—a manifold given in intuition. We do well here to recall Kant's definition of judgment in the third *Critique*: the thought of a particular as contained under a universal (*Judgment*, 5:179).

Now, the principle of a subsumption only yields contention without any solution by means of proofs if it is not capable of conceptually determining the particular that it subsumes; as Kant puts it: if it is not the principle of a determinant judgment. If it, instead, subsumes, and therefore unifies, without determining either what the intuited manifold *is*—from the theoretical point of view, or what such a manifold *ought to be*—from the practical (be it a technically practical, morally practical, or pathologically conditioned) point of view; if this is the principle of the search for a conceptually determinant unity; if it is an heuristic-indeterminate principle, then the judgment in which it performs the role of a determining ground will be termed "reflective" (*reflektierend*). Laying claim here to universal assent amounts to bringing about contention.

The solution to the Antinomy of Taste—and consequently to the historical aesthetic controversy between the thesis of a private subjective beauty and that of a universally objective beauty—rests upon the very nature of the determining ground of the judgment of taste (that is, the aesthetic reflective judgment). The nonlogical, nonobjective, nonconceptual, and indemonstrable universality of beauty is the enigmatic universality of the principle to which we refer the representation of a beautiful object of nature or art.

This indefinite universal principle has been variously characterized throughout the *Critique of Aesthetic Judgment*. Unfortunately, we cannot presently analyze each of these definitions—there are at least five—furnished by Kant. We can, however, join them together in classes, characterize these classes, and ask (1) for the necessity of such a diversity, and (ii) for the connection between the various *formulae* that are meant to cohere, so that the essential claims of Kant's aesthetics remain problematic, but not schizoid.

The aim of the present paper is to shed some light on the enigmatic intersubjective structure at the basis of the problematic universality of the beautiful; to argue that this structure, albeit problematic, is unified; and to defend the claim that its various characterizations are necessary for the construction of its meaning.

I'll call "logical" or "epistemological" the first class of characterizations of the subjective principle of taste.[2] They are available in the Analytic of the Beautiful, particularly in §9—the last one in Kant's account of the judgment of taste's quantity; in the fourth moment of the Analytic—which deals with the modality of the aesthetic reflective judgment; and, finally, in the deduction (§38)—and in the immediately foregoing paragraphs. What justifies the term "epistemological" for this class of characterizations is the fact that they connect beauty immediately with cognition. They make explicit the logical relation between the cognitive faculties in the production of aesthetic response. In broad outlines, following the guidance of the first edition's account of the schematism, this relation can be depicted as follows:

First of all, imagination, considered as the faculty of synthesis, synthesizes a sensibly apprehended manifold. Second, it reproduces such a synthesized manifold under the unity claim laid by the conceptual principle of understanding. To synthesize means here: to assign the manifold a form—so far as it cannot possess one out of the realm of subjectivity—that is still not the conceptual discursive determination of this manifold's unity *per notas communes*.

Now, in the current cognitive process, this something previously synthesized would be simply recognized in the third synthesis of imagination—the conceptual recognition. Strangely, the third *Critique* characterizes this process with the expression "objective schematism." A tautology? If not, it's because there is a schematism through which no object of cognition is constituted. In the third *Critique*, the beauty issue, the theme of the judgment of taste and the question of the problematic nonconceptual universality of a feeling, is the problem of a subjective schematism. Despite the unavailability of conceptual recognition, of sensible transposition of the concepts of understanding and determination of what the given manifold is or ought to be, there is still schematism, judgment, and a form, which is preconceptually represented and felt by the subject in its pure aesthetic pleasure.

The manifold content previously synthesized by the imagination under the unity claim of understanding—but not recognized by the understanding—stimulates, intensifies—as Kant puts it—vivifies (*belebt*) the harmonious accordance of these two powers of representation, which are together responsible for the cognitive synthesis and, consequently, for the accomplishment of knowledge. Nevertheless, the recognition operation, which aims at the conformity between the reproduced data and a concept of understanding, can occasionally fail, and whenever this occurs, the mutually quickening activity of the imagination in its freedom and the understanding with its conformity to law is intensified. Such an endeavor and vivification doesn't occur whenever knowledge takes place and doesn't bring about any knowledge. The access we can have to such a subjective principle is an awareness of it in the feeling of our state of mind; a feeling of pleasure (*Wohlgefallen*) that is sensibly distinguished from feelings of satisfaction derived from any ends. That is to say, the subjective *Stimmung* provoked by beauty mentioned above rests at the basis of a feeling of pleasure that, in Kant's terms, takes no interest in the existence of its object.

It follows that Kant's solution to the Antinomy of Taste can be so presented: the determining ground of the aesthetic reflective judgment is a subjective *Stimmung*, and not an objective connection between the faculties involved in the process of cognition. The universality of beauty is nothing but that already deduced in the first *Critique*, that is to say, the universality of knowledge, or better, the universality of the possibility of cognition, inasmuch as we deal here with reflecting faculties in their failed endeavor to achieve objective knowledge. Beautiful is thus the representation that we do not subsume under a conceptual principle, but rather under the preconceptual common accord between the faculty of concepts and the faculty of intuitions;[3] the representation that we refer to this *Stimmung* as a universal, albeit conceptually undetermined, principle; thus as a universal but nonobjective, hence intersubjective, principle. And since subsuming a manifold amounts to assigning it the form (be it determinate or not) of a principle belonging to subjectivity, judging something as beautiful amounts to assigning it the indeterminate form of the possibility (not the reality) of its occurrence as an object of knowledge.

Hence, the principle of the pure judgments of taste being a *Stimmung* between faculties belonging to the universal structure of subjectivity, this judgment engenders contention, and the claim upon universal assent for taste appreciation is meaningful. Since, however, such a *Stimmung* is not an objective rule, there is no sense in attempting to determine a priori—or to furnish a deduction of—what is or should be beautiful, and these conditions license only nondisputative contention about the beauty of an object. This turns out to mean: there can be no deduction of a universal model of correct beauty appreciation.

Summed up, this is Kant's epistemological solution: the determining ground of the judgment of taste connected with the universality of cognition. The *Bestimmungsgrund* of beauty, a subjective common accord between the spontaneous and the receptive faculties as a subjective condition of knowledge. The judgment of taste as the subsumption of *data* under a universally valid subjective element, which, in the course of a successful objective schematism resulting in the achievement of knowledge, remains latent, but not absent. The harmonic accord of the cognitive faculties is that subjective element that, insofar as it responds to the very possibility of knowledge, emerges particularly in the unsuccessful cognitive effort, whereby it is intensified and vivified so as to gain knowledge and finally gets its heuristic character subjectively schematized in the outlines of a beautiful object.

Given this sketch, we could ask: what else does Kant need in order to establish the possibility of a simultaneously universal and aesthetic estimate? Nothing, presumably. Nevertheless, the author writes an Introduction and an analytic exposition of the judgments of taste from the point of view of its relation to ends, probably because he deems it necessary to explain the principle of such a judgment differently. We will call this second mode of the characterization of taste's *Bestimmungsgrund* "practical," because it expounds the principle of taste as the principle of the purposiveness (*Zweckmässigkeit*) of nature and because, as we shall see in the sequel, the purposiveness of nature is a concept belonging to the realm of practical thought.

There are good reasons to identify in the third *Critique* a relevant concern about the systematic unity of transcendental philosophy. *Critique of the Power of Judgment* would possess the capacity of joining together the disconnected parts of the critical doctrine and of unifying its different objects. The issue raises, however, some difficulties that must be dealt with:

1. What exactly does Kant understand by the phrase "purposiveness of nature"?
2. Which role can the purposiveness principle perform in the third *Critique*'s systematicity claim?
3. Does this tendency explain the connection between purposiveness and taste in the third *Critique*? Or could it be for another reason that the two determinations of the principle of taste, which we will call "epistemological" and "practical," need to exist together as the basis of the foundation of the determining of taste in reflective judgment?

First point. As is well known, a principle is the ground from which something starts, but it is more than a mere beginning. It is a force that commands and determines what starts from it. Principle is for Kant always the principle of determination (*Bestimmungsgrund*). Since purposiveness (*Zweckmässigkeit*) is designated as the principle of a judgment, we could say that the "thought of a particular as contained under a universal" can be commanded and determined by purposiveness. But purposiveness can only determine a thought by assuming the role of the "universal" upon which is based the sense of the particular there contained. We should then ask what the universal principle named purposiveness precisely commands, prescribes, determines, or fails to determine regarding the particular that it founds and contains.

What is thought under the unity of the universal principle of purposiveness is considered in light of an heuristic presupposition, so argues Kant. We presuppose, that is, on the basis of our consideration of the object taken under the concept of purposiveness—and this in order to search for something (*heurisco*)—we first posit the thesis that its existence is due to some creator, to the volition of some understanding, which is certainly not ours. To think an object under the concept of purposiveness, that is, to judge something as final regarding this determining ground amounts to considering it under the hypothesis that it is not simply an object of nature, subordinated to the necessary rules of phenomenal causality, but rather that it is the outcome of a process whereby some superior intentional understanding has set this object before itself as an end.[4]

Such determining ground belongs neither to the faculty of knowledge nor to that of desire. It is an idea stemming from our *Urteilskraft*. While performing under the determination of such an idea, the faculty of judgment exerts what can be termed "judicative autonomy." This faculty, which is our power of connecting particular representations with universal ones, can operate either in the theoretical or in the practical context. In the first, it is responsible for cognitive synthesis; it refers an intuited manifold to a theoretical concept containing its connecting rule. In the second, it is responsible for practical knowledge, comparing an intuited manifold to the concept of what it *ought to be*, rather than to one of what it *is*; that is to say, to the concept through which reason determines the faculty of desire to want something in particular; as simply put, to the concept of something as an end of will.

Kant designates as "practical judgment"—be it morally practical, concerning the internal perfection of the judged object, or technically practical, when the object is considered in the judgment from the point of view of its utility—the kind of judgment that expresses such a reference and assigns its subject the predicate "good."

Now, it can happen that the faculty of judgment does not find itself compelled to serve one of the remaining superior faculties of the mind—

knowledge and desire. This is precisely what is considered in the admittedly principal half of the third *Critique*; in fact, a critique of aesthetic judgment wouldn't have any place if our judging faculty operated exclusively under the legislative authority of the determinant powers of subjectivity: the objective categorical and moral subsumption.[5] If we can meaningfully "criticize" the aesthetic judgment, it is because the faculty of judgment occasionally operates autonomously, independently of the others. Autonomy of the pure power of judgment is precisely what is at issue when we experience beauty.

The experience of beauty can be thus depicted as the result of the process whereby a manifold apprehended in sensibility puts the faculty of judgment into motion and simultaneously refuses to submit to those objective principles of cognition, through which objective schematism is gained. Here, the power of judgment can be encountered as such. Given the unavailability of a determined concept of understanding or of reason, the apprehended manifold remains related exclusively to the *possibility of a subsumption*, or to what renders possible its judicative recognition. The subjective power that is responsible for the cognitive synthesis (or, as Kant puts it, that subjective condition of the possibility of knowledge) is lifted out of the refuge it occupies in a successful cognition and has now to account for the failure of that which it should tacitly guarantee. Now, the superior power of *Gemüt* responsible for a subsumption in general is the faculty of "thinking a particular as contained under a universal," which is precisely the definition of the faculty of judgment. It is in this sense that we shall grasp the characterization, in §35, of the principle of the judgment of taste. This principle, already designated in the Introduction as the purposiveness principle of reflective judgments in general, and in §9 as a subjective *Stimmung* between understanding and imagination, is now characterized as the "*Urteilskraft* or the faculty for judging itself."[6] The faculty of judgment is designated as the principle and determining ground of its own judicative activity. The previously apprehended manifold, which had not been conceptually recognized, is here subsumed under the judging faculty (*Urteilskraft*), itself considered as a subjective condition of the possibility of cognitive subsumption. This amounts to saying: the manifold is in the judgment referred to the judging power alone, and will hence assume the conceptually indeterminate form of the possibility of knowledge.[7]

This is, in a few words, the principle of the purposiveness of nature, the reflective judgment's highest and "*heautonomous*" principle: the *Bestimmungsgrund* of those judgments whereby the judging faculty heuristically refers a given representation to itself as the subjective condition of the possibility of a definite knowledge.

We are now able to face the question: what role does the principle of purposiveness have as the basis of the third *Critique*'s systematicity claim? The statement, in the Introduction, of the systematic-unity purpose (the unity between the previously criticized realms of nature and freedom) appears to be meaningful because: (1) the third *Critique* intends to be an investigation into the judging faculty as such; (2) the judging faculty as such, that is, not subordinated to the other superior faculties of mind (namely, the cognitive and the faculty of desire), makes itself properly available to an analysis while operating as a reflective faculty; (3) the superior principle of the reflective judging faculty is precisely the principle of purposiveness of nature; and finally (4) the principle of purposiveness of nature is the principle of the thought of the realm of natural necessity as the purpose and the end of an hypothetical intentional understanding.

To think natural causality as the end of a free causality, as a heuristic strategy seeking increase in knowledge, to find out a subjective condition of the possibility of cognition and to meet the solution to the historical aesthetic controversy surrounding the problem of the universality of beauty: this is the mixture of results that the third *Critique* offers, without much pedagogical courtesy, to the reader's discomfort. Whatever it be, the announced bridge over the gulf between the two realms of nature and freedom, established in the purposive and reflective thought of a nature created by a free will (albeit not ours), seems to be an established thought.

This given, let us face the last question: does the goal, briefly expressed and quite uncertain, of providing systematic unity for the above-mentioned realms really justify the assignment of the status of the determining ground of aesthetic judgment to the purposiveness of nature? Or could this unification be rather a consequence of an independent investigation into the aesthetic issue? Is the explanation of taste compelled to accept the principle of purposiveness because of the fact that Kant made the decision to join together two investigations—the aesthetic and the systematic—in the same book entitled *Critique of the Power of Judgment?*

If this is so, we could give up the unfortunate enterprise of grasping what a hypothetical intentional understanding has to do with our spontaneous estimate of beauty. But if this is not so, then our interpretation must justify the necessity of the principle of purposiveness without quitting the aesthetic sphere, that is, within the boundaries of an investigation into the power of aesthetic judgment, even though the results of such an investigation are suitable for further and different theoretical purposes.

Now, to justify the necessity of the principle of purposiveness within the aesthetic sphere of an account of the judging faculty means: to show that purposiveness belongs necessarily to the pure aesthetic judgment's determining ground, whose analysis properly elucidates our power of judgment as such. This amounts to arguing that purposiveness is not a transcendental concept devised in order to provide the unity between cognition and morality in an aesthetic realm; rather, such a unity makes sense because, independently of the systematicity purpose, our current and disinterested estimate of beauty is, as it were, a final judgment.

* * *

The Analytic of Aesthetic Judgment is an intense endeavor to analyze and deduce the problematic, nonconceptual, subjective, and indemonstrable universality of the beautiful. We saw the solution Kant advanced in the Antinomy of Taste. Universality of taste makes sense insofar as it is not a logical one, founded upon the concepts of understanding or of reason, but rather a aesthetic one, which can be contingently experienced through a disinterested feeling of pleasure termed "favor" (*Gunst*). Such a feeling is nothing but the state of mind (*Gemütszustand*) brought about by the subjective precognitive common accord between the faculties involved in the cognitive process, namely, understanding and imagination. This accord, inasmuch as it functions as the principle to which we refer a given representation, is the determining ground of the judgment of taste on the beautiful.

Now, the judgment of taste belongs to the class of the reflective judgments, such as the aesthetic case, and the Introduction affirms repeatedly that the determining ground of the reflective judgments in general, that is, nondeterminants, a class that includes, therefore, the judgment of taste, is the principle of the purposiveness of nature (*Zweckmässigkeit*). Accordingly, the third Moment of the Analytic states explicitly that the judgment of taste upon the beautiful presupposes a certain purposiveness connecting the given representation with the subjective principle under which it is subsumed. We repeat our question: why this double characterization? Or better, why the second, if the first one had already furnished a sufficient explanation of the universality and necessity of this kind of reflective judgment?[8]

We believe the question can be answered this way: because without the principle of purposiveness, the aesthetic character of the judgment of taste cannot be grounded. By means of the *Stimmung* between the cognitive faculties, Kant provides an explanation of the universality and necessity of the experienced beauty. He stands, however, in need of the reflective principle of purposiveness to explain precisely that beauty can be experienced, that is to say, that we are able to gain access to it. This point deserves more attention.

In this respect, a briefly announced thesis of the Introduction, precisely in its section VI, is determinant. Kant states: "In fact, although in the concurrence of perceptions with laws in accordance with universal concepts of nature (the categories) we do not encounter the least effect on the feeling of pleasure in us nor can encounter it, because here the understanding proceeds unintentionally, in accordance with its nature" (*Judgment*, 5:187). Kant expresses here, unfortunately without further discussion, an essential proposition of the third *Critique*, namely, that a feeling of pleasure can only obtain as the outcome of the realization of an aim or an intention. The subsumption of a particular representation under a universal principle can only bring about a *Wohlgefallen*, be it pure or empirical, if it is constituted as a final relation, which is equivalent to saying: if the principle of the subsumption is the representation of an end. Kant's proposition can be summed up this way: from the judgment of *data* under the categories of understanding no feeling of pleasure can arise, for the reason that the categories do not contain the rule according to which any one is to be compelled to recognize what an object or state of things *ought to be*; rather they are responsible for the recognition of what an object *is*.

As a matter of fact, the Introduction thesis seems to complicate, rather than to overcome the stalemate—more precisely, the antinomy—of the Dialectic. All pleasure, it is said, is necessarily coupled with the attainment of an aim. But it is also said that all feeling stemming from the realization of an aim is connected with the representation of the existence of the object, arises from the final conformity of such an existence to a previously represented concept of an end, and is called interest. Now, the quality of pleasure in the beautiful is designated precisely as the disinterestedness. It should hence follow that the pleasure in the beautiful, disinterested, unintentional, and disconnected with the existence of objects could be anything but a feeling of pleasure; neither *Wohlgefallen* nor *Befriedigung*.

Moreover, section VI of the Introduction muddies the waters: "The attainment of every aim is combined with the feeling of pleasure," reaffirms Kant, but he adds: in taste, pleasure arises "merely through the relation of the object to the faculty of cognition, without the concept of purposiveness in this case having the least regard to the faculty of desire, and thus being entirely distinct from any practical purposiveness of nature" (*Judgment*, 5:187). So construed, the argument amounts to saying that the feeling of pleasure is, to be sure, a feeling, which requires accomplishment of aims, but also one that, strangely, dismisses the slightest connection with faculty of desire; strangely because, if our interpretation is correct, taking something as an end is equivalent to having one's faculty of desire determined through the representation of this end. Furthermore, Kant's puzzling account seems to imply that the feeling of pleasure, in addition to its distinctness from the desiring faculty, arises from the attachment of an object to the faculty of cognition, even though it has been affirmed several times that such a cognitive subordination does not involve any feeling of pleasure.

We believe Kant's solution to these difficulties can be summed up as follows:

1. Doubtless, what we experience in the appreciation of beauty is properly a feeling of pleasure.

2. The thesis of the association of pleasure with the attainment of purposes remains intact.
3. Pleasure, and consequently intention and purposiveness, can be founded upon a judicative operation that does not consist in the subsumption of a given representation under a principle of the desiring faculty. This is precisely the case in taste.
4. Subjectivity can gain access to purposiveness and intentionality also by means of the cognitive faculties, and not only through will.

We shall confine our attention to items 2, 3, and 4.

Item 2, concerning the thesis of the association between pleasure and intentionality: First, we observe that as laid out in the Introduction, this thesis functions, as it were, as an axiom all along the Analytic. Kant simply does not discuss the possibility of a pleasure apart from the attainment of an aim, be it determined or not, material or formal. The analysis of taste from the point of view of its quality, before arguing for the disinterestedness of our aesthetic appreciation, insists on the distinction between judgment of taste and judgment of knowledge, ascribing to the latter the status of an absolutely nonaesthetical judgment.[9] Supposedly, it means that in such a case the predicate is not united to the subject on the basis of a feeling, that the subsumption here is strictly conceptual, and "there is no transition from concepts to the feeling of pleasure or displeasure" (*Judgment*, 5:211). Only after this consideration does Kant begin to talk about interest, only then does he start to deal with the two classes of judgments that could be mistakenly taken for judgments of taste, precisely because they involve some feeling, they operate in the intentional context, and they relate to attainment of aims; these are the judgment upon the agreeable and the judgment upon the good. It is clear from the foregoing that the ground of his analysis and distinctions, whenever taste is at issue, is the ground of the final judgments, or better, of those judgments grounded upon an intentional principle.

We do well to observe, second, that in only two passages does Kant seem to allow room for discussion of the subject.[10] In both, the problem is related to the controversial status of moral respect. The question is then: if all feeling presuppose satisfaction of aspirations, and if moral respect is a feeling, what are the ends or aims to whose satisfaction moral respect corresponds? Coherently, Kant does not argue that it is the representation of the *Endzweck*, of a moral world considered as the end of our rationally determined will. For there is, to be sure, a satisfaction in the conformity of an action to the superior principle of morality. We even express it in judgments classified as morally practical, which constitute a subclass of those termed judgments upon the good. Nevertheless, we must emphasize that satisfaction belonging to such a final conformity is not moral respect. As clearly put in §12, respect, as an a priori feeling, cannot be inferred as a consequence from any purposiveness connection. Such a cause-effect connection is always empirical and therefore can only be cognized a posteriori. The feeling of moral respect, hence, does not arise from any satisfaction resulting from conformity to ends;[11] rather it is the state of mind produced by the determination of the will through the moral law (*Judgment*, §12, 5:222). Such a determination is, in fact, the representation of an end to be attained, which will likely bring about some pleasure, but one that must be differentiated from respect, namely, a practical pleasure as an a posteriori occurrence in a practical judgment; following Kant's classification, in a judgment upon the internal perfection of an object.

So construed, the argument seems to entail the conclusion that moral respect is a feeling of pleasure dissociated of all intentionality. Such an inference is, however, dismissed in §42 of the *Critique*, where Kant deals with the possibility of an interest in the beautiful. Succinctly: moral respect is not an effect (*Wirkung*) of a final causality, and therefore does not depend upon interest. Nonetheless, as a state of mind connected to the determination of the will through the moral law, it produces (*hervorbringt*) an interest in morality: it determines our desiring faculty to will something as an end. Moral respect, hence, only makes sense within the purposiveness sphere, namely, a morally practical purposiveness, so that the thesis of the necessary link between feeling and purposiveness remains intact.

Item 3, whose proposition is: there is a feeling of pleasure, and therefore a final judgment, which does not depend on our faculty of desire. Kant conceives of the principle of purposiveness as the highest principle of the faculty of judgment precisely in order to provide an elucidation of the possibility of a disinterested pleasure. There is interest, that is, a kind of pleasure that is different from the one related to beauty, whenever we refer a given representation to ends belonging to our desiring faculty, be they rational or pathological. Judgments that express such a "material"[12] purposiveness are called judgments upon the good and upon the agreeable. On the other hand, there is no pleasure at all in the reference of this representation to a theoretical concept of the understanding. If, however, we refer a given representation to the ideal presupposition that its existence is an end of a certain intentional principle, in such a case we neither cognize it nor aim at its existence, and therefore there won't be either knowledge or interest. And yet, subjectivity is not lifted out of the sphere of the concept of purposiveness, hence, that of the feeling of pleasure. The principle of purposiveness employed by the judging faculty in its autonomous activity—not subordinated to cognition or desire—does not require from subjectivity a representation of an end or its interest in some existence. This is why Kant asserts that, so employed, the *heautonomous* heuristic presupposition of a creating understanding is the principle of a formal purposiveness, which amounts to saying: a purposiveness existing apart from an end, a purposiveness without an end. If in the determining ground of the judgment of taste upon the beautiful the principle of purposiveness were lacking, if such a determining ground were delineated exclusively as the free play of our powers of cognition, then the reference of a supposedly beautiful object to the subjective *Stimmung* wouldn't engender any pleasure. For, if theoretical cognition, if objective schematism by itself does not bring about any pleasure, why should we expect to find some in the mere subjective *Stimmung* of the faculties conditioning the possibility of cognition?

Finally, item 4 raises the question of how epistemological and practical versions of the principle of taste coexist in the determining ground of the aesthetic reflective judgment. In other words, what connects the subjective harmonic play of the powers of cognition to the principle of purposiveness of nature, both identified as the ground of the judgment of the beautiful in different places of the third *Critique*? Viewed in light of the preceding considerations, this question becomes more precise: how can our cognitive faculties, displayed in mutual quickening activity by a given representation deserving the predicate "beautiful," produce a final relation between representations and, consequently, raise pleasure apart from the faculty of desire? In this question, what is at stake is, to be sure, the general problem of the systematic unity of the transcendental philosophy, but also, moreover, the specific problem of the cohesion, the coherence, and the intelligibility of the *Critique of the Power of Judgment*, which must first be treated.

Notes

1. A non-apodeictic necessity, that is, an exemplary nondemonstrable one, is the main subject of the fourth moment of the Analytic of the Beautiful, which deals with the aesthetic reflective judgment—following the guidance of the logical functions of judging—from the point of view of its modality (*Judgment*, §§18–22, 5:236–40). Considering that we mentioned a non-apodeictic "universality" as that to which the judgment of taste lays claims, and not a "necessity" of that kind, as Kant puts it the Analytic, we owe an explanation. Kant normally assigns a deductive section in the critical works the task of providing a deduction of the necessity of the judgment at issue. Accordingly, a proof of the aesthetic reflective judgment's necessity is what can be expected from §38 of the *Critique of the Power of Judgment*. This deduction, however, is a quite unusual one, compared to those of theoretical and practical judgments. The reason is that what is at stake here is the demonstration of the necessity of a judgment whose necessity is precisely a non-apodeictic one (literally: nondemonstrable); an exemplary (*exemplarisch*) one. This particular situation compromises, as it were, the clear distinction between necessity and universality regarding the deduction's task.

It is worthwhile to lay out in barest outline Salim Kemal's plausible thesis of the distinction between "deduction of universality" and "deduction of necessity" in the *Critique* in *Kant's Aesthetic Theory* (London: St. Martin's Press, 1992). Kemal argues that the deduction of the judgments of taste is committed to a double enterprise. The first is to prove "the possibility of making judgments of taste at all" (89); that "aesthetic judgments generally are possible" (88). According to the author, such a task is successfully accomplished by the deduction, where Kant "is concerned with the a priori conditions of judgments of taste generally" (86). There would be, however, another task beyond that of demonstrating the subjective principles upon which aesthetic and simultaneously universally valid judgments must be based. The task of proving that and when we make aesthetic universally valid judgments. Given that "in the deduction Kant is not considering particular actual judgments and how we must treat them," that "the general possibility of judgments [does not] tell us how we assess particular cases," and that knowing "generally that aesthetic judgments are possible" does not amount to knowing "which if any actual instances are judgments of taste" (86); in few words, considering the "distinction between possible and actual judgments," Kemal asserts that "we also need to justify the necessity of actual instances of such putative judgments" (89). He suggests, hence, that we should save the term "necessity" only for "actual instances" to each particular case of aesthetic predication. So far as Kant's deduction is not concerned with them, it would be merely a deduction of the "universality of aesthetic judgments," which means: of the logical possibility of making a simultaneously aesthetic and universally valid subsumption. For further discussion on the subject and particularly about the specificity of the third *Critique*'s deduction, see Pedro Costa Rego, *A improvável unanimidade do belo: Sobre a estética de Kant* [The improbable unanimity of beauty: On Kant's aesthetics] (Rio de Janeiro: 7Letras, 2002), 157–72.

2. "Epistemological" is the term employed by some commentators of the third *Critique*, namely, Paul Guyer and Donald Crawford, to refer to Kant's endeavor to furnish a proof of the universality and necessity of the judgment of taste. Beyond this "epistemological deduction," Kant would have tried another one, termed by them a "moral deduction," in the Dialectic of the Aesthetic Judgment. See Paul Guyer, *Kant and the Claims of Taste*, reprint ed. (Cambridge: Cambridge University Press, 1997), 246–47; and Donald Crawford, *Kant's Aesthetic Theory* (Madison: University of Wisconsin Press, 1974). I prefer to save the term "epistemological" to express a *formula* of the determining ground of the judgment of taste, and I do not oppose to her a "moral," but rather a "practical" *formula*, which takes place, as we shall see, not in the Dialectic, but in the Introduction, in the form of the "heautonomous" principle of *Zweckmässigkeit*.

3. Which is not sensibility, as we could expect on the basis of Kant's first *Critique* and *Logic*, but imagination. See, comparatively, section VII of the introduction to *Judgment*, 5:189–92; and §35, 5:287; and *Logic*, 9:11.

4. The complete and literal formulation of the purposiveness of nature is presented by Kant in the Introduction of the *Judgment* in the following terms: "Now this principle can be nothing other than this: that since universal laws of nature have their ground in our understanding, which precribes them to nature (although only in accordance with the universal concept of it as nature), the particular empirical

laws, in regard to that which is left undetermined in them by the former, must be considered in terms of the sort of unity they would have if an understanding (even if not ours) had likewise given them for the sake of our faculty of cognition, in order to make possible a system of experience in accordance with particular laws of nature. Not as if in this way such an understanding must really be assumed" (*Judgment*, 5:180).

5. It is worthwhile at this point to mention that it is exactly the fact that human beings act on concepts, as is done generally in theoretical cognition, that is, subordinated to the principles belonging to the cognitive faculties, that deprives teleological judgment of the status of a main theme in the third *Critique*, in spite of its reflective character. As Kant puts it, at least "as far as its application is concerned it belongs to the theoretical part of philosophy" to which the aesthetic power of judgment is completely excluded, so far as it judges its objects under the principle of the formal purposiveness of nature and is therefore the unique possessing "a principle that the power of judgment lays at the basis of its reflection on nature entirely a priori." Aesthetically judging under formal purposiveness, and not teleologically under objective purposiveness, amounts to being lifted out of the logical sphere of objective concepts. See *Judgment*, Introduction, §VIII, 5:192–94.

6. In Kant's words: "Now since the concepts in a judgment constitute its content (that which pertains to the cognition of the object), but the judgment of taste is not determinable by means of concepts, it is grounded only on the subjective formal condition of a judgment in general. The subjective condition of all judgments is the faculty for judging itself, or the power of judgment" (*Judgment*, §35, 5:287).

7. This seems to be the logical consequence of the fact that the determining ground of the judgment of taste, defined from the "epistemological" point of view as the mutually quickening harmonic activity of imagination and understanding, is made intelligible as a subjective condition of the possibility of cognition in general. By referring the judged object to itself as to a subjective condition of the possibility of conceptually definite judgment, the faculty of judgment indeed judges it, but not under definite concepts, not in a determinate fashion. To judge free from the legislative authority of the concepts of understanding and of the ideas of reason amounts to reflecting upon the form of the object.

8. At least this seems to be the thesis of the deduction in the third *Critique*. To perform a deduction, notes Kant, means: to prove the objective validity of a certain principle or concept through demonstration that it is the condition of the possibility of the cognition of an object that is given elsewhere (*anderwärts*). Accordingly, the third *Critique*'s deduction need not argue that the connection between the object and its determining ground in judgment of taste is a final one in order to provide a proof that the subjective *Stimmung* between understanding and imagination operates as a condition of the possibility of "cognizing" the aesthetic character of a given object. Regarding Kant's definition of the deduction's task, see *Practical Reason* 5:46, and the analysis of Guido Antônio de Almeida, "Critique, Deduction, and the Fact of Reason," chapter 7 of this volume.

9. Naturally, in the sense that the *Critique of the Power of Judgment* ascribes to the term "aesthetic."

10. Namely, in §12 and §42, a point that will be explained in the sequel.

11. This term translates *Befriedigung* rather than *Wohlgefallen*.

12. The term "matter" is employed in §38, in the *formula* of the deduction. It delineates a criterion that ultimately distinguishes the class of the pure aesthetic judgments from those involving a feeling of pleasure. Disinterested, the pleasure of pure taste is the only one produced by the mere "form" of purposiveness.

18

Freedom in Appearance

Notes on Schiller and His Development of Kant's Aesthetics

Christian Hamm

In the first pages of the second edition of the 1794 treatise *Religion within the Boundaries of Mere Reason* one finds a long footnote in which Kant acknowledges the objections of an eminent critic of his writings and justifies once more his "rigorist" ethics, elaborated in the *Groundwork of the Metaphysics of Morals*, in the second *Critique* and in the first edition of *Religion* itself, according to which can be admitted in his doctrine of morals no "intermediate moral concept." We read this:

> Professor Schiller, in his masterful treatise on *gracefulness* and *dignity* in morality (Thalia, 1793, 3rd issue), disapproves of this way of representing obligation, because it carries with it the frame of mind of a Carthusian. Since we are however at one upon the most important principles, I cannot admit disagreement on this one, if only we can make ourselves clear to one another. —I readily grant that I am unable to associate *gracefulness* with the *concept of duty*, by reason of its very dignity. For the concept of duty includes unconditional necessitation, to which gracefulness stands in direct contradiction. The majesty of the law (like the law on Sinai) instills awe (not dread, which repels; and also not fascination, which invites familiarity); and this awe arouses the respect of the subject toward his master, except that in this case, since the master lies in us, it arouses a *feeling of the sublimity* of our own vocation that enraptures us more than any beauty. (*Religion*, 6:23)

Schiller mentions this note in a letter of May 18, 1794, to his friend and adviser Gottfried Körner, in which he demonstrates his pleasure with Kant's positive reception of his work:

This article was originally published as "Liberdade na aparência: Anotações sobre Schiller e sua complementação da estética kantiana," in *Filosofia: Diálogos de horizonte*, ed. Cirne Lima/Feltes/Moraes/Zilles (Caxias do Sul: Editora da UCS, 2001), 369–85. Translated by the author and Adriano Perin.

> In the new edition of his philosophical doctrine of religion, Kant has expressed his opinion about my new writing on grace and dignity and defended himself against the offense contained in it. He talks about my writing with respect and calls it a masterly work. I just cannot explain how satisfied I feel with the fact that he read my writing and that it impressed him so much.[1]

On June 13, four weeks later, he writes to Kant himself:

> I cannot miss this opportunity of showing you gratitude, reverend Sir, for the attention given to my little work and for being so indulgent with me. . . . It was just the liveliness of my desire to make the results of your doctrine of morals more accessible to a part of the public that seems to avoid this and . . . to conciliate it with the rigor of your system, what made me for a moment look like your opponent, something to which, actually, I do not have either ability or inclination. With immense joy I realized from your note that you did not interpret my intention in the wrong way.[2]

If it is true that Schiller's intention was, as he pointed out, to conciliate "a part of the public" with the rigor of Kant's moral philosophy—and we have no reason to doubt the honesty of this declaration or Schiller's profound admiration for Kant's ideas in general—it is still worth asking if this was his only intention or if he had other reasons to express his objections and critical improvements and, therefore, to risk the conflict with Kant.

In fact, in several of Schiller's commentaries one can find out that he was far from considering his theoretical studies a simple analysis or exegesis of Kant's work. On the other hand, he was thinking of a systematic increase and improvement of it, and, with this, of his own new contribution to Kant's thought. As a new contribution it is doubted that it could go hand in hand with his master's theory. Perhaps the commentary in which Schiller's real intention is most evident is this: "Where I merely tear down and attack other opinions I am rigorously Kantian; only where I build am I in opposition to Kant."[3]

Therefore, "to reconcile the public with the rigor of Kant's doctrine" cannot be understood as a simple attempt to settle this doctrine, in the sense of making it more accessible to its readers, through a mere *internal* harmonization of elements that are at first opposed to each other or in contradiction. It means, however, to develop *out of* Kant's theory—even though *from and grounded on Kant's critical-transcendental principles* and mainly in compatibility with them—an additional constructive proposal. Such a proposal, in Schiller's understanding, would be able to cope with those problems that Kant could not solve properly because he was too close to his own critical apparatus. Thus, it seems to be quite possible that Kant's praise for Schiller in the above quote is, at least in part, due to a misunderstanding:

that of having underestimated the constructive aspect of Schiller's intention. Likewise, Schiller's enthusiastic reaction could be grounded on his—mistaken—impression, at least at this moment ("We are in agreement on the most fundamental principles," "I cannot establish a disagreement"),[4] of Kant's whole consent to his undertaking.

Following Schiller's letters to Gottfried Körner of 1793, which are entitled *Kallias, or On Beauty*, the dissertation *On Grace and Dignity* of the same year constitutes his second great aesthetic-philosophical essay. In both these works the question of the possibility of an objective concept of the beautiful is at the heart of Schiller's efforts. This means the possibility of a constitutive systematic connection of the concept of the beautiful with the idea of morality—a theme that, at least at first sight, seems to be very far from Kant's own thought.

Kant's main thesis concerning the beautiful, which is systematically developed in the first part of his *Critique of the Power of Judgment*, states that beauty cannot be conceived as an objective quality of the object itself, but merely as a *relation* (specifically "aesthetical") between the subject who aesthetically judges and the object to be judged. The accomplishment of such a judgment, understood as a reflective (i.e., not determinative) activity of the power of judgment, requires, in what concerns the subject, "disinterested satisfaction," which necessarily presupposes a "free play" of the faculties—understanding and imagination—involved in this activity. With the introduction of the figures of disinterested satisfaction and free play Kant seeks to assure the universal validity of aesthetic judgment: having as a ground of determination neither something that is subjectively agreeable nor something that is objectively determined by concepts. On the other hand, in a judgment of taste, what allows us "to impute to anyone" a "common agreement" or to speak of the beautiful *as if it were* a quality of the object is only the "state of mind" itself, which results from the referred free play on the occasion of the judgment of an object through a sensation without any interest, that is, the feeling of a genuinely aesthetical pleasure and, therefore, the *"universal communicability" of this state* (*Judgment*, 5:216).

After long and intense studies Schiller was quite familiar not only with Kant's own argumentation but also with the great classical aesthetics and with the conceptions of Kant's immediate predecessors, from Shaftesbury and Burke to Baumgarten and Winckelmann. Thus, he was aware of the difficulties in these philosophers and of the difficulties that he himself would face in the search of another way to ground the beautiful: "The revolution in the philosophical world," he wrote in a letter of February 1793, "shook the ground on which aesthetic was established, and its traditional system, if one can attribute to it such a name, was torn down." In this situation, he continues, it was Kant, "in his critique of the power of aesthetical judgment, who *began* to apply the principles of the critical philosophy . . . to taste, and, if he did not established them, he at least *prepared the grounds* for a new theory of art."[5] Without any possibility of going back to the traditional solutions and without having yet a positive alternative it seems to Schiller himself a "daring idea" to assume, as he intends to, the role of the "nobleman" of this new theory and make of it a genuine "philosophical science."

Nevertheless, the reason for Schiller's dedication to quite a daring employment did not only consist of merely theoretical concern with the closing of a systematic gap left open or disregarded by his predecessors in its demanded clarity by the transcendental philosophy. On the other hand, what was under consideration, prior to this, was his own *existential interest* in the determination and clarification of the theoretical ground and the practical principles of his artistic-literary work. That is, Schiller was considering his role as a poet and playwright in a time marked by revolutions and profound changes in almost all segments of political, social, economical, and cultural life. It is with regard to this idea of a necessary justification of the artistic production and the purpose of this production that Schiller cannot admit that art, "the instructor of the soul," "the most effective of all the incentives of the human spirit," lies as objectively indeterminate, and that its object, the beautiful, is a mere function of sensation or of subjective imagination, being this either in the empiric-psychological or in the productive-transcendental sense. His letter of 1793 continues: "When I reflect on the relation of the feeling of the beautiful . . . to your human nature . . . I cannot regard it as a simple play of the sensible faculty, which is only capable of empirical rules. Beauty as well, I think, must rest, like truth and right, on eternal grounds, and the original laws of reason must be also the rules of taste."

Schiller knows, however, that the fact that we only *feel* but do not know beauty can "frustrate all hope of finding a universally valid principle to it" since "every judgment proceeding from this spring represents only a judgment of experience." This difficulty, which is actually manifested in the common procedure of "examining the aesthetic principles according to our feelings," instead of to "examine and correct your feelings according to principles," constitute to him the "crux, to which even Kant, regretfully, considered it impossible to give a solution."[6]

Regardless of this rather unoptimistic diagnosis, it turns out to be clear to Schiller that, whichever solution the problem may have, it can only be searched for and, perhaps, found on the basis of the "grounds prepared" by Kant:

> In fact, I would never have had the courage to attempt a solution to the problem . . . had not Kant's philosophy provided me with the proper resources. This fruitful philosophy . . . also furnishes the solid fundamental stones with which to erect a system of aesthetics, and the fact that it was also not provided with this merit I can only explain as a premeditated idea of its author. Far from

> considering myself the one to whom this is reserved, I only want to seek until where this discovered path can bring me.[7]

At this moment, Schiller's rearticulated opinion, according to which Kant's aesthetics constitutes only a preparatory work or the initial part of a new philosophical theory of art to be still developed, as well as his speculations on Kant's possible motives to leave his theory unfinished, deserve a commentary. Initially, it is worth asking if Schiller's position deals with simply what is said to be the "fundamental stones," that is, a fragment; and, second and more precisely, if it is true that Kant was not able to "undo" that psychological-conceptual "crux" referred to before by Schiller, or, as we can read in another place, if Kant really had a motive to "lose hope" at the task of finding "the objective concept of beauty, which serves also as an objective principle of taste."[8]

With regard to the first point, it seems evident that at least Kant did not have any doubt about the complete character of his aesthetic proposal, in the sense of it being composed by a set of theorems and arguments, which in their whole, and according to their specifically transcendental mode of foundation, could guarantee, far from any arbitrary or dogmatic conceptualization, an unequivocal and coherent definition of the central theoretical figure of every aesthetics, namely, the *beautiful*. Furthermore, even though constituting, as already referred, only a *function of* (aesthetic) *judgment*, the beautiful could even be qualified, in good sense, as objective. This is because, according to Kant's argumentation, it is necessarily based on the principle of "universal communicability." Unable to be grounded *in the object*, but merely in the particular mode of judging it, the referred objectivity in Kant is undoubtedly not the one Schiller is searching for. Moreover, just because Kant's mode of judging represents quite more than "a simple play of the sensible faculty, which is only capable of empirical rules," does not mean that it is manifested any less. That is why it does not seem right, or at least seems problematic, to speak, as Schiller does, of a "hopeless" Kant in face of the problem of the determination of an objective principle of taste.

In what concerns such discrepancies it is worth remembering that all that we, as well as Schiller, call "Kant's aesthetics" was elaborated under the title of a "*critique of the power of* aesthetic *judgment*." As it is known, this critique is a part of a wider employment, namely, the transcendental foundation of a new type of judgment—the reflective judgment—upon whose harmonious integration in the corpus of the transcendental theory will depend not only the justification of our judgments on the beautiful, but also, and primarily, the solution to the more basic question of how it is possible to justify the idea of a necessary connection between the theoretically necessary principles of our experience of nature and the practically necessary principles of freedom.

In this context, aesthetic judgment, or judgment of taste, represents only *one type* of reflective judgment, one that is, however, highly interesting from the systematic point of view because it illuminates—and this in a clearer manner than teleological judgment, precisely because of the nonconceptual determinability of its objects—the formal structure of any reflective judgment and its peculiar connection with the "receptivity of a pleasure from reflection" simply on the "forms" of things, which, in Kant's words, "indicates not only a purposiveness of the objects in relation to the reflecting power of judgment . . . in the subject, but also, conversely, one of the subject . . . with regard to the objects" (*Judgment* 5:192). Without going into saying that in view of this, all of Kant's aesthetic investigations can or must be read exclusively from the perspective of a systematic foundation of the transcendental principle of reflective judgment, it is, however, unquestionable that *one* of Kant's motives for dedicating himself to these aesthetic investigations was eminently systematic; it means that none of its results can be interpreted *out of* this systematic-transcendental perspective. Any corrective reading guided by the idea of a disconnection of the specifically aesthetic doctrines from their transcendental basis would immediately affect the internal logic of the transcendental construction in its entirety; as also, vice versa, the coherence of a specifically aesthetic argumentation can only be guaranteed through reference to elementary transcendental principles. This is the reason for Kant's rigorous insistence on the maintenance of the strictly formal character and the absolute purity of his argumentation.

We must remember this when we read Schiller's intention of being "rigorously Kantian" in his critique to the others, but "in opposition to Kant" in the constructive part of his own work. Therefore the question is: how to solve this dilemma of constructing a theory with Kant and also against Kant?

We can find a first answer in the *Kallias*, where Schiller begins to sketch the general lines of his proposal and to prepare and determine the first pieces of his argumentation—pieces that are all derived from Kant's theorems—in order to construct his own theory. In this context, Schiller's concern is especially caused by *one* point that is one of the necessary and most important consequences of the transcendental foundation of the beautiful in general. That is, the fact that, by reason of it being dependent on the mere *free* play of the faculties of knowledge in the accomplishment of a judgment of taste, the beautiful can be *any object*—of nature or of art—that is capable of acting as an impulse to the aesthetic perception. Nevertheless, Schiller wants to examine if between all the possible candidates for an aesthetic judgment there are some specific objects or determinate forms that perhaps can provoke, more than other objects, an aesthetic reaction; and if it is possible to identify in this privileged objects some qualities that would make possible, in difference with Kant's manner, a deduction of the beautiful, not of the subject but of the *object* of judgment, that is, a foundation of an *objective* concept of the beautiful.

Thus, what would these qualities be? To explain this Schiller appeals to the central thesis of Kant's practical philosophy, in reference to which he develops a new concept, namely, that of a *beautiful action*. In Schiller's conception such an action differs from a purely moral action, as Kant's conceives it, by the fact that it is practiced neither "against the interests of the senses" nor merely "for the respect for the moral law." On the other hand, it would be practiced in whole harmony between reason and sensibility, that is, in accordance with both the moral law and the senses.

The starting point of Schiller's reasoning is the Kantian concept of an "action of the will" [*Willenshandlung*] or "moral action."[9] This action is characterized, in transcendental terms, by its exclusively formal determination, which means that it constitutes a product of *pure* will, that is, of the will autonomously determined by its own form (and not by contingent matters). Unlike this moral action, of which practical reason *categorically requires* that it be determined by its own pure form, a natural action, or better, an action resulting from a mere "effect of nature" [*Naturwirkung*], is realized and practiced mainly on the basis of and according to "natural laws" and, by this fact, not under the domain of the practical reason, in a way that this cannot *require* anything from such a (necessary) effect of nature, but—and here starts Schiller's own argumentation—simply "*desire*" that this "be *by itself*, that it **shows** autonomy" (italics in original; emphasis added in bold).

Schiller is wholly conscious that, in order to make this figure of "desire of reason" work, he has to conceive of it in such a way that the accomplishment of the desire by reason cannot be interpreted as a real inference (read moral) of the latter in the mechanism of nature. The autonomy of a natural object cannot be understood as a work or as an effect of the action of practical reason since, in this case, the referred object would automatically lose its natural autonomy and, therefore, would be heteronomous, that is, it would be determined no more by itself, but by an external will, alien to it. In the same way that a rational being [*Vernunftwesen*] that wants to show pure autonomy always has to act by pure reason, so a natural being [*Naturwesen*] has to "act by *pure nature*, if he wants to show pure autonomy," because "the proper [*das Selbst*] of the rational being is reason and the proper of the natural being is nature."

Based on this idea of a natural being capable of acting by pure nature, Schiller is able to define more precisely what can and even must constitute the activity and the specific role of practical reason in the sought after foundation of the beautiful: if practical reason "discovers . . . in the contemplation of a natural being" that this being is determined by itself, it "will attribute to the same being a *similarity with freedom*, or, finally, *freedom*." However, by the fact that this freedom can only be "lent" to the object by reason, since "nothing can be free except for the supernatural," and "freedom, in itself, can never be the object of the senses," the respective object to which reason lends freedom, *is* not in fact free, but only "*appears*" or "*seems*" to be free.[10] According to Schiller, under consideration here is a mere "analogy of an object with the form of practical reason," not of freedom in actual fact, but only of "*freedom in appearance*" or "*freedom in the phenomenon*."[11] Nevertheless, Schiller thinks that it is possible to establish, based on this new systematic construction, a new mode of judgment. That is, besides the *logical* judgment of concepts, the *teleological* judgment of intuitions, both according to the form of knowledge and the *moral* judgment of free effects (i.e., of moral actions), this according to the form of pure will, the new and fourth mode would be the judgment of nonfree actions, but still according to the form of pure will, that is, of a genuinely aesthetic judgment. In the same manner that the agreement of the concept with the form of knowledge expresses *purposiveness* with reason, the analogy of intuition with the form of knowledge *similarity* with reason, and the agreement of an action with the form of pure will *morality*, so the analogy of a phenomenon with the form of pure will, or of freedom, expresses *beauty*. Therefore, beauty is nothing more than "freedom in appearance" or "freedom in the phenomenon."[12]

Schiller is convinced that it is possible to verify this freedom in the phenomena, that is, he believes in the existence of such a beauty both in the objects of nature and, above all, in the cultural and artistic manifestations of the human. Schiller points to a widely discussed model in the aesthetics of the time, that is, the so-called line of beauty and grace, a term coined by the artist and writer William Hogarth,[13] as an exemplary case of this beauty contained in the aesthetical object. The same model is characterized by a wavy line that causes—unlike, for instance, a jagged line—the impression that it passes without ruptures and without any external intervention. It is in this lack of abrupt alterations, in this (apparent) independence of any external will that Schiller sees—in analogy with the "equilibrate acting" of nature, which also "does not like leaps"[14]—an element of freedom: precisely that freedom "in appearance" that, according to what was said earlier, does not manifest itself through a predeterminate physical quality of the object, but rather in the specific "form" of its presentation. Hence his conclusion, which seems to be pertinent:

> Given that *beauty* is not restricted to any matter . . . and given that all that is presented to the senses can appear as . . . free or nonfree, it follows that the sphere of the beautiful has a very wide extension, since reason can and must call for freedom in everything that sensibility and reason immediately present to it. Therefore, the realm of taste is a realm of freedom—the beautiful world of the

> senses is the happy symbol of how the moral (world) must be, and every beautiful natural being out of myself a happy citizen that calls me: be happy like me![15]

Yet, in a more concrete and more dramatic manner than in the case of the beautiful line, the idea of freedom shows itself in appearance, where one considers the presentation of *human acting* in its beautiful form, that is, where one considers not objects but the already mentioned *beautiful actions*—actions that, as we can now say, must have the appearance of "free effects of nature."[16] Furthermore, in appearance one considers not only the artistic presentation of these actions, but also—in accordance with the appeal: "be happy like me!"—their possible transformation in *real* beautiful actions. This in a form of behavior, a lifestyle oriented by the principle of a happy harmonization of the moral ought with the necessities of nature.

It is regarding this point that Schiller, still in the context of the *Kallias*, formulates for the first time his critique of Kant's rigorist ethics. Although without mentioning Kant, in this work Schiller manifests his dissatisfaction with the force that practical reason has been exercising over our inclinations in the moral determinations of the will. With the consideration that this force is opposed to any mediate intention and, therefore, always has "something humiliating and unpleasant in appearance," Schiller reaches the conclusion that moral actions can never be beautiful if they contain an element of coercion, if we are supposed to attend "the procedure by which they" are "extorted from sensibility."[17]

Schiller returns to this thought and tries to make it more specific and stronger in his work *On Grace and Dignity*. In the context of the previous meaning, he presents, already in the first pages of this work, beauty as a "citizen of two worlds," one to which "it belongs by birth" and the other to which it belongs "by adoption." Receiving "its existence in the sensible nature" and acquiring "its citizenship in the intelligible world," the role or employment of beauty consists in the aesthetic mediation between these two worlds. By the fact that the approach is concerned not with objects but with beautiful *actions* Schiller focuses his exposition on the human being *in movement*, or, more precisely, on that specific form of movement by which the beautiful is revealed: the gracious movement.

Unlike merely architectonic beauty, which Schiller considers to be the (aesthetic) beauty of the human body produced by nature and whose purpose and technical perfection directly correspond to an idea of reason, in the case of grace what is mainly under consideration is a *beauty produced by the subject*. By means of a classic allegory in which a magic belt that gives grace to the one who wears it is attributed to the goddess of beauty, Schiller develops the concept of a beauty produced by the subject showing that grace represents, according to this mythological figure, a "beauty *in movement*," that is, "a beauty that can causally originate itself in the subject and cease in the same way." According to Schiller, this is the reason why the referred beauty is distinguished from "fixed beauty that is necessarily given with the subject itself." Nevertheless, being the "explicit sense" of the Greek myth that the belt gives "the *objective* quality of grace" to the person adorned with it—and not, as it happens with other adornments, "its impression subjectively in the representation of the others"—grace makes it possible that the "belt's bearer not just *seems* to be but *is* endearing."[18]

Given, on the one hand, the *movable* and *nonnatural* character of such beauty and, on the other, its applicability merely to the domain of *human* beauty, it is obvious that not all human movements can be endowed with grace, but only the nonnatural, that is, the *voluntary* ones. Moreover, within this last group, only those that, according to the myth's idea, represent an *extension* of the naturally causal, namely, movements that are "expressions of *moral* feelings," can be endowed with grace. Because of this, Schiller concludes that wherever grace is presented "there the soul is the moving principle, and it is *in it* that is contained the cause of beauty of movement."[19]

With this formulation Schiller is resuming his previous argumentation: to speak of grace as an expression of moral feelings and as "beauty produced by the subject itself" means nothing more than to presuppose—not as an aesthetic illusion, but as an objective quality—something supernatural in the natural, that is, "freedom in the phenomenon."

Nevertheless, the approach of grace as a beauty not given by nature, but rather produced by the subject, and its description as a quality not grounded in the object, but rather as a kind not of object but of *action*, represents more than a variation or specification of the previous thesis. More clearly than the initial argumentation it reveals that the main motive of Schiller's aesthetic investigations into the beautiful is, basically, an eminently moral-practical motive. We can see now that Schiller's main concern is not the correction or the weakness of the Kantian aesthetic categories and, then, a new foundation to the beautiful, but the foundation of a new ethical perspective, in which the beautiful would occupy a constitutive place. The argumentative line that concerns this starts exactly where Schiller is speaking of the *soul* as an animated force *behind* all the human works and actions that are manifested in the senses as beautiful works and actions. Therefore, it is not surprising that, from now on, Schiller's discourse gets more and more distant from the analysis of the aesthetic-poetic moments to assume an explicitly practical-pedagogic character. The question concerning the creation of beautiful forms that show "freedom in appearance" becomes, thus, a question concerning the moral formation of character: the theme is not the production of an outer beautiful in relation to ourselves, but rather the formation of beauty in us, the beauty of the soul itself, that is, the "*beautiful soul*."[20]

This formation [*Bildung*] of character or of soul can simply consist, according to the aforesaid, in the learning of a determinate form—the beautiful form—in order to manage our sensible nature according to rational principles, that is, in the accomplishment of a process of compatibility, a harmonious adaptation of our inclinations to the apodictic requirements of reason. Certainly, the motive for the domestication of our instincts is or must be always moral and, therefore, of an absolutely unquestionable necessity. But, since "where the *moral* feeling finds satisfaction" there also "the *aesthetic* feeling does not want to be reduced" and the "agreement with an idea" cannot "cost any sacrifice in the phenomenon," then the spirit of the human being, whose destiny is "to be active and morally feel," is responsible for creating the necessary conditions to the harmonious coexistence of the good with the beautiful. In other words, the formation required from the spirit, "once the human being acquires conscience of his moral destiny," constitutes a work that, even thought not *morally* motivated, has to present itself to the senses by means of the results that are also *aesthetically* perceptible. Showing the "trails" of the work to which the spirit submitted itself, this formation must, as a result, be an "expressive formation" [*sprechende Bildung*] able to "speak for itself, that is, [a formation] that expresses a way of feeling adequate to its destiny, a moral aptitude."[21]

Schiller distinguishes, in what concerns the manner and the respective degree of this expressive formation, three relations that the human being can establish with respect to itself: in a first relation, he or she represses the requirements of his or her sensible nature to behave according to the "most elevated" requirements of reason; in a second relation, conversely, he or she subjects the rational part of his or her being to the sensible part, following simply "the impulse according to which natural necessity drags him as other phenomena"; in a third, finally, natural impulses and laws of reason are at balance. Logically, it is this third relation that characterizes the last phase of the formation of the spirit (and this is the only one that would make possible the so desired "free appearance" of beauty); "since, if *neither reason that dominates sensibility nor sensibility that dominates reason* match the beauty of expression, the condition under which the beauty of the play produces itself will be (and there is no fourth alternative) that state of mind *in which reason and sensibility*—ought and inclination—harmonize."[22]

In grounding beauty in the process of a specifically moral formation of the spirit, Schiller is able to approach more precisely that systematic question already at the idea of a "borrowed freedom" in the *Kallias* and at the allegory of Aphrodite's magic belt. That is, the question of how to connect *in the same object* something that is, at the same time, an expression of morality and also, as a gracious movement, an expression of beauty. Since, in the case of a virtually beautiful action, a positive conclusion is presupposed concerning the formation of the spirit, the result of this moral formation—precisely because it is the result of an obligated action of reason—is necessarily reflected as a beautiful quality in the phenomenon. Schiller can, in this sense, call beauty an "*obligation* of phenomena" and also justify this fact, provided that "the necessity which is referred to it in the subject is grounded in reason itself and, therefore, is general and necessary."[23] Furthermore, in his conception, because of the free character, that is, the independence of the beautiful from any conceptual determination, this obligation of the phenomena constitutes even a "*prior* obligation," since "before understanding starts its work sensibility already judged." Such "judgment of the senses" is possible not only because the will has, in general, "a connection more immediate to the faculty of the senses than to the faculty of knowledge," but also, and above all, because "in many cases"—that is, exactly in these cases that are exemplars of the accomplishment and evaluation of beautiful actions—it would be even against its own interests if it were supposed to guide itself first by reason:

> The man who is so unable to trust the voice of his instinct, who needs always to adjust it according to the moral principle does not inspire my sympathy; but one has great esteem for the man who securely places his trust in instinct without danger of being diverted by it. Therefore, this proves that both principles are in that harmony which is the stamp of a perfect humanity, and which is understood as a beautiful soul.[24]

With these words Schiller shows that he has, in fact, moved very far from the domain of Kant's own argumentation, in whose practical philosophy, as is known, there is no room either for an "obligation in the phenomena" or for the "voice of instinct." That Schiller himself has full consciousness of this is revealed by his explicit complaints, in this context of the exposition of his ideal of a beautiful soul, about the rigorous character of Kant's moral philosophy. According to Schiller, in this philosophy "the idea of the *ought* is presented with such a hardness that it drives away all Graces and could easily tempt a weak understanding to reach moral perfection by means of a dark and monastic asceticism." Considering that the "rigorous and raw contraposition of both principles that act on the human being's will" would not enable the systematic integration of the beautiful with the concept of a moral action, Schiller continues insisting on the necessity of a conciliation between sensibility and reason, between ought and inclination, as the only way to institute a criteria to determine what constitutes the human being's moral perfection. Man, we read once more in this respect, is not "destined" to practice this or that moral action, but rather "to *be a moral being*," what is prescribed to this moral being "are not *virtues*, but *the virtue*," and this is not originated in the *conflict* between ought and inclination, but is "nothing more than '*an inclination to the ought*.'"[25]

The meaning of this provocative (even though concurring with the spirit of his well-known arguments) formulation is not that there is or cannot be any *objective* opposition between actions performed by the ought and others performed by inclinations, between that which one wants and that which one must do, but simply this: that the human has, as a rational being, the "natural" commitment to do everything to solve such conflicts and, second and more important, to *willingly* do this. That is to say, "that, in the objective sense, not only *can* he connect pleasure with the ought but also *must* do this," that he "*must happily obey his reason*":[26]

> In making him a sensible and a rational being, nature . . . already imposed on [man] the obligation to maintain together what it has united; to keep himself connected to the purest manifestations of his divine part as well as with his sensible part and to not ground the triumph of the former in the oppression of the latter. Only when his character springs from *his whole humanity* as a united effect of both principles, *when he constitutes his own nature*, is he assured; because while moral spirit continues to make force, natural instinct still will have to show its *power* to it. A simply *collapsed* enemy can get up again, only a *resigned* enemy is truly beaten.[27]

Coming back once more to the initial question about the compatibility between Schiller's argumentation and Kant's position, it is worth asking if, in the latter, one does not find any place for the idea of a possible reconciliation between duty and desire, that is, if Kant's concern regarding a latitudinary interpretation of the concept of duty definitely prevents any possibility of a moral action that, even though accomplished according to a genuinely moral maxim, can *also* please the one who accomplishes it or someone else who sees a person accomplishing it. Does not Kant himself speak of a "duty concerning the culture" of the human being and, therefore, understand the obligation to strive the most one can so as to reach one's moral improvement in a way similar to Schiller's? Does not Kant also declare, on various occasions, that inclination to an action that "conforms with duty (e.g., to beneficence)" is not only possible but even desirable, since it "can indeed greatly facilitate the effectiveness of *moral* maxims" (*Practical Reason*, 5:118)?

This is, in fact, presented in a gentle and pacifying manner, but one could still ask what is really shown by it. It shows, above all, that Kant, with all his efforts to establish an exclusively transcendental foundation of morality, was also conscious that the domain to which this theory is related and in which it becomes real and has to prove, every time again, his universal validity, is not an abstract realm outside us, but the concrete world of our experience, the domain of empirical actions of every individual, whose preferences, interests, and dispositions can naturally be the most varied ones. This would be a way that, for example, something that represents a serious conflict to someone, would represent to someone else—who, according to the preceding, has a certain ability to cope with his or her inclinations—a salutation that is not even conflicting. In other words: Kant admits, in the apparently less rigorous observations presented earlier, merely the (relatively trivial) fact that, empirically, there are and always will be different degrees of moral comprehension and, on account of this, more and less fortunate ways of solving the respective conflicts between ought and inclination. Although it is always possible to relate such empirical data with a supposed "ideal of morality" and to determine, from this operation, the "moral value" of this or that action, it is clear that none of these data have something to do with or can become a part of the *transcendental* reflection on the *foundation* of morality as such.

At this level of the foundation any appeal to a determinate state of development reached by the sensible part and/or by the rational part of human nature in the process of formation of the spirit would automatically imply, as already said, in the infraction of the (transcendental) rules of argumentation, from which this foundation is solely possible. Furthermore, the integration of the element of a natural harmonization of the conflict between duty and inclination in transcendental reasoning would necessarily result in the abandonment or, according to the initially mentioned constructive sense, in the defeat of this manner of argumentation. What for Schiller represents an act of emancipation or of the autonomy of human nature, for Kant remains, within his strictly transcendental perspective, exactly the contrary, namely, a heteronomy. That is, the *heteronomy of the will*, which, being not subjected to material determinations, does not have another field to act autonomously except that which is marked by the *conflict* between ought and inclination, by the alternatives to act according to a moral or nonmoral manner. Thus, for Kant there is no other way to prove freedom of the will save by the unrestricted recognition of its obligation to make "free" decisions, that is, motivated exclusively by the ought, by the respect to the moral law, and not by the idea—perhaps aesthetically more attractive—of a harmonization of this law with the desirable ideal of morally beautiful actions.

Now we can say that it is the establishment of the will solely based on duty, on respect for the moral law, and also on its independence from any concept or value outside of it, that made Kant, in the commentary quoted in the beginning of this paper, pronounce himself—in spite of his "agreement on the most fundamental principles"[28]—clearly against a connection between beauty and morality, that is, against an immediate association of grace with the concept of the ought. It is not the *foundation* of morality in duty, but only the possible *consequence* of this foundation, "*virtue*," understood as a "firmly grounded disposition [*Gesinnung*] to strictly fulfill our duty," that can be associated with beauty and, as a "splendid picture of humanity," allows "the attendance of the *Graces*," which, "when one still speaks of the ought," cannot "meddle in the business of determination" of it, "in order to try to provide incentives of action," but must always "keep a respectful distance" (*Religion*, 6:23–24).

According to Kant's transcendental perspective, that the moral act of the human being has grace, that there are beautiful actions and, as their ground, a "beautiful soul," which is the expression of "the moral destiny of humanity," represent nothing more than *regulative principles* (of action and of moral behavior), or principles of *application*, but not *constitutive principles* of the *foundation* of morality as such.

In what concerns Schiller's perspective, on the other hand, it is known that he did not simply accept the final verification of the incompatibility of his ethical-aesthetic proposal with Kant's transcendental basic principles, but rather continued "constructively" working on the elaboration of his central ideas on the necessity of the moral manifestation of beautiful actions of the human being and the foundation of this beauty in a pure concept of reason. This work culminated in the publication of his last great philosophical-pedagogic study on the topic, namely, *The Aesthetic Education of Man* (1795), in which, by means of an audacious synthesis of his previous ethical and aesthetic reflections and the historical and political speculations resulting from them, he finally succeed in grounding his conception of the human as a rational being who is ethical and aesthetically formed and who, owing to the harmonious development of his natural dispositions, is predestined to the construction of a happy society.

Nevertheless, it is worth considering that in this work—in spite of the extension of the perspective and the new argumentative apparatus used in it—the systematic connection with Kant's doctrine is clearly maintained.[29] Therefore, the immanent tension between the transcendental part and the constructive moment of Schiller's own discourse is also maintained. This tension, which already marked the previous argumentation, is the reason why Schiller's theory, even in its mature version, keeps holding its systematic ambiguity. This means that, in its entirety, Schiller's theory, far from constituting a definitive systematization or integration in a philosophical horizon already finished, represents more an incentive for the effort to present a possible systematic connection between the good and the beautiful than an accurate solution to this problem.

Notes

1. Friedrich Schiller, *Gesamtausgabe*, ed. Gerhard Fricke, 20 vols. (Munich: Deutscher Taschenbuch Verlag, 1966), 18:136.
2. Ibid.

3. Letter to Friedrich Heinrich Jacobi, June 29, 1795, in ibid.

4. That is, a year before the letter to Jacobi of June 29.

5. Letter to Prince Friedrich Christian von Schleswig-Holstein-Augustenburg, February 9, 1793, in Schiller, *Gesamtausgabe*, 19:223 (my emphasis added).

6. Schiller, *Gesamtausgabe*, 19:224.

7. Ibid.

8. Letter to Gottfried Körner, December 21, 1792, in Schiller, *Gesamtausgabe*, 17:233.

9. The exposition of Schiller's arguments (including the literal quotations) in the next paragraphs are drawn from Schiller, *Gesamtausgabe*, 17:166–74.

10. In the German text Schiller uses the word *erscheinen*, which in general means "to appear." But in this specific context in which he points out the difference between *to be free* and *to seem to be free* (without in fact being free) it is better to translate it as "to seem" (*scheinen*).

11. Concerning the translation of the German word *Erscheinung*, consider the following note.

12. The German word "*Erscheinung*," in Schiller's famous formula "*Schönheit ist Freiheit in der Erscheinung*," means both "appearance" and "phenomenon." We can find in some translations the word "phenomenon." Even though it is not so close to Schiller's linguistic intentions, this option is wholly defensible since the context in itself sufficiently explains in what manner and in which sense the *phenomenon* allows the *appearance* of the beauty of the object.

13. It was Gottfried Körner who, in a letter of January 18, 1793, called Schiller's attention to the English painter William Hogarth (1697–1764) who wrote about this line in *The Analysis of Beauty* (1753) (Schiller, *Gesamtausgabe*, 19:189).

14. Schiller, *Gesamtausgabe*, 17:189.

15. Ibid.

16. Ibid., 17:173.

17. Ibid.

18. Ibid., 18:5–6 (emphasis mine).

19. Ibid., 18:8.

20. Ibid.

21. Ibid., 18:26–27.

22. Ibid., 18:31.

23. Ibid., 18:16 (all quotations in this paragraph).

24. Ibid., 18:35–36.

25. Ibid., 18:32–33 (emphasis mine).

26. This and the following quotation in ibid., 18:33 (emphasis mine).

27. Schiller defends himself against this critique (18:32) even before the publication of the second edition of Kant's writing on religion, that is, without being aware of Kant's commentaries concerning the theses expressed in *On Grace and Dignity*.

28. Schiller, *Gesamtausgabe*, 8:136.

29. Following the very same meaning of what Schiller wrote two years previously in his letters to Jacobi and Prince Friedrich Christian, we read in the First Letter that Schiller "does not [want] to hide that, to a great extent, it is on Kantian principles that the affirmations that will follow are grounded" (*Gesamtausgabe*, 9:5).

19

Reading the Appendix to Kant's *Critique of the Teleological Power of Judgment*

Pedro Pimenta

Nature in its purposive forms speaks figuratively to us, says Kant; the interpretation of its cipher yields us the phenomenon of freedom in ourselves.

F. W. J. von Schelling, *System of Transcendental Idealism*

The subject of this article is the second part of Kant's *Critique of the Power of Judgment*, concerning teleological judgment. The aim is to show through a close reading of the appendix the role of reflective teleological judgments in promoting the connection or transition (*Übergang*) between the theoretical and the practical principles of reason as a single faculty. Such a reading implies that the text of the appendix is a consistent and coherent part of Kant's exposition in the third *Critique*. That the third *Critique* deals with this connection in its different configurations is what Kant states in both introductions, the definitive and the discarded, to the *Critique of the Power of Judgment* (5:176–79 and 20:193–208). Within the scope of the critical examination of reflective judgment in its teleological function, the connection between practical and pure reason discovers itself in a manner that shows that a transcendental meaning, rather than transcendent, must be attributed to the concepts examined in the second *Critique* concerning *practical reason*, namely, those of a highest good, of a deity, of the immortality of the soul, and of freedom.

The appendix is entitled Doctrine of the Method of the Teleological Power of Judgment. Having presented a close inspection of the transcendental principles of teleological judgment, Kant goes on to show what use is to be made of teleological judgments or, in other words, what their legitimate use is from a critical point of view. From the outset the appendix brings home the point that

This article was originally published as "Relexão e finalidade: A finitude da razão na *Crítica do juízo*," in *Discurso* 32 (2002): 193–234. Translated by the author.

teleology as a discipline cannot be a part of science as such, because so far as human reason goes this species of judgment is not concerned with the explanation of things in nature, but only with describing them.

> Strictly speaking, positing ends of nature in its products, insofar as it constitutes a system in accordance with teleological concepts, belongs only to the description of nature, which is composed in accordance with a particular guideline, in which reason certainly plays a role that is magnificently instructive and purposive in many respects, but in which it provides no information at all about the origination and the inner possibility of these forms, although it is that with which theoretical natural science is properly concerned. (*Judgment*, 5:417)

The distinction between *describing* and *explaining* duplicates that between *subjective maxims* and *objective principles*, stated by Kant in the *Groundwork of the Metaphysics of Morals* and fully exploited in the *Critique of Practical Reason* (*Groundwork*, 4:420–21 note; *Practical Reason*, 5:19). *To explain* is the task of the understanding, concerned as it is with syntheses of sensible data by means of concepts or categories. As the first *Critique* plainly states, the concept of a purposiveness of nature is not among those of the understanding, and is to be considered transcendent from the point of view of knowledge.[1] On the other hand, *to describe* is just that: to find a concept for a particular object that can be satisfactorily understood by means of such concept. This applies to judgments of taste as well as to teleological judgments. The problem, Kant seems to imply, is that human reason tends to take descriptions for explanations, or rather to see in our capacity to describe the possibility of explaining. Description is the operation of reflective judgments by means of which human reason can make sense of things without actually knowing them. It is one thing to talk about natural beings as products of art, it is another to pretend to account for organic forms in terms of the supposed laws that would render them possible as such, as intrinsically different from mechanical aggregates. In the first instance we have at our disposal, that is, within the bounds of human reason, an art of describing; in the second, we enter the uncertain realm of speculation (*Judgment*, 5:197).[2]

The power of describing without explaining allow us, on the other hand, to think of things described in terms of purposiveness as belonging to a system. And it is here that we come to understand what the object of speculation is that human reason pursues in teleology. The description of natural beings as organisms leads us to infer a principle of formation underlying all form. Modern philosophers such as Ralph Cudworth referred to this principle in terms of a "plastic of nature." Kant rejects what he considers to be such imprecise vocabulary and talks of a "technique of nature," a principle *of* the judgment and *for* the judgment that does not concern "things in themselves" (*First Introduction*, 20:232, note; *Judgment*, 5:365).

This in turn explains why teleology is part of a doctrine, *Lehre*, but not of a science, *Wissenschaft*, and also why, nevertheless, it is perfectly legitimate from a critical point of view to describe nature in teleological terms—provided this does not develop to an ontological statement concerning things in themselves.[3] The distinction between doctrine and science also prevents us from taking a transcendental principle (technique of nature) for a transcendent principle (plastics). The subjective origins of the principle of purposiveness prohibits teleology from becoming part of a theoretical science that is prone to metaphysical speculation. In short, reason should rest satisfied with having a "negative influence" as teleology both on a doctrine of nature and on a theological doctrine (*Judgment*, 5:416–17). This already indicates in clear terms that reflective judgment is equidistant from theoretical and practical reason.[4]

To determine more precisely the role of teleology in the system of philosophy, Kant has to draw a careful if controversial distinction between two species of reflective judgments of purposiveness. First, there are judgments that describe beings, and especially those that manifest some sort of life as organisms, that is, as organized systems, complete in themselves. This species of purposiveness seems to be clearly in breach of the laws of nature such as are conceived in the understanding through which one can consider the same sort of being by mere mechanical principles. But the contradiction is merely apparent, as Kant explains:

> Just as the mechanism of nature . . . is not by itself sufficient for conceiving of the possibility of an organized being . . . the mere teleological ground of such a being is equally inadequate for considering and judging it as a product of nature unless the mechanism of the latter is associated with the former, as if it were the tool of an intentionally acting cause to whose ends nature is subordinated, even in its mechanical laws. (*Judgment*, 5:421–42)

This species of purposiveness is then coherent with mechanical principles, since one principle of judgment, far from excluding the other, complements it: teleology enriches our *knowledge* of natural beings, allowing reason to call them organisms—or systems.[5] This would be impossible within the limits of the understanding, since systematic comprehension of natural beings concerns their manner of formation (*Judgment*, 5:417–18). This kind of purposiveness (*Zweckmässigkeit*), postulated by reflective judgment, is intrinsic (*inneren*) and concerns merely the form of the thing under consideration (*Judgment*, 5:424).[6]

> But intrinsic or internal purposiveness leads the mind to a further consideration:
>
> Now things that have no internal purposiveness or presuppose none for their possibility, e.g., soils, air, water, etc., can nevertheless be quite purposive externally, i.e., in relation to other beings; but these must always be

> organized beings, i.e., natural ends, for otherwise the former could not be judged as means at all. (*Judgment*, 5:425)

Kant introduces here a difficult point he had been dealing with since 1763. For "extrinsic purposiveness" (*äussern Zweckmässigkeit*) can only be admitted in a general system of beings in which some of them operate as ends while others function as means to those ends. This is "an entirely different concept" (*ein ganz anderes Begriff*) from that of "intrinsic purposiveness," for while we can discern the *function* of a single organized being by examining the relations between its constitutive parts, the same cannot be said of a system of nature as a whole, or at least not without risking the reintroduction of old philosophical prejudices.[7]

Unorganized things must be judged as means conformable to organized things as ends. But in pursuing an answer to the question, why do these creatures exist?, human reason tends to offer an answer along the lines of "for the human being, . . . and he is the ultimate end of creation here on earth" (*Judgment*, 5:426). Indeed, Kant accepts this anthropomorphic argument, but with a twist that proves to be decisive. For to say something like that and to remain within the limits of mere reason is possible only if we take the meaning of the sentence "the human being is the ultimate end (*letzter Zweck*) of creation" to be that human reason, in considering nature as a system, is led to the conclusion that the place of the human being in this system is at the end, that is to say, that one's own intelligence and comprehension depends the possibility of such a system (*Judgment*, 5:428–29). In the same manner that things as *phenomena* cannot be said to have intrinsic ends *in themselves*, it is a mistake to assert, as metaphysicians and natural historians alike are prone to do, that extrinsic purposiveness belongs to nature as a system in itself: it is reflective judgment that makes it a principle that nature *must* be considered as a system so that experience in general becomes possible.[8]

In what sense, then, are human beings said to be nature's *letzter Zweck*?

> Now if that which is to be promoted as an end through the human being's connection to nature is to be found within the human being himself, then it must be either the kind of end that can be satisfied by the beneficence of nature itself, or it is the aptitude and skill for all sorts of ends for which he can use nature (external and internal). The first end of nature would be the *happiness*, the second the *culture* of the human being. (*Judgment*, 5:429–30)

These two ends—happiness and culture—sufficiently show that there is no reason for us to inquire concerning transcendent intentions implanted in nature by an intelligent being in our favor. Happiness, as argued in the second *Critique* (5:34–35), is an end of the imagination, whose attributes cannot be known or determined a priori. Instead of leading us to the enjoyment of such a state, maxims aiming at it only lead us astray from moral or rational ends. Which leads us to the following conclusion:

> It is so far from being the case that nature has made the human being its special favorite and favored him with beneficence above all other animals, that it has rather spared him just as little as any other animal from its destructive effects, whether of pestilence, hunger, danger of flood, cold, attacks by other animals great and small, etc.; even more, the conflict in the natural predispositions of the human being, reduces himself and others of his own species, by means of plagues that he invents for himself . . . to such need, and he works so hard for the destruction of his own species, that even if the most beneficent nature outside of us had made the happiness of our species its end, that end would not be attained in a system of nature upon the earth, because the nature inside of us is not receptive to that. (*Judgment*, 5:430–31)

This implies that to speak of a *letzter Zweck*, or of an ultimate end, is to refer nature as a system to the human being as a principle. But to think of the human being as a principle is to exceed the realm of nature as articulated by the reflective judgment, since it is clear that a human being, in its creative relation with nature, does not meet the ends that it finds inscribed in its rational faculties. Nature is not at our entire disposal, it only answers to ends proposed by reason insofar as they involve in their conception some kind of sensible element. Culture (*Kultur*), on the other hand, is a kind of activity that displays the seeds, so to speak, of the superior forms of rationality that human beings are capable of. Human nature has an animal as well as a rational, nobler side: "The production of the aptitude of a rational being for any ends in general (thus those of his freedom) is *culture*. Thus only culture can be the ultimate end that one has cause to ascribe to nature in regard to the human species" (*Judgment*, 5:431).

The improvement of natural dispositions in the human being, the advancement of *Bildung*, is precisely that which enhances the difference between natural and rational disposition in the mind of the human being, that is, the natural capacity of overcoming mere natural dispositions. It is here that *purposiveness* becomes *teleology*. The human being is not merely the ultimate end of nature, it is also its *Endzweck*, or its "final end."[9]

This consideration of reflective judgment enables us to describe nature as a system. As a mediate faculty, reflective judgment formulates a teleology as a doctrine that does not belong to either practice or theory. The remaining systematic task for Kant is to show the terms in which it is possible to speak of a transcendental connection between practical and theoretical reason by means of reflective teleological judgments.

Such a connection has already been suggested, in a manner, by the text of the appendix itself. When Kant speaks of the human being as *letzter Zweck*, an ultimate end, he is describing the human being as both a natural and intellectual being, capable of partially imposing rational concepts or ideas on materials of sensibility comprehended through laws of the understanding. The difference between hypothetical and categorical imperatives, stated in the *Groundwork*, is reinforced here through a different approach. Whereas in the *Groundwork* Kant stresses the negative aspect of such difference, showing the human being's sensible nature as kind of restraint to its rational nature, in the appendix the determining of the power of choice (*Willkür*) aiming at sensible objects serves as an instance of the rationality, albeit incomplete, that is the main feature of human nature. Once this positive approach is adopted, hypothetical imperatives can be seen rather as inferior instances of the pure determination of the will (*Willen*) by the idea of reason, which Kant denominates by the term "autonomy" (*Groundwork*, 4:446).[10]

But an *ultimate goal* is not, as we have seen, the same as a *final end*—an *Endzweck*: culture does not equate with morality (*Idea*, seventh proposition, 8:24–26). By definition, a final end is that which, in order to be made possible, does not require any other end beyond itself (*Judgment*, 5:434). This includes in rational perspective all natural, subordinate ends, for

> there is nothing in nature (as a sensible being) the determining ground of which, itself found in nature, is not always in turn conditioned; and this holds not merely for nature outside of us (material nature), but also for nature inside of us (thinking nature)—as long as it is clearly understood that I am considering only that within me which is nature. (*Judgment*, 5:435)

By *Endzweck*—a term whose sense implies what in us *is not* strictly nature—Kant means then an end whose sole condition is the idea of it (*Judgment*, 5:435). In this sense, the human being is first an intellectual, then a sensible being. Culture and happiness are its natural goals; but the human being is in nature the "only natural being in which we can nevertheless cognize, on the basis of its own constitution, a supersensible faculty (*freedom*) and even the law of the causality together with the object that it can set for itself as the highest end (the highest good in the world)" (*Judgment*, 5:435). The theological, anthropomorphic philosophical formula, "The human being as the end of creation" is reduced by Kant to a moral-rational imperative. It is due to the constitution of our faculties that we are led to conceive our place in nature as the ultimate term, as an end that is absolute only in reference to all other sensible things. Nature is at the disposal of reason only insofar as the human being behaves in a rational manner or, in Kantian terms, as it acts freely through the rational determination of the will.

The recognition of this capacity leads to an inversion of perspective, for now it is clear that to have an idea of an ultimate end is the same as to have a priori purely formal conditions of proposing ends in general, including sensible ends:

> Now if things in the world, as dependent beings as far as their existence is concerned, need a supreme cause acting in accordance with ends, then the human being is the final end of creation; for without him the chain of ends subordinated to one another would not be completely grounded; and only in the human being, although in him only as a subject of morality, is unconditional legislation with regard to ends to be found, which therefore makes him alone capable of being a final end, to which the whole of nature is teleologically subordinated. (*Judgment*, 5:435–36)

The place assigned by Kant to a doctrine of teleological judgment corresponds precisely to the intermediate position of the faculty of judgment in relation to theoretical and practical uses of reason. Such a doctrine does not belong either to theory (the knowledge of nature) or to practice (the laws of morality), but rather connects the concepts of the understanding and the ideas of reason through a common principle, namely, purposiveness of nature. This arrangement is made possible by the very nature of each of these faculties, understanding and reason. To understand is to conceive nature in mechanical terms; to reason is to conceive it in teleological terms. Purposiveness is the reflective principle that connects, in the human mind, mechanism and teleology, allowing us to know particular nature in such terms as are made to be compatible with the ideas we have of it as a system.

But the appendix inquires further into the developments of such a discipline of the rational faculty as a doctrine of the method of teleological judgment. These can be easily discerned. Systematic comprehension of nature leads reason to formulate a doctrine that Kant calls "physical theology" (§85). At this point, the tone of the appendix becomes overtly polemical, since it inevitably tackles traditional philosophical issues concerning the being and attributes of God.

In the context of eighteenth-century thought, physical theology is a term that can be understood in general as the demonstration of the existence of an intelligent being, the author of nature, from empirical data taken as rational evidence of this. The *Critique of the Teleological Power of Judgment* implies that for Kant such a philosophical task is absurd per se, if by empirical data one means either perceptions summoned by the understanding or representations of natural beings as organisms, since both of these are transcendental constructions, not empirical evidence that could be taken as natural signs of order. The doctrine delineated in the appendix serves not for theological purposes; rather, it shows how theological categories arise from reason alone. If human reason speaks of a God, there must be a rationale for this within human faculties, and such as is sufficient to show the necessity of the admission of the existence of God without any further empirical evidence of order. Thus, reflective judgment of the teleological kind, going beyond mere mechanism and mere purposiveness, requires that a natural order or disposition of things be explained by a concept of a sufficient cause capable of articulating such an order by virtue of its "infinite intelligence."

It is here that the "concept of a divinity" underlying natural order, as reflected by human judgment, becomes necessary. Such a necessity is understood by Kant as subjective, that is, as being valid only insofar as it concerns human reason and its ends (i.e., practical ends) (*Judgment*, 5:441).[11] The moral perspective is that which allows sound human reason, and critical philosophy, to postulate the existence of God without recourse to the transcendent realm cheered by metaphysicians of old. To be necessary, the existence of God depends on the human being recognizing itsef as a moral agent, or, in the context of the appendix, recognizing in nature something else beyond "a mere desert" of creation (*Judgment*, 5:442), the "realm of ends" in which to effectuate the ends of practical reason:

> We have . . . a ground for a principle for conceiving, for the relation of natural ends to an intelligent world-cause that is necessary given the constitution of our reason, of the nature and the properties of this first cause as the supreme ground in the realm of ends, and so for determining the concept of it—which physical teleology, which could only produce concepts that are indeterminate and for that very reason unsuited for both theoretical as well as practical use, could not do. (*Judgment*, 5:444)[12]

But in order that the "immeasurable gap" (*unsehebares Kluft*) between practical and theoretical reason be definitively surpassed, a further step is required. And here reflective judgment gives way to practical reason, or rather the connection between practical and theoretical reason is shown to be dependent on practical reason, whose interest is said by Kant to be the "highest" (*höchsten*). Or, in the words of the second *Critique*: "In the union of pure speculative with pure practical reason in one cognition, the latter has primacy, assuming that this union is not *contingent* and discretionary but based *a priori* on reason itself and therefore *necessary*" (*Practical Reason*, 5:121). It is with its own practical interest in view that reason is justified in assuming the existence of an infinite intelligent being that is also "a moral cause of the world" (*Judgment*, 5:450). It is by means of an inference, then, that we arrive at the conclusion of the existence of God:

> Now the only concept of this sort to be encountered in human reason is the concept of the freedom of human beings under moral laws, together with the final end that reason prescribes by means of this law, the first of which is suitable for ascribing to the author of nature and the second of which is suitable for ascribing to human beings those properties that contain the necessary

> condition for the possibility of both—so that the existence and the constitution of this being who is otherwise entirely hidden from us can be inferred from this very idea. (*Judgment*, 5:473–74)

This moral concept of God belongs to reason; it is an idea dependent on the freedom of the agent who follows the moral law and who requires, as a necessary condition for its own acting, a disposition of the world as moral system. God is here a concept that allows reason to interpret nature as a system favorable to the effectuation of moral laws (*Judgment*, 5:451). The disparity between the sensible and the supersensible is replaced, in the operation of reflective judgments, by that coordination of perspectives in the same representation that Kant sees as the highest aim of all critical philosophy, as conductive to a new form of metaphysics (*Judgment*, 5:456; and *Pure Reason*, B29–30).[13]

The appendix further articulates the relation between the practical concept of the existence of God with those of immortality of the soul, freedom, happiness, and a kingdom of ends.[14] But to infer the existence of a suprasensible God, of the immortality of the soul, and of a supreme good in which virtue and happiness finally meet is only to conclude that freedom, in determining the will of the human being, opens up a new perspective that requires the human being to review the sensible world so that it can make sense from a suprasensible point of view:

> Here we have to do (or are playing) merely with ideas created by reason itself, whose objects (if they have any) lie wholly beyond our field of vision (*Gesichtskreis*); although they are transcendent for speculative cognition, they are not taken as empty, but with a practical intent they are made available to us by lawgiving reason itself, yet not in order to brood over their objects as to what they are in themselves and in their nature, but rather how we have to think of them in behalf of moral principles directed toward the final end of all things. (*End*, 8:332–33)

The appendix is not by any means Kant's final word on the subject of the relation between morals and religion. Transcendental as well as empirical aspects of the matter will be further discussed by the philosopher in important writings such as the *Religion within the Boundaries of Mere Reason* (1793) and the *Conflict of the Faculties* (1798). The contribution of a close, albeit short reading of some passages of the appendix such as we have tried to offer here may perhaps lie in the fact that it illuminates the decisive point that Kant's critical philosophy conceives religious notions as having a purely transcendental origin. In that sense, we can speak of a natural religion within the limits of pure reason as being for Kant the only true religion as such. If metaphysics is to have a new meaning, why should theology and religion be exempted from some kind of radical redefinition?[15]

From a more systematic point of view, the appendix is the final occasion for Kant to reinforce the role of the *Critique of the Power of Judgment* as part of the system of critical philosophy. It is true that in a sense each and every part of the *Critique of the Power of Judgment* is a constant reminder of the connections or transitions that critical philosophy discovers in the human mind between the different and complementary legislations of pure and practical reason. The scope of the discussion advanced by Kant in the appendix allows him to evince any further objections concerning the critical concept of nature as referred to moral ends. Reflective judgment, in its teleological configuration, shows that moral ends and ends said to be in nature are fundamentally the same, as both stem from the same source, human reason.[16]

Given this, if the nature of religious objects constitutes such an important issue in the appendix, it is mainly because it is a *theme* arising from the close inspection of that obscure region in which practical and theoretical reason meet. Reflective judgment, far from being a lesser, unimportant part of Kant's philosophy, is the necessary confirmation of the conclusion stated in the *Critique of Pure Reason* and in the *Critique of Practical Reason*. In surveying those regions of the mind where metaphysical notions are engendered, the third *Critique* brings to light the connections between the higher faculties of the *Gemüt* so as to show that, if philosophy is necessarily a system, it is by virtue of reason being a kind of organization that operates from systematic principles. And surely one of the paradoxes stemming from this new "way of thinking" (*Denkungsart*) is that, without adding to the rational faculty any "principle of insight" (*Grundsatz der Einsichten*), critical philosophy is able to discover a "subjective principle" (*Orient*, 8:137, 140) that is sufficient for the satisfaction of the most ambitious goals of reason—those concerning the principles of moral rectitude.[17]

Notes

Epigraph. F. W. J. von Schelling, *System of Transcendental Idealism*, trans. Peter Heath (Charlottesville: University Press of Virginia, 1978), par. 608, 215–16.

1. This is discussed by Kant in the appendix to the Transcendental Dialectic. As is well known, both the *First Introduction* and the second book of the third *Critique* offer a substantial reappraisal of that section.

2. See also the translator's notes in Alexis Philonenko, *Critique de faculté de juger* (Paris: Vrin, 1993), 358; Antonio Marques, *Organismo e sistema em Kant* [Organism and system in Kant] (Lisbon: Presença, 1987), 336–37; and Gérard Lebrun, *Kant et la fin de la métaphysique* (Paris: Colin, 1970), 112–14.

3. Concerning this point, see J. D. MacFarland, *Kant's Concept of Teleology* (Edinburgh: University Press, 1970), esp. chapter 1, "The Justification of Natural Science."

4. J. A. Gianotti, *Kant e o espaço da história universal* [Kant and the place of universal history] (São Paulo: Martins Fontes, 2005), 106–7.

5. The analogy between these two terms is explicitly suggested by Kant in the *Prolegomena*, 4:263; and in the second preface to the *Critique of Pure Reason*, B38.

6. The point of Kant's argument, frequently misunderstood, is that since purposiveness concerns the *form* of the representation, and since form is a word that applies merely to the human manner of intuition, to concepts of the understanding and to relations between our faculties, it does not and cannot concern any matter whatsoever of knowledge. It is in this sense that the concept of an end (*Zweck*) is said by Kant to be subjective. The same applies to the judgments of taste dealt with in the first part of the *Critique of the Power of Judgment*: to have a sentiment (*Gefühl*) in a representation does not require any kind of knowledge, but merely certain configurations between the different powers of the mind. See Louis Guillermit, *L'élucidation critique du jugement de goût* (Paris: CNRS, 1986), 78–84.

7. See Lebrun, *Kant et la fin*, 672–73.

8. See Lebrun, *Kant et la fin*, 724–25; and Marques, *Organismo e sistema*, 344, 348.

9. This is Kant's ultimate solution for the conceptual problems posed in the essay *Idea for a Universal History*. See Ricardo R. Terra, *A política tensa: Idéia e realidade na filosofia da história da Kant* (Sao Paulo: Iluminuras, 1997), esp. chapter 2, part 3.

10. The definitive study is still, in many aspects, that of H. J. Paton: *The Categorial Imperative* (Philadelphia: University of Pennsylvania Press, 1948).

11. See also *Progress in Metaphysics* (20:304); and the different approaches of Philonenko, *Critique*, 414; and Eric Weil, "Penser et connaître," in Eric Weil, *Problèmes kantiennes* (Paris: Vrin, 1970), 51–52.

12. See Lebrun, *Kant et la fin*, 761–62; and Lebrun, "La raison pratique dans la *Critique du jugement*," in Gérard Lebrun, *Sobre Kant* [On Kant] (Sao Paulo: Iluminuras, 1993), 103.

13. See Rubens R. Torres, *Ensaios de filosofia ilustrada* [Essays on enlightened philosophy], 2nd ed. (São Paulo: Iluminuras, 2004), 187–88.

14. The reader will find an interesting exposition of this in Allen Wood, *Kant's Moral Religion* (Ithaca: Cornell University Press, 1970).

15. See the important study of Jean-Louis Bruch, *La philosophie kantienne de la réligion* (Paris: Aubier, 1968).

16. For a closer inspection of this point, see Thomas Auxter's fine book, *Kant's Moral Teleology* (Macon: Mercer University Press, 1982), 65–80.

17. I would like to express my sincere gratitude to Professor Ricardo R. Terra at the University of São Paulo, Brazil.

20

Symbolization in Kant's Critical Philosophy

Joãosinho Beckenkamp

Just as he concluded in great style the secular development of philosophical enlightenment, Kant also opened a new space in which the programs of subsequent philosophy would be developed. In particular, German Idealism owes a great deal to him concerning the conceptions of reason, idea, and even philosophy itself.

I would like to show that Kant can also be considered the philosopher who marked the place in which both idealists and romantics would soon lay claim to what they called a "new mythology." Therefore, I will begin with a short text first published in 1917 by Franz Rosenzweig, "Das älteste Systemprogramm des deutschen Idealismus" (The oldest system program of German idealism), that can be considered a real program of post-Kantian German philosophy at the end of eighteenth century.

Dated from 1796, or at the latest 1797, this fragment has been the object of an endless debate that has even involved the question of its authorship; it is sometimes attributed to Hegel, sometimes to Schelling or even Hölderlin. This difficulty in determining the authorship of the text clearly points to these authors' community of purpose, at least at that moment. Without exaggeration, one could consider this fragment a shared program of both romantics and idealists until the end of eighteenth century. Thus, this program raises various issues about Kant's critical philosophy.

The system program does this directly by putting itself in a line of continuity with Kant's practical philosophy: "Since all metaphysics will henceforth fall into *morals*—for which Kant, with both of his practical postulates, has only given an *example* and *exhausted* nothing—, so this ethics will contain nothing other than a complete system of all ideas or, what is the same, of all practical postulates."[1] Future metaphysics would be thus a systematic development of the ideas of reason, of which Kant, in his doctrine of practical postulates, had

This article was originally published as "Simbolização na filosofia crítica kantiana," in *Kant e-Prints* 1, no. 1 (2002): 1–8; ftp://logica.cle.unicamp.br/pub/kant-e-prints/simbol.pdf. Translated by the author.

touched only upon the ideas of God and immortality. The task we are now to undertake is a complete analysis of the ideas of reason now founded in morals. This development of ideas is first conceived of as a development of reason in its own element, therefore as a philosophical program in a traditional sense.

But the most interesting suggestion in order to localize future developments in German idealism and romanticism consists of giving a sensible aspect to the ideas of reason for the sake of acquiring the people's interest. This suggestion appears as a response to the necessity of a sensible religion or mythology: "At the same time, we so often hear that the great multitude should have a *sensual religion*. Not only the great multitude, but even philosophy needs it. Monotheism of reason and the heart, polytheism of the imagination and art, that is what we need!"[2] So that the ideas of reason to be developed in the way suggested by Kant may become part of the life of the great mass, it is necessary that they assume the form of imagination and art, that is, they must become sensible. But this form of imagination, so much appreciated by the people, is largely found in the fables of mythology. A new mythology, therefore, is needed to present the ideas of reason in a sensible form, sufficient for imagination and art: "we must have a new mythology, this mythology must, however, stand in the service of ideas, it must become a mythology of *reason*."[3] The program proposes, therefore, the introduction of a new mythology so that the ideas of reason may penetrate the domain of the sensible, particularly through imagination and art. The necessity of this new mythology is explicitly presented as a necessity for the collective, since we shouldn't await a greater penetration of reason in the great popular mass without a corresponding sensible form: "Until we make ideas aesthetic, i.e., mythological, they hold no interest for the *people*, and conversely, before mythology is reasonable, the philosopher must be ashamed of it. Thus finally the enlightened and unenlightened must shake hands; mythology must become philosophical, and the people reasonable, and philosophy must become mythological in order to make philosophy sensual."[4] So that the people and philosophers do not become estranged from each other and, above all, so that the real unity of all elements of a people comes to be, the mythology of the people must be pervaded by reason, and the reason of philosophers must be made sensible by the sensible form of mythology. From this program we can understand a series of developments within both German idealism and romanticism.

We can see also to what extent these developments could come out of Kant's philosophy, in which we find the great practical change of modern philosophy toward morality or ethics. Practically all philosophy in the future should be developed from the demands of morality. Concerning the development of ideas of reason in its philosophical element, the program can be understood without difficulty as a continuation of Kant's work. What we want to show here is that we can also find in Kant the elements with which to address the demand of a sensibilization of the ideas of reason, thereby preparing the grounds on which it became possible to formulate the demand for a new mythology. Since, in Kant's critical philosophy, the demand to make sensible the ideas of reason is addressed by the process of symbolizing, this topic will allow us to decide to what extent Kant laid the foundations for a renewal of interest in mythology within the Enlightenment itself.

Symbolizing is a type of exhibition, an exhibition of ideas of reason. Generally, Kant's critical philosophy is characterized by the thesis that all knowledge we can have depends on two essential elements, the conceptual and the intuitive. In order to have objective validity, a concept must be related to intuition or some intuitive element. In the case of empirical concepts, we address this demand for an intuitive instance simply by giving an example, that is, by showing an example of empirical intuition (*Judgment*, 5:354). The case of pure concepts is more difficult, since they don't allow empirical exemplification. The intuitive relation of pure concepts cannot be given by a sensible intuition or an empirical instance, because they have to show that they can be related to a pure intuition. This provides the organization of the general problem of the exhibition (*Darstellung*) of pure concepts, of which there are two types: understanding and reason. As we have seen, the question of exhibition is of great importance in Kant's transcendental philosophy because the pure concepts of understanding and reason, since they have no empirical anchorage, are suspected of possibly having no sense at all.[5] The failure in the exhibition of a pure concept would imply its emptiness: "Where we are unable to achieve this [to represent a pure concept], the concept is empty, i.e., it suffices for no knowledge" (*Progress in Metaphysics*, 20:279). That is, if we cannot give objective reality to a pure concept, whether of understanding or of reason, exhibiting it in its connection with an object of possible experience, then this concept is empty and cannot contribute to knowledge. Consequently, if a pure concept should have any theoretical relevance, it must be possible to exhibit it, that is, there must be a procedure for its exhibition.

In his transcendental philosophy, Kant was very careful to show that the pure concepts of understanding (categories) are of a very different nature than the concepts of pure reason (ideas). Thus it is that he conceives a procedure of direct exhibition in intuition for the pure concepts of understanding, a procedure called schematism, while for the pure concepts of reason no such procedure of direct exhibition is given, that is, any true exhibition (*Progress in Metaphysics*, 20:279). So we have two kinds of exhibition of pure concepts, one, properly speaking, for the exhibition of pure concepts of understanding, and another, in a broader sense, for the indirect exhibition of pure concepts of reason, called "symbolizing" by Kant: "If it cannot be presented immediately, but only in its consequences (*indirecte*), it [the act of representing the concept] may be called the symbolization of the concept. The first occurs with concepts of the sensible, the second is an expedient for concepts of the super-sensible which are therefore not truly presented, and can be given in no possible experience, though they still necessarily appertain to a cognition, even if it were possible merely as a practical one" (*Progress in Metaphysics*, 20:279–80). The process of symbolizing thus becomes essential for the representation of concepts of the supersensible and, therefore, for all metaphysics. What is in question here is the very significance of these concepts, since there is a strong suspicion that they may not have any meaning at all.

Even if this question about the significance of pure concepts of reason has in Kant its importance in relation with certain presuppositions of morality, the above-mentioned postulates of practical reason, the question can also be raised in relation with the theoretical domain, as Zeljko Loparic has shown in his transcendental semantics. In the theoretical domain, the question of the meaning of the ideas of reason is positively introduced insofar as Kant's transcendental philosophy conceives a regulative use of these ideas in the constitution of a scientific theory or, as Kant expresses himself, in the systematization of the knowledge of understanding. It wouldn't be possible to use, even in a mere regulative function, a concept without meaning. For this reason, it is not surprising that the problem is formulated already in the *Critique of Pure Reason*, in particular when dealing with the regulative use of the ideas of reason (*Pure Reason*, A664/B692). Here we also find a first approach to the procedure that makes it possible to relate ideas of reason with sensible elements, that is, the analogical procedure (*Pure Reason*, A665/B693).

Both the question of the significance of the ideas of reason and its recourse to analogy are later treated in detail in paragraphs 57 and 58 of the *Prolegomena*, where a treatment of the use of ideas of reason in the theoretical domain is also dealt with (*Prolegomena*, 4:350–60). In these paragraphs can be found a direct answer to the attack made by Hume on analogical procedures in general in his *Dialogues Concerning Natural Religion*, whose German translation appeared in 1781, two years before the *Prolegomena*. Hume's attack was directed against a traditional procedure that takes analogical reasoning as an inference from the resemblance of effects to the resemblance of causes. Kant's definition of analogy, on the other hand, is based on the resemblance of relations: "This type of cognition is cognition *according to analogy*, which surely does not signify, as the word is usually taken, an imperfect similarity between two things, but rather a perfect similarity between two relations in wholly dissimilar things" (*Prolegomena*, §58, 4:357). The traditional conception of analogical procedure, demolished by Hume, suggested for example that it is possible to draw an analogy between human reason, which produces artifacts, and the reason of the supreme being, which produces the universe, simply by establishing an imperfect resemblance between two things. Based on this resemblance, even if imperfect, the impression is raised that one knows at least something of this supreme being. Kant insists now that the analogical procedure conceived in this way isn't sustainable, because we do not have any knowledge of the cause of the world that could allow us to speak of a resemblance with our artisan reason.

On the other hand, Kant is convinced that an analogy of relations can resist Hume's attacks very well, since in this kind of analogy we have no pretension to any knowledge of the supersensible element used as an unknown in the analogy. From this comes his effort to explain what an analogy conceived in this way is, even through examples: "By means of such an analogy I can therefore provide a concept of a relation to things that are absolutely unknown to me. E.g., the promotion of the happiness of the children = a is to the love of the parents = b as the welfare of humankind = c is to the unknown in God = x, which we call love: not as if this unknown had the least similarity with any human inclination, but because we can posit the relation between God's love and the world to be similar to that which things in the world have to one another. But here the concept of the relation is a mere category, namely the concept of cause, which has nothing to do with sensibility" (*Prolegomena*, §58; 4:357 note). This means that we reach here the limits of what it is possible to know on the basis of experience and, with the help of a precarious analogical procedure, we try to determine, for thinking's sake, the relation that can be established between the sensible, the object of our knowledge, and the supersensible, the object of our thought. In the theoretical domain, the gain is really modest and certainly doesn't concern a pretended knowledge of supersensible objects, but rather the systematization of the knowledge of objects of sensible intuition.

Thought by analogy cannot pretend to get a theoretical knowledge of the supersensible, because we have theoretical knowledge only in the sphere defined by the sensible. So the analogical procedure acquires a function very different from the traditional, and Kant can say: "In this way I can indeed have no theoretical knowledge of the supersensible, e.g., of God, but can yet have a knowledge by analogy, and such as it is necessary for reason to think" (*Progress in Metaphysics*, 20:280). The analogy remains a necessary instrument for reason to be able to think about or to reflect on things from a perspective drawn from its ideas. In the terminology of the *Critique of the Power of Judgment* we can characterize this new function of analogy as follows: the analogical procedure has, by way of determinant judgments, no function in the knowledge of an object, but does, by way of reflexive judgments, have a function in reflection. With respect to this new function of the analogical procedure, one can at least say that Hume's objection does not apply, since it was directed against the traditional cognitive function of analogy, criticized and also abandoned by Kant.

The analogical procedure constitutes, furthermore, the methodological kernel of symbolism: "The symbol of an Idea (or a concept of reason) is a representation of the object by analogy" (*Progress in Metaphysics*, 20:280). In order to have a determined representation of the supersensible as envisioned by the idea, reason must make use of the analogy with something that can be given in intuition. Its symbol is the representation of the supersensible according to the analogy with something given in intuition. The symbols exhibit the ideas or pure concepts of reason in an indirect way, that is, "by means of an analogy (for which empirical intuitions are also employed), in which the power of judgment performs a double task, first applying the concept to the object of a sensible intuition, and then, second, applying the mere rule of reflection on that intuition to an entirely different object, of which the first is only the symbol" (*Judgment*, 5:352). In fact, the analogy can be drawn in relation to an object of empirical intuition just as it can be in relation to an object of pure intuition. So, for example, the eagle, an object of empirical intuition, can symbolize intellect, and the circle, an object of pure intuition, can symbolize perfection.

Kant's example in §59 of the *Critique of the Power of Judgment* is taken from the context in which it was articulated at the end of eighteenth century, the demand for the sensification of the ideas of reason. This example deals with the idea of state, that is, an idea of practical reason. Reason distinguishes between a state that represents the will of all citizens and a despotic state, which is easier to grasp in following analogical representation: "Thus a monarchical state is represented by a body with a soul if it is ruled in accordance with laws internal to the people, but by a mere machine (like a handmill) if is it ruled by a single absolute will, but in both cases it is represented only symbolically. For between a despotic state and a handmill there is, of course, no similarity, but there is one between the rule for reflecting on both and their causality" (*Judgment*, 5:352). This example allows us to show how the analogical thought or reflection operates to exhibit an idea of reason. On the one hand, we have a state in which all relations are organic, in which the state and all of its members constitute only one totality. Using the concept of an organism, in which all of the parts and the whole constitute only one indivisible unity, we obtain a rule with which to reflect on this kind of state. On the other hand, we could use the concept of a machine to reflect on the despotic state, because, just as in a machine everything works through mechanical relations, so too in the despotic state are the established relations of a mechanical, and not an organic, nature: the despot commands like someone who pushes a button or pulls a lever that in turn sets in motion the next piece, and so on until the order is definitively carried out. What is gained by this analogy is, precisely, perceptiveness, since we have now an object of empirical intuition (the living body or the machine) as reference for our reflection. This object is not of course an instance of the concept of reason, but only its symbol.

This much is enough to get a notion of what the process of symbolizing is as conceived by Kant. It remains our task, however, to see to what extent Kant explores this process in the direction of what would come to be called the mythology of reason. Of course, the new mythology deals much more with a universal symbolism,[6] to be shared by an entire people, whereas for Kant, the necessity to symbolize ideas derives from the limits of reason, so that "we always need a certain analogy with natural being in order to make supersensible characteristics comprehensible to us" (*Religion*, 6:65 note). What must become more comprehensive are the ideas of reason, in particular the ideas of freedom, immortality, and God. These ideas have objective reality in the practical domain, since they derive directly from the demands of pure practical reason, whose command is felt in the moral imperative. It is therefore essential to understand right away that the supersensible dispositions mentioned in the text are not attributes of divinity, but moral dispositions like the submission to the command of pure reason, the sacrifice of natural appetites in favor of moral order, and so on. To make these dispositions more comprehensive and give them a sensible figure, comprehensible to the imagination, narratives about the uses of embodied law and other similar things are very useful, provided that the analogical symbolism isn't confused with an ontological statement. So Kant warns, considering the symbolizing of moral ideas through biblical narratives: "We have here (as means of elucidation) a schematism of analogy, with which we cannot dispense. To transform it, however, into a schematism of object-determination (as means for expanding our cognition) constitutes anthropomorphism, and from the moral point of view (in religion) this has most injurious consequences" (*Religion*, 6:65 note). The result of an ontological interpretation of all those images and narratives, intended to symbolize concepts of morality (of the supersensible), is a certain dogmatic anthropomorphism (anthropomorphic representation of God), pernicious in so far as it transforms a symbol of moral interest into an object of interest for technical reason (to guarantee one's own future happiness).

So, in the context of Christian religion, Kant explains that this symbolic illustration must be in fact understood as speaking of moral relations: concerning the categoricalness of moral law, we are ourselves like the son who must sacrifice himself, and the voice that commands this moral law as a categorical one is that of the father who prefers to see his son crucified, and so on. In Christ we have the "Personified Idea of the Good Principle" (*Religion*, 6:60), the "ideal of moral perfection" (6:61). His incarnation and sacrifice constitute appropriate symbols to reflect on the supersensible that appears with respect to the moral law. But the concepts of the supersensible are the concepts of pure practical reason or morality. Therefore "from the practical point of view, this idea [of an ideal of moral perfection] has complete reality within itself. For it resides in our morally-legislative reason. We *ought* to conform to it, and therefore we must also *be able* to" (6:62). The narratives about Christ as a personified moral principle constitute in this way a set of symbolic representations that can make the ideas of reason more perceptive. For Kant this symbolizing of the ideas is essential, since otherwise we could neither make these relations perceptive nor make them accessible to our limited understanding. A discursive intellect like our own must separate and distinguish in order to later understand the conjunction made by itself; thus, in the case of the relation of a sensible and limited being to the pure law of will, we think of there being two separate things for what is actually the unique relation of moral law to the will that must submit itself to this law that it itself imposes. In fact, they are not really two separate things, but rather it is the same will, the same practical reason that gives itself a law that it may or may not submit to, father and son being, in the end, the same thing. What is truly supersensible and cannot be submitted to the conditions of sensibility, such as space and time, acquires a sensible figure, and the narrative makes possible, clearly only by analogy, a representation in space and time of that which neither time nor space allow. So the narrative of the sacrifice of God's son represents by analogy, that is, presents in a narrative within space and time, the pure relation of will and law, and thereby we can contemplate in some way what originally had almost disappeared in pure conceptual relations.

If, on the one hand, the narratives of Christ are suitable to symbolize the ideal of moral perfection, on the other hand there are, in the book of *Genesis*, narratives suitable to symbolize the origin of evil. In the first part of his text on religion, Kant deals with new elements to examine the origin of evil, a very grave difficulty for all philosophy, insofar as moral evil must have a rational origin, since it is almost impossible to conceive how an originally good reason can give rise to evil. After drawing the conceptual frame in which to examine the problem, Kant points to the biblical narrative as a useful analogy: "Now, the mode of representation which the Scriptures use to depict the origin of evil, as having a beginning in human nature, well agrees with the foregoing; for the Scriptures portray this beginning in a narrative, where what must be thought as objectively first by nature (without regard to the condition of time) appears as a first in time" (*Religion*, 6:41). According to the narrative, mankind begins in a state of innocence, but soon infringes upon the law and falls into evil. The story of the original fall represented at the time an original act of reason through which man assumes as a supreme principle of his will something that is not the moral principle given by reason. This subversion of principles in human will, in fact the origin of all evil, is incomprehensible, since "this propensity to evil, remains inexplicable to us" (6:43). The biblical narrative would allow this same incomprehensibility to be represented symbolically through the figure of a "seductive spirit," the fallen angel that seduced the first human couple. In this way, the original fall is transferred to the sphere of pure spirituality, far beyond all spirituality that mankind can reach, in which is situated the incomprehensibility of an original transition from good to evil (6:43–44).

Since mankind is in a world in which good and evil are in permanent conflict, we can even admit those Christian narratives of combat between the prince of darkness and his followers on the one hand, and good men on the other hand, stories about the struggle of good and evil, of God and the devil as symbolism suited to reason. However, Kant insists on the mere symbolic character of these stories: "This expression does not appear to be intended to extend our cognition beyond the world of the senses but only to make intuitive, for practical use, the concept of something to us unfathomable" (*Religion*, 6:59). In this case, the adhesion of will to the principle of evil is incomprehensible since will was originally composed of a natural disposition toward good. The hypostasis of good and evil in a kingdom of light and a kingdom of darkness illustrates the original relation of the will to good and evil, making it thereby comprehensible to imagination or intuition.

Particularly interesting with regard to the subsequent development of idealist and romantic philosophy would be an eschatological expectation according to which the highest good will finally be realized in this world. This eschatological expectation has a symbolic configuration in the image of a Kingdom of God on earth, in which the whole historical journey of mankind would end. With regard to the sensification of the idea of the highest good being realized in the world, even the eschatological and apocalyptical narratives of the Scriptures can be useful: "Now the Kingdom of Heaven can be interpreted as a symbolic representation aimed merely at stimulating greater hope and courage and effort in achieving it, if to this narrative there is attached a prophecy (just as in the Sibylline books) of the consummation of this great cosmic revolution, in the image of a visible Kingdom of God on earth" (*Religion*, 6:134). The idea that must guide these symbolic representations of the arrival of a new world and a new kingdom of good on earth, according to critical philosophy, is the idea of the highest good, in which morality and happiness are realized at the same time. Amid the historical journey man can only hope that the highest good that reason demands as a duty or an aim to be reached will finally be realized. Both the hope and the effort to finally reach the highest good are permanently revived and encouraged by those symbolic representations in which the imagination foresees the return of goodness in person with the arrival of His triumphant kingdom, that is, with God's kingdom on earth.

Thereby a symbolism of reason is obtained that in its subsequent development leads directly to the mythology of reason, just as the demand of universal communicability[7] of the ideas of pure practical reason is raised. Kant recognized the popularity of Christian narratives, suggesting at the same time that their rational kernel is not limited to Christian faith: "It is easy to see, once we divest of its mystical cover this vivid mode of representing things, apparently also the only one at the time suited to the common people, why it (its spirit and rational meaning) has been valid and binding practically, for the whole world and at all times; because it lies near enough to every human being for each to recognize his duty in it" (*Religion*, 6:83). Of course, Kant is more interested in showing the kernel of rationality than in exploring the sensible covering with which to make the ideas of reason more popular or accessible to the great mass. But just as he determines in his critical philosophy the place of a symbolism of reason he is at the same time opening the way for others to subsequently demand the formation of a new mythology or a universal symbolism, this time as a mythology of reason.

It is even possible to get a preliminary characteristic of German idealism and romanticism from this relation between the ideas of reason and their symbolic representation, insofar as idealism would develop toward a progressive representation of ideas in reason's own conceptual element, while romanticism has a tendency to incorporate more and more elements of the sensible covering or symbolism supplied by religion, coming to preach in its latest reactionary form for a return to medieval Christianism. For the investigation of German romanticism, particularly in its early manifestation at the end of the eighteenth century, it is essential to put its preoccupation with mythology and religion in a line of continuity with the programmatic demand for a mythology of reason, since this is the only way to understand romanticism in continuity with the Enlightenment, whose rationalistic ideas end up demanding the penetration of the popular masses. For the investigation of German idealism, on the other hand, the program of a mythology of reason allows us to put the question more clearly of the relation between mythology and reason, between religion and philosophy, in its various representations. This relation is conceived in one way by Kant, in another way by Schelling, and still in another by Hegel, but the place of mythology and religion in the system of the ideas of reason was determined by Kant's critical philosophy, insofar as he recognized the necessity of a symbolism for the ideas of reason.

Notes

1. "Das älteste Systemprogramm des deutschen Idealismus," in *Mythologie der Vernunft*, ed. Christoph Jamme and Helmut Schneider (Frankfurt am Main: Suhrkamp, 1984), 11. English translation by Diana Behler, "The Oldest Systematic Program of German Idealism," in *Philosophy of German Idealism*, ed. Ernst Behler, vol. 23 of The German Library (New York: Continuum, 1987), 161–63.

2. Behler, "Oldest Systematic Program," 162.

3. Ibid.

4. Ibid., 162–63.

5. This problem of exhibition could nowadays be defined as a problem of an a priori semantics, for in Kantian terms the possibility of presentating the concept is an essential condition to its having meaning. The procedures of exhibition are, for this reason, the central theme of a semantic interpretation of Kant's transcendental philosophy as proposed by Zeljko Loparic, *A semântica transcendental de Kant* [Kant's transcendental semantics] (Campinas: Col. CLE, 2000). In this project, the section on the Schematism of Pure Concepts of Understanding is naturally emphasized, as it was earlier in Heidegger's phenomenological interpretation of Kant's transcendental philosophy (in both *Kant und das Problem der Metaphysik* and *Phänomenologische Interpretation von Kants Kritik der reinen Vernunft*). The program of a semantic interpretation of transcendental philosophy leads, then, to the exploration of various places in which Kant makes use of symbolizing for the concepts of pure reason.

6. The expression "universal symbolism" is first used by Schelling in a lecture of 1804. See Friedrich W. J. Schelling, *Sämtliche Werke*, Part 1, vol. 6, ed. Karl F. A. Schelling (Stuttgart: Cotta, 1856), 571.

7. Friedrich Schlegel uses the expression "universal communicability" in *Rede über die Mythologie*. See Friedrich Schlegel, *Schriften zur Literatur*, ed. Wolfdietrich Rasch (Munich: Deutscher Taschenbuch Verlag, 1985), 303. This speech aims to reproduce Schelling's position at the time (1799). Among the romanticists the problem of universal communicability is the problem of popularity or the penetration of the masses, which is essential for the ideas of philosophers to become a common good of a people. Kant also knows the problem of universal communicability, although not related to the ideas of reason as such (which for Kant constitutes knowledge, communicable without more ado), but rather a state of mind, the feeling of pleasure with beauty (*Judgment*, 5:216–17).

Bibliography of Works in German and English

Some Brazilian scholars have already published material in English or German. This bibliography, though undoubtedly incomplete, provides citations to that material in order to facilitate further exploration and incorporation of Brazilian scholars' work by the anglophone reader. Excluded from this bibliography are the extensive number of publications in English or German in the Proceedings from the São Paulo Kant Congress in 2005: *Recht und Frieden in der Philosophie Kants: Akten des X. Internationalen Kant-Kongresses*. Edited by Valerio Rohden, Ricardo Terra, Guido de Almeida, and Margit Ruffing. 5 vols. Berlin: Walter de Gruyter, 2008. A list of the names of Brazilian and Portuguese contributors to the proceedings appears at the end of this bibliography to facilitate identification of the Brazilian contributors both in the proceedings and elsewhere.

Alves, Pedro M. S. "The Concept of a Transcendental Logic." *Kant e-Prints*, 2nd ser., 5, no. 3 (2010): 132–44. http://www.cle.unicamp.br/kant-e-prints/index_arquivos/kant-vol5-n3.htm.

Bonaccini, Juan Adolfo. "Concerning the Relationship between Non-Spatiotemporality and Unknowability of Things in Themselves in Kant's *Critique of Pure Reason*." *The Paideia Project Online: Proceedings of the Twentieth World Congress of Philosophy* (August 10–15, 1998). http://www.bu.edu/wcp/Papers/Mode/ModeBona.htm.

———. "A Short Account of the Problem of Apriority of Space and Time." In Horstmann, *Akten des IX. Internationalen Kant-Kongresses*, 2:129–35.

Borges, Maria de Lordes Alves. "Actions and Feelings." *Kant e-Prints*, 2nd ser., 3, no. 2 (2008): 115–22. http://www.cle.unicamp.br/kant-e-prints/index_arquivos/kant-vol3-n2.htm.

———. "Hegel and Kant on the Ontological Argument." *The Paideia Project Online: Proceedings of the Twentieth World Congress of Philosophy* (August 10–15, 1998). http://www.bu.edu/wcp/Papers/Mode/ModeDeLo.htm.

———. "Kant on Sympathy and Moral Incentives." *Ethic@* 1, no. 2 (2002): 183–99. http://www.cfh.ufsc.br/ethic@/ETICA6.PRN.pdf.

———. "Kant on Women and Morality." *Kant e-Prints*, 2nd ser., 5, no. 3 (2010): 145–61. http://www.cle.unicamp.br/kant-e-prints/index_arquivos/kant-vol5-n3.htm.

———. "Sympathy in Kant's Moral Theory." In Horstmann, *Akten des IX. Internationalen Kant-Kongresses*, 3:152–58.

———. “War and Perpetual Peace.” *Ethic@* 5 (2006): 81–90. http://www.cfh.ufsc.br/ethic@/Capa51ok.htm.

———. “What Can Kant Teach Us about Emotions?” *Journal of Philosophy* 101 (2004): 140–58.

Bueno, Vera Cristina de Andrade. “Reflecting Judgment and Metaphysics.” *Kant e-Prints*, 2nd ser., 3, no. 2 (2008): 95–102. http://www.cle.unicamp.br/kant-e-prints/index_arquivos/kant-vol3-n2.htm.

Dall’Agnol, Darlei. “Kant and Contemporary Philosophy in Brazil: Problems and Perspectives.” *Kant e-Prints*, 2nd ser., 2, no. 2 (2007): 95–98. http://www.cle.unicamp.br/kant-e-prints/index_arquivos/Page504.htm.

Esteves, Julio. “Kants Widerlegung des ontologischen Beweises.” In Horstmann, *Akten des IX. Internationalen Kant-Kongresses*, 3:665–73.

———. “Musste Kant Thesis und Antithesis der dritten Antinomie der *Kritik der reinen Vernunft* vereinbaren?” *Kant-Studien* 95 (2004): 146–70.

Faggion, Andrea. “On Transcendental Semantics beyond the Critique of Pure Reason.” *Kant e-Prints*, 2nd ser., 2, no. 2 (2007): 165–70. http://www.cle.unicamp.br/kant-e-prints/index_arquivos/Page613.htm.

———. “What Has Transcendental Deduction Proven?” *Kant e-Prints*, 2nd ser., 3, no. 2 (2008): 287–92. http://www.cle.unicamp.br/kant-e-prints/index_arquivos/kant-vol3-n2.htm.

Figueiredo, Gilberto Vilela. “The Medicine and GERD of Immanuel Kant (1724–1804).” *Otolaryngology—Head and Neck Surgery* 140 (January 2009): 9–12.

Frangiotti, M. A. “The Ideality of Time.” *Manuscrito* 17 (1994): 135–58.

———. “The Kantian ‘I Think,’ the Cartesian Soul, and the Humean Mind.” In *Proceedings of the Eighth International Kant Congress*, vol. 2, edited by Hoke Robinson, 207–15. Marquette: Marquette University Press, 1995.

———. “Refuting Kant’s ‘Refutation of Idealism.’” *Idealistic Studies* 25 (1995): 93–106.

———. “Skepticism, Metaphysical Realism, and Transcendental Arguments.” *Dialogos* 66 (1995): 88–99.

———. “Transcendental Idealism and Phenomenalism.” *Critica Revista Hisponamericana de Filosofia* 26 (1994): 73–95.

Greimann, Dirk. “Ist die Ethik Kants ontologisch unschuldig?” *Kant-Studien* 95 (2004): 107–27.

Heck, José. “Gerechtigkeit als Vereinbarung: Kant und der moderne Kontraktualismus.” *Kant e-Prints* 3, no. 1 (2004): 1–14. ftp://ftp.cle.unicamp.br/pub/kant-e-prints/vol.3-n.1-2004.pdf.

Horstmann, Rolf-Peter, Thomas Seebohm, and Volker Gerhardt, eds. *Akten des IX. Internationalen Kant-Kongresses*. 5 vols. Berlin: Walter de Gruyter, 2001.

Klotz, Christian. “Schritte auf dornichten Pfaden: Zu neuerer Kantliteratur.” *Philosophische Rundschau* 42 (1995): 11–34.

Loparic, Zeljko. “Das Faktum der Vernunft—Eine semantische Auslegung.” In Horstmann, *Akten des IX. Internationalen Kant-Kongresses*, 3:63–71.

———. “Finitude of Reason.” *Synthesis Philosophica* 6 (1991): 215–29.

———. “Is the Enlightenment an Outdated Program?” *Proceedings of the Twentieth World Congress of Philosophy*, vol. 7, edited by Mark Gedney, 211–20. Bowling

Green: Bowling Green State University, Philosophy Documentation Center, 2000.

———. "Kant's Dialectic." *NOUS* 21 (1987): 573–93.

———. "Kant on Indirect Proofs." *O Que Nos Faz Pensar* 4 (1991): 56–60.

———. "Kant's Philosophical Method (I)." *Synthesis Philosophica* 6 (1991): 467–83.

———. "Kant's Philosophical Method (II)." *Synthesis Philosophica* 7 (1992): 361–81.

———. "Kant's Semantic Turn." *Kant e-Prints*, 2nd ser., 2, no. 1 (2007): 105–15. http://www.cle.unicamp.br/kant-e-prints/index_arquivos/Page504.htm.

———. "The Logical Structure of the First Antinomy." *Kant-Studien* 81 (1990): 280–303.

———. "On the Unavoidable Tasks of Reason." *Kant e-Prints*, 2nd ser., 3, no. 2 (2008): 193–209. http://www.cle.unicamp.br/kant-e-prints/index_arquivos/kant-vol3-n2.htm.

———. "System-Problems in Kant." *Synthese* 74 (1988): 107–40.

Marques, José Oscar de Almeida. "Harmony and Melody in Kant's Second Analogy of Experience." *Kant e-Prints*, 2nd ser., 5, no. 3 (2010): 57–65. http://www.cle.unicamp.br/kant-e-prints/index_arquivos/kant-vol5-n3.htm.

Mendonça, Wilson P. "Is There a Way of Making the Right Prior to the Good?" *Studia Kantiana* 1 (1998): 323–40.

———. "Die Person als Zweck an sich." *Kant-Studien* 84 (1993): 167–84.

———. Der Psychophysische Materialismus in der Perspektive Kants und Wittgensteins." *Kant-Studien* 81 (1990): 277–97.

Oliveira, Nythamar Hylário Fernandes de. "Between Aesthetics and Ethics." *International Studies in Philosophy* 31 (1999): 83–100.

———. "Critique of Public Reason Revisited: Kant as Arbiter between Rawls and Habermas." *Veritas* 45 (2000): 583–606.

———. "Dialectic and Existence in Kant and Kierkegaard." *Veritas* 46 (2001): 231–53.

———. "Kant, Rawls, and the Foundations of a Theory of Justice." In Horstmann, *Akten des IX. Internationalen Kant-Kongresses*, 3:286–95.

Peres, Daniel Tourinho. "Imagination and Practical Reason." *Kant e-Prints*, 2nd ser., 3, no. 2 (2008): 293–96. http://www.cle.unicamp.br/kant-e-prints/index_arquivos/kant-vol3-n2.htm.

Perez, Daniel Omar. "Madness as a Semantic Question: A Kantian Interpretation." *Trans-Form-Acao* 32 (2009): 95–117.

Perez, Daniel Omar, and Juan Adolfo Bonaccini. "On Kantian Studies and Kant's Influence in Brazil." *Kant e-Prints*, 2nd ser., 4, no. 1 (2009): 23–41. http://www.cle.unicamp.br/kant-e-prints/index_arquivos/kant-vol4-n1.htm.

Pinto, Silvio. "Transcendental Analytic as a Constructive Semantics." *Kant e-Prints* 2, no. 4 (2003): 1–20. http://www.cle.unicamp.br/kant-e-prints/index_arquivos/Page400.htm.

Pinzanni, Alessandro. "Kant on Sovereignty." *Kant e-Prints*, 2nd ser., 3, no. 2 (2008): 229–36. http://www.cle.unicamp.br/kant-e-prints/index_arquivos/kant-vol3-n2.htm.

———. "Reflecting Judgment and Metaphysics." *Kant e-Prints*, 2nd ser., 3, no. 2 (2008): 229–36. http://www.cle.unicamp.br/kant-e-prints/index_arquivos/kant-vol3-n2.htm.

———. "Der systematische Stellenwert der pseudo-ulpianischen Regeln in Kants Rechtslehre." *Zeitschrift für Philosophische Forschung* 59 (2005): 71–94.

Portal, Mario Ariel Gonzales. "Cassirer und Kant." *Cassirer Forschungen* 2 (1996): 20–40.

Rancan, Ubirajara. "Bemerkungen über die Kant-Forschung in Brasilien." *Kant-Studien* 100 (2009): 369–78.

Rohden, Valerio. "Die handschriftlichen Korrekturen im Erlanger Originalexemplar der Kritik der praktischen Vernunft." *Kant-Studien* 95 (2004): 135–45.

Souza, Jario José. "Feuerbach und die Ethik Kants." In Horstmann, *Akten des IX. Internationalen Kant-Kongresses*, 5:600–608.

Vaccari, Ulisses Razzante. "Kant and Nature Admiration." *Trans-Form-Acao* 32 (2009): 85–94.

Brazilian and Portuguese contributions to *Recht und Frieden in der Philosophie Kants: Akten des X. Internationalen Kant-Kongresses*. Edited by Valerio Rohden, Ricardo Terra, Guido de Almeida, and Margit Ruffing. 5 vols. Berlin: Walter de Gruyter, 2008. Note that some of the Brazilian contributors moved to Brazil from elsewhere to accept teaching positions. Portuguese contributors are noted in parenthesis.

Guido Antônio de Almeida
Silvia Altmann
Pedro M. S. Alves (Portugal)
Paulo Roberto Monteiro de Araujo
Marcelo Aversa
Joãosinho Beckenkamp
Juan Adolfo Bonaccini
Maria Borges
Antonio Frederico Saturnino Braga
Eduardo Brandão
Adriano Naves de Brito
Vera Cristina de Andrade Bueno
Maria Lúcia Caciola
Jairo Dias Carvalho
Fernando Henrique Castanheira
Arthur E. Grupillo Chagas
Flávia Carvalho Chagas
Leonardo Antônio Cisneiros Arrais
Luciano Codato
Renato Valois Cordeiro
Pedro Paulo Coroa

José Humberto de Brito Cruz
Darlei Dall'Agnol
Rodrigo Duarte
Aylton Barbieri Durão
Delamar José Volpato Dutra
Julio Esteves
Andréa Faggion
Tiago Fonseca Falkenbach
Juliano Fellini
Sofia Helena Gollnick Ferreira
Vinicius Berlendis de Figueiredo
Virginia Figueiredo
Fábio François Mendonça da Fonseca
Renato Duarte Fonseca
Ivanilde A. V. C. Fracalossi
Miguel Gally
Rosa Gabriella de Castro Gonçalves
José Arthur Giannotti
Dirk Greimann
Alexandre Hahn
Christian Hamm
José N. Heck
Edgard José Jorge Filho
Telêmaco Jucá
Maurício Cardoso Keinert
Patricia Kauark-Leite
Raúl Landim
Erick de Lima
Orlando Bruno Linhares
Zeljko Loparic
Ana Maria D'Ávila Lopes
Gerson Luiz Louzado
Angela Maroja
António Marques (Portugal)
Ubirajara Rancan de Azevedo Marques
António Manuel Martins (Portugal)
Clélia Aparedica Martins
Tobias Alécio Mattei
Fernando Costa Mattos
Agostinho de Freitas Meirelles
Edmilson Menezes
Solange de Moraes

Cinara Nahra
Amós Nascimento
Marcos Nobre
Paulo César Nodari
Soraya Nour
Manfredo Araújo de Oliveira
Nythamar de Oliveira
Daniel Tourinho Peres
Adriano Perin
Olavo C. Pimenta
Pedro Paulo Garrido Pimenta
Celso de Moraes Pinheiro
Alessandro Pinzani
Luis Cesar Yanzer Portela
Lúcio Lourenço Prado
Cesar Augusto Ramos
Pedro Costa Rego
Thiago Reis
Valerio Rohden
Paulo Roberto Licht dos Santos
Marcos César Seneda
Marco Aurélio Oliveira da Silva
Luís Eduardo Ramos de Souza
Ricardo Ribeiro Terra
João Carlos Brum Torres
Ulisses Razzante Vaccari

Contributors

Guido Antônio de Almeida is professor emeritus at the Federal University of Rio de Janeiro and a CNPq researcher. He is the author of *Sinn und Inhalt in der genetischen Phänomenologie E. Husserls* and, with Raúl Landim, of *Filosofia da linguagem e lógica* (Philosophy of language and logic). Kantian philosophy has been his major field of interest for some time. Besides a number of articles on Kant's theoretical and practical philosophy, he has recently published an annotated translation into Portuguese of Kant's *Groundwork of the Metaphysics of Morals* and an earlier translation of the *Jäsche Logik*.

Joãosinho Beckenkamp is professor at the Federal University of Minas Gerais. He has published translations of Kant's *Dreams of a Spirit-Seer*, *Doctrine of Right*, and the *Duisburg Nachlaß*. His interests in post-Kantian German Idealism are reflected in his books *Entre Kant e Hegel* (Between Kant and Hegel) and *O jovem Hegel: Formação de um sistema pós-kantiano* (The young Hegel: Formation of a post-Kantian system).

Juan Adolfo Bonaccini is professor at the Federal University of Pernambuco and a CNPq researcher. He is the author of *Kant e o problema da coisa em si no idealismo alemão* (Kant and the problem of the thing in itself in German idealism) and many articles on theoretical issues in Kant. He has recently translated Kant's *Metaphysik Dohna Lectures* into Portuguese.

Maria de Lourdes Borges is professor of philosophy at the Federal University of Santa Catarina and a CNPq researcher. She has published many articles on Kant, including "What Can Kant Teach Us about the Emotions?," "Physiology and the Controlling of Affects in Kant's Philosophy," and "O belo como símbolo do bom, ou a estetização da moralidade" (Beauty as a symbol of the good, or the aestheticization of morality).

Darlei Dall'Agnol is professor of philosophy at the Federal University of Santa Catarina and a CNPq researcher. He has published *Ética e linguagem: Uma introdução ao Tractatus de Wittgenstein* (Ethics and language: An introduction to Wittgenstein's *Tractatus*); *Valor intrínseco—Metaética, ética normative, e ética prática em G. E. Moore* (Intrinsic value—Metaethics, normative ethics, and practical ethics in G. E. Moore); and *Bioética* (Bioethics) in addition to articles on Kant and other subjects.

JULIO ESTEVES is professor at Northern Fluminense State University and a CNPq researcher. Among his articles on Kant's practical philosophy are "Mußte Kants Thesis und Antithesis der dritten Antinomie der 'Kritik der reinen Vernunft' vereinbaren?" in *Kantstudien*; "Kant, santos, e heróis" (Kant, saints, and heroes); and "A liberdade no canon da razão pura: Uma interpretação alternative" (Freedom in the canon of pure reason: An alternative interpretation).

CHRISTIAN HAMM is professor at the Federal University of Santa Maria. He is the author of *Textinterpretation und Ästhetische Erfahrung* and *Philosophie*. Other publications include articles on Kant's ethics and aesthetics. He is currently vice president of the Brazilian Kant Society and has been editor of the journal *Studia Kantiana*.

JOSÉ NICOLAU HECK is dean of research and postgraduate studies, professor of philosophy at the Federal University of Goiás and at the Catholic University of Goiás, and a CNPq researcher. His main interests are in political philosophy and philosophy of law. His books include *Direito e moral: Duas lições sobre Kant* (Right and morality: Two lectures on Kant), Da razão prática ao Kant tardio (From practical reason to the late Kant), and *Thomas Hobbes: Passado e futuro* (Thomas Hobbes: Past and future).

RAÚL LANDIM is professor at the Federal University of Rio de Janeiro and a CNPq researcher. He is the author of *Evidência e verdade em Descartes* (Evidence and truth in Descartes) and of numerous articles both on Kant's theory of judgment and Descartes' epistemology. His recent works are about the semantic conception of predication and judgment in Aquinas, the Port Royal Logic, and Kant.

ZELJKO LOPARIC is professor emeritus at the State University of Campinas and a CNPq researcher. Among his many publications are the books *A semântica transcendental de Kant* (Kant's transcendental semantics), *Heidegger réu* (Heidegger on trial), and *Éthica e finitude* (Ethics and finitude). He was the Mary Gregor Memorial Lecturer for the North American Kant Society in 2007. He was a cofounder and the first president of the Brazilian Kant Society.

SORAYA NOUR teaches at the University Lille II and the Collège International de Philosophie, Paris. She has published À *Paz perpétua de Kant: Filosofia do direito internacional e das relações internacionais* (Kant's *Toward Perpetual Peace:* The philosophy of international right and international relations) and is editor of *The Minority Issue: Law and the Crisis of Representation*.

Her articles include "Weltöffentlichkeit als Völkerrechtliche Kategorie" and "Kelsen as Reader of Freud."

Daniel Tourinho Peres is professor at the Federal University of Bahia and a CNPq researcher. His main interests are political philosophy and metaphysics, especially Kant and German philosophy. He has published *Kant: Metafisica e política* (Kant: Metaphysics and politics) and several articles on these subjects.

Daniel Omar Perez is professor at the Pontifical University of Parana and a CNPq researcher. His books include *Kant e o problema da significacão* (Kant and the problem of meaning), and he is editor of the collection *Kant no Brasil* (Kant in Brazil) from which several of the articles in this volume are drawn. He is editor of the online journal *Kant e-Prints*.

Pedro Pimenta is professor at the University of São Paulo. He is the author of *A linguagem das formas: Natureza e arte em Shaftesbury* (The language of forms: Nature and art in Shaftesbury) and *Reflexão e moral em Kant* (Reflection and morality in Kant). He is currently working on a research project concerning some aspects of eighteenth-century thought on language.

Pedro Costa Rego taught at Parana State University before becoming professor of philosophy at Rio de Janeiro State University and a CNPq researcher. He is the author of *A improvável unanimidade do belo—Sobre a estética de Kant* (The improbable unanimity of the beautiful: On Kant's aesthetics). His articles include various other studies of Kant's aesthetics and of Kant in general.

Valerio Rohden was professor emeritus at the Federal University Rio Grande do Sul, a CNPq researcher, and, until his death in 2010, professor at the Lutheran University of Brazil. He translated all three of Kant's *Critiques* into Portuguese. He was one of the founders of the Brazilian Kant Society and served as its first president. He was president during the planning and realization of the Tenth International Kant Congress in São Paulo in 2005.

Ricardo Ribeiro Terra is professor at the University of São Paulo and a CNPq and CEBRAP researcher. He is the author of *A política tensa: Idéia e realidade na filosofia da história de Kant* (Political tension: Idea and reality in Kant's philosophy of history) and *Passagens: Estudos sobre a filosofia de* Kant (Transitions: Studies in Kant's philosophy). He was a cofounder and recently served as president of the Brazilian Kant Society in addition to past service as editor of *Studia Kantiana*.

João Carlos Brum Torres is professor emeritus at the Federal University of Rio Grande do Sul, Professor at the University of Caxias do Sul, and a CNPq researcher. He has authored the books *Transcendentalismo e dialetica* (Transcendentalism and dialectic), *Valor e forma do valor* (Value and the form of value), and *Figuras do estado moderno* (Forms of the modern state), as well as numerous articles on Kant. Outside academia he has served as secretary of state for coordination and planning in the government of the state of Rio Grande de Sul and has held other government posts.

Index